Readings

from the

Illustrious

Eleventh

Edition

of the

Encyclopaedia

Britannica

SIMON & SCHUSTER
NEW YORK LONDON TORONTO SYDNEY TOKYO SINGAPORE

ALL

THERE

IS

TO

KNOW

EDITED BY
ALEXANDER COLEMAN
AND CHARLES SIMMONS

SIMON & SCHUSTER
Rockefeller Center
1230 Avenue of the Americas
New York, New York 10020

Designed by Hyun Joo Kim
Manufactured in the United States of America

1   3   5   7   9   10   8   6   4   2

Library of Congress Cataloging-in-Publication Data

All there is to know : readings from the illustrious eleventh edition of the Encyclopaedia Britannica / edited by Alexander Coleman and Charles Simmons.
                    p.   cm.
Based on the 28-volume, eleventh edition of the Encyclopaedia Britannica.
1. Encyclopedias and dictionaries.   I. Coleman, Alexander.   II. Simmons,
        Charles, 1924–   .   III. Encyclopaedia Britannica.
                AG5.A38   1994
031—dc20   93-5297
                                                                 CIP

ISBN 0-671-76747-X

This work is based on the 28-volume eleventh edition of
the *Encyclopaedia Britannica, A Dictionary of Arts, Sciences, Literature
and General Information,* published in 1910 and 1911.

CONTENTS

The Invisible World 120

Natural Selections 147

The Literary Life   171

Peoples   209

PROLOGUE

For the culture that produces it, an encyclopedia contains all the world, summed up in words. Almost no nation or race is without its own; each one has something sacred or definitive about it, because it tells people who they are and where they came from. The tradition of the West has been reflected over the years in successive editions of many encyclopedias, the most famous in English being the *Encyclopaedia Britannica*, the first edition of which was published in Edinburgh, in three volumes, between 1768 and 1771. The *Britannica*, as it is familiarly known, always offered a canonic view of things, a set of assumptions and conclusions about culture and shared knowledge.

In a home where English is spoken and where there is at least some cultural ambition, an edition of the *Britannica* is almost surely to be found. An encyclopedia in the home can give a child his or her first glimpse of a larger world, and adults often fondly recall their first encounter with those heavy volumes. As we progress in formal education we tend to use an encyclopedia for quick information and as a useful summary of complex subjects. But almost any page of an encyclopedia can evoke the surprise and joy of discovery we first felt as children.

Encyclopedias have also been thought of as a sort of manual for the young, providing spiritual formation and cultural guidance, and this has much to do with the etymology of the word. The Greeks called their ideals of education *enkyklio paideia*, variously translated as "rounded-out training," "the circle of learning," or "all-round general education."

Makers of encyclopedias will always be torn between contradictory goals: brevity or completeness. The dilemma will never be substantially resolved since a perfect balance is impossible. An encyclopedia can provide an exhaustive treatise on each subject, with all details in their proper order, or it can break up elements within the whole and alphabetize each separately—a procedure that gives these elements status and attention. However, alphabetizing the details of a grand subject puts the reader at risk of losing a total view of the subject.

How to make an encyclopedia? Should knowledge be organized thematically, with dominant and subservient categories, or should this same *summa* be divided up into the more convenient, if less connective, method of fragmented alphabetization? It is not an idle matter. For instance, to the organic imagination, everything in reality is connected to everything else. Recourse to the alphabet in an encyclopedia is a resignation to chaos, ill representing the world in its interlaced unity.

The last attempt to organize an encyclopedia along organic, thematic lines in the nineteenth century was the failed endeavor of Samuel Taylor Coleridge and his projected *Encyclopaedia Metropolitana,* where the philosopher and poet envisioned a "First Division" of pure sciences (grammar, logic, mathematics, morals, and theology), to be followed by a "Second Division" of mixed and applied sciences (philosophy, fine arts, "useful" art, and medicine), while a "Third Division" would contain biographies and history in chronological arrangement, and then finishing up this stupendous conception with a "Fourth Division," which would contain a "gazeteer or complete vocabulary of Geography, and a philosophical and etymological lexicon of the English language...." Not surprisingly, this visionary plan was rejected by Coleridge's publisher, and the philosopher removed himself from the project, but not without a final and most memorable salvo against the facile alphabetizers:

> To call a huge unconnected miscellany of *omni scibile,* in an arrangement determined by the accident of initial letters, to call it an encyclopaedia, is the impudent ignorance of your Presbyterian bookmakers.

The one encyclopedia of the twentieth century to avow a Coleridgean "faith in the unity of knowledge," to use Mortimer Adler's phrase, is the latest (fifteenth) edition of the *Encyclopaedia Britannica.* This newest *Britannica* offers a special solution to the quandary posed by the advantages and disadvantages of thematic organization versus alphabetization. The totality of the material has been divided into two major parts, the first being the "Macropaedia" of nineteen volumes, accompanied by a second part—the "Micropaedia"—of ten volumes, and finally the one-volume "Propaedia," the last being both an index and a general outline of the knowledge contained in the first two major divisions of the whole. The "Micro-paedia" is a traditional alphabetized encyclopedia consisting of short articles that give an introduction to a particular subject. The "Ma-cropaedia," on the other hand, gives us some four thousand essays, sometimes of treatise length, which are closely cross-referenced to the alphabetized materials in the "Micropaedia." The plan and its meticulous realization fulfill, in contemporary terms, the fullest possible implications of the term *en-cyclo-paedia*.

Editors are at the mercy of the scholars who are at the forefront of their disciplines. The specialist must be able to examine closely every tree in the forest and still be able to give an overall view of that same forest. Often, the limitations of space available may dismay such a scholar who is asked to summarize the essence of a life's work in two or three thousand words. The writing of such concentrated ar-ticles is an art in itself, often more difficult than the writing of a scholarly paper. This is also not the place for the display of the ego of the individual scholar. Knowledge is nobody's private property, and often the best of any encyclopedia is in unsigned pieces. This anonymity is due to the fact that all submissions are so constantly subjected to reconsideration, editing, checking, and updating as to lose their original identification.

All cross-references must match. Unimaginable would be contri-butions by various authorities in which one contradicts another. Over the years, revisions have been carried out by the publication of suc-cessive editions, or by issuing supplementary volumes to the previ-ously published whole edition. The practice today—constant retouching of all volumes—has been the rule since the publication of the ever-changing fifteenth edition of the *Britannica,* aided by the flexibility offered by computer technology.

Each encyclopedia is distinct from any other. The commonality of knowledge might imply that they cannot help but echo one another in an endlessly boring unanimity of exposition, but this is rarely the case. In spite of all aspirations to objectivity, a latent eccentricity of purpose and design makes each of them different and interesting in its own way. They all may try to cover "the world," but it is the world as *they*—the editors and contributors born in a certain time and place—perceive it to be. Any encyclopedia must embody the uncon-scious assumptions (usually of some kind of superiority) or a partic-ular ethnocentric point of view, and it is also difficult to imagine one without at least a tinge of national bias. In the ninth edition of the *Britannica,* for instance, it was not unusual to read the phrase "in our country" scattered throughout the articles. This kind of allegiance was excised in later editions, if for no other motive than to further acceptance of the *Britannica* in the United States. Politics and national ambitions of the moment may loom large, as the encyclopedias produced under Mussolini or Stalin demonstrate on so many of their pages.

Older encyclopedias are certainly worth reading, but they have the relevance of last year's newspapers. Because of their dusty bulk and our misguided sense that an "outdated" work is no longer of any use, a past edition can become a rarity for bibliophiles within a decade of its being superseded by a new edition. They are the mainstays of tag sales and local library benefits. At the very worst, and it happens all the time, the trash can beckons. But there are some past editions of encyclopedias that certainly deserve to be looked at today, and not just because they respond to the idle curiosity of the antiquarian.

With its special combination of high literary style and narrative panache, the eleventh edition of the *Britannica* has rightly attained a unique place, because it displays with such ebullience, authority, and wit the essence of the Victorian point of view. The queen had died some ten years before the publication of the eleventh edition, but the contributors were formed during the latter years of her reign, and they are proud to tell us about the achievements of the age into which they were born. In the words of one observer, the eleventh "represents the pinnacle of literary taste before the world turned sour. . . . though sociologically behind the times, for the Humanities [it] was supreme." For the avid youngster rummaging about the library at home, for the literate adult in the decades after its publication in 1910 and 1911, the eleventh was a magical door onto the world.

Here is the testimony of Sir Kenneth Clark (b. 1903), in his self-portrait entitled *Another Part of the Wood,* recalling a convalescence in Bath when he was fourteen years old. It is then he opens the eleventh for the first time:

> I wanted information. So what I valued most in the bookcase was the eleventh edition of the *Encyclopaedia Britannica.* It is indeed a masterly piece of editing, for it retains the best of the old articles . . . and contributions from the best critics of the nineties—Gosse, Leslie Stephen, Morley and John Addington Symonds, all doing their best, which subsequent contributors to encyclopaedias have not done. . . . In consequence, one leaps from one subject to another, fascinated as much by the play of mind and the idiosyncrasies of the authors

as by the facts and dates. It must be the last encyclopaedia
in the tradition of Diderot which assumes that information can be made memorable only when it is slightly
coloured by prejudice. When T. S. Eliot wrote "Soul
curled up on the window seat reading the *Encyclopaedia
Britannica*" he was certainly thinking of the eleventh edition, and he accurately describes my condition.

An equally vivid memory of the attractions of the *Encyclopaedia* to
a child was noted by the Argentinean writer Jorge Luis Borges, born
into a family of Anglophiles in 1899. In his "Autobiographical Essay,"
he tells us that

> If I were to name the chief event in my life, I should say
> my father's library. In fact I sometimes think I have never
> strayed outside that library. I can still picture it. . . . I
> vividly remember so many of the steel engravings in
> *Chambers' Encyclopaedia* and in the *Britannica*.

Much later in his life Borges was to give more evidence of the
meaning of the *Britannica* to him as a fledgling critic and future writer
of fictions: After winning the Second Municipal Prize of the city of
Buenos Aires for a book of essays in 1929, Borges used part of what
he thought to be a "lordly sum" to buy a secondhand set of the
eleventh edition of the *Encyclopaedia Britannica*.

Clark and Borges are not alone in esteeming the particular qualities
of the eleventh edition as they remember it. There are good reasons
for distinguishing this edition from all previous and all subsequent
editions. Although it was very much an Anglo-American enterprise,
the eleventh still retains the scholarly authority associated with the
universities of Edinburgh, Glasgow, Oxford, and Cambridge, as did
all previous editions. The eleventh, however, contained elements new
in the making of a *Britannica*. Not only was the number of entries on
United States and Canadian subjects markedly increased, but the
disposition of the material was revised to give it a more popular air,
a tone for the whole of the book in which journalistic clarity accompanied, without compromise in quality, the august scholarly tradition
already established by previous editions. In contrast to the meager
sales of the ninth edition (the most direct precedent of the eleventh,
since the tenth edition was made up of the ninth plus supplementary
volumes), the eleventh was a best-seller among encyclopedias of any
age. When a final tally was made just prior to the revision of the work
that would become the twelfth edition, some 395,000 sets of the

twenty-eight volumes and the one-volume index had been sold throughout the world, and this does not take into account the photographically miniaturized "Handy Volume" edition sold through the Sears, Roebuck catalog from 1915 on, or such variants as the *Junior Britannica* and many pirated editions.

The sales in the United States were a token of the response by an avid public to an encyclopedia that, for the first time, took full cognizance of its history and culture; Canadian readers responded in a parallel fashion. By the time of its publication in 1910–11, a grand market for reading materials had been created not only by the increasing literacy of the population on the entire eastern seaboard but also by the newly prosperous beneficiaries of westward expansion both in the United States and in Canada. There were growing numbers of citizens from a fundamentally agrarian economy whose thirst for education and culture was not easily satisfied. Bookstores were nonexistent save in major cities or towns. But in the United States, with the establishment of Rural Free Delivery (popularly known as RFD) in 1896, books were brought to the mailbox, or even to the door, by the postman. New advertising campaigns in local newspapers and journals promoted new titles (and encyclopedias in particular), on a scale heretofore unimaginable.

Although sales of the eleventh edition of the *Britannica* were remarkable, the success was more of an intellectual than a pecuniary triumph. Two men were responsible for this achievement: the American-born Horace Everett Hooper, a visionary of cultural entrepreneurship whose enthusiasm and financial backing brought the eleventh into being in just over seven years, and the British journalist and man of letters Hugh Chisholm, the editor-in-chief, who was responsible for the structure, the commissioning of articles, the editing, and the supervision of the enterprise. Chisholm professed to have meticulously read 90 percent of the articles in the twenty-eight volumes, and could prove it by citing details whenever a doubter dared question his command of a particular entry.

Hooper and Chisholm differed sharply in their education, cultural assumptions, and approaches to life. Soon after his arrival in London in 1897, Horace Hooper gained notoriety in English publishing circles as a brash "ranker," someone who aspired to a station in British life which he would clearly not be permitted to attain. Furthermore, he was looked down upon as the aggressive salesman he most certainly was, a proponent of a newly despised "American" (i.e., vulgar) method of advertisement frowned upon by cultured readers. Hugh Chisholm was an incarnation of just those same establishment values

Hooper was later destined to shake to their foundations. He was the typical literary journalist in the London of his time, someone who closely identified himself with *The Times* and other distinguished literary magazines, all exemplifying the high taste of the age. He was a frequent contributor to those weeklies and occasionally served as an admired editor. A friend later recalled, "Chisholm's views were early fixed and they were, I am tempted to say, somewhat old-fashioned. He still saw the world as Disraeli [d. 1881] saw it." There was considerable divergence between the impeccable content of the encyclopedia and its energetic marketing, but each effort was splendidly accomplished in its own way.

Horace Everett Hooper was born into an old Yankee family in Worcester, Massachusetts, on December 8, 1859. Though he attended schools in Worcester and Washington, D.C., and later Princeton, he quickly shed all pretense to formal schooling and took off for Denver, Colorado, where he founded the Western Book and Stationery Company, a warehouse and distributing center for books both practical and literary. Hooper was a special brand of entrepreneur from early on, with a particularly "self-made" zest characterizing many autodidacts, but this does not mean that he was just a peddler of culture, merely turning a profit by the printed page. When he declared much later that "it is immoral for invaluable information to be shut off away from the people," he was not eyeing a market, but giving evidence of the driving force of his life—cultural evangelism. At the same time, he was a canny businessman who knew what he wanted, one of the many merchant giants of the age who, like Aaron Montgomery Ward, Richard Warren Sears, and Alvah Curtis Roebuck, began to use the increasingly efficient services of the U.S. postal system and other commercial carriers for the transportation of wares that were being ordered through catalog and newspaper advertisements. A potential customer of Sears, Roebuck who leafed through the 1897 catalog of the firm would find that it offered, along with the Bible, maps of the world, globes, manuals for apprentice electricians and plumbers, primers in the law (*Law at a Glance, or Every Man His Own Counselor*), public speaking guides (*The Tuxedo Reciter*), instruction books for future railroad engineers (*The Locomotive Catechism*), and works such as Macaulay's *History of England* in five volumes, much of Twain, Hugo, George Eliot, Scott, and Fenimore Cooper. The mass marketing of books through catalogs was a sign of the times, and it did not take long for the young Hooper to become a major figure in this specialized retailing. In 1893 he moved to Chicago to join the firm of James Clark, producer of cheap editions of major authors,

known as "cheap Johns." The Clark firm also published a pirated
ninth edition of the *Encyclopaedia Britannica,* and it held the rights to
the then popular *Century Dictionary,* which, by the time of Hooper's
arrival in Chicago, was suffering flagging sales. Aided by one Henry
Haxton, who was to become a life-long associate and creator of lurid
advertisements, Hooper devised a bombastic campaign to revive the
sales of the dictionary, offering special Christmas rates, with only a
small down payment required for the delivery of the entire set—"An
ideal Christmas present! Take advantage of this never-again offer!
BUY NOW! A GREAT BOON!" The many remaining sets sold out quickly.
It was a prophetic commercial triumph. Both Hooper and Haxton
rewarded themselves with extended vacations to England, where they
took their ease and also explored opportunities in the book trade.

A significant change was taking place in the history of British
journalism—one that had echoes in the making and marketing of
books. Tastes in reading were changing along with a massive expansion of the reading public, newly literate where their parents or
grandparents were not. On the most elementary level, that of newspaper readers, much of this change was marked by the journalistic
revolution brought about by Alfred Harmsworth, later Lord Northcliffe. In 1894 Harmsworth purchased the London *Daily News* and
immediately converted it into a paradigm of popular journalism, the
yellow press being its most extreme variant. There was a rich array
of graphics, photographs, cartoons and drawings, women's columns,
serials, and much social gossip. These were the tactics also used by
William Randolph Hearst in the United States, and by Lord Beav-
erbrook in England later. Harmsworth's influence was expanded and
intensified by his acquisition of the *Daily Mail* in 1896 and the *Daily
Mirror* in 1903. Hooper soon saw that English journalism and, indirectly but no less potently, English popular literary taste were in a
process of transformation not at all elitist. As Q. D. Leavis, an observer
of Northcliffe's activities, has described it, "The traditional editorial
style—the rounded and majestic period, the elaborate argument, the
moderate tone—had to go; it was replaced by the bright, snappy style
that picks out the 'human features' of a topic in three simple paragraphs. It was Northcliffe's discovery of 'tabloid journalism.' "

The new reading habits of the British working class brought into
being what has been called "middle-brow culture," which in turn led
to the phenomenon of adult education, new possibilities for advance-
ment, the ethic of self-improvement and self-help. It was also the age
of the "bestseller," with formerly unimaginable sales of works by Sir
Henry Rider Haggard, Marie Corelli, Rudyard Kipling, and the

young H. G. Wells. The adventure story was especially celebrated, since its heroics mirrored the triumph of the Empire. Public acclaim accorded to the new kind of literature was a matter of much anguish to another kind of novelist, Henry James, for example, whose delicate exploration of the inner world sharply contrasted with this bracing world of the triumphant ego. In any case, the financial success of these bestsellers demonstrated that print was no longer dominated by the tastes of an elite. It was a propitious time for an American cultural entrepreneur to arrive in London.

As a reader, Hooper preferred history, biography, popular science, practical manuals of all kinds, and, of course, encyclopedias. He had a marked aversion to fiction. He saw himself as a propagator of culture for the masses, that burgeoning public represented by the ambitious working man on both sides of the Atlantic. He knew about the thirst for knowledge in America, and he was ready for the challenge in the British Isles. After all, his American publicity stunts, appeals to culture in their own peculiar way, were mightily successful, and England could be fertile ground with just a bit more prodding. As he pored over the magazines, literary reviews, and newspapers during his London stay, Hooper was struck by their dullness, so different from home. The advertisements for books and works of learning in general gave the impression that the publisher was appealing only to those few who hardly needed any inducement to purchase the book in question. The excessive modesty of tone resulted in poor sales, and, even more painful to a businessman of Hooper's temperament, the ads were not reaching enough people. As Herman Kogan, the historian of the *Encyclopaedia Britannica,* put it,

> Most publishers [at that time] simply inserted small ads
> containing the name of the firm, the title of the book,
> and its author, occasionally adding a favorable comment
> from a reviewer. It was considered bad taste to engage
> in the new kind of advertising puffery for cultural
> products.

Ballyhoo in advertising was confined to soap, cigarettes, cereals, and the like.

Always on the lookout for a business opportunity, Hooper discovered that two major institutions, bulwarks of intellectual life in England, were in serious financial straits: the *Encyclopaedia Britannica,* then in its ninth edition, and *The Times* of London, the latter suffering from declining revenues and circulation—only 36,000 copies then being sold daily. The Northcliffe revolution was having its effect upon the staid *Times,* and it was losing out to the newcomers.

As for the ninth edition of the *Encyclopaedia Britannica,* 60,000 sets had been sold throughout the world, and only 10,000 in Great Britain. The owners believed that the market for the work had been exhausted. Serial publication of successive volumes of the same edition taking place over more than two decades resulted in early volumes becoming out-of-date well before the last volume of the edition was issued. A change of editorship of the ninth along the way only added to the impression of intellectual and chronological disarray.

But Hooper believed that the market for the work had barely been tapped. He immediately set out to bring *The Times* and the *Britannica* together for their mutual benefit. With the aid of the Clark firm and the American bookseller Walter Montgomery Jackson, a contract was drawn up with the owners of the *Britannica* in which they agreed to permit the reissue of the ninth edition. A royalty would accrue to the financially beleaguered newspaper in exchange for the loan of its reputation and also for the use of a few offices in Printing House Square. The edition of the ninth was to be offered at the low price of fourteen guineas, the equivalent of about seventy-five dollars today. Inevitably, there was an "American" inducement—the encyclopedia was to be made available to any purchaser with a down payment of only one guinea, the rest to be paid on the installment plan—a first in British bookselling. Within three months, some 10,000 sets were sold, and some 50,000 in the next five years. By 1898 *The Times* had received some twelve thousand pounds in royalties.

There were complaints. Some subscribers had assumed they were purchasing a revised or updated version of the ninth. On Fleet Street, the witticism circulated that *"The Times* is behind the Encyclopaedia and the Encyclopaedia is behind the times." A few sets were returned, but nonetheless, the association of *The Times,* "The Thunderer," as it was known, with the enterprising Americans helped stabilize the finances of the company. More importantly, the new habit of buying a major cultural product such as the *Britannica* on the installment plan had been firmly established in British retailing.

Hooper quickly bought out the Edinburgh owners of the *Encyclopaedia Britannica,* and made a further move to free himself from the association with the Clark company. With the newly founded Hooper and Jackson, Ltd., plans were made to revise the ninth into a tenth edition, one that would consist of the original volumes plus ten more as supplements. In the energetic advertising campaign for the new version, emphasis was placed on being up-to-date. As one notice put it, "Biography since Dickens, Statistics since the Census of '71, Philosophy since Mill, Surgery since Ascepticism, Politics since Peel, Sports since the Safety Bicycle, Electricity since Incandescent Lighting. . . ." The volumes were issued on the same pay-as-you-go basis as the former edition, and the advertising copywriters began to hit their stride. There were "Going! Going! Gone!" headlines, along with contests, offers of scholarships to Oxford and Cambridge to winners, immediate follow-up to inquiries, even prepaid telegrams needing only a return signature to authorize purchase and delivery.

Some members of *The Times* board looked down their noses. One tired editor balefully recalled the campaign for the tenth edition:

> Flight was useless . . . the whole country from Land's End to John O'Groats and from Yarmouth to Dunmore Head was pervaded by the *EB*. It loaded the British breakfast table with the morning coffee and lay, hard and knobby, under British pillows throughout uneasy nights. There was no escape from the torrent of "follow-ups" save by the dispatch of a firm order to purchase accompanied by an installment of one guinea. . . .

It is not difficult to imagine the unease, if not outrage, that certain British readers felt at this crass promotion of what had been an icon of dignified learning and scholarly respectability. Though some 70,000 sets of the tenth edition were sold within a few years, there was lingering wrath expressed by recipients of these missives. Historian Herman Kogan has dug up a few of the more memorable examples: "From my bath, I curse you!," read one telegram, while another, sent by a retired member of Parliament, raged, "You have made a damnable hubbub, sir, and an assault upon my privacy with your American tactics." Hooper was on the watch for slackers who did not keep up their monthly payments. He once envisioned hiring a six-foot-six-inch retired New York policeman who would drive a small van painted vermilion with the words "Debt Collection Agency" inscribed in bright yellow on its sides. Though he threatened to deploy this one-man army, he never did, since the number of defaulters was insignificant. This was, after all, London at the beginning of the twentieth century.

In May 1904, Hooper was appointed advertisement director of *The Times,* while his partner Jackson took up the post of circulation manager. It was an unthinkable American coup. Immediately, there were changes in layout and tone of the pictorial advertisements and the accompanying copy. Pen drawings became common in advertisements, taking up two, three, or even six columns. Older readers were horrified to see block invitations to purchase Martell's Three-Star Brandy nudging columns reporting Parliamentary deliberations.

Hooper devised other lures. In 1905, The Times Book Club was created, a richly stocked lending library in the center of London, where the latest books were available for borrowing without cost, but open *only* to subscribers to *The Times*. This tactic set Hooper, Jackson, and the *Times* administration on a collision course with the Publisher's Association and such figures as Frederick Macmillan and C. J. Longman, who correctly saw the latest American outrage as an assault on their price-fixing monopoly as they marketed their books. Intrepid as always, Hooper delighted in the adverse publicity surrounding this "Book War," as it is known in the histories of British journalism, and it proceeded until reaching a boiling point. The distressed owners of *The Times,* divided among themselves about what to do with the intruders, sold out to Alfred Harmsworth, by then Lord Northcliffe, in the late spring of 1908.

Hooper had been dealing with Harmsworth surreptitiously, and he expected to be treated well by the new owner. But Harmsworth was unfaithful. Hooper and Jackson were removed from their posts, they lost control of the book club, and the ongoing association of *The Times* with the *Britannica* was severed. It was a shock. By 1908, Hooper had looked forward to sponsorship by *The Times* during the years of preparation of the envisioned eleventh edition. Some forty thousand articles had already been commissioned, many of them written, edited, and in galley form. Hooper himself had, by the fall of 1909, disbursed some $700,000 (partly his own money, some from loans) for payments to staff, contributors, and typesetters in England and in the United States. He began a search for a sponsor of equal, if not superior, reputation. This new sponsor would have to lend intellectual allure to the enterprise, and would also have to provide an image of stability to the banks, who needed assurances that the new *Britannica* was worthy of continued support. Hooper's failure to entice the Oxford University Press, to whose directors he offered a generous royalty of 10 percent on all sales, did not discourage him. Always the entrepreneur, Hooper instructed his agent to try his luck with the syndics of the Cambridge University Press, noting drily that "Oxford thought I was trying to bribe them. I offered them too much. You go to Cambridge now—and offer them just half." After a final presentation by Hooper himself, the name of Cambridge University was lent to the eleventh edition of the *Encyclopaedia Britannica*. The agreement was signed on July 31, 1910, barely three months before the first set of volumes was placed on sale. At a dinner honoring the staff and collaborating scholars at Claridge's in London in late October of that same year, the chancellor of the University, Lord Rayleigh, candidly confessed that "Cambridge did not make it. Cambridge did nothing as to the planning of this work or as to the choice of writers. Neither did Cambridge do anything beyond looking into the question of testing its intellectual merits."

Hooper's daring and panache were also brought to bear on the matter of the dedication in the front pages of the first volume. It had been the custom to dedicate all editions of the *Britannica* to the then-reigning monarch in the year of initial publication, and it would seem that the procedure was followed in this case:

DEDICATED BY PERMISSION

TO

HIS MAJESTY GEORGE THE FIFTH
King of Great Britain and Ireland
And of The British Dominions Beyond the Seas
Emperor of India
AND TO
WILLIAM HOWARD TAFT
President of the United States of America

Horace Hooper's brother, employed in the New York office of the *Britannica,* wrote to President Taft, asking permission for the dedication. Two days later, Taft's secretary phoned, wanting to know the order in which the two names would appear. Franklin Hooper thought fast and said that "beginning with this edition," the sets sold in the United States would have the dedicatory page with President Taft's name appearing first. "That is quite satisfactory," was the reply, "and the president says you have his consent."

The present writer has examined many editions of the eleventh printed in America and has yet to find a single volume one in which the name of William Howard Taft precedes that of His Majesty George the Fifth. Given the hucksterish character of both Hoopers, the chances are that the promise to President Taft could not be conveniently fulfilled in the final rush toward publication at the end of 1910.

Doubtless, Hooper's ways of doing things were intrusive for their times. As an admiring associate of his recalled much later,

> We were unused in those days to American methods of
> salesmanship. It had hardly occurred to us to reckon the

sale of a reference book in tens of thousands, and the
devices adopted to attain those figures were the jest of
literary London for several merry months. But "H. E."
[Hooper] had a way with him in gauging the public's
taste in advertisements and a skill second to none in
creating an unfelt want. "How many sets did you sell in
Great Britain?" someone once asked him, and, on hearing the figure, "Dear me! I shouldn't have thought as
many people as that wanted the *Encyclopaedia.*" "They
didn't," said "H. E.," "I made 'em."

A more delicate view of the effect of Hooper's method as it related
to the ongoing history of *The Times* before Northcliffe was given by
The Times itself much later, when it noted that

the production and delivery of the ninth and tenth editions had been from one point of view almost too successful, and a repetition of that experience on an even
larger scale would have meant the creation of a distinct
and extensive business not wholly reconcilable with the
primary objects of this journal.

The masterly editing that characterized the eleventh from start to
finish was the achievement of Hugh Chisholm, who had already
worked well with Hooper in the composition of the supplementary
volumes of the tenth edition, and who was appointed in 1903 chief
editor of the projected eleventh. But as noted, it was a union of
contraries between the two of them. A friend and collaborator of
Chisholm's, Janet Courtney (responsible for the monumental index
volume), recalled that

each could supply what the other lacked—Hooper the
imaginative force and fertility in invention, Chisholm the
scholarship and the knowledge of English life and
thought which the American businessman necessarily
lacked. And between them there was affection, mutual
trust and perfect confidence

Hugh Chisholm was born in London on February 22, 1866,
graduated from Corpus Christi College at Oxford in 1886, and went
to London, where he was called to the bar in 1892. He never practiced
law, but opted for a career in journalism—eventually as editor of the
St. James's Gazette. He was a gregarious figure in the London of his

time, well over six feet tall, broad-shouldered, and of a distinctly authoritative mien. A collaborator on the staff recalled after Chisholm's death in 1924 that he had "a confidence in statement and assumption of superior knowledge which clung to him through life and did injustice to a personality simple and far from arrogant. Combined with his fine features and commanding inches this manner gave him, now and again, the air of Mussolini." The *St. James's Gazette,* typifying the gentility and literary conservatism of the time, was a congenial place for Chisholm. His tastes—the novels of George Meredith and the plays of Sir James Barrie—matched those of his public. In 1900, he left the *Gazette* to become chief writer for the *London Standard.* But this lasted only a few months, since in mid-1900 he was invited by Hooper and Jackson to become joint editor of the tenth edition then in the making. After its publication in 1902, he became the chief editor for the eleventh. It was determined early on that 90 percent of the new encyclopedia needed freshly commissioned pieces. Although he was always tempted to return to *The Times,* Chisholm chose to stay with Hooper and the *Britannica* staff after the events of 1908, and became the eleventh's most voluble publicist in England and abroad as he checked over the new pieces. He did rejoin the staff of *The Times* as financial editor between 1914 and 1920, well after the appearance of the eleventh, but he left it once again when Hooper urged him to assist in the preparation of the supplementary volumes to the eleventh. In 1922 these three volumes were published, making up what is known as the twelfth edition. Hugh Chisholm died at the early age of fifty-eight.

By the time he was called to work on the tenth, and then on to the eleventh edition, Chisholm had already earned a reputation as a superbly educated journalist of vision who knew everything he felt impelled to know. His obituary in *The Times* caught the blithe sense of assurance he always carried with him:

> He had read and thought much, having a great capacity
> of rapid assimilation, and the quickness, almost amount-
> ing to impatience, of his intellectual grasp, added to a
> scholarly and pointed style, gave an individuality to his
> numerous articles, whether they concerned politics, fi-
> nance, or literature. Chisholm also possessed a gift for
> organization, for the exercise of which he was soon to
> find almost ideal scope.

Janet Courtney noted that

> [he] came near being the ideal editor of an encyclopae-
> dia, who should, I take it, be a man of the world as well
> as a scholar, possessed of the widest knowledge, but no
> pedant. His mind should be evenly balanced, but his
> imagination should spring ahead of it. He should be able
> to weigh in the balance all new subjects, to decide which
> are mere fads and fashions of the moment and which
> belong to the future. He must be capable of realizing
> what posterity will want, for he has to anticipate its judge-
> ments. And he should be able to withstand the verbose
> and conceited contributor.

On another occasion, she recalled that

> Chisholm could map out a subject . . . better than the
> expert he was inviting to write on it. In these long [plan-
> ning] letters, which he wrote all in his own hand and
> had duplicated in smudgy copying books—his office
> methods were prehistoric and the despair of New York
> when he and I were over there—he would build up the
> framework of an article so that we marvelled why he
> could not dictate them, but he always said he couldn't
> and never would try.

In commissioning a piece, Chisholm's loyalties, prejudices, and
intellectual facility often got the upper hand, and he was apt to employ old friends and journalistic colleagues to execute the initial draft
of a new article. That a person "had worked with me on the *St. James's*"
settled the matter. He had a weak grasp of the sciences in general,
but did not feel compelled to delegate major responsibilities in these
areas to more qualified specialists.

There was something Dickensian in the working methods and general amateurishness of the administration of the eleventh, yet the
edition came to triumph due to Chisholm's unerring sense of scholarly journalism, that the French think of as *la haute vulgarisation*. The
fresh clarity of the articles in the eleventh was a happy change from
the forbidding monumentality of the treatises found in the ninth
edition. These innovations are not especially evident now at a distance
of some eighty years, but for the time it did constitute a new meth-
odology for a modern encyclopedia.

The most obvious point to be made about the eleventh is the
simplest and the most impressive—the eleventh was not published
sequentially in successive volumes. The whole enterprise remained

in a state of adjustable galley proof, constantly subject to revision, until the very last moment, late summer of 1910. The first fourteen volumes were put on sale *en bloc* in the autumn of 1910; the second set of the remaining fourteen volumes in early 1911. This was a "first" in the history of multivolume reference publications, since all other major works in the genre—*The Oxford English Dictionary* (which began publication of its first volumes in 1888 and was still incomplete in 1910), *The Dictionary of National Biography*—were all published in successive volumes over the years, a fatal defect. Chisholm was eloquent on this point in his "Editorial Introduction" to the eleventh:

> In an encyclopaedia, it is only the alphabetization of the headings which causes them to fall in distinct volumes, and the accident of position separates the treatment of the same or closely related subjects in such a way that, if they are discussed from the point of view of widely different dates, the organic unity of the work is entirely lost. . . . Since none of the work was printed or published until the whole of it was ready, new headings could always be introduced with their appropriate matter. . . . The execution of the Eleventh edition could proceed in all its parts *pari passu*, the various articles being kept open for revision or rewriting, so as to represent the collective knowledge and the contemporary standpoint of the date at which the whole was issued.

As an instance of the impressive flexibility that Chisholm had at his disposal during the years of writing and assembling this new edition, the original plan of the work envisaged twenty-seven volumes of text, to be complemented by the exhaustive index volume, which would make up the twenty-eighth. However, in spite of Chisholm's best efforts at getting concision and compression from his contributors in the years just prior to publication, it became clear at a very late stage that an additional volume had to be added in order to insure volumes of uniform size. This was done, although the well-advertised wooden bookcase containing the whole (a distinct and inviting feature of the campaign) had already been measured to fit the original twenty-seven volumes plus the index. The decision to use thin India paper in the printing of the work made it possible to accommodate the extra volume; it was a very tight squeeze.

The eleventh, along with all its predecessors back to the first edition, reflected the changing cultural patterns of its various makers. The participants in the eleventh shared in the Victorian beliefs by

which they were formed. Their vision of its objective permanence
led to a belief in a set of laws of progress in history and culture. The
eleventh is the incarnation of this particular world view, and it is that
of an assured citizen of the British Empire. The belief in the rightness
of the Colonial adventure, expansion, and dominion is often expressed in a bluff, no-nonsense manner. It was in the voice of the
time.

After all, the era between 1870 and 1914 was a time for the wholesale creation of what now seem to us to be hallowed traditions. This
is the age of the "Invention of Tradition," to use Eric Hobsbawm's
phrase (and title for his study of the subject). Events with mass participation give foundation to the citizen's spirit and suggest a permanence for the order fostering such "traditions"—the old school
ties, the reunions, the Royal Jubilees, Bastille Day, May Day, the Olympic Games, the Cup Final, and the Tour de France, even the founding
of the Boy Scouts—all of these are important and expected markers
in the routine of any year now, but they did not gain their preeminence in the calendar until relatively recently. The eleventh served
the same purpose.

As one of many spiritual centers of gravity, solid bulwarks against
turbulence and uncertainty, it would have been unimaginable to expect a critical view of the monarchy or the empire in the eleventh,
or to see them treated with irony in the manner later made famous
by Lytton Strachey; this was a phenomenon of English literary life
after the Great War, a collapse of heroic values. The eleventh responded to a need and a belief in an ordered universe, a kind of
innocence. Eccentricity was allowed and indeed given surprisingly
loose rein at times, but this only lent a surface piquancy and attractive
oddity to the inner calm of the book as a whole.

It is easy to look back now and say that in Chisholm's celebration
of the past he saw nothing of the future and thus understood little
of the portents in his own age. But how many observers of the first
ten years of this century could or did imagine what was coming, what
was about to engulf them all? It is true that the backward glance, the
revivalist sense does seem to offer too many delights as it suffocates
the critical inquiring spirit. And so, the intellectual and spiritual up-
heavals that might have been evident to a prescient editor were not
perceived by Hugh Chisholm. The names of Planck, Einstein, Freud,
Mahler, or even the Wright Brothers are hardly given their due,
though they do get a mention here and there. The eleventh peered
only dimly into the future. And too, a tone of paternalistic benevo-

lence toward "primitive" societies and cultures is evident, and we have
not refrained from giving some alarming examples under the rubric
"Peoples." The most poisonous article in this regard is unquestionably
the piece on "The Negro," a nadir of its kind. These things still do
occur in the eleventh, in spite of new-found strength in the fields of
anthropology and ethnology, and the pervasive influence of the distinguished contributor to the ninth edition, Sir James Frazier, the
first volume of whose masterpiece *The Golden Bough* was already
twenty years in print when the eleventh was published.

Characterization of people and races from an imperialist perspective occurs frequently in the eleventh. At the turn of the century, the
culture of progressivism and liberalism in both England and in the
United States was founded upon a delicate balance between an op-
timistic faith in the fraternity of mankind and the need to impose
order upon the world's diversity and general rambunctiousness. The
sustaining ideal of nation or empire won out over the consideration
of ethnic autonomy or individuality. The "melting pot" idea, well
propagated in the United States at the time of the great immigrations,
was felt to be a liberal impulse, part of a program for nationhood.
It was not viewed as especially repressive, though it does seem to be
so today. Cecil Rhodes was its embodiment within the British Empire,
and this drive toward cohesion had its American representatives. For
instance, Theodore Roosevelt warned his countrymen in 1916 that
"if our various constituent strains endeavor to keep themselves separate from the rest of their fellow-countrymen by the use of hyphens,
they are doing all in their power to prevent themselves and ourselves
from ever becoming a real nationality at all."

The eleventh speaks in a tone that, in the worst of cases, descends
to bluster. After all, this was the age of materialism, *realpolitik,* the
application of business methods to all realms of human activity, along
with the attendant social Darwinism and its pervasive notion of "the
survival of the fittest." At the same time, the eleventh sustained a
strong spiritual bond with the values and the ideals upon which the
ninth edition was formulated. This intellectual atmosphere is not easy
to describe; let it be said that it was a milieu in which severely critical
approaches toward reality were often stilled by the deadening pres-
sures of conventional wisdom, of what most people assumed to be
the truth. The drive toward order, evident everywhere in the eleventh, was a matter of faith to Hugh Chisholm. He would not have
countenanced anything else, as his article on Queen Victoria in volume twenty-eight suggests so eloquently. The spiritual links of the

eleventh to the ninth edition cannot be overemphasized, but this allegiance to its predecessor was not especially a good thing, in the end.

As Alasdair MacIntyre, a critical observer of the cultural assumptions of the ninth edition, has noted, "To think and speak of truth, knowledge, duty, and right in the late nineteenth century mode, the mode in fact of the ninth edition, is to give evidence of membership in a culture in which lack of self-knowledge has been systematically institutionalized." The connections between the effusive, self-assured spirit of the ninth and the ongoing outlook of the eleventh were openly displayed by Hugh Chisholm himself at the Claridge's dinner when he proudly affirmed that "there had been no change in the general spirit, standard and ideal of the present edition as compared with the ninth edition." Without acknowledging any partiality in the making of either the ninth or the eleventh edition, he insisted that the new work "takes no side or party; it attempts to give representation to all parties, sects and sides." And he assured his listeners and prospective readers that "the idea which ran through the whole of the new edition was that British interests were best served by giving the reader all the relevant information about any subject, whether it affected foreign countries or the homeland." More tellingly, he noted that it was his own feeling "that British interests covered the whole world." By that norm a survey of that same world from this perspective was wholly justified.

In the critical reception of the work, much was made of the supposed "Americanization" of the *Britannica,* a code word for less treatiselike exposition of knowledge and more parceling of information. The matter of the biographies of living people caused trouble— indeed, some scholars who had particpiated in the previous edition refused the call this time, since they had such serious objections in principle to including biographies of still-living persons. The expansion in number of entries, from approximately 17,000 in the ninth edition to more than 40,000 in the eleventh, did seem to affect the majestic appearance and tone that had so imposingly characterized the ninth edition. But if this was "Americanization," it did not impede the production of an encyclopedia of the highest quality and attractiveness, although written and edited with differing principles of cultural communication and with the aforementioned deficiencies in both social and physical sciences.

The potential market in the United States was a considerable reason for the breakup of the old structure. Even the ninth edition had ten times more sales in the United States than it had in the whole of the British Empire. The greater attention to American and Canadian subjects resulted in an office in New York City. This was organized under the supervision of Charles C. Whinery, then a graduate student in history at Cornell, who ran the office under his intellectual mentor, Professor James Shotwell, a Canadian by birth, but who by that time was a renowned professor of American history at Columbia. Hooper and Shotwell had an uncommon sympathy for each other. In fact, at one moment in 1904 Hooper had dismissed Chisholm as editor over some minor matter, and had offered the job to Shotwell, who happened to be in London on sabbatical. As Shotwell recalled, "I refused the offer, for I had never lived in that commercial world where such ruthless things are done. I saw Chisholm and liked him. He came to terms with Hooper, who, however, insisted that I was to be managing editor with the same salary as if I were editor-in-chief."

Nonetheless, the American element was minor; of the staff of departmental editors under Chisholm in London, forty-three were British and four were American. Of the fifteen hundred contributors to the new edition, approximately 77 percent were British and 11 percent American. The statistics are misleading, however, and may give the false impression of an excessive British bias. Chisholm was an ultraconservative observer of English politics and letters while at the same time an open-minded liberal as he approached the vastness of the United States and its culture in the making at the beginning of the century. As a spokesman for the *Britannica,* he traveled throughout the United States on five separate trips before, during, and after the completion of his work with the eleventh. He enjoyed the vivacity and surge of American life and at the same time felt more comfortable in older institutions here—he considered the staid and patrician Lotos Club on East 66th Street in New York City his home away from home.

The "Anglo-American fusion" has many explanations. A sympathetic observer from *The Times* noted around the time of the publication of the eleventh that

> the Americans have a reading public much larger than
> we have; their universities, their public schools, and their
> free libraries are always on the look-out for first-rate
> books of reference; and they have such a just pride in
> their own country and its history that they would very
> naturally be set against a book professing to cover the
> whole ground of knowledge that did not deal adequately
> with their great events and their great men.

Chisholm took great care to expand the treatment of major American cities, states, and territories, as a reading of what now seem to be the quaint entries on Newark, New Jersey, or Los Angeles, California, reveals. He was also meticulous in bringing forth and updating major articles from the ninth on American subjects.

As was common practice in previous editions, the authors of major pieces were identified by their initials, and we have identified those contributors in an appended list. In the eleventh itself, a complete list of named contributors to each volume was placed at the beginning, but with one odd touch—to identify A. L., let us say, one must look up under "A" and *not* "L" to find that these initials identify the distinguished classicist, translator of Homer, and specialist in paraspiritual matters Andrew Lang. Much of the richness of the eleventh, however, derives from the innumerable anonymous contributions, "many of which," Chisholm noted, "have indeed equally high authority behind them."

As for the statistical distribution of the materials contained in the eleventh, geography, pure and applied science, and history head the list, with the highest proportion of contributions (29, 17, and 17 percent respectively), followed by literature, fine arts, and the social sciences (11, 9, and 7 percent respectively). The least number of articles within the whole is given to psychology and philosophy (1.7 and .8 percent respectively).

The eleventh edition was to last for more than its share of years, since the outbreak of World War I prevented a prompt and timely revision. A twelfth edition, comprising the eleventh plus three supplementary volumes, was not brought out until 1922. A thirteenth soon followed, then a markedly different fourteenth edition, which appeared in 1929. After the fourteenth, there were no more identifiable "editions" as such; rather, the later work ("the fifteenth") underwent constant revision as is the practice today. In the early forties, the *Britannica* incorporated itself as an autonomous entity and began a long and fruitful association with the University of Chicago.

The eleventh edition stands today as a unique monument to Oxbridge culture at the turn of the century, a moment where the apparent differences between the British and American outlooks were submerged in a common ideal of educational and informational reform directed to the public at large. As our selections suggest, the articles retained the personal stamp of their authors, and it is that quality that makes it a joy to read. To quote Sir Kenneth Clark once again, "It must be the last encyclopaedia . . . which assumes that information can be made memorable only when it is slightly coloured by prejudice."

Indeed, the charms of the eleventh's quirky integrity spring from this passionate, wayward celebration of life, caught in time just a few years before the assassination of Archduke Franz Ferdinand at Sarajevo.

—Alexander Coleman

A NOTE ON THE TEXT

The thought of cruising through the eleventh edition of the *Britannica,* plucking articles for this anthology, seemed, in anticipation, like a heavenly pastime to two compulsive readers like Alexander Coleman and me. Coleman, I recall, when we began the search two years ago, was looking forward to adding another layer to his understanding of the Western world. Less learned, less disciplined, and less ambitious than Coleman, I merely pictured myself walking along a shell-rich beach, picking up a treasure here and there.

The reality of dealing with the 44 million words that comprise the eleventh was quite a different experience. But it was an experience. First and last there was the sheer bulk. Forty-four million, to most of us, is an unenvisionable number. In terms of words, even more so. But to describe the length of the eleventh as equal to 440 good-sized novels might give an idea of the task we had set ourselves. There were times when the spirit was willing but the eye was weak; and there were times when the spirit, too, was limp.

For us to *read* the eleventh would have taken years of doing that and nothing else, so out of necessity we formed strategies. As we gained experience we developed a sense of what to read, even study, what to scan, and what to skip. Material on applied science, like hydraulics and electricity, we could skip without danger. Biographies of, say, contemporary government and military figures whose names were unfamiliar and whose inclusion in the eleventh was a kind of *Who's Who* gesture could be scanned quickly.

On the other hand, anything written by a person well known to us today called for careful consideration. Contributors included many celebrated figures of the nineteenth and early twentieth centuries—Macaulay, Swinburne, Donald Tovey, Prince Kropotkin, Edmund Gosse, George Saintsbury, Andrew Lang, Thomas Huxley, to mention only a few. Some of these articles did not live up to the names of their authors, and some were masterpieces—Macaulay's piece on Samuel Johnson, for instance.

Articles on nations and races had to be watched for extraordinary examples of turn-of-the-century prejudices about the character and characteristics of various peoples. Some of the assertions were amusing, and some were shocking. The question arose: would we by including the shockers be perpetuating racial libels, or would we be revealing a crucial aspect of the pre–World War I British mind? We decided that if we explained ourselves we would be doing the latter. We hope that proves to be the case.

All the major articles in the eleventh are signed. In the eleventh there are many remarkable brief, unsigned pieces, and sometimes one yearns to know who wrote them. Take for instance the 700-word entry on Henry James, who, in 1911, had five more years to live. The piece appears in the text, but a few sentences here: "As a novelist, Henry James is a modern of the moderns both in subject matter and in method. . . . His characters are for the most part people of the world who conceive of life as a fine art and have the leisure to carry out their theories. . . . They are specialists in conduct and past masters in casuistry, and are full of variations and shadows of turning. . . ." One is not likely to find the phrase "shadows of turning" in an encyclopedia published last Tuesday. As I say, one longs to know who wrote a brief notice like this—quite possibly it was a youngish person, as yet to be celebrated. In 1911 E. M. Forster was thirty-two, Ford Madox Ford thirty-eight, Rebecca West nineteen.

Known and unknown. Most of the signers in the eleventh are now complete strangers, some of them, from the quality of their contributions, unjustly. One in particular wrote on a startlingly high level—Thomas Seccombe; Balliol, Oxford; lecturer in history at the University of London. His essay on Dickens, reprinted here, is quite brilliant, as are his entries on Marlowe, Boswell, Smollett, Leslie Stephen, and his part of the eleventh's massive article on English literature. Coleman tells us about him in his prefatory note to the Dickens piece.

Reading through the eleventh, one learned to keep an eye open for certain strengths—articles on birds, particularly, and beasts in general; and for peculiarities—means of torture and eccentrics. Some of the articles are stunningly wrongheaded and had to be included, and some notably prescient, reflecting at the start attitudes about to develop.

Some long articles we have reprinted in full (Macaulay's Johnson), and from some we have stolen snippets (from the article on Charles Darwin, a few sentences about his daily routine; from Robert Louis Stevenson a passage on his character). Our one criterion of choice, however, has been good reading—which does not always mean good writing. A few entries are included because of their absurdity. So this is not a book to be read through. It's a bedside book, a hammock book, a companion to take on a trip.

Coleman in his introduction discusses the pros and cons of the alphabetical arrangement of material in an encyclopedia. We faced the question ourselves in deciding how to order the anthology. Using the alphabet would have been true to the original; on the other hand we had not intended to make a miniencyclopedia; we had composed a reader. So we compromised, divided our finds into categories, and arranged the selections alphabetically within each category. In this way, we felt, we had avoided the look and feel of an encyclopedia and yet availed ourselves of the alphabet's serendipitous abutments. Finally, we have excerpted without notice and elided without ellipses.

—Charles Simmons

BRIEF LIVES

Of the many hundreds of biographical sketches contained in the whole of the eleventh, we have chosen some twenty-nine lives. The reasons for excluding so many and including these have to do more with their vivacious style and their narrative dispatch than anything else. We did not want to include just a list of the great and famous, but neither are they characters from the past who have all gone unrecognized over the years; the names of Barnum, Brummel, Marquise de Pompadour, or Jonathan Wild still have some resonance, each for different reasons. On the other hand, we chose them because each contained sufficient oddity, surprise, heroic nobility, or plain craziness to warrant our consideration. Concise synthesis and appropriate stylistic finish were essential. Only eight of these sketches carry with them identifiable authorship, and this fact reminds us as always of the excellence of so many anonymous contributions to the eleventh. Everything is done in broad strokes, of course, but here and there a trivial detail is a telling mark of the retold life, a sign for the character's destiny. They live in their differences; the life of one of the earliest practitioners of biography, John Aubrey, seems the most amusingly erratic; the life of Edmund Campion the most noble and pious; the most rabid that of Anne Josèphe Théroigne de Méricourt; the most valiant that of Marquise de Pompadour; the most unsettling that of Major John André, the most alluring that of the Greek courtesan Phryne, and finally the most entertainingly fraudulent that of Comte de Saint-Germain, alias "Der Wundermann."

ACCORAMBONI, VITTORIA (1557–1585), an Italian lady famous for her great beauty and accomplishments and for her tragic history. She was born in Rome of a family belonging to the minor *noblesse* of Gubbio, which migrated to Rome with a view to bettering their fortunes. After refusing several offers of marriage for Vittoria, her father betrothed her to Francesco Peretti (1573), a man of no position, but a nephew of Cardinal Montalto, who was regarded as likely to become pope. Vittoria was admired and worshipped by all the cleverest and most brilliant men in Rome, and being luxurious and extravagant although poor, she and her husband were soon plunged in debt. Among her most fervent admirers was P. G. Orsini, duke of Bracciano, one of the most powerful men in Rome, and her brother Marcello, wishing to see her the duke's wife, had Peretti murdered (1581). The duke himself was suspected of complicity, inasmuch as he was believed to have murdered his first

wife, Isabella de' Medici. Now that Vittoria was free he made her an offer of marriage, which she willingly accepted, and they were married shortly after. But her good fortune aroused much jealousy, and attempts were made to annul the marriage; she was even imprisoned, and only liberated through the interference of Cardinal Carlo Borromeo. On the death of Gregory XIII., Cardinal Montalto, her first husband's uncle, was elected in his place as Sixtus V. (1585); he vowed vengeance on the duke of Bracciano and Vittoria, who, warned in time, fled first to Venice and thence to Salò in Venetian territory. Here the duke died in November 1585, bequeathing all his personal property (the duchy of Bracciano he left to his son by his first wife) to his widow. Vittoria, overwhelmed with grief, went to live in retirement at Padua, where she was followed by Lodovico Orsini, a relation of her late husband and a servant of the Venetian republic, to arrange amicably for the division of the property. But a quarrel having arisen in this connexion Lodovico hired a band of bravos and had Vittoria assassinated (22nd of December 1585). He himself and nearly all his accomplices were afterwards put to death by order of the republic. (L.V.)

ANDRÉ, JOHN (1751–1780), British soldier, was born in London in 1751 of Genevese parents. Accident brought him in 1769 to Lichfield, where, in the house of the Rev. Thomas Seward, whose daughter Anna was the centre of a literary circle, he met the beautiful Miss Honora Sneyd. A strong attachment sprang up between the two, but their marriage was disapproved of by Miss Sneyd's family, and André was sent to cool his love in his father's counting-house in London and on a business tour to the continent. Commerce was, however, too tame an occupation for his ambitious spirit, and in March 1771 he obtained a commission in the Seventh (Royal Fusiliers), which, after travel in Germany, he joined in Canada in 1774. Here his character, conduct and accomplishments gained him rapid promotion. Miss Sneyd in 1773 married R. L. Edgeworth, the father of the novelist, Maria Edgeworth, having previously refused Thomas Day, the author of *Sandford and Merton;* but André remained faithful to his love for her. In a letter to Anna Seward, written shortly after being taken prisoner by the Americans at the capitulation of St John's on the 3rd of November 1775, he states that he has been "stripped of everything except the picture of Honora, which I concealed in my mouth. Preserving this I yet think myself fortunate." Exchanged towards the close of 1776, André became in succession aide-de-camp to General Grey and to the commander-in-chief of the British forces, Sir Henry Clinton, who raised him to the rank of major and appointed him adjutant-general of the forces in 1778. Early in 1780 the American general, Benedict Arnold, thinking himself injuriously treated by his colleagues, made overtures to the British to betray to them the important fortress of West Point on the Hudson river, the key of the American position, of which he was commandant. This seemed to Sir Henry Clinton a favourable opportunity for concluding the war, and Major André was appointed to negotiate with Arnold. For this purpose he landed from a vessel bearing a flag of truce and had an interview with Arnold, who delivered to him full particulars and plans of the fortress of West Point, and arranged with him to co-operate with the British during an attack which was to be made in a few days. Unfortunately for André, the British vessel was fired on before the negotiations were finished and obliged to drop down the river. André, therefore, could not return by the way he came and was compelled to pass the night within the American lines. After making the fatal mistake of exchanging his uniform for a civilian disguise, he set out next day by land for New York, provided by Arnold with a passport, and succeeded in passing the regular American outposts undetected. Next day, however, just when all danger seemed to be over, André was stopped by three American militiamen, to whom he gave such contradictory answers that, in spite of Arnold's pass, they searched him and discovered in his boots the fatal proofs of his negotitions for the betrayal of West Point. Notwithstanding his offer of a large sum for his release, his captors delivered him up to the nearest American officer. Washington, although admitting that André was "more unfortunate than criminal," sent him before a court-martial, by which, notwithstanding a spirited defence, he was, in consequence of his own admissions, condemned to death as a spy. In spite of the protests and entreaties of Sir Henry Clinton and the threats of Arnold he was hanged at Tappan on the 2nd of October 1780. Arnold, warned by the unfortunate André, escaped by flight the punishment he so richly merited. The justice of André's execution has been a fruitful theme for discussion, but both British and American military writers are agreed that he undoubtedly acted in the character of a spy, although under orders and entirely contrary to his own feelings. Washington's apparent harshness in refusing the condemned man a soldier's death by shooting has also been censured, but it is evident that no other course was open to the American commander, since a mitigation of the sentence would have implied a doubt as to its justice. Besides courage and distinguished military talents, Major André was a proficient in drawing and in music, and showed considerable poetic talent in his humorous *Cow-chase*, a kind of parody on *Chevy-chase*, which appeared in three successive parts at New York, the last on the very day of his capture. His fate excited universal sympathy both in America and Europe, and the whole British army went into mourning for him. A mural sculptured monument to his memory was erected in Westminster Abbey by the British government when his remains were brought over and interred there in 1821; and a memorial has been erected to him by Americans on the spot where he was taken. André's military journal, giving an interesting account of the British movements in America from June 1777 to the close of 1778, was taken to England in 1782 by General Grey, whose descendant, Earl Grey, discovered it in 1902 and disposed of it to an American gentleman.

ANDREA, GIOVANNI (1275–1348), Italian canonist, was born at Mugello, near Florence, about 1275. He studied canon law at Bologna, where he distinguished himself in this subject so much that he was made professor at Padua, and later at Pisa and Bologna, rapidly acquiring a high reputation for his learning and his moral character. Curious stories are told of him; for instance, that by way of self-mortification he lay every night for twenty years on the bare ground with only a bear's skin for a covering; that in an audience he had with Pope Boniface VIII. his extraordinary shortness of stature led the pope to believe he was kneeling, and to ask him three times to rise, to the immense merriment of the cardinals; and that he had a daughter, Novella, so accomplished in law as to be able to read her father's lectures in his absence, and so beautiful, that she had to read behind a curtain lest her face should distract the attention of the students. He is said to have died at Bologna of the plague in 1348, and an epitaph in the church of the Dominicans in which he was buried, calling him *Rabbi Doctorum, Lux, Censor, Normaque Morum,* testifies to the public estimation of his character.

ANNE OF CLEVES (1515–1557), fourth wife of Henry VIII., king of England, daughter of John, duke of Cleves, and Mary, only daughter of William, duke of Juliers, was born on the 22nd of September 1515. Her father was the leader of the German Protestants, and the princess, after the death of Jane Seymour, was regarded by Cromwell as a suitable wife for Henry VIII. She had been brought up in a narrow retirement, could speak no language but her own, had no looks, no accomplishments and no dowry, her only recommendations being her proficiency in needlework, and her meek and gentle temper. Nevertheless her picture, painted by Holbein by the king's command (now in the Louvre, a modern copy at Windsor), pleased Henry and the marriage was arranged, the treaty being signed on the 24th of September 1539. The princess landed at Deal on the 27th of December; Henry met her at Rochester on the 1st of January 1540, and was so much abashed at her appearance as to forget to present the gift he had brought for her, but nevertheless controlled himself sufficiently to treat her with courtesy. The next day he expressed openly his dissatisfaction at her looks; "she was no better than a Flanders mare." The attempt to prove a precontract with the son of the duke of Lorraine broke down, and Henry was forced to resign himself to the sacrifice. On the wedding morning, however, the 6th of January 1540, he declared that no earthly thing would have induced him to marry her but the fear of driving the duke of Cleves into the arms of the emperor. Shortly afterwards Henry had reason to regret the policy which had identified him so closely with the German Protestantism, and denied reconciliation with the emperor. Cromwell's fall was the result, and the chief obstacle to the repudiation of his wife being thus removed, Henry declared the marriage had not been and could not be consummated; and did not scruple to cast doubts on his wife's honour. On the 9th of July the marriage was declared null and void by convocation, and an act of parliament to the same effect was passed immediately. Henry soon afterwards married Catherine Howard. On first hearing of the king's intentions, Anne swooned away, but on recovering, while declaring her case a very hard and sorrowful one from the great love which she bore to the king, acquiesced quietly in the arrangements made for her by Henry, by which she received lands to the value of £4000 a year, renounced the title of queen for that of the king's sister, and undertook not to leave the kingdom. In a letter to her brother, drawn up by Gardiner by the king's direction, she acknowledged the unreality of the marriage and the king's kindness and generosity. Anne spent the rest of her life happily in England at Richmond or Bletchingley, occasionally visiting the court, and being described as joyous as ever, and wearing new dresses every day! An attempt to procure her reinstalment on the disgrace of Catherine Howard failed, and there was no foundation for the report that she had given birth to a child of which Henry was the reputed father. She was present at the marriage of Henry with Catherine Parr and at the coronation of

Mary. She died on the 28th of July 1557 at Chelsea, and was buried in Westminster Abbey. (P.C.Y.)

⟨⟩ **AUBREY, JOHN** (1626–1697), English antiquary, was born at Easton Pierse or Percy, near Malmesbury, Wiltshire, on the 12th of March 1626, his father being a country gentleman of considerable fortune. He was educated at the Malmesbury grammar school under Robert Latimer, who had numbered Thomas Hobbes among his earlier pupils, and at his schoolmaster's house Aubrey first met the philosopher about whom he was to leave so many curious and interesting details. He entered Trinity College, Oxford, in 1642, but his studies were interrupted by the Civil War. In 1646 he became a student of the Middle Temple, but was never called to the bar. He spent much of his time in the country, and in 1649 he brought into notice the megalithic remains at Avebury. His father died in 1652, leaving to Aubrey large estates, and with them, unfortunately, complicated lawsuits. Aubrey, however, lived gaily, and used his means to gratify his passion for the company of celebrities and for every sort of knowledge to be gleaned about them. Anthony à Wood prophesied that he would one day break his neck while running downstairs after a retreating guest, in the hope of extracting a story from him. He took no active share in the political troubles of the time, but from his description of a meeting of the Rota Club, founded by James Harrington, the author of *Oceana,* he appears to have been a theorizing republican. His reminiscences on this subject date from the Restoration, and are probably softened by considerations of expediency. In 1663 he became a member of the Royal Society, and in the next year he met Joan Somner, "in an ill hour," he tells us. This connexion did not end in marriage, and a lawsuit with the lady complicated his already embarrassed affairs. He lost estate after estate, until in 1670 he parted with his last piece of property, Easton Pierse. From this time he was dependent on the hospitality of his numerous friends. In 1667 he had made the acquaintance of Anthony à Wood at Oxford, and when Wood began to gather materials for his invaluable *Athenae Oxonienses,* Aubrey offered to collect information for him. From time to time he forwarded memoranda to him, and in 1680 he began to promise the "Minutes for Lives," which Wood was to use at his discretion. He left the task of verification largely to Wood. As a hanger-on in great houses he had little time for systematic work, and he wrote the "Lives" in the early morning while his hosts were sleeping off the effects of the dissipation of the night before. He constantly leaves blanks for dates and facts, and many queries. He made no attempt at a fair copy, and, when fresh information occurred to him, inserted it at random. He made some distinction between hearsay and authentic information, but had no pretence to accuracy, his retentive memory being the chief authority. The principal charm of his "Minutes" lies in the amusing details he has to recount about his personages, and in the plainness and truthfulness that he permits himself in face of established reputations. In 1592 he complained bitterly that Wood had destroyed forty pages of his MS., probably because of the dangerous freedom of Aubrey's pen. Wood was prosecuted eventually for insinuations against the judicial integrity of the earl of Clarendon. One of the two statements called in question was certainly founded on information provided by Aubrey. This perhaps explains the estrangement between the two antiquaries and the ungrateful account that Wood gives of the elder man's character. "He was a shiftless person, roving and magotie-headed, and sometimes little better than crased. And being exceedingly credulous, would stuff his many letters sent to A. W. with follies and misinformations, which sometimes would guide him into the paths of errour." In 1673 Aubrey began his "Perambulation" or "Survey" of the county of Surrey, which was the result of many years' labour in collecting inscriptions and traditions in the country. He began a "History of his Native District of Northern Wiltshire," but, feeling that he was too old to finish it as he would wish, he made over his material, about 1695, to Thomas Tanner, afterwards bishop of St Asaph. In the next year he published his only completed, though certainly not his most valuable work, the *Miscellanies*, a collection of stories on ghosts and dreams. He died at Oxford in June 1697, and was buried in the church of St Mary Magdalene.

🙠 **BARNUM, PHINEAS TAYLOR** (1810–1891), American showman, was born in Bethel, Connecticut, on the 5th of July 1810, his father being an inn- and store-keeper. Barnum first started as a store-keeper, and was also concerned in the lottery mania then prevailing in the United States. After failing in business, he started in 1829 a weekly paper, *The Herald of Freedom*, in Danbury; after several libel suits and a prosecution which resulted in imprisonment, he moved to New York in 1834, and in 1835 began his career as a showman, with his purchase and exploitation of a coloured woman, Joyce Heth, reputed to have been the nurse of George Washington, and to be over a hundred and sixty years old. With this woman and a small company he made well-advertised and successful tours in America till 1839, though Joyce Heth died in 1836, when her age was proved to be not more than seventy. After a period of failure, he purchased Scudder's American Museum, New York, in 1841; to this he added considerably, and it became one of the most popular shows in the United States. He made a special hit by the exhibition, in 1842, of Charles Stratton, the celebrated "General Tom Thumb." In 1844 Barnum toured with the dwarf in England. A remarkable instance of his enterprise was the engagement of Jenny Lind to sing in America at $1000 a night for one hundred and fifty nights, all expenses being paid by the *entrepreneur*. The tour began in 1850. Barnum retired from the show business in 1855, but had to settle with his creditors in 1857, and began his old career again as showman and museum proprietor. In 1871 he established the "Greatest Show on Earth," a travelling amalgamation of circus, menagerie and museum of "freaks," &c. This show, incorporated in the name of "Barnum, Bailey & Hutchinson," and later as "Barnum & Bailey's" toured all over the world. In 1907 the business was sold to Ringling Brothers. Barnum wrote several books, such as *The Humbugs of the World* (1865), *Struggles and Triumphs* (1869), and his *Autobiography* (1854, and later editions). He died on the 7th of April 1891.

BARRINGTON, GEORGE (b. 1755), an Irishman with a curious history, was born at Maynooth on the 14th of May 1755, the son of a working silversmith named Waldron. In 1771 he robbed his schoolmaster at Dublin and ran away from school, becoming a member of a touring theatrical company under the assumed name of Barrington. At Limerick races he joined the manager of the company in pocket-picking. The manager was detected and sentenced to transportation, and Barrington fled to London, where he assumed clerical dress and continued his pocket-picking. At Covent Garden theatre he robbed the Russian prince Orlov of a snuff-box, said to be worth £30,000. He was detected and arrested, but as Prince Orlov declined to prosecute, was discharged, though subsequently he was sentenced to three years' hard labour for pocket-picking at Drury Lane theatre. On his release he was again caught at his old practices and sentenced to five years' hard labour, but influence secured his release on the condition that he left England. He accordingly went for a short time to Dublin, and then returned to London, where he was once more detected pocket-picking, and, in 1790, sentenced to seven years' transportation. On the voyage out to Botany

Bay a conspiracy was hatched by the convicts on board to seize the ship. Barrington disclosed the plot to the captain, and the latter, on reaching New South Wales, reported him favourably to the authorities, with the result that in 1792 Barrington obtained a warrant of emancipation (the first issued), becoming subsequently superintendent of convicts and later high constable of Paramatta. In 1796 a theatre was opened at Sydney, the principal actors being convicts, and Barrington wrote the prologue to the first production. This prologue has obtained a wide publicity. It begins:—

> From distant climes, o'er widespread seas, we come,
> Though not with much *éclat* or beat of drum;
> True patriots we, for, be it understood,
> We left our country for our country's good.

Barrington died at a ripe old age at Paramatta, but the exact date is not on record. He was the author of *A Voyage to Botany Bay* (London, 1801); *The History of New South Wales* (London, 1802); *The History of New Holland* (London, 1808).

BARTON, ELIZABETH (*c.* 1506–1534),

"the maid of Kent," was, according to her own statement, born in 1506 at Aldington, Kent. She appears to have been a neurotic girl, subject to epilepsy, and an illness in her nineteenth year resulted in hysteria and religious mania. She was at the time a servant in the house of Thomas Cobb, steward of an estate near Aldington owned by William Warham, archbishop of Canterbury. During her convalescence she passed into trances lasting for days at a time, and in this state her ravings were of such "marvellous holiness in rebuke of sin and vice" that the country folk believed her to be inspired. Cobb reported the matter to Richard Masters, the parish priest, who in turn acquainted Archbishop Warham. The girl having recovered, and finding herself the object of local admiration, was cunning enough, as she confessed at her trial, to feign trances, during which she continued her prophecies. Her fame steadily growing, the archbishop in 1526 instructed the prior of Christ Church, Canterbury, to send two of his monks to hold an inquiry into the case. One of these latter, Edward Bocking, obtained her admission as a nun to St Sepulchre's convent, Canterbury. Under Bocking's instruction Barton's prophecies became still more remarkable, and attracted many pilgrims, who believed her to be, as she asserted, in direct communication with the Virgin Mary. Her utterances were cunningly directed towards political matters, and a profound and widespread sensation was caused by her declaration that should Henry persist in his intention of divorcing Catherine he "should no longer be king of this realm . . . and should die a villain's death." Even such men as Fisher, bishop of Rochester, and Sir Thomas More, corresponded with Barton. On his return from France in 1532 Henry passed through Canterbury and is said to have allowed the nun to force herself into his presence, when she made an attempt to terrify him into abandoning his marriage. After its solemnization in May 1533, her utterances becoming still more treasonable, she was examined before Cranmer (who had in March succeeded to the archbishopric on Warham's death) and confessed. On the 25th of September Bocking and another monk, Hadley, were arrested, and in November, Masters and others were implicated. The maid and her fellow prisoners were examined before the Star Chamber, and were by its order publicly exposed at St Paul's Cross, where they each read a confession. In January 1534 by a bill of attainder the maid and her chief accomplices were condemned to death, and were executed at Tyburn on the 20th of April. It has been held that her confession was extracted by force, and therefore valueless, but the evidence of her imposture seems conclusive.

BLOOMER, AMELIA JENKS (1818–1894),

American dress-reformer and women's rights advocate, was born at Homer, New York, on the 27th of May 1818. After her marriage in 1840 she established a periodical called *The Lily*, which had some success. In 1849 she took up the idea—previously originated by Mrs Elizabeth Smith Miller—of a reform in woman's dress, and the wearing of a short skirt, with loose trousers, gathered round the ankles. The name of "bloomers" gradually became popularly attached to any divided-skirt or knickerbocker dress for women. Until her death on the 30th of December 1894 Mrs Bloomer took a prominent part in the temperance campaign and in that for woman's suffrage.

BOLEYN (or BULLEN), ANNE (c. 1507–

1536), queen of Henry VIII. of England, daughter of Sir Thomas Boleyn, afterwards earl of Wiltshire and Ormonde, and of Elizabeth, daughter of Thomas Howard, earl of Surrey, afterwards duke of Norfolk, was born, according to Camden, in 1507, but her birth has been ascribed, though not conclusively, to an earlier date (to 1502 or 1501) by some later writers. In 1514 she accompanied Mary Tudor

to France on the marriage of the princess to Louis XII., remained
there after the king's death, and became one of the women in waiting
to Queen Claude, wife of Francis I. She returned in 1521 or 1522
to England, where she had many admirers and suitors. Among the
former was the poet Sir Thomas Wyatt, and among the latter, Henry
Percy, heir of the earl of Northumberland, a marriage with whom,
however, was stopped by the king and another match provided for
her in the person of Sir James Butler. Anne Boleyn, however, remained unmarried, and a series of grants and favours bestowed by
Henry on her father between 1522 and 1525 have been taken, though
very doubtfully, as a symptom of the king's affections. Unlike her
sister Mary, who had fallen a victim to Henry's solicitations, Anne
had no intention of being the king's mistress; she meant to be his
queen, and her conduct seems to have been governed entirely by
motives of ambition. The exact period of the beginning of Anne's
relations with Henry is not known. They have been surmised as
originating as early as 1523; but there is nothing to prove that Henry's
passion was anterior to the proceedings taken for the divorce in May
1527, the celebrated love letters being undated. Her name is first
openly connected with the king's as a possible wife in the event of
Catherine's divorce, in a letter of Mendoza, the imperial ambassador,
to Charles V. of the 16th of August 1527, during the absence in
France of Wolsey, who, not blinded by passion like Henry, naturally
opposed the undesirable alliance, and was negotiating a marriage
with Renée, daughter of Louis XII. Henry meanwhile, however, had
sent William Knight, his secretary, on a separate mission to Rome to
obtain facilities for his marriage with Anne; and on the cardinal's
return in August he found her installed as the king's companion and
proposed successor to Catherine of Aragon. After the king's final
separation from his wife in July 1531, Anne's position was still more
marked, and in 1532 she accompanied Henry on the visit to Francis
I., while Catherine was left at home neglected and practically a prisoner. Soon after their return Anne was found to be pregnant, and
in consequence Henry married her about the 25th of January 1533
(the exact date is unknown), their union not being made public till
the following Easter. Subsequently, on the 23rd of May, their marriage
was declared valid and that with Catherine null, and in June Anne
was crowned with great state in Westminster Abbey. Anne Boleyn
had now reached the zenith of her hopes. A weak, giddy woman of
no stability of character, her success turned her head and caused her
to behave with insolence and impropriety, in strong contrast with
Catherine's quiet dignity under her misfortunes. She, and not the

king, probably was the author of the petty persecutions inflicted upon Catherine and upon the princess Mary, and her jealousy of the latter showed itself in spiteful malice. Mary was to be forced into the position of a humble attendant upon Anne's infant, and her ears were to be boxed if she proved recalcitrant. She urged that both should be brought to trial under the new statute of succession passed in 1534, which declared her own children the lawful heirs to the throne. She was reported as saying that when the king gave opportunity by leaving England, she would put Mary to death even if she were burnt or flayed alive for it. She incurred the remonstrances of the privy council and alienated her own friends and relations. Her uncle, the duke of Norfolk, whom she was reported to have treated "worse than a dog," reviled her, calling her a "grande putaine." But her day of triumph was destined to be even shorter than that of her predecessor. There were soon signs that Henry's affection, which had before been a genuine passion, had cooled or ceased. He resented her arrogance, and a few months after the marriage he gave her cause for jealousy, and disputes arose. A strange and mysterious fate had prepared for Anne the same domestic griefs that had vexed and ruined Catherine and caused her abandonment. In September 1533 the birth of a daughter, afterwards Queen Elizabeth, instead of the long-hoped-for son, was a heavy disappointment; next year there was a miscarriage, and on the 29th of January 1536, the day of Catherine's funeral, she gave birth to a dead male child.

On the 1st day of May following the king suddenly broke up a tournament at Greenwich, leaving the company in bewilderment and consternation. The cause was soon known. Inquiries had been made on reports of the queen's ill-conduct, and several of her reputed lovers had been arrested. On the 2nd Anne herself was committed to the Tower on a charge of adultery with various persons, including her own brother, Lord Rochford. On the 12th Sir Francis Weston, Henry Norris, William Brereton and Mark Smeaton were declared guilty of high treason, while Anne herself and Lord Rochford were condemned unanimously by an assembly of twenty-six peers on the 15th. Her uncle, the duke of Norfolk, presided as lord steward, and gave sentence, weeping, that his niece was to be burned or beheaded as pleased the king. Her former lover, the earl of Northumberland, left the court seized with sudden illness. Her father, who was excused attendance, had, however, been present at the trial of the other offenders, and had there declared his conviction of his daughter's guilt. On the 16th, hoping probably to save herself by these means, she informed Cranmer of a certain supposed impediment to her mar-

riage with the king—according to some accounts a previous marriage
with Northumberland, though the latter solemnly and positively denied it—which was never disclosed, but which, having been considered by the archbishop and a committee of ecclesiastical lawyers, was
pronounced, on the 17th, sufficient to invalidate her marriage. The
same day all her reputed lovers were executed; and on the 19th she
herself suffered death on Tower Green, her head being struck off
with a sword by the executioner of Calais brought to England for
the purpose. She had regarded the prospect of death with courage
and almost with levity, laughing heartily as she put her hands about
her "little neck" and recalled the skill of the executioner. "I have seen
many men" (wrote Sir William Kingston, governor of the Tower) "and
also women executed, and all they have been in great sorrow, and to
my knowledge this lady has much joy and pleasure in death." On the
following day Henry was betrothed to Jane Seymour.

Amidst the vituperations of the adherents of the papacy and the
later Elizabethan eulogies, and in the absence of the records on which
her sentence was pronounced, Anne Boleyn's guilt remains unproved. To Sir William Kingston she protested her entire innocence,
and on the scaffold while expressing her submission she made no
confession. Smeaton alone of her supposed lovers made a full confession, and it is possible that his statement was drawn from him by
threats of torture or hopes of pardon. Norris, according to one account, also confessed, but subsequently declared that he had been
betrayed into making his statement. The others were all said to have
"confessed in a manner" on the scaffold, but much weight cannot be
placed on these general confessions, which were, according to the
custom of the time, a declaration of submission to the king's will and
of general repentance rather than acknowledgment of the special
crime. "I pray god save the king," Anne herself is reported to have
said on the scaffold, "and send him long to reign over you, for a
gentler nor a more merciful prince was there never; and to me he
was ever a good, a gentle and sovereign lord." A principal witness
for the charge of incest was Rochford's own wife, a woman of infamous character, afterwards executed for complicity in the intrigues
of Catherine Howard. The discovery of Anne's misdeeds coincided
in an extraordinary manner with Henry's disappointment in not
obtaining by her a male heir, while the king's despotic power and the
universal unpopularity of Anne both tended to hinder the administration of pure justice. Nevertheless, though unproved, Anne's guilt
is more than probable. It is almost incredible that two grand juries,
a petty jury, and a tribunal consisting of nearly all the lay peers of

England, with the evidence before them which we do not now possess, should have all unanimously passed a sentence of guilt contrary to the facts and their convictions, and that such a sentence should have been supported by Anne's own father and uncle. Every year since her marriage Anne had given birth to a child, and Henry had no reason to despair of more; while, if Henry's state of health was such as was reported, the desire for children, which Anne shared with him, may be urged as an argument for her guilt. Sir Francis Weston in a letter to his family almost acknowledges his guilt in praying for pardon, especially for offences against his wife; Anne's own conduct and character almost prepare us for some catastrophe. Whether innocent or guilty, however, her fate caused no regrets and her misfortunes did not raise a single champion or defender. The sordid incidents of her rise, and the insolence with which she used her triumph, had alienated all hearts from the unhappy woman. Among the people she had always been intensely disliked; the love of justice, and the fear of trade losses imminent upon a breach with Charles V., combined to render her unpopular. She appealed to the king's less refined instincts, and Henry's deterioration of character may be dated from his connexion with her. She is described as "not one of the handsomest women in the world; she is of a middling stature, swarthy complexion, long neck, wide mouth, bosom not much raised, and in fact has nothing but the English king's great appetite, and her eyes which are black and beautiful, and take great effect." Cranmer admired her—"sitting in her hair" (*i.e.* with her hair falling over her shoulders, which seems to have been her custom on great occasions), "upon a horse litter, richly apparelled," at her coronation. (P.C.Y.)

BRINVILLIERS, MARIE MADELEINE MARGUERITE D'AUBRAY, MARQUISE DE (*c.* 1630–1676), French poisoner, daughter of Dreux d'Aubray, civil lieutenant of Paris, was born in Paris about 1630. In 1651 she married the marquis de Brinvilliers, then serving in the regiment of Normandy. Contemporary evidence describes the marquise at this time as a pretty and much-courted little woman, with a fascinating air of childlike innocence. In 1659 her husband introduced her to his friend Godin de Sainte-Croix, a handsome young cavalry officer of extravagant tastes and bad reputation, whose mistress she became. Their relations soon created a public scandal, and as the marquis de Brinvilliers, who had left France to avoid his creditors, made no effort to terminate them, M. d'Aubray secured the arrest of Sainte-Croix on a *lettre de cachet*.

For a year Sainte-Croix remained a prisoner in the Bastille, where he is popularly supposed to have acquired a knowledge of poisons from his fellow-prisoner, the Italian poisoner Exili. When he left the Bastille, he plotted with his willing mistress his revenge upon her father. She cheerfully undertook to experiment with the poisons which Sainte-Croix, possibly with the help of a chemist, Christopher Glaser, prepared, and found subjects ready to hand in the poor who sought her charity, and the sick whom she visited in the hospitals. Meanwhile Sainte-Croix, completely ruined financially, enlarged his original idea, and determined that not only M. Dreux d'Aubray but also the latter's two sons and other daughter should be poisoned, so that the marquise de Brinvilliers and himself might come into possession of the large family fortune. In February 1666, satisfied with the efficiency of Sainte-Croix's preparations and with the ease with which they could be administered without detection, the marquise poisoned her father, and in 1670, with the connivance of their valet La Chaussée, her two brothers. A post-mortem examination suggested the real cause of death, but no suspicion was directed to the murderers. Before any attempt could be made on the life of Mlle Thérèse d'Aubray, Sainte-Croix suddenly died. As he left no heirs the police were called in, and discovered among his belongings documents seriously incriminating the marquise and La Chaussée. The latter was arrested, tortured into a complete confession, and broken alive on the wheel (1673), but the marquise escaped, taking refuge first probably in England, then in Germany, and finally in a convent at Liège, whence she was decoyed by a police emissary disguised as a priest. A full account of her life and crimes was found among her papers. Her attempt to commit suicide was frustrated, and she was taken to Paris, where she was beheaded and her body burned on the 16th of July 1676.

❧ BRUMMELL, GEORGE BRYAN (1778–1840), English man of fashion, known as "BEAU BRUMMELL," was born in London on the 7th of June 1778. His father was private secretary to Lord North from 1770 to 1782, and subsequently high sheriff of Berkshire; his grandfather was a shopkeeper in the parish of St James, who supplemented his income by letting lodgings to the aristocracy. From his early years George Brummell paid great attention to his dress. At Eton, where he was sent to school in 1790, and was extremely popular, he was known as Buck Brummell, and at Oxford, where he spent a brief period as an undergraduate of Oriel

College, he preserved his reputation, and added to it that of a wit and good story-teller, while the fact that he was second for the Newdigate prize is evidence of his literary capacity. Before he was sixteen, however, he left Oxford, for London, where the prince of Wales (afterwards George IV.), to whom he had been presented at Eton, and who had been told that Brummell was a highly amusing fellow, gave him a commission in his own regiment (1794). Brummell soon became intimate with his patron—indeed he was so constantly in the prince's company that he is reported not to have known his own regimental troop. In 1798, having then reached the rank of captain, he left the service, and next year succeeded to a fortune of about £30,000. Setting up a bachelor establishment in Mayfair, he became, thanks to the prince of Wales's friendship and his own good taste in dress, the recognized *arbiter elegantiarum.* His social success was instant and complete, his repartees were the talk of the town, and, if not accurately speaking a wit, he had a remarkable talent for presenting the most ordinary circumstances in an amusing light. Though he always dressed well, he was no mere fop—Lord Byron is credited with the remark that there was nothing remarkable about his dress save "a certain exquisite propriety." For a time Brummell's sway was undisputed. But eventually gambling and extravagance exhausted his fortune, while his tongue proved too sharp for his royal patron. They quarrelled, and though for a time Brummell continued to hold his place in society, his popularity began to decline. In 1816 he fled to Calais to avoid his creditors. Here he struggled on for fourteen years, receiving help from time to time from his friends in England, but always hopelessly in debt. In 1830 the interest of these friends secured him the post of British consul at Caen, to which a moderate salary was attached, but two years later the office was abolished. In 1835 Brummell's French creditors in Calais and Caen lost patience and he was imprisoned, but his friends once more came to the rescue, paid his debts and provided him with a small income. He had now lost all his interest in dress; his personal appearance was slovenly and dirty. In 1837, after two attacks of paralysis, shelter was found for him in the charitable asylum of Bon Sauveur, Caen, where he died on the 30th of March 1840.

BURKE, WILLIAM (1792–1829), Irish criminal, born in Ireland in 1792. After trying his hand at a variety of trades there, he went to Scotland about 1817 as a navvy, and in 1827 was living in a lodging-house in Edinburgh kept by William Hare, another Irish labourer. Towards the end of that year one of Hare's lodgers, an old army pensioner, died. This was the period of the body-snatchers or Resurrectionists, and Hare and Burke, aware that money could always be obtained for a corpse, sold the body to Dr Robert Knox, a leading Edinburgh anatomist, for £7, 10s. The price obtained and the simplicity of the transaction suggested to Hare an easy method of making a profitable livelihood, and Burke at once fell in with the plan. The two men inveigled obscure travellers to Hare's or some other lodging-house, made them drunk and then suffocated them, taking care to leave no marks of violence. The bodies were sold to Dr Knox for prices averaging from £8 to £14. At least fifteen victims had been disposed of in this way when the suspicions of the police were aroused, and Burke and Hare were arrested. The latter turned king's evidence, and Burke was found guilty and hanged at Edinburgh on the 28th of January 1829. Hare found it impossible, in view of the strong popular feeling, to remain in Scotland. He is believed to have died in England under an assumed name. From Burke's method of killing his victims has come the verb "to burke," meaning to suffocate, strangle or suppress secretly, or to kill with the object of selling the body for the purposes of dissection.

⌒⌒⌒ BUXTON, JEDEDIAH (1707–1772), English arithmetician, was born on the 20th of March 1707 at Elmton, near Chesterfield, in Derbyshire. Although his father was school-master of the parish, and his grandfather had been the vicar, his education had been so neglected that he could not write; and his knowledge, except of numbers, was extremely limited. How he came first to know the relative proportions of numbers, and their progressive denominations, he did not remember; but on such matters his attention was so constantly riveted, that he frequently took no cognizance of external objects, and when he did, it was only with reference to their numbers. He measured the whole lordship of Elmton, consisting of some thousand acres, simply by striding over it, and gave the area not only in acres, roods and perches, but even in square inches. After this, he reduced them into square hairs'-breadths, reckoning forty-eight to each side of the inch. His memory was so great, that in resolving a question he could leave off and resume the operation again at the same point after the lapse of a week, or even of several months. His perpetual application to figures prevented the smallest acquisition of any other knowledge. His wonderful faculty was tested in 1754 by the Royal Society of London, who ac-

knowledged their satisfaction by presenting him with a handsome gratuity. During his visit to the metropolis he was taken to see the tragedy of *Richard III.* performed at Drury Lane theatre, but his whole mind was given to the counting of the words uttered by David Garrick. Similarly, he set himself to count the steps of the dancers; and he declared that the innumerable sounds produced by the musical instruments had perplexed him beyond measure. He died in 1772.

CAMPION, EDMUND (1540–1581), English Jesuit, was born in London, received his early education at Christ's Hospital, and, as the best of the London scholars, was chosen in their name to make the complimentary speech when Queen Mary visited the city on the 3rd of August 1553. He went to Oxford and became fellow of St John's College in 1557, taking the oath of supremacy on the occasion of his degree in 1564, in which year he was orator in the schools. He had already shown his talents as a speaker at the funeral of Amy Robsart in 1560; and when Sir Thomas White, the founder of the college, was buried in 1564, the Latin oration fell to the lot of Campion. Two years later he welcomed Queen Elizabeth to the university, and won a regard, which the queen preserved until the end. Religious difficulties now began to beset him; but at the persuasion of Edward Cheyney, bishop of Gloucester, although holding Catholic doctrines, he took deacon's orders in the English Church. Inwardly "he took a remorse of conscience and detestation of mind." Rumours of his opinions began to spread and, giving up the office of proctor, he left Oxford in 1569 and went to Ireland to take part in a proposed restoration of the Dublin University. The suspicion of papistry followed him; and orders were given for his arrest. For some three months he eluded pursuit, hiding among friends and occupying himself by writing a history of Ireland (first published in Holinshed's *Chronicles*), a superficial work of no real value. At last he escaped to Douai, where he joined William Allen and was reconciled to the Roman Church. After being ordained subdeacon, he went to Rome and became a Jesuit in 1573, spending some years at Brünn, Vienna and Prague. In 1580 the Jesuit mission to England was begun, and he accompanied Robert Parsons who, as superior, was intended to counterbalance Campion's fervour and impetuous zeal. He entered England in the characteristic guise of a jewel merchant, arrived in London on the 24th of June 1580, and at once began to preach. His presence became known to the authorities and an indiscreet decla-

ration, "Campion Brag," made the position more difficult. The hue
and cry was out against him; henceforth he led a hunted life, preach-
ing and ministering to Catholics in Berkshire, Oxfordshire, North-
amptonshire and Lancashire. During this time he was writing his
Decem Rationes, a rhetorical display of reasons against the Anglican
Church. The book was printed in a private press at Stonor Park,
Henley, and 400 copies were found on the benches of St Mary's,
Oxford, at the Commencement, on the 27th of June 1581. The sensation was immense, and the pursuit became keener. On his way to
Norfolk he stopped at Lyford in Berkshire, where he preached on
the 14th of July and the following day, yielding to the foolish im-
portunity of some pious women. Here he was captured by a spy and
taken to London, bearing on his hat a paper with the inscription,
"Campion, the Seditious Jesuit." Committed to the Tower, he was
examined in the presence of Elizabeth, who asked him if he acknowledged her to be really queen of England, and on his replying
straightly in the affirmative, she made him offers, not only of life but
of wealth and dignities, on conditions which his conscience could not
allow. He was kept a long time in prison, twice racked by order of
the council, and every effort was made to shake his constancy. Despite
the effect of a false rumour of retraction and a forged confession,
his adversaries in despair summoned him to four public conferences
(1st, 18th, 23rd and 27th of September), and although still suffering,
and allowed neither time nor books for preparation, he bore himself
so easily and readily that he won the admiration of most of the
audience. Racked again on the 31st of October, he was indicted at
Westminster that he with others had conspired at Rome and Reims
to raise a sedition in the realm and dethrone the queen. On the 20th
of November he was brought in guilty before Lord Chief Justice
Wray; and in reply to him said: "If our religion do make traitors we
are worthy to be condemned; but otherwise are and have been true
subjects as ever the queen had." He received the sentence of the
traitor's death with the *Te Deum laudamus,* and, after spending his
last days in pious exercises, was led with two companions to Tyburn
(1st of December 1581) and suffered the barbarous penalty. Of all
the Jesuit missionaries who suffered for their allegiance to the ancient
religion, Campion stands the highest. His life and his aspirations were
pure, his zeal true and his loyalty unquestionable. He was beatified
by Leo XIII, in 1886. (E.Tn.)

◯◠◠◯ **CAPPELLO, BIANCA** (1548–1587), grand duchess of Tuscany, was the daughter of Bartolommeo Cappello, a member of one of the richest and noblest Venetian families, and was famed for her great beauty. At the age of fifteen she fell in love with Pietro Bonaventuri, a young Florentine clerk in the firm of Salviati, and on the 28th of November 1563 escaped with him to Florence, where they were married and she had a daughter named Pellegrina. The Venetian government made every effort to have Bianca arrested and brought back, but the grand duke Cosimo de' Medici intervened in her favour and she was left unmolested. However she did not get on well with her husband's family, who were very poor and made her do menial work, until at last her beauty attracted Francesco, the grand duke's son, a vicious and unprincipled rake. Although already married to the virtuous and charming Archduchess Giovanna of Austria, he seduced the fair Venetian and loaded her with jewels, money and other presents. Bianca's accommodating husband was given court employment, and consoled himself with other ladies; in 1572 he was murdered in the streets of Florence in consequence of some amorous intrigue, though possibly Bianca and Francesco were privy to the deed. On the death of Cosimo in 1574 Francesco succeeded to the grand duchy; he now installed Bianca in a fine palace close to his own and outraged his wife by flaunting his mistress before her. As Giovanna had borne Francesco no sons, Bianca was very anxious to present him with an heir, for otherwise her position would remain very insecure. But although she resorted to all sorts of expedients, even to that of trying to pass off a changeling as the grand duke's child, she was not successful. In 1578 Giovanna died; a few days later Francesco secretly married Bianca, and on the 10th of June, 1579, the marriage was publicly announced. The Venetian government now put aside its resentment and was officially represented at the magnificent wedding festivities, for it saw in Bianca Cappello an instrument for cementing good relations with Tuscany. But the long expected heir failed to come, and Bianca realized that if her husband were to die before her she was lost, for his family, especially his brother Cardinal Ferdinand, hated her bitterly, as an adventuress and interloper. In October 1587 both the grand duke and his wife died of colic within a couple of days of each other. At the time poison was suspected, but documentary evidence has proved the suspicion to be unfounded. (L.V.)

FREDEGOND (*Fredigundis*) (d. 597), Frankish queen. Originally a serving-woman, she inspired the Frankish king, Chilperic I., with a violent passion. At her instigation he repudiated his first wife Audovera, and strangled his second, Galswintha, Queen Brunhilda's sister. A few days after this murder Chilperic married Fredegond (567). This woman exercised a most pernicious influence over him. She forced him into war against Austrasia, in the course of which she procured the assassination of the victorious king Sigebert (575); she carried on a malignant struggle against Chilperic's sons by his first wife, Theodebert, Merwich and Clovis, who all died tragic deaths; and she persistently endeavoured to secure the throne for her own children. Her first son Thierry, however, to whom Bishop Ragnemod of Paris stood godfather, died soon after birth, and Fredegond tortured a number of women whom she accused of having bewitched the child. Her second son also died in infancy. Finally, she gave birth to a child who afterwards became king as Clotaire II. Shortly after the birth of this third son, Chilperic himself perished in mysterious circumstances (584). Fredegond has been accused of complicity in his murder, but with little show of probability, since in her husband she lost her principal supporter.

Henceforth Fredegond did all in her power to gain the kingdom for her child. Taking refuge at the church of Notre Dame at Paris, she appealed to King Guntram of Burgundy, who took Clotaire under his protection and defended him against his other nephew, Childebert II., king of Austrasia. From that time until her death Fredegond governed the western kingdom. She endeavoured to prevent the alliance between King Guntram and Childebert, which was cemented by the pact of Andelot; and made several attempts to assassinate Childebert by sending against him hired bravoes armed with poisoned *scramasaxes* (heavy single-edged knives). After the death of Childebert in 595 she resolved to augment the kingdom of Neustria at the expense of Austrasia, and to this end seized some cities near Paris and defeated Theodebert at the battle of Laffaux, near Soissons. Her triumph, however, was short-lived, as she died quietly in her bed in 597 soon after her victory. (C.Pf.)

GILBERT, MARIE DOLORES ELIZA ROSANNA ["Lola Montez"] (1818–1861), dancer and adventuress, the daughter of a British army officer, was born at Limerick, Ireland, in 1818. Her father dying in India when she was seven years old, and her mother marrying again, the child was sent to Europe to be educated, subsequently joining her mother at Bath. In 1837 she made a runaway match with a Captain James of the Indian army, and accompanied him to India. In 1842 she returned to England, and shortly afterwards her husband obtained a decree *nisi* for divorce. She then studied dancing, making an unsuccessful first appearance at Her Majesty's theatre, London, in 1843, billed as "Lola Montez, Spanish dancer." Subsequently she appeared with considerable success in Germany, Poland and Russia. Thence she went to Paris, and in 1847 appeared at Munich, where she became the mistress of the old king of Bavaria, Ludwig I.; she was naturalized, created comtesse de Landsfeld, and given an income of £2000 a year. She soon proved herself the real ruler of Bavaria, adopting a liberal and anti-Jesuit policy. Her political opponents proved, however, too strong for her, and in 1848 she was banished. In 1849 she came to England, and in the same year was married to George Heald, a young officer in the Guards. Her husband's guardian instituted a prosecution for bigamy against her on the ground that her divorce from Captain James had not been made absolute, and she fled with Heald to Spain. In 1851 she appeared at the Broadway theatre, New York, and in the following year at the Walnut Street theatre, Philadelphia. In 1853 Heald was drowned at Lisbon, and in the same year she married the proprietor of a San Francisco newspaper, but did not live long with him. Subsequently she appeared in Australia, but returned, in 1857, to act in America, and to lecture on gallantry. Her health having broken down, she devoted the rest of her life to visiting the outcasts of her own sex in New York, where, stricken with paralysis, she died on the 17th of January 1861.

GWYN, NELL [ELEANOR] (1650–1687), English actress, and mistress of Charles II., was born on the 2nd of February 1650/1, probably in an alley off Drury Lane, London, although Hereford also claims to have been her birthplace. Her father, Thomas Gwyn, appears to have been a broken-down soldier of a family of Welsh origin. Of her mother little is known save that she lived for some time with her daughter, and that in 1679 she was drowned, apparently when intoxicated, in a pond at Chelsea. Nell Gwyn, who sold oranges in the precincts of Drury Lane Theatre, passed, at the age of fifteen, to the boards, through the influence of the actor Charles Hart and of Robert Duncan or Dungan, an officer of the guards who had interest with the management. Her first recorded appearance on the stage was in 1665 as Cydaria, Montezuma's daughter, in Dryden's *Indian Emperor,* a serious part ill-suited to her. In the following year she was Lady Wealthy in the Hon. James Howard's comedy *The English Monsieur.* Pepys was delighted with the playing of "pretty, witty Nell," but when he saw her as Florimel in Dryden's *Secret Love, or the Maiden Queen,* he wrote "so great a performance of a comical part was never, I believe, in the world before" and, "so done by Nell her merry part as cannot be better done in nature" (*Diary,* March 25, 1667). Her success brought her other leading rôles—Bellario, in Beaumont and Fletcher's *Philaster;* Flora, in Rhodes's *Flora's Vagaries;* Samira, in Sir Robert Howard's *Surprisal;* and she remained a member of the Drury Lane company until 1669, playing continuously save for a brief absence in the summer of 1667 when she lived at Epsom as the mistress of Lord Buckhurst, afterwards 6th earl of Dorset. Her last appearance was as Almahide to the Almanzor of Hart, in Dryden's *The Conquest of Granada* (1670), the production of which had been postponed some months for her return to the stage after the birth of her first son by the king.

As an actress Nell Gwyn was largely indebted to Dryden, who seems to have made a special study of her airy, irresponsible personality, and who kept her supplied with parts which suited her. She excelled in the delivery of the risky prologues and epilogues which were the fashion, and the poet wrote for her some specially daring examples. It was, however, as the mistress of Charles II. that she endeared herself to the public. Partly, no doubt, her popularity was due to the disgust inspired by her rival, Louise de Kéroualle, duchess of Portsmouth, and to the fact that, while the Frenchwoman was a Catholic, she was a Protestant. But very largely it was the result of exactly those personal qualities that appealed to the monarch himself. She was *piquante* rather than pretty, short of stature, and her chief beauty was her reddish-brown hair. She was illiterate, and with difficulty scrawled an awkward E. G. at the bottom of her letters, written for her by others. But her frank recklessness, her generosity, her invariable good temper, her ready wit, her infectious high spirits and amazing indiscretions appealed irresistibly to a generation which welcomed in her the living antithesis of Puritanism. "A true child of the London streets," she never pretended to be superior to what she was, nor to interfere in matters outside the special sphere assigned her; she made no ministers, she appointed to no bishoprics, and for the high issues of international politics she had no concern. She never forgot her old friends, and, as far as is known, remained faithful to her royal lover from the beginning of their intimacy to his death, and, after his death, to his memory.

Of her two sons by the king, the elder was created Baron Hedington and earl of Burford and subsequently duke of St Albans; the younger, James, Lord Beauclerk, died in 1680, while still a boy. The king's death-bed request to his brother, "Let not poor Nelly starve," was faithfully carried out by James II., who paid her debts from the Secret Service fund, provided her with other moneys, and settled on her an estate with reversion to the duke of St Albans. But she did not long survive her lover's death. She died in November 1687, and was buried on the 17th, according to her own request, in the church of St Martin-in-the-Fields, her funeral sermon being preached by the vicar, Thomas Tenison, afterwards archbishop of Canterbury, who said "much to her praise." Tradition credits the foundation of Chelsea Hospital to her influence over the king.

HAMILTON, EMMA, LADY (*c.* 1765–1815), wife of Sir William Hamilton, the British envoy at Naples, and famous as the mistress of Nelson, was the daughter of Henry Lyon, a blacksmith of Great Neston in Cheshire. The date of her birth cannot be fixed with certainty, but she was baptized at Great Neston on the 12th of May 1765, and it is not improbable that she was born in that year. Her baptismal name was Emily. As her father died soon after her birth, the mother, who was dependent on parish relief, had to remove to her native village, Hawarden in Flintshire. Emma's early life is very obscure. She was certaintly illiterate, and it appears that she had a child in 1780, a fact which has led some of her biographers to place her birth before 1765. It has been said that she was first the mistress of Captain Willet Payne, an officer in the navy, and that she was employed in some doubtful capacity by a notorious quack of the time, Dr Graham. In 1781 she was the mistress of a country gentleman, Sir Harry Featherstonhaugh, who turned her out in December of that year. She was then pregnant, and in her distress she applied to the Hon. Charles Greville, to whom she was already known. At this time she called herself Emily Hart. Greville, a gentleman of artistic tastes and well known in society, entertained her as his mistress, her mother, known as Mrs Cadogan, acting as housekeeper and partly as servant. Under the protection of Greville, whose means were narrowed by debt, she acquired some education, and was taught to sing, dance and act with professional skill. In 1782 he introduced her to his friend Romney the portrait painter, who had been established for several years in London, and who admired her beauty with enthusiasm. The numerous famous portraits of her from his brush may

have somewhat idealised her apparently robust and brilliantly coloured beauty, but her vivacity and powers of fascination cannot be
doubted. She had the temperament of an artist, and seems to have
been sincerely attached to Greville. In 1784 she was seen by his uncle,
Sir William Hamilton, who admired her greatly. Two years later she
was sent on a visit to him at Naples, as the result of an understanding
between Hamilton and Greville—the uncle paying his nephew's debts
and the nephew ceding his mistress. Emma at first resented, but then
submitted to the arrangement. Her beauty, her artistic capacity, and
her high spirits soon made her a great favourite in the easy-going
society of Naples, and Queen Maria Carolina became closely attached
to her. She became famous for her "attitudes," a series of *poses plas-
tiques* in which she represented classical and other figures. On the
6th of September 1791, during a visit to England, she was married
to Sir W. Hamilton. The ceremony was required in order to justify
her public reception at the court of Naples, where Lady Hamilton
played an important part as the agent through whom the queen
communicated with the British minister—sometimes in opposition
to the will and the policy of the king. The revolutionary wars and
disturbances which began after 1792 made the services of Lady Hamilton always useful and sometimes necessary to the British government. It was claimed by her, and on her behalf, that she secured
valuable information in 1796, and was of essential service to the
British fleet in 1798 during the Nile campaign, by enabling it to obtain
stores and water in Sicily. These claims have been denied on the rather
irrelevant ground that they are wanting in official confirmation, which
was only to be expected since they were *ex hypothesi* unofficial and
secret, but it is not improbable that they were considerably exaggerated, and it is certain that her stories cannot always be reconciled
with one another or with the accepted facts. When Nelson returned
from the Nile in September 1798 Lady Hamilton made him her hero,
and he became entirely devoted to her. Her influence over him indeed
became notorious, and brought him much official displeasure. Lady
Hamilton undoubtedly used her influence to draw Nelson into a most
unhappy participation in the domestic troubles of Naples, and when
Sir W. Hamilton was recalled in 1800 she travelled with him and
Nelson ostentatiously across Europe. In England Lady Hamilton insisted on making a parade of her hold over Nelson. Their child,
Horatia Nelson Thompson, was born on the 30th of January 1801.
The profuse habits which Emma Hamilton had contracted in Naples,
together with a passion for gambling which grew on her, led her into
debt, and also into extravagant ways of living, against which her

husband feebly protested. On his death in 1803 she received by his will a liferent of £800, and the furniture of his house in Piccadilly. She then lived openly with Nelson at his house at Merton. Nelson tried repeatedly to secure her a pension for the services rendered at Naples, but did not succeed. On his death she received Merton, and an annuity of £500, as well as the control of the interest of the £4000 he left to his daughter. But gambling and extravagance kept her poor. In 1808 her friends endeavoured to arrange her affairs, but in 1813 she was put in prison for debt and remained there for a year. A certain Alderman Smith having aided her to get out, she went over to Calais for refuge from her creditors, and she died there in distress if not in want on the 15th of January 1815. (D.H.)

LAMBERT, DANIEL (1770–1809), an Englishman famous for his great size, was born near Leicester on the 13th of March 1770, the son of the keeper of the jail, to which post he succeeded in 1791. About this time his size and weight increased enormously, and though he had led an active and athletic life he weighed in 1793 thirty-two stone (448 lb). In 1806 he resolved to profit by his notoriety, and resigning his office went up to London and exhibited himself. He died on the 21st of July 1809, and at the time measured 5 ft. 11 in. in height and weighed 52¾ stone (739 lb). His waistcoat, now in the Kings Lynn Museum, measures 102 in. round the waist. His coffin contained 112 ft. of elm and was built on wheels. His name has been used as a synonym for immensity. George Meredith describes London as the "Daniel Lambert of cities," and Herbert Spencer uses the phrase "a Daniel Lambert of learning." His enormous proportions were depicted on a number of tavern signs, but the best portrait of him, a large mezzotint, is preserved at the British Museum in Lyson's *Collectanea*.

McGILLIVRAY, ALEXANDER (c. 1739–1793), American Indian chief, was born near the site of the present Wetumpka, in Alabama. His father was a Scotch merchant and his mother the daughter of a French officer and an Indian "princess." Through his father's relatives in South Carolina, McGillivray received a good education, but at the age of seventeen, after a short experience as a merchant in Savannah and Pensacola, he returned to the Muscogee Indians, who elected him chief. He retained his connexion with business life as a member of the British firm of Panton, Forbes

& Leslie of Pensacola. During the War of Independence, as a colonel in the British army, he incited his followers to attack the western frontiers of Georgia and the Carolinas. Georgia confiscated some of his property, and after the peace of 1783 McGillivray remained hostile. Though still retaining his British commission, he accepted one from Spain, and during the remainder of his life used his influence to prevent American settlement in the south-west. So important was he considered that in 1790 President Washington sent an agent who induced him to visit New York. Here he was persuaded to make peace in consideration of a brigadier-general's commission and payment for the property confiscated by Georgia; and with the warriors who accompanied him he signed a formal treaty of peace and friendship on the 7th of August. He then went back to the Indian country, and remained hostile to the Americans until his death. He was one of the ablest Indian leaders of America and at one time wielded great power—having 5000 to 10,000 armed followers. In order to serve Indian interests he played off British, Spanish and American interests against one another, but before he died he saw that he was fighting in a losing cause, and, changing his policy, endeavoured to provide for the training of the Muscogees in the white man's civilization. McGillivray was polished in manners, of cultivated intellect, was a shrewd merchant, and a successful speculator; but he had many savage traits, being noted for his treachery, craftiness and love of barbaric display. (W.L.F.)

NASH, RICHARD (1674–1762), English dandy, better known as "BEAU NASH," was born at Swansea on the 18th of October 1674. He was descended from an old family of good position, but his father from straitened means had become partner in a glass business. Young Nash was educated at Carmarthen grammar school and at Jesus College, Oxford. He obtained a commission in the army, which, however, he soon exchanged for the study of law at the Temple. Here among "wits and men of pleasure" he came to be accepted as an authority in regard to dress, manners and style. When the members of the Inns of Court entertained William III. after his accession, Nash was chosen to conduct the pageant at the Middle Temple. This duty he performed so much to the satisfaction of the king that he was offered knighthood, but he declined the honour, unless accompanied by a pension. As the king did not take the hint, Nash found it necessary to turn gamester. The pursuit of his calling led him in 1705 to Bath, where he had the good fortune almost immediately to succeed Captain Webster as master of the ceremonies. His qualifications for such a position were unique, and under his authority reforms were introduced which rapidly secured to Bath a leading position as a fashionable watering-place. He drew up a new code of rules for the regulation of balls and assemblies, abolished the habit of wearing swords in places of public amusement and brought duelling into disrepute, induced gentlemen to adopt shoes and stockings in parades and assemblies instead of boots, reduced refractory chairmen to submission and civility, and introduced a tariff for lodgings. Through his exertions a handsome assembly-room was also erected, and the streets and public buildings were greatly improved. Nash adopted an outward state corresponding to his nominal dignity. He wore an immense white hat as a sign of office, and a dress adorned with rich embroidery, and drove in a chariot with six greys, laced lackeys and French horns. When the act of parliament against gambling was passed in 1745, he was deprived of an easy though uncertain means of subsistence, but the corporation afterwards granted him a pension of six score guineas a year, which, with the sale of his snuff-boxes and other trinkets, enabled him to support a certain faded splendour till his death on the 3rd of February 1762. He was honoured with a public funeral at the expense of the town. Notwithstanding his vanity and impertinence, the tact, energy and superficial cleverness of Nash won him the patronage and notice of the great, while the success of his ceremonial rule, as shown in the increasing prosperity of the town, secured him the gratitude of the corporation and the people generally. He was a man of strong personality, and considerably more able than Beau Brummell, whose prototype he was.

PHRYNE, Greek courtesan, lived in the 4th century B.C. Her real name was Mnesarete, but owing to her complexion she was called Phryne (toad), a name given to other courtesans. She was born at Thespiae in Boeotia, but seems to have lived at Athens. She acquired so much wealth by her extraordinary beauty that she offered to rebuild the walls of Thebes, which had been destroyed by Alexander the Great (336), on condition that the words "Destroyed by Alexander, restored by Phryne the courtesan," were inscribed upon them. On the occasion of a festival of Poseidon at Eleusis she laid aside her garments, let down her hair, and stepped into the sea in the sight of the people, thus suggesting to the painter Apelles his great picture of Aphrodite Anadyomene, for which Phryne sat as

model. She was also (according to some) the model for the statue of
the Cnidian Aphrodite by Praxiteles. When accused of profaning the
Eleusinian mysteries, she was defended by the orator Hypereides,
one of her lovers. When it seemed as if the verdict would be unfa-
vourable, he rent her robe and displayed her lovely bosom, which so
moved her judges that they acquitted her. According to others, she
herself thus displayed her charms. She is said to have made an attempt
on the virtue of the philosopher Xenocrates. A statue of Phryne, the
work of Praxiteles, was placed in a temple at Thespiae by the side of
a statue of Aphrodite by the same artist.

◈◈◈ POMPADOUR, JEANNE ANTOI-NETTE POISSON LE NORMANT D'ÉTIOLES,

Marquise de (1721–1764), mistress of Louis XV., was born in Paris
on the 29th of December 1721, and baptized as the legitimate daughter of François Poisson, an officer in the household of the duke of
Orleans, and his wife, Madeleine de la Motte, in the church of St
Eustache; but she was suspected, as well as her brother, afterwards
marquis of Marigny, to be the child of a very wealthy financier and
farmer-general of the revenues, Le Normant de Tournehem. He at
any rate took upon himself the charge of her education; and, as from
the beauty and wit she showed from childhood she seemed to be
born for some uncommon destiny, he declared her "un morceau de
roi," and specially educated her to be a king's mistress. This idea was
confirmed in her childish mind by the prophecy of an old woman,
whom in after days she pensioned for the correctness of her prediction. In 1741 she was married to a nephew of her protector and
guardian, Le Normant d'Étioles, who was passionately in love with
her, and she soon became a queen of fashion. Yet the world of the
financiers at Paris was far apart from the court world, where she
wished to reign; she could get no introduction at court, and could
only try to catch the king's eye when he went out hunting. But Louis
XV. was then under the influence of Mme de Mailly, who carefully
prevented any further intimacy with "la petite Étioles," and it was not
until after her death that the king met the fair queen of the financial
world of Paris at a ball given by the city to the dauphin in 1744, and
he was immediately subjugated. She at once gave up her husband,
and in 1745 was established at Versailles as "maîtresse en titre." Louis
XV. bought her the estate of Pompadour, from which she took her
title of marquise (raised in 1752 to that of duchess). She was hardly

established firmly in power before she showed that ambition rather than love had guided her, and began to mix in politics. Knowing that the French people of that time were ruled by the literary kings of the time, she paid court to them, and tried to play the part of a Maecenas. Voltaire was her poet in chief, and the founder of the physiocrats, Quesnay, was her physician. In the arts she was even more successful; she was herself no mean etcher and engraver, and she encouraged and protected Vanloo, Boucher, Vien, Greuze, and the engraver Jacques Guay. Yet this policy did not prevent her from being lampooned, and the famous poissardes against her contributed to the ruin of many wits suspected of being among the authors, and notably of the Comte de Maurepas. The command of the political situation passed entirely into her hands; she it was who brought Belle-Isle into office with his vigorous policy; she corresponded regularly with the generals of the armies in the field, as her letters to the Comte de Clermont prove; and she introduced the Abbé de Bernis into the ministry in order to effect a very great alteration of French politics in 1756. The continuous policy of France since the days of Richelieu had been to weaken the house of Austria by alliances in Germany; but Mme de Pompadour changed this hereditary policy because Frederick the Great wrote scandalous verses on her; and because Maria Theresa wrote her a friendly letter she entered into an alliance with Austria. This alliance brought on the Seven Years' War, with all its disasters, the battle of Rosbach and the loss of Canada; but Mme de Pompadour persisted in her policy, and, when Bernis failed her, brought Choiseul into office and supported him in all his great plans, the Pacte de Famille, the suppression of the Jesuits, and the peace of Versailles. But it was to internal politics that this remarkable woman paid most attention; no one obtained office except through her; in imitation of Mme de Maintenon, she prepared all business for the king's eye with the ministers, and contrived that they should meet in her room; and she daily examined the letters sent through the post office with Janelle, the director of the post office. By this continuous labour she made herself indispensable to Louis. Yet, when after a year or two she had lost the heart of her lover, she had a difficult task before her; to maintain her influence she had not only to save the king as much trouble as possible, but to find him fresh pleasures. When he first began to weary of her she remembered her talent for acting and her private theatricals at Étioles, and established the "thé-âtre des petits cabinets," in which she acted with the greatest lords about the court for the king's pleasure in tragedies and comedies, operas and ballets. By this means and the "concerts spirituels" she kept in favour for a time; but at last she found a surer way, by encouraging the king in his debaucheries, and Louis wept over her kindness to his various mistresses. Only once, when the king was wounded by Damiens in 1757, did she receive a serious shock, and momentarily left the court; but on his recovery she returned more powerful than ever. She even ingratiated herself with the queen, after the example of Mme de Maintenon, and was made a lady-in-waiting; but the end was soon to come. "Ma vie est un combat," she said, and so it was, with business and pleasure she gradually grew weaker and weaker, and when told that death was at hand she dressed herself in full court costume, and met it bravely on the 15th of April 1764, at the age of forty-two.

SAINT-GERMAIN, Comte de (*c.* 1710–*c.* 1780) called *der Wundermann*, a celebrated adventurer who by the assertion of his discovery of some extraordinary secrets of nature exercised considerable influence at several European courts. Of his parentage and place of birth nothing is definitely known; the common version is that he was a Portuguese Jew, but various surmises have been made as to his being of royal birth. It was also stated that he obtained his money, of which he had abundance, from acting as spy to one of the European courts. But this is hard to maintain. He knew nearly all the European languages, and spoke German, English, Italian, French (with a Piedmontese accent), Portuguese and Spanish. Grimm affirms him to have been the man of the best parts he had ever known. He was a musical composer and a capable violinist. His knowledge of history was comprehensive, and his accomplishments as a chemist, on which be based his reputation, were in many ways real and considerable. He pretended to have a secret for removing flaws from diamonds, and to be able to transmute metals. The most remarkable of his professed discoveries was of a liquid which could prolong life, and by which he asserted he had himself lived 2000 years. After spending some time in Persia, Saint-Germain is mentioned in a letter of Horace Walpole's as being in London about 1743, and as being arrested as a Jacobite spy and released. Walpole says: "He is called an Italian, a Spaniard, a Pole; a somebody that married a great fortune in Mexico and ran away with her jewels to Constantinople; a priest, a fiddler, a vast nobleman." At the court of Louis XV., where he appeared about 1748, he exercised for a time extraordinary influence and was employed on secret missions by Louis XV.; but, having interfered in the dispute between Austria and France, he was compelled in June 1760, on account of the hostility of the duke of Choiseul, to remove to England. He appears to have resided in London for one or two years, but was at St Petersburg in 1762, and is asserted to have played an important part in connexion with the conspiracy against the emperor Peter III. in July of that year, a plot which placed Catherine II. on the Russian throne. He then went to Germany, where, according to the *Mémoires authentiques* of Cagliostro, he was the founder of freemasonry, and initiated Cagliostro into that rite. He was again in Paris from 1770 to 1774, and after frequenting several of the German courts he took up his residence in Schleswig-Holstein, where he and the Landgrave Charles of Hesse pursued together the study of the "secret" sciences. He died at Schleswig in or about 1780–1785, although he is said to have been seen in Paris in 1789.

SERRES, OLIVIA (1772–1834), an English imposter, who claimed the title of Princess Olive of Cumberland, was born at Warwick on the 3rd of April 1772. She was the daughter of Robert Wilmot, a house-painter in that town, who subsequently moved to London. In 1791 she married her drawing-master, John Thomas Serres (1759–1825), marine painter to George III., but in 1804 separated from him. She then devoted herself to painting and literature, producing a novel, some poems and a memoir of her uncle, the Rev. Dr Wilmot, in which she endeavoured to prove that he was the author of the *Letters of Junius*. In 1817, in a petition to George III., she put forward a claim to be the natural daughter of Henry Frederick, duke of Cumberland, the king's brother, and in 1820, after the death of George III., claimed to be the duke's legitimate daughter. In a memorial to George IV. she assumed the title of Princess Olive of Cumberland, placed the royal arms on her carriage and dressed her servants in the royal liveries. Her story represented that her mother was the issue of a secret marriage between Dr Wilmot and the princess Poniatowski, sister of Stanislaus, king of Poland, and that she had married the duke of Cumberland in 1767 at the London house of a nobleman. She herself, ten days after her birth, was, she alleged, taken from her mother, and substituted for the still-born child of Robert Wilmot. Mrs Serres's claim was supported by documents, and she bore sufficient resemblance to her alleged father to be able to impose on the numerous class of persons to whom any item of so-called secret history is attractive. In 1823 Sir Robert Peel, then Home Secretary, speaking in parliament, declared her claims unfounded, and her husband, who had never given her pretensions any support, expressly denied his belief in them in his will. Mrs Serres died on the 21st of November 1834, leaving two daughters. The eldest, who married Antony Ryves, a portrait painter, upheld her mother's claims and styled herself Princess Lavinia of Cumberland. In 1866 she took her case into court, producing all the documents on which her mother had relied, but the jury, without waiting to hear the conclusion of the reply for the crown, unanimously declared the signatures to be forgeries. Mrs Serres's pretensions were probably the result of an absurd vanity. Between 1807 and 1815 she had managed to make the acquaintance of some members of the Royal family, and from this time onwards seems to have been obsessed with the idea of raising herself, at all costs, to their social level. The tale once invented, she brooded so continuously over it that she probably ended by believing it herself.

⟨◈⟩ **THÉROIGNE DE MÉRICOURT, ANNE JOSÈPHE** (1762–1817), a Frenchwoman who was a striking figure in the Revolution, was born at Marcourt (from a corruption of which name she took her usual designation), a small town in Luxembourg, on the banks of the Ourthe, on the 13th of August 1762. She was the daughter of a well-to-do farmer, Peter Théroigne. She appears to have been well educated, having been brought up in the convent of Robermont; she was quick-witted, strikingly handsome in appearance and intensely passionate in temper; and she had a vigorous eloquence, which she used with great effect upon the mobs of Paris during that short space of her life (1789–93) which alone is of historical interest. The story of her having been betrayed by a young *seigneur,* and having in consequence devoted her life to avenge her wrongs upon aristocrats, a story which is told by Lamartine and others, is unfounded, the truth being that she left her home on account of a quarrel with her stepmother. In her career as courtesan she visited London in 1782, was back in Paris in 1785, and in Genoa in 1788, where she was a concert singer. In 1789 she returned to Paris. On the outbreak of the Revolution, she was surrounded by a coterie of well-known men, chief of whom were Pétion and Desmoulins; but she did not play the rôle which legend assigned her. She took no part in the taking of the Bastille nor in the days of the 5th and 6th of October, when the women of Paris brought the king and queen from Versailles. In 1790 she had a political salon and spoke once at the club of the Cordeliers. The same year she left Paris for Marcourt, whence after a short stay she proceeded to Liège, in which town she was seized by warrant of the Austrian Government, and conveyed first to Tirol and thereafter to Vienna, accused of having been engaged in a plot against the life of the queen of France. After an interview, however, with the emperor Leopold II., she was released; and she returned to Paris in January 1792, crowned of course with fresh laurels because of her captivity, and resumed her influence. In the clubs of Paris her voice was often heard, and even in the National Assembly she would violently interrupt the expression of any moderatist views. Known henceforth as "la belle Liégoise," she appeared in public dressed in a riding habit, a plume in her hat, a pistol in her belt and a sword dangling at her side, and excited the mob by violent harangues. Associated with the Girondists and the enemies of Robespierre, she became in fact the "Fury of the Gironde." She commanded in person the 3rd corps of the so-called army of the faubourgs on the 20th of June 1792, and again won the gratitude of the people. She shares a heavy responsibility for her connexion with the riots of the 10th of August. A certain contributor to the journal, the *Acts of the Apostles,* Suleau by name, earned her savage hatred by associating her name, for the sake of the play upon the word, with a deputy named Populus, whom she had never seen. On the 10th of August, just after she had watched approvingly the massacre of certain of the national guard in the Place Vendôme, Suleau was pointed out to her. She sprang at him, dragged him among the infuriated mob, and he was stabbed to death in an instant. She took no part in the massacres of September, and, moderating her conduct, became less popular from 1793. Towards the end of May the Jacobin women seized her, stripped her naked, and flogged her in the public garden of the Tuileries. The following year she became mad, a fate not surprising when one considers her career. She was removed to a private house, thence in 1800 to La Salpetrière for a month, and thence to a place of confinement called the Petites Maisons, where she remained—a raving maniac—till 1807. She was then again removed to La Salpetrière, where she died, never having recovered her reason, on the 9th of June 1817.

WILD, JONATHAN (*c.* 1682–1725), English criminal, was born about 1682 at Wolverhampton, where his father was a wig-maker. After being apprenticed to a local buckle-maker, he went to London to learn his trade, and, getting into debt, was imprisoned for several years. The acquaintance of many criminals which he made in prison he turned to account after his release by setting up as a receiver of stolen goods. Wild shrewdly realized that it was safer, and in most cases more profitable, to dispose of such property by returning it to its legitimate owners than to sell it, with the attendant risks, in the open market, and he thus built up an immense business, posing as a recoverer of stolen goods, the thieves receiving a commission on the price paid for recovery. A special act of parliament was passed by which receivers of stolen property were made accessories to the theft, but Wild's professed "lost property office" had little difficulty in evading the new law, and became so prosperous that two branch offices were opened. From profiting by robberies in which he had no share, Wild naturally came to arrange robberies himself, and he devised and controlled a huge organization, which plundered London and its approaches wholesale. Such thieves as refused to work with him received short shrift. The notorious Jack Sheppard, wearied of Wild's exactions, at last refused to deal with him, whereupon Wild secured his arrest, and himself arrested Sheppard's confederate, "Blueskin." In return for Wild's services in tracking down such thieves as he did not himself control, the authorities for some time tolerated the offences of his numerous agents, each a specialist in a particualr kind of robbery, and so themselves strengthened his position. If an arrest were made, Wild had a plentiful supply of false evidence at hand to establish his agents' *alibi,* and he did not hesitate to obtain the conviction, by similar means, of such thieves as refused to recognize his authority. Such stolen property as could not be returned to the owners with profit was taken abroad in a sloop purchased for this work. At last either the authorities became more strict or Wild less cautious. He was arrested, tried at the Old Bailey, and after being acquitted on a charge of stealing lace, found guilty of taking a reward for restoring it to the owner without informing the police. He was hanged at Tyburn on the 24th of May 1725.

As we leafed through the twenty-eight volumes of the eleventh, we noted that editor Hugh Chisholm had commissioned essays on—and must have taken interest in—many very gruesome methods of torture and execution as administered throughout the ages. We have here included a number of convincingly gory examples, but in order to alleviate what otherwise would be a too-macabre portion of the whole book, we grant the reader some relief by including two irresistible narrations of mild crime—one, the admirably narrated (and anonymous) "Affair of the Diamond Necklace," a tale of intrigue in the court of Louis XVI, and the other, a brisk recounting of a display of such effrontery and impudence that it must or should have ranked high already in the history of imposture: "The Tichborne Claimant."

Here is the history of a four-hundred-pound butcher from Wagga Wagga, Queensland, named Arthur Orton (alias Tom Castro, alias Roger Charles Tichborne), who came surprisingly close to making off with one of the great ancestral fortunes still available to swindlers in Victorian England. Evident here are the supreme narrative talents of Thomas Seccombe, one of editor Hugh Chisholm's most valued contributors (and whose trenchant essay on Charles Dickens we have included later in this volume). The story of the "Claimant," as he was popularly known, is done with a keen style, precise condensation of materials, and oblique but ever-present moral judgment. The story as we read it in the eleventh attracted the attention of the inveterate eleventh reader Jorge Luis Borges, who, with the supplementary aid of Bram Stoker's portrait of Orton in his *Famous Imposters*, wrote a comic variant on the material he found in Seccombe's piece, retitled it "Tom Castro, the Implausible Impostor," and produced another minor masterpiece "overlaid," as it were, over Seccombe's narration. It is now collected and can be found in Borges's *A Universal History of Infamy*, first published in Buenos Aires in 1935 and now available in English translation.

BLINDING, a form of punishment anciently common in many lands, being inflicted on thieves, adulterers, perjurers and other criminals. The inhabitants of Apollonia (Illyria) are said to have inflicted this penalty on their "watch" when found asleep at their posts. It was resorted to by the Roman emperors in their persecutions of the Christians. The method of destroying the sight varied. Sometimes a mixture of lime and vinegar, or barely scalding vinegar alone, was poured into the eyes. Sometimes a rope was twisted round the victim's head till the eyes started out of their sockets. In the middle ages the punishment seems to have been changed from total blindness to a permanent injury to the eyes, amounting, however, almost to blindness, produced by holding a red-hot iron dish or basin before the face. Under the forest laws of the Norman kings of England blinding was a common penalty. Shakespeare makes King John order his nephew Arthur's eyes to be burnt out.

BOILING TO DEATH, a punishment once common both in England and on the continent. The only extant legislative notice of it in England occurs in an act passed in 1531 during the reign of Henry VIII., providing that convicted prisoners should be boiled to death; it is, however, frequently mentioned earlier as a punishment for coining. The *Chronicles of the Grey Friars* have an account of boiling for poisoning at Smithfield in the year 1522, the man being fastened to a chain and lowered into boiling water several times until he died. The preamble of the statute of Henry VIII. (which made poisoning treason) in 1531 recites that one Richard Roose (or Coke), a cook, by putting poison in some food intended for the household of the bishop of Rochester and for the poor of the parish of Lambeth, killed a man and woman. He was found guilty of treason and sentenced to be boiled to death without benefit of clergy. He was publicly boiled at Smithfield. In the same year a maid-servant for poisoning her mistress was boiled at King's Lynn. In 1542 Margaret Davy, a servant, for poisoning her employer, was boiled at Smithfield. In the reign of Edward VI., in 1547, the act was repealed.

BRANDING (from Teutonic *brinnan,* to burn), in criminal law a mode of punishment; also a method of marking goods or animals; in either case by stamping with a hot iron. The Greeks branded their slaves with a Delta, Δ, for Δσυλοδ. Robbers and runaway slaves were marked by the Romans with the letter F (*fur, fugitivus*); and the toilers in the mines, and convicts condemned to figure in gladiatorial shows, were branded on the forehead for identification. Under Constantine the face was not permitted to be so disfigured, the branding being on the hand, arm or calf. The canon law sanctioned the punishment, and in France galley-slaves could be branded "TF" (*travaux forcés*) until 1832. In Germany, however, branding was illegal. The punishment was adopted by the Anglo-

Saxons, and the ancient law of England authorized the penalty. By the Statute of Vagabonds (1547) under Edward VI. vagabonds, gipsies and brawlers were ordered to be branded, the first two with a large V on the breast, the last with F for "fraymaker." Slaves, too, who ran away were branded with S on cheek or forehead. This law was repealed in 1636. From the time of Henry VII. branding was inflicted for all offences which received benefit of clergy, but it was abolished for such in 1822. In 1698 it was enacted that those convicted of petty theft or larceny, who were entitled to benefit of clergy, should be "burnt in the most visible part of the left cheek, nearest the nose." This special ordinance was repealed in 1707. James Nayler, the mad Quaker, who in the year 1655 claimed to be the Messiah, had his tongue bored through and his forehead branded B for blasphemer.

In the Lancaster criminal court a branding-iron is still preserved in the dock. It is a long bolt with a wooden handle at one end and an M (malefactor) at the other. Close by are two iron loops for firmly securing the hands during the operation. The brander, after examination, would turn to the judge and exclaim, "A fair mark, my lord." Criminals were formerly ordered to hold up their hands before sentence to show if they had been previously convicted.

Cold branding or branding with cold irons became in the 18th century the mode of nominally inflicting the punishment on prisoners of higher rank. "When Charles Moritz, a young German, visited England in 1782 he was much surprised at this custom, and in his diary mentioned the case of a clergyman who had fought a duel and killed his man in Hyde Park. Found guilty of manslaughter he was *burnt* in the hand, if that could be called burning which was done with a cold iron" (Markham's *Ancient Punishments of Northants*, 1886). Such cases led to branding becoming obsolete, and it was abolished in 1820 except in the case of deserters from the army. These were marked with the letter D, not with hot irons but by tattooing with ink or gunpowder. Notoriously bad soldiers were also branded with BC (bad character). By the British Mutiny Act of 1858 it was enacted that the court-martial, in addition to any other penalty, may order deserters to be marked on the left side, 2 in. below the armpit, with the letter D, such letter to be not less than 1 in. long. In 1879 this was abolished.

CAMORRA, a secret society of Naples associated with robbery, blackmail and murder. The origin of the name is doubtful. Probably both the word and the association were introduced into Naples by Spaniards. There is a Spanish word *camorra* (a quarrel), and similar societies seem to have existed in Spain long before the appearance of the Camorra in Naples. It was in 1820 that the society first became publicly known. It was primarily social, not political, and originated in the Neapolitan prisons then filled with the victims of Bourbon misrule and oppression, its first purpose being the protection of prisoners. In or about 1830 the Camorra was carried into the city by prisoners who had served their terms. The members worked the streets in gangs. They had special methods of communicating with each other. They mewed like cats at the approach of the patrol, and crowed like cocks when a likely victim approached. A long sigh gave warning that the latter was not alone, a sneeze meant he was not "worth powder and shot," and so on. The society rapidly extended its power, and its operations included smuggling and blackmail of all kinds in addition to ordinary road-robberies. Its influence grew to be considerable. Princes were in league with and shared the profits of the smugglers: statesmen and dignitaries of the church, all classes in fact, were involved in the society's misdeeds. From brothels the Camorra drew huge fees, and it maintained illegal lottery offices. The general disorder of Naples was so great and the police so badly organized that merchants were glad to engage the Camorra to superintend the loading and unloading of merchandise. Being non-political, the government did not interfere with the society; indeed its members were taken into the police service and the Camorra sometimes detected crimes which baffled the authorities. After 1848 the society became political. In 1860, when the constitution was granted by Francis II., the *camorristi* then in gaol were liberated in great numbers. The association became all-powerful at elections, and general disorder reigned till 1862. Thereafter severe repressive measures were taken to curtail its power. In September 1877 there was a determined effort to exterminate it: fifty-seven of the most notorious camorristi being simultaneously arrested in the market-place. Though much of its power has gone, the Camorra has remained vigorous. It has grown upwards, and highly-placed and well-known camorristi have entered municipal administrations and political life. In 1900 revelations as to the Camorra's power were made in the course of a libel suit, and these led to the dissoultion of the Naples municipality and the appointment of a royal commissioner. A government inquiry also took place. As the result of this investigation the Honest Government League was formed, which succeeded in 1901 in entirely defeating the Camorra candidates at the municipal elections.

The Camorra was divided into classes. There were the "swell mobs-men," the camorristi who dressed faultlessly and mixed with and levied fines on people of highest rank. Most of these were well connected. There were the lower order of blackmailers who preyed on shopkeepers, boatmen, &c.; and there were political and murdering camorristi. The ranks of the society were largely recruited from the prisons. A youth had to serve for one year an apprenticeship so to speak to a fully admitted camorrista when he was sometimes called *picciotto d'honore,* and after giving proof of courage and zeal became a *picciotto di sgarro,* one, that is, of the lowest grade of members. In some localities he was then called *tamurro.* The initiatory ceremony for full membership is now a mock duel in which the arm alone is wounded. In early times initiation was more severe. The camorristi stood round a coin laid on the ground, and at a signal all stooped to thrust at it with their knives while the novice had at the same time to pick the coin up, with the result that his hand was generally pierced through in several places. The noviciate as *picciotto di sgarro* lasted three years, during which the lad had to work for the camorrista who had been assigned to him as master. After initiation there was a ceremony of reception. The camorristi stood round a table on which were a dagger, a loaded pistol, a glass of water or wine supposed to be poisoned and a lancet. The *picciotto* was brought in and one of his veins opened. Dipping his hand in his own blood, he held it out to the camorristi and swore to keep the society's secrets and obey orders. Then he had to stick the dagger into the table, cock the pistol, and hold the glass in his mouth to show his readiness to die for the society. His master now bade him kneel before the dagger, placed his right hand on the lad's head while with the left he fired off the pistol into the air and smashed the poison-glass. He then drew the dagger from the table and presented it to the new comrade and embraced him, as did all the others. The Camorra was divided into centres, each under a chief. There were twelve at Naples. The society seems at one time to have always had a supreme chief. The last known was Aniello Ansiello, who finally disappeared and was never arrested. The chief of every centre was elected by the members of it. All the earnings of the centre were paid to and then distributed by him. The camorristi employ a whole vocabulary of cant terms. Their chief is *masto* or *sì masto,* "sir master." When a member meets him he salutes with the phrase *Masto, volite niente?* ("Master, do you want anything?"). The members are addressed simply as *sì.*

≪≫ DIAMOND NECKLACE, THE AFFAIR

OF THE, a mysterious incident at the court of Louis XVI. of France, which involved the queen Marie Antoinette. The Parisian jewellers Boehmer and Bassenge had spent some years collecting stones for a necklace which they hoped to sell to Madame Du Barry, the favourite of Louis XV., and after his death to Marie Antoinette. In 1778 Louis XVI. proposed to the queen to make her a present of the necklace, which cost 1,600,000 livres. But the queen is said to have refused it, saying that the money would be better spent equipping a man-of-war. According to others, Louis XVI. himself changed his mind. After having vainly tried to place the necklace outside of France, the jewellers attempted again in 1781 to sell it to Marie Antoinette after the birth of the dauphin. It was again refused, but it was evident that the queen regretted not being able to acquire it.

At that time there was a personage at the court whom Marie Antoinette particularly detested. It was the cardinal Louis de Rohan, formerly ambassador at Vienna, whence he had been recalled in 1774, having incurred the queen's displeasure by revealing to the empress Maria Theresa the frivolous actions of her daughter, a disclosure which brought a maternal reprimand, and for having spoken lightly of Maria Theresa in a letter of which Marie Antoinette learned the contents. After his return to France the cardinal was anxious to regain the favour of the queen in order to obtain the position of prime minister. In March 1784 he entered into relations with a certain Jeanne de St Remy de Valois, a descendant of a bastard of Henry II., who after many adventures had married a *soi-disant* comte de Lamotte, and lived on a small pension which the king granted her. This adventuress soon gained the greatest ascendancy over the cardinal, with whom she had intimate relations. She persuaded him that she had been received by the queen and enjoyed her favour; and Rohan resolved to use her to regain the queen's good will. The comtesse de Lamotte assured the cardinal that she was making efforts on his behalf, and soon announced to him that he might send his justification to Marie Antoinette. This was the beginning of a pretended correspondence between Rohan and the queen, the adventuress duly returning replies to Rohan's notes, which she affirmed to come from the queen. The tone of the letters became very warm, and the cardinal, convinced that Marie Antoinette was in love with him, became ardently enamoured of her. He begged the countess to obtain a secret interview for him with the queen, and a meeting took place in August 1784 in a grove in the garden at Versailles between him and a lady whom the cardinal believed to be the queen herself. Rohan offered her a rose, and she promised him that she would forget the past. Later a certain Marie Lejay (renamed by the comtesse "Baronne Gay d'Oliva," the last word being apparently an anagram of Valoi), who resembled Marie Antoinette, stated that she had been engaged to play the role of queen in this comedy. In any case the countess profited by the cardinal's conviction to borrow from him sums of money destined ostensibly for the queen's works of charity. Enriched by these, the countess was able to take an honourable place in society, and many persons believed her relations with Marie Antoinette, of which she boasted openly and unreservedly, to be genuine. It is still an unsettled question whether she simply mystified people, or whether she was really employed by the queen for some unknown purpose, perhaps to ruin the cardinal. In any case the jewellers believed in the relations of the countess with the queen, and they resolved to use her to sell their necklace. She at first refused their commission, then accepted it. On the 21st of January 1785 she announced that the queen would buy the necklace, but that not wishing to treat directly, she left the affair to a high personage. A little while later Rohan came to negotiate the purchase of the famous necklace for the 1,600,000 livres, payable in instalments. He said that he was authorized by the queen, and showed the jewellers the conditions of the bargain approved in the handwriting of Marie Antoinette. The necklace was given up. Rohan took it to the countess's house, where a man, in whom Rohan believed he recognized a valet of the queen, came to fetch it. Madame de Lamotte had told the cardinal that Marie Antoinette would make him a sign to indicate her thanks, and Rohan believed that she did make him a sign. Whether it was so, or merely chance or illusion, no one knows. But it is certain that the cardinal, convinced that he was acting for the queen, had engaged the jewellers to thank her; that Boehmer and Bassenge, before the sale, in order to be doubly sure, had sent word to the queen of the negotiations in her name; that Marie Antoinette had allowed the bargain to be concluded, and that after she had received a letter of thanks from Boehmer, she had burned it. Meanwhile the "comte de Lamotte" appears to have started at once for London, it is said with the necklace, which he broke up in order to sell the stones.

When the time came to pay, the comtesse de Lamotte presented the cardinal's notes; but these were insufficient, and Boehmer complained to the queen, who told him that she had received no necklace and had never ordered it. She had the story of the negotiations repeated for her. Then followed a *coup de théâtre*. On the 15th of August 1785, Assumption day, when the whole court was awaiting the king and queen in order to go to the chapel, the cardinal de Rohan, who was preparing to officiate, was arrested and taken to the Bastille. He was able, however, to destroy the correspondence exchanged, as he thought, with the queen, and it is not known whether there was any connivance of the officials, who did not prevent this, or not. The comtesse de Lamotte was not arrested until the 18th of August, after having destroyed her papers. The police set to work to find all her accomplices, and arrested the girl Oliva and a certain Reteaux de Villette, a friend of the countess, who confessed that he had written the letters given to Rohan in the queen's name, and had imitated her signature on the conditions of the bargain. The famous charlatan Cagliostro was also arrested, but it was recognized that he had taken no part in the affair. The cardinal de Rohan accepted the parlement of Paris as judges. A sensational trial resulted (May 31, 1786) in the acquittal of the cardinal, of the girl Oliva and of Cagliostro. The comtesse de Lamotte was condemned to be whipped, branded and shut up in the Salpetrière. Her husband was condemned, in his absence, to the galleys for life. Villette was banished.

Public opinion was much excited by this trial. It is generally believed that Marie Antoinette was stainless in the matter, that Rohan was an innocent dupe, and that the Lamottes deceived both for their own ends. People, however, persisted in the belief that the queen had used the countess as an instrument to satisfy her hatred of the cardinal de Rohan. Various circumstances fortified this belief, which contributed to render Marie Antoinette very unpopular—her disappointment at Rohan's acquittal, the fact that he was deprived of his charges and exiled to the abbey of la Chaise-Dieu, and finally the escape of the comtesse de Lamotte from the Salpetrière, with the connivance, as people believed, of the court. The adventuress, having taken refuge abroad, published *Mémoires* in which she accused the queen. Her husband also wrote *Mémoires,* and lived until 1831, after having, it is said, received subsidies from Louis XVIII.

DRAWING AND QUARTERING, part of the penalty anciently ordained in England for treason. Until 1870 the full punishment for the crime was that the culprit be dragged on a hurdle to the place of execution; that he be hanged by the neck but not till he was dead; that he should be disembowelled or drawn and his entrails burned before his eyes; that his head be cut off and his body divided into four parts or quartered. This brutal penalty was first inflicted in 1284 on the Welsh prince David, and on Sir

William Wallace a few years later. In Richard III.'s reign one Col-
lingbourne, for writing the famous couplet "The Cat, the Rat and
Lovel the Dog, Rule all England under the Hog,'" was executed on
Tower Hill. Stow says, "After having been hanged, he was cut down
immediately and his entrails were then extracted and thrown into
the fire, and all this was so speedily done that when the executioners
pulled out his heart he spoke and said 'Jesus, Jesus.' " Edward Marcus
Despard and his six accomplices were in 1803 hanged, drawn and
quartered for conspiring to assassinate George III. The sentence was
last passed (though not carried out) upon the Fenians Burke and
O'Brien in 1867. There is a tradition that Harrison the regicide, after
being disembowelled, rose and boxed the ears of the executioner.

⌒⌒⌒ DUCKING AND CUCKING STOOLS,

chairs used for the punishment of scolds, witches and prostitutes in
bygone days. The two have been generally confused, but are quite
distinct. The earlier, the Cucking-stool or Stool of Repentance, is of
very ancient date, and was used by the Saxons, who called it the
Scealding or *Scolding Stool*. Seated on this stool the woman, her head
and feet bare, was publicly exposed at her door or paraded through
the streets amidst the jeers of the crowd. The Cucking-stool was used
for both sexes, and was specially the punishment for dishonest brewers and bakers. Its use in the case of scolding women declined on
the introduction in the middle of the 16th century of the Scold's
Bridle, and it disappears on the introduction a little later of the
Ducking-stool. The earliest record of the use of this latter is towards
the beginning of the 17th century. It was a strongly made wooden
armchair (the surviving specimens are of oak) in which the culprit
was seated, an iron band being placed around her so that she should
not fall out during her immersion. Usually the chair was fastened to
a long wooden beam fixed as a seesaw on the edge of a pond or river.
Sometimes, however, the Ducking-stool was not a fixture but was
mounted on a pair of wooden wheels so that it could be wheeled
through the streets, and at the river-edge was hung by a chain
from the end of a beam. In sentencing a woman the magistrates
ordered the number of duckings she should have. Yet another type
of Ducking-stool was called a tumbrel. It was a chair on two wheels
with two long shafts fixed to the axles. This was pushed into the pond
and then the shafts released, thus tipping the chair up backwards.
Sometimes the punishment proved fatal, the unfortunate woman
dying of shock. Ducking-stools were used in England as late as the

beginning of the 19th century. The last recorded cases are those of a Mrs Ganble at Plymouth (1808); of Jenny Pipes, "a notorious scold" (1809), and Sarah Leeke (1817), both of Leominster. In the last case the water in the pond was so low that the victim was merely wheeled round the town in the chair.

FETTERS AND HANDCUFFS, instruments for securing the feet and hands of prisoners under arrest, or as a means of punishment. The old names were manacles, shackbolts or shackles, gyves and swivels. Until within recent times handcuffs were of two kinds, the figure-8 ones which confined the hands close together either in front or behind the prisoner, or the rings from the wrists were connected by a short chain much on the model of the handcuffs in use by the police forces of to-day. Much improvement has been made in handcuffs of late. They are much lighter and they are adjustable, fitting any wrist, and thus the one pair will serve a police officer for any prisoner. For the removal of gangs of convicts an arrangement of handcuffs connected by a light chain is used, the chain running through a ring on each fetter and made fast at both ends by what are known as *end-locks*. Several recently invented appliances are used as handcuffs, *e.g.* snaps, nippers, twisters. They differ from handcuffs in being intended for one wrist only, the other portion being held by the captor. In the snap the smaller circlet is snapped to on the prisoner's wrist. The nippers can be instantly fastened on the wrist. The twister, not now used in England as being liable to injure prisoners seriously, is a chain attached to two handles; the chain is put round the wrist and the two handles twisted till the chain is tight enough.

Leg-irons are anklets of steel connected by light chains long enough to permit of the wearer walking with short steps. An obsolete form was an anklet and chain to the end of which was attached a heavy weight, usually a round slot. The Spanish used to secure prisoners in bilboes, shackles round the ankles secured by a long bar of iron. This form of leg-iron was adopted in England, and was much employed in the services during the 17th and 18th centuries. An ancient example is preserved in the Tower of London. The French marine still use a kind of leg-iron of the bilbo type.

GUILLOTINE, who was born at Saintes, May 28, 1738, and elected to the Constituent Assembly in 1789, brought forward on the 1st December of that year two propositions regarding capital punishment, the second of which was that, "in all cases of capital punishment it shall be of the same kind—that is, decapitation—and it shall be executed by means of a machine." The reasons urged in support of this proposition were that in cases of capital punishment the privilege of execution by decapitation should no longer be confined to the nobles, and that it was desirable to render the process of execution as swift and painless as possible. The debate was brought to a sudden termination in peals of laughter caused by an indiscreet reference of Dr Guillotine to his machine, but his ideas seem gradually to have leavened the minds of the Assembly, and after various debates decapitation was adopted as the method of execution in the penal code which became law on the 6th October 1791. At first it was intended that decapitation should be by the sword, but on account of a memorandum by M. Sanson, the executioner, pointing out the expense and certain other inconveniences attending that method, the Assembly referred the question to a committee, at whose request Dr Antoine Louis, secretary to the Academy of Surgeons, prepared a memorandum on the subject. Without mentioning the name of Guillotine, it recommended the adoption of an instrument similar to that which was formerly suggested by him. The Assembly decided in favour of the report, and the contract was offered to the person who usually provided the instruments of justice; but, as his terms were considered exorbitant, an agreement was ultimately come to with a German of the name of Schmidt, who, under the direction of M. Louis, furnished a machine for each of the French departments. After satisfactory experiments had been made with the machine on several dead bodies in the hospital of Bicêtre, it was erected on the Place de Grève for the execution of the highwayman Pelletier on the 25th April 1792. While the experiments regarding the machine were being carried on, it received the name *Louisette* or *La Petite Louison,* but the mind of the nation seems soon to have reverted to Guillotine, who first suggested its use; and in the *Journal des révolutions de Paris* for 28th April 1792 it is mentioned as *la guillotine,* a name which it thenceforth bore both popularly and officially. In 1795 the question was much debated as to whether or not death by the guillotine was instantaneous, and in support of the negative side the case of Charlotte Corday was adduced whose countenance, it is said, blushed as if with indignation when the executioner, holding up the head to the public gaze, struck it with his fist. The connexion of the instrument with the horrors of the Revolution has hindered its introduction into other countries, but in 1853 it was adopted under the name of

Fallschwert or *Fallbeil* by the kingdom of Saxony; and it is used for the execution of sentences of death in France, Belgium and some parts of Germany. It has often been stated that Dr Guillotine perished by the instrument which bears his name, but it is beyond question that he survived the Revolution and died a natural death in 1814.

⟨◦∼⟩ **PEINE FORTE ET DURE** (French for "hard and severe punishment"), the term for a barbarous torture inflicted on those who, arraigned of felony, refused to plead and stood silent, or challenged more than twenty jurors, which was deemed a contumacy equivalent to a refusal to plead. By early English law a prisoner, before he could be tried, must plead "guilty" or "not guilty." Before the 13th century it was usual to imprison and starve till submission, but in Henry IV.'s reign the *peine* was employed. The prisoner was stretched on his back, and stone or iron weights were placed on him till he either submitted or was pressed to death. Pressing to death was abolished in 1772; "standing mute" on an arraignment of felony being then made equivalent to conviction. By an act of 1828 a plea of "not guilty" was to be entered against any prisoner refusing to plead, and that is the rule to-day. An alternative to the *peine* was the tying of the thumbs tightly together with whipcord until pain forced the prisoner to speak. This was said to be a common practice at the Old Bailey up to the 19th century.

⟨◦∼⟩ **SCALPING,** the custom of removing the skin of the skull, with hair attached. Though generally associated with the North American Indians, the practice has been common in Europe, Asia and Africa. The underlying idea, as of similar mutilations of those slain in battle, is the warrior's wish to preserve a portable proof or trophy of his prowess. Scalping was the usual form of mutilation from the earliest times. Herodotus describes the practice among the Scythians. The Abbé Emmanuel H. D. Domenech (*Seven Years' Residence in the Great Desert of North America*, ch. 39) quotes the *decalvare* of the ancient Germans, the *capillos et cutem detrahere* of the code of the Visigoths, and the *Annals* of Flodoard, to prove that the Anglo-Saxons and the Franks still scalped about A.D. 879. In Africa it was, and doubtless is, as prevalent as are all barbarous mutilations.

Among the North American Indians scalping was always in the nature of a rite. It was common to those tribes east of the Rocky Mountains, in the south-west and upper Columbia; but unknown apparently among the Eskimo, along the north-west coast, and on the Pacific coast west of the Cascade range and the Sierras, except among some few Californian tribes, or here and there in Mexico and southward. Properly the scalp could only be taken after a fair fight; in more recent times there seems to have been no such restriction. To facilitate the operation the braves wore long war-locks or scalping-tufts, as an implied challenge. These locks were braided with bright ribbons or ornamented with a feather. After the successful warrior's return the scalp or scalps captured were dried, mounted and consecrated by a solemn dance. Some tribes hung the scalps to their bridles, others to their shields, while some ornamented with them the outer seams of their leggings. Scalping was sometimes adopted by the whites in their wars with the Redskins, and bounties have been offered for scalps several times in American history.

∽∽∽ **TARRING AND FEATHERING,** a method of punishment at least as old as the Crusades. The head of the culprit was shaved and hot tar poured over it, a bag of feathers being afterwards shaken over him. The earliest mention of the punishment occurs in the orders of Richard Cœur de Lion, issued to his navy on starting for the Holy Land in 1191. "Concerning the lawes and ordinances appointed by King Richard for his navie the forme thereof was this . . . item, a thiefe or felon that hath stolen, being lawfully convicted, shal have his head shorne, and boyling pitch poured upon his head, and feathers or downe strawed upon the same whereby he may be knowen, and so at the first landing-place they shall come to, there to be cast up." A later instance of this penalty being inflicted is given in *Notes and Queries,* which quotes one James Howell writing from Madrid, in 1623, of the "boisterous Bishop of Halverstadt," who, "having taken a place where there were two monasteries of nuns and friars, he caused divers feather beds to be ripped, and all the feathers thrown into a great hall, wither the nuns and friars were thrust naked with their bodies oiled and pitched and to tumble among these feathers, which makes them here (Madrid) presage him an ill-death." In 1696 a London bailiff, who attempted to serve process on a debtor who had taken refuge within the precincts of the Savoy, was tarred and feathered and taken in a wheelbarrow to the Strand, where he was tied to the Maypole which stood by what is now Somerset House. It is probable that the punishment was never regarded as legalized, but was always a type of mob vengeance.

⟨⟨⟩⟩ **THUGS.** That the Sanskrit root *sthag* (Pali, *thak*), to cover, to conceal, was mainly applied to fraudulent concealment, appears from the noun *sthaga*, a cheat, which has retained this signification in the modern vernaculars, in all of which it has assumed the form *thag* (commonly written *thug*), with a specific meaning. The Thugs were a well-organized confederacy of professional assassins, who in gangs of whom 10 to 200 travelled in various guises through India, wormed themselves into the confidence of wayfarers of the wealthier class, and, when a favourable opportunity occurred, strangled them by throwing a handkerchief or noose round their necks, and then plundered and buried them. All this was done according to certain ancient and rigidly prescribed forms and after the performance of special religious rites, in which the consecration of the pickaxe and the sacrifice of sugar formed a prominent part. From their using the noose as an instrument of murder they were also frequently called *Phansigars,* or "noose-operators." Though they themselves trace their origin to seven Mahommedan tribes, Hindus appear to have been associated with them at an early period; at any rate, their religious creed and practices as stanch worshippers of Kali (Devi, Durga), the Hindu goddess of destruction, had certainly no flavour of Islam in them. Assassination for gain was with them a religious duty, and was considered a holy and honourable profession. They had, in fact, no idea of doing wrong, and their moral feelings did not come into play. The will of the goddess by whose command and in whose honour they followed their calling was revealed to them through a very complicated system of omens. In obedience to these they often travelled hundreds of miles in company with, or in the wake of, their intended victims before a safe opportunity presented itself for executing their design; and, when the deed was done, rites were performed in honour of that tutelary deity, and a goodly portion of the spoil was set apart for her. The fraternity possessed also a jargon of their own (*Ramasi*), as well as certain signs by which its members recognized each other in the remotest parts of India. Even those who from age or infirmities could no longer take an active part in the operations continued to aid the cause as watchers, spies, or dressers of food. It was owing to their thorough organization, the secrecy and security with which they went to work, but chiefly to the religious garb in which they shrouded their murders, that they could, unmolested by Hindu or Mahommedan rulers, recognized as a regular profession and paying taxes as such, continue for centuries to practise their craft. Both the fractions into which they were divided by the Nerbudda river laid claim to antiquity: while the northern, however, did not trace their origin further back than the period of the early Mahommedan kings of Delhi, the southern fraction not only claimed an earlier and purer descent, but adhered also with greater strictness to the rules of their profession. (R.R.)

CRLS **TICHBORNE CLAIMANT, THE.** Roger Charles Tichborne (1829–1854), whose family name became a household word on account of an attempt made by an impostor in 1868 to personate him and obtain his heritage, was the eldest grandson of Sir Edward Tichborne, the 9th baronet, of a very ancient Hampshire family. Sir John de Tichborne, sheriff of Southampton, was created a baronet by James I. in 1621, and from him his descendants inherited great wealth and the position of one of the leading Roman Catholic families in the south of England. Roger Charles, born at Paris on the 5th of January 1829, was the eldest son of James Francis Doughty-Tichborne (who subsequently became 10th baronet and died in 1862) by Henriette Felicité, natural daughter of Henry Seymour of Knoyle, in Wiltshire. This lady, who hated England, was intent upon bringing up her son as a Frenchman; the result was that he got hardly any education until he went in 1846 to Stonyhurst, whence he proceeded in 1849 to Dublin and joined the 6th Dragoon Guards. His eccentricity and his French accent made him a butt in his regiment, and, being disappointed of war service, he sold out in 1852, and in the following year proceeded on a trip to South America. He sailed in March 1853 from Havre for Valparaiso, whence he crossed the Andes, reaching Rio de Janeiro in 1854. In April of that year he sailed from Rio in the "Bella" and was lost at sea, the vessel foundering with all hands. His insurance was paid and his will proved in July 1855. The baronetcy and estates passed in 1862 to Roger's younger brother, Sir Alfred Joseph Doughty-Tichborne, who died in 1866. The only person unconvinced of Roger's death was his mother the dowager Lady Tichborne, from whom every tramp-sailor found a welcome at Tichborne Park. She advertised largely and injudiciously for the wanderer, and in November 1865 she learnt, through an agency in Sydney, that a man "answering to the description of her son" had been found in the guise of a small butcher at Wagga Wagga, in Queensland. As a matter of fact, the supposed Sir Roger did not correspond at all to the lost heir, who was slim, with sharp features and straight black hair, whereas the claimant was enormously fat, with wavy, light-brown hair. His first letter to Lady Tichborne was not only ignorant and illiterate, but appealed to circumstances (notably a birth-mark and an incident at Brighton) of which she admitted that she had no recollection. But so great was her infatuation with her fixed idea, that she soon overcame the first qualms of distrust and advanced money for the claimant to return to Europe. Like all pretenders, this one was impelled by his entourage, who regarded him in the light of an investment. He himself was reluctant to move, but the credulity of persons under the influence of a romantic story soon came to his aid. Thus an old friend of Sir James Tichborne's at Sydney, though puzzled by the claimant's answers, was convinced by a resemblance to his supposed father. At Sydney, too, he made the acquaintance of Bogle, a negro servant of a former baronet. Bogle sailed with him from Sydney in the summer of 1866, and coached him in the rudiments of the rôle which he was preparing to play. On reaching London on Christmas Day 1866 the claimant paid a flying visit to Tichborne House, near Alresford, where he was soon to obtain two important allies in the old family solicitor, Edward Hopkins, and a Winchester antiquary, Francis J. Baigent, who was intimately acquainted with the Tichborne family history. He next went over to Paris, where in an hotel bedroom on a dark January afternoon he was promptly "recognized" by Lady Tichborne. This "recognition" naturally made an enormous impression upon the English public, who were unaware that Lady Tichborne was a monomaniac. That such a term is no exaggeration is shown by the fact that she at once acquiesced in her supposed son's absolute ignorance of French. She allowed the claimant £1000 a year, accepted his wife, a poor illiterate girl, whom he had married in Queensland, and handed over to him the diaries and letters written by Roger Tichborne from South America. From these documents the claimant now carefully studied his part; he learnt much, too, from Baigent and from two carabiniers of Roger's old regiment, whom he took into his service. The villagers in Hampshire, a number of the county families, and several of Tichborne's fellow officers in the 6th Dragoons, became eager victims of the delusion. The members of the Tichborne family in England, however, were unanimous in declaring the claimant to be an impostor, and they were soon put upon the track of discoveries which revealed that Tom Castro, as the claimant had been called in Australia, was identical with Arthur Orton (1834–1898), the son of a Wapping butcher, who had deserted a sailing vessel at Valparaiso in 1850, and had received much kindness at Melipilla in Chile from a family named Castro, whose name he had subsequently elected to bear during his sojourn in Australia. It was discovered, too, that Roger Tichborne was never at Melipilla, an assertion to which the claimant, transferring his own adventures in South America to the account of the man whom he impersonated, had committed himself in an affidavit. These discoveries and the deaths of Lady Tichborne and Hopkins were so discouraging that the "claimant" would gladly have "retired" from the baronetage; but the pressure of his creditors, to whom he owed vast sums, was importunate. A number of "Tichborne bonds" to defray the expenses of litigation were taken up by the dupes of the imposture, and an ejectment action against the trustees of the Tichborne estates (to which the heir was the 12th baronet, Sir Henry Alfred Joseph Doughty-Tichborne, then two years old) finally came before Chief Justice Bovill and a special jury at the court of common pleas on the 11th of May 1871. During a trial that lasted over one hundred days the claimant exhibited an ignorance, a cunning and a bulldog tenacity in brazening out the discrepancies and absurdities of his depositions, which have probably never been surpassed in the history of crime. Over one hundred persons swore to the claimant's identity, the majority of them—and they were drawn from every class—being evidently sincere in their belief in his cause. It was not until Sir John Coleridge, in a speech of unparalleled length, laid bare the whole conspiracy from its inception, that the result ceased to be doubtful. The evidence of the Tichbornes finally convinced the jury, who declared that they wanted no further evidence, and on the 5th of March 1872 Serjeant Ballantine, who led for the claimant, elected to be non-suited. Orton was immediately arrested on a charge of perjury and was brought to trial at bar before Chief Justice Cockburn in 1873. The defendant showed his old qualities of impudence and endurance, but the indiscretion of his counsel, Edward Kenealy, the testimony of his former sweetheart, and Kenealy's refusal to put the Orton sisters in the box, proved conclusive to the jury, who, on the one hundred and eighty-eighth day of the trial, after half-an-hour's deliberation found that the claimant was Arthur Orton. Found guilty of perjury on two counts, he was sentenced on the 28th of February 1874 to fourteen years' penal servitude. The cost of the two trials was estimated at something not far short of £200,000, and of this the Tichborne estates were mulcted of fully £90,000. The claimant's better-class supporters had deserted him before the second trial, but the people who had subscribed for his defence were stanch, while the populace were convinced that he was a persecuted man, and that the Jesuits were at the bottom of a deep-laid plot for keeping him out of his own. There were symptoms of a riot in London in April 1875, when parliament unanimously rejected a motion (by Kenealy) for referring the Tichborne case to a royal commission, and the military had to be held in readiness. But the agitation subsided, and when Orton emerged from gaol in 1884 the fickle public took no interest in him. The sensation of ten years earlier could not be galvanized into fresh life either by his lectures or his alternate confessions of imposture and reiterations of innocence, and Orton sank into poverty and oblivion, dying in obscure lodgings in Marylebone on the 2nd of April 1898. (T.Se.)

TREAD-MILL, a penal appliance introduced by Sir William Cubitt in 1818 and intended by him as a means of employing criminals usefully. It was a large hollow cylinder of wood on an iron frame, round the circumference of which were a series of steps about 7½ in. apart. The criminal, steadying himself by hand-rails on either side, trod on these, his weight causing the mill to revolve and compelling him to take each step in turn. In the brutalizing system formerly in vogue the necessary resistance was obtained by weights, thus condemning the offender to useless toil and defeating the inventor's object. The tread-mill, however, was subsequently utilized for grinding corn, pumping water and other prison purposes. The speed of the wheel was regulated by a brake. Usually it revolved at the rate of 32 ft. per minute. The prisoner worked for 6 hours each day, 3 hours at a time. He was on the wheel for 15 minutes and then rested for 5 minutes. Thus in the course of his day's labour he climbed 8640 ft. Isolation of prisoners at their work was obtained by screens of wood on each side of the mill, converting the working space into a separate compartment. Each prisoner was medically examined before going to the mill.

By the Prison Act 1865 every male prisoner over 16, sentenced to hard labour, had to spend three months at least of his sentence in labour of the first class. This consisted primarily of the tread-mill, or, as an alternative, the crank. The latter consisted of a small wheel, like the paddle-wheel of a steamer, and a handle turned by the prisoner made it revolve in a box partly filled with gravel. The amount of gravel regulated the hard labour; or the necessary resistance was obtained by a brake, by which a pressure, usually of 12 lb, was applied. The prisoner had to make 8000 or 10,000 revolutions during his 6 hours' work, according to his strength, the number being registered on a dial. The crank too, however, was subsequently made to serve useful purposes. Both tread-mill and crank have gradually been abolished; in 1895 there were 39 tread-mills and 29 cranks in use in

English prisons, and these had dwindled down to 13 and 5 respectively in 1901. They are now disused.

The fundamental idea of Cubitt's invention, *i.e.* procuring rotary motion for industrial purposes by the weight of men or animals, is very old. "Tread-wheels," of this type, usually consist of hollow cylinders, round the inner surface of which a horse, dog or man walks, foothold being kept by slabs of wood nailed across at short intervals.

❧ **WHIPPING,** or FLOGGING, a method of corporal punishment which in one from or another has been used in all ages and all lands. In ancient Rome a citizen could not be scourged, it being considered an infamous punishment. Slaves were beaten with rods. Similarly in early medieval England the whip could not be used on the freeman, but was reserved for the villein. The Anglo-Saxons whipped prisoners with a three-corded knotted lash. It was not uncommon for mistresses to whip or have their servants whipped to death. William of Malmesbury relates that as a child King Æthelred was flogged with candles by his mother, who had no handier weapon, until he was insensible with pain. During the Saxon period whipping was the ordinary punishment for offences, great or small. Payments for whipping figure largely in municipal and parish accounts from an early date. The abolition of the monasteries, where the poor had been sure of free meals, led during the 16th century to an increase of vagrancy, at which the Statute of Labourers (1350) and its provisions as to whipping had been early aimed. In the reign of Henry VIII. was passed (1530) the famous Whipping Act, directing vagrants to be carried to some market town or other place "and there tied to the end of a cart naked and beaten with whips throughout such market town till the body shall be bloody." In the 39th year of Elizabeth a new act was passed by which the offender was to be stripped to the waist, not quite naked. It was under this statute that whipping-posts were substituted for the cart. Many of these posts were combined with stocks, as that at Waltham Abbey, which bears date "1598." It is of oak, 5 ft. 9 in. high, with iron clasps for the hands when used for whipping, and for the feet when used as stocks. Fourpence was the old charge for whipping male and female rogues. At quarter-sessions in Devonshire at Easter 1598 it was ordered that the mothers of bastard children should be whipped; the reputed fathers suffering a like punishment. In the west of England in 1684, "certain Scotch pedlars and petty chapmen being in the habit of selling their goods to the greate damage and hindrance of shoppe-keepers," the court ordered them to be stripped naked and whipped. The flogging of women was common. Judge Jeffreys, in so sentencing a female prisoner, is reported to have exclaimed, "Hangman, I charge you to pay particular attention to this lady. Scourge her soundly, man: scourge her till her blood runs down! It is Christmas: a cold time for madam to strip. See that you warm her shoulders." Lunatics, too, were whipped, for in the Constable's Accounts of Great Staughton, Hunts, occurs the entry, "1690–1, Paid in charges taking up a distracted woman, watching her and whipping her next day—8/6d." A still more remarkable entry is "—1710–1, Pd. Thomas Hawkins for whipping two people yt had smallpox—8d." In 1764, the *Public Ledger* states that a woman who is described as "an old offender" was taken from the Clerkenwell Bridewell to Enfield and there publicly whipped at the cart's tail by the common hangman for cutting wood in Enfield Chase. A statute of 1791 abolished the whipping of females.

FUN AND GAMES

Faced with such a plethora of games and pastimes described in the eleventh, we were first tempted to fill our collection with games that are of curiosity value to us today, in that they are no longer frequently played, but are constantly referred to in any social literature touching upon daily life in the late nineteenth or early twentieth century. We were considering, for instance, the detailed descriptions of such card games as skat (the favorite of composer Richard Strauss, who played it maniacally with friends), or whist, without which the visitors to a respectable American or English parlor of the time would be at a loss as to how to pass the time. But these same descriptions seemed a bit prosaic, and instead we have included a series of games or contest descriptions that are still well known to us today (bear-baiting being the obvious exception), and where the history of the activity or the method of execution offered both interest and amusement. "Pugilism" and "Mountaineering" represent two newly prized Victorian rituals that receive careful and meticulous descriptions. At the same time, there are other activities in this area that have an unintended comic effect when read, where the authors describe the most ordinary movement of the body in excruciatingly specific and gradualized terms, slowing down the activity as we read of it, resulting in prose that is strange in its slow-motion absurdity and quite wonderful. The best examples here refer to the art of mounting a horse in "Riding," and the disquisitions on floating and diving in the article "Swimming."

BASE-BALL (so-called from the bases and ball used), the national summer sport of the United States, popular also throughout Canada and in Japan. Its origin is obscure. According to some authorities it is derived from the old English game of rounders, several variations of which were played in America during the colonial period; according to other authorities, its resemblance to rounders is merely a coincidence, and it had its origin in the United States, probably at Cooperstown, New York, in 1839, when, it is said, Abner Doubleday (later a general in the U.S. army) devised a scheme for playing it. About the beginning of the 19th century a game generally known as "One Old Cat" became popular with schoolboys in the North Atlantic states; this game was played by three boys, each fielding and batting in turn, a run being scored by the batsman running to a single base and back without being put out. Two Old Cat, Three Old Cat, and Four Old Cat were modifications of this game, having respectively four, six, and eight players. A development of this game bore the name of town-ball, and the Olympic Town-Ball Club of Philadelphia was organized in 1833. Matches between organized baseball clubs were first played in the neighbourhood of New York, where the Washington Baseball Club was founded in 1843. The first regular code of rules was drawn up in 1845 by the Knickerbocker Baseball Club and used in its matches with the Gotham, Eagle and Empire clubs of New York, and the Excelsior, Putnam, Atlantic and Eckford clubs of Brooklyn. In 1858 the first National Association was organized, and, while its few simple laws were generally similar to the corresponding rules of the present code, the ball was larger and "livelier," and the pitcher was compelled to deliver it with a full toss, no approach to a throw being allowed. The popularity of the game spread rapidly, resulting in the organization of many famous clubs, such as the Beacon and Lowell of Boston, the Red Stockings of Cincinnati, the Forest City of Cleveland and the Maple Leaf of Guelph, but, owing to the sharp rivalry between the foremost teams, semi-professionalism soon crept in, although in those days a man who played for a financial consideration always had some other means of livelihood, as the income to be derived from playing ball in the summer time was not enough to support him throughout the year. In spite of its popularity, the game acquired certain undesirable adjuncts. The betting and pool selling evils became prominent, and before long the game was in thorough disrepute. It was not only generally believed that the matches were not played on their merits, but it was known that players themselves were not above selling contests. At that time many of the journals of the day foretold the speedy downfall of the sport. A convention of those interested financially and otherwise in the game, was held in 1867 in Philadelphia, and an effort was made to effect a reformation. That the sport even then was by no means insignificant can be seen from the fact that in that convention some 500 organizations were represented. While the work done at the convention did not accomplish all that was expected, it did produce certain reforms, and the sport grew rapidly thereafter both in the eastern and in the middle western part of the United States. In the next five years the interest in the game became so great that it was decided to send a representation of American base-ball players to England; and two clubs, the Bostons, who were the champions that year, and the Athletics, former champions, crossed the Atlantic and played several exhibition games with each other. While successful in exciting some interest, the trip did not succeed in popularizing base-ball in Great Britain. Fifteen years later two other nines of representative American base-ball players made a general tour of Australia and various other countries, completing their trip by a contest in England. This too, however, had little effect, and later attempts to establish base-ball in England have likewise been unsuccessful. But in America the game continued to prosper. The first entirely professional club was the Cincinnati Red Stockings (1868). Two national associations were formed in 1871, one having jurisdiction over professional clubs and the other over amateurs. In 1876 was formed the National League, of eight clubs under the presidency of Nicholas E. Young, which contained the expert ball-players of the country. There were so many people in the United States who wanted to see professional base-ball that this organization proved too small to furnish the desired number of games, and hence in 1882 the American Association was formed. For a time it seemed that there would be room for both organizations; but there was considerable rivalry, and it was not until an agreement was made between the two organizations that they were able to work together in harmony. They practically controlled professional base-ball for many years, although there were occasional attempts to overthrow their authority, the most notable being the formation in 1890 of a brotherhood of players called the Players' League, organized for the purpose of securing some of the financial benefits accruing to the managers, as well as for the purpose of abolishing black-listing and other supposed abuses. The Players' League proved not sufficiently strong for the task, and fell to pieces. For some years the National League consisted of twelve clubs organized as stock companies, representing cities as far apart as Boston and St. Louis, but in 1900 the number was reduced to eight, namely, Boston, Brooklyn, Chicago, Cincinnati, New York, Pittsburg, Philadelphia and St. Louis. Certain aggressive and dissatisfied elements took advantage of this change to organize a second great professional association under the presidency of B. B. Johnson, the "American League," of eight clubs, six of them in cities where the National League was already represented. Most of the clubs of both leagues flourish financially, as also do the many minor associations which control the clubs of the different sections of the country, among which are the Eastern League, the American Association, Western League, Southern Association, New England League, Pacific League and the different state leagues. Professional base-ball has not been free from certain objectionable elements, of which the unnecessary and rowdyish fault-finding with the umpires has been the most evident, but the authorities of the different leagues have lately succeeded, by strenuous legislation, in abating these.

⟨᠅⟩　BEAR-BAITING and BULL-BAITING,

sports formerly very popular in England but now suppressed on account of their cruelty. They took place in arenas built in the form of theatres which were the common resort even of cultivated people. In the bear-gardens, which are known to have existed since the time of Henry II., the bear was chained to a stake by one hind leg or by the neck and worried by dogs. Erasmus, writing (about 1500) from the house of Sir Thomas More, spoke of "many herds of bears maintained in the country for the purpose of baiting." Sunday was the favourite day for these sports. Hentzner, writing in 1598, describes the bear-garden at Bankside as "another place, built in the form of a theatre, which serves for the baiting of Bulls and Bears. They are fastened behind, and then worried by great English bull-dogs, but not without great risk to the dogs from the horns of the one and the teeth of the other, and it sometimes happens they are killed upon the spot; fresh ones are immediately supplied in the places of those that are wounded or tired." He also describes the whipping of a blinded bear, a favourite variation of bear-baiting. For a famous baiting which took place before Queen Elizabeth in 1575 thirteen bears were provided. Of it Robert Laneham (fl. 1575) wrote, "it was a sport very pleasant to see, to see the bear, with his pink eyes, tearing after his enemies' approach; the nimbleness and wait of the dog to take his advantage and the force and experience of the bear again to avoid his assaults: if he were bitten in one place how he would pinch in another to get free; that if he were taken once, then by what shift with biting, with clawing, with roaring, with tossing and tumbling he would work and wind himself from them; and when he was loose to shake his ears twice or thrice with the blood and the slaver hanging about his physiognomy." The famous "Paris Garden" in Southwark was the chief bear-garden in London. A Spanish nobleman of the time, who was taken to see a pony baited that had an ape tied to its back, expressed himself to the effect that "to see the animal kicking amongst the dogs, with the screaming of the ape, beholding the curs hanging from the ears and neck of the pony, is very laughable." Butler describes a bear-baiting at length in the first canto of his *Hudibras*.

The Puritans endeavoured to put an end to animal-baiting, although Macaulay sarcastically suggested that this was "not because it gave pain to the bear, but because it gave pleasure to the spectators." The efforts of the Puritans seem, however, to have had little effect, for we find the sport flourishing at the Restoration; but the conscience of cultivated people seems to have been touched, for Evelyn wrote in his *Diary*, under the date of June 16th, 1670: "I went with some friends to the bear-garden, where was cock-fighting, dog-fighting, bear and bull baiting, it being a famous day for all these butcherly sports, or rather barbarous cruelties. The bulls did exceedingly well, but the Irish wolf-dog exceeded, which was a tall greyhound, a stately creature indeed, who beat a cruel mastiff. One of the bulls tossed a dog full into a lady's lap, as she sat in one of the boxes at a considerable height from the arena. Two poor dogs were killed, and so all ended with the ape on horseback, and I most heartily weary of the rude and dirty pastime, which I had not seen, I think, in twenty years before." Steele also attacked these cruel sports in the *Tatler*. Nevertheless, when the tsar Nicholas I. visited England as cesarevich, he was taken to see a prize-fight and a bull-baiting. In this latter form of the sport the bull's nose was usually blown full of pepper to render him the more furious. The bull was often allowed a hole in the ground, into which to thrust his nose and lips, his most vulnerable parts. Sometimes the bull was tethered, and dogs, trained for the purpose, set upon him one by one, a successful attack resulting in the dog fastening his teeth firmly in the bull's snout. This was called "pinning the bull." A sport called bull-running was popular in several towns of England, particularly at Tutbury and Stamford. Its establishment at Tutbury was due to John of Gaunt, to whose minstrels, on the occasion of their annual festival on August 16th the prior of Tutbury, for his tenure, delivered a bull, which had his horns sawn off, his ears and tail cut off, his nostrils filled with pepper and his whole body smeared with soap. The minstrels gave chase to the bull, which became the property of any minstrel of the county of Stafford who succeeded in holding him long enough to cut off a lock of his hair. Otherwise he was returned to the prior. At the dissolution of the monasteries this tenure devolved upon the dukes of Devonshire, who suppressed it in 1788. At Stamford the running took place annually on November 13th, the bull being provided by the butchers of the town, the townspeople taking part in the chase, which was carried on until both people and beast were exhausted, and ended in the killing of the bull. Certain rules were strictly observed, such as the prohibition of carrying sticks or staves that were shod with iron. The Stamford bull-running survived well into the 19th century. Bear-baiting and bull-baiting were prohibited by act of parliament in 1835.

COCK-FIGHTING, or Cocking, the sport of pitting game-cocks to fight, and breeding and training them for the purpose. The game-fowl is now probably the nearest to the Indian jungle-fowl (*Gallus ferrugineus*), from which all domestic fowls are believed to be descended. The sport was popular in ancient times in India, China, Persia and other eastern countries, and was introduced into Greece in the time of Themistocles. The latter, while moving with his army against the Persians, observed two cocks fighting desperately, and, stopping his troops, inspired them by calling their attention to the valour and obstinacy of the feathered warriors. In honour of the ensuing victory of the Greeks cock-fights were thenceforth held annually at Athens, at first in a patriotic and religious spirit, but afterwards purely for the love of the sport. Lucian makes Solon speak of quail-fighting and cocking, but he is evidently referring to a time later than that of Themistocles. From Athens the sport spread throughout Greece, Asia Minor and Sicily, the best cocks being bred in Alexandria, Delos, Rhodes and Tanagra. For a long time the Romans affected to despise this "Greek diversion," but ended by adopting it so enthusiastically that Columella (1st century A.D.) complained that its devotees often spent their whole patrimony in betting at the pit-side. The cocks were provided with iron spurs (*tela*), as in the East, and were often dosed with stimulants to make them fight more savagely.

From Rome cocking spread northwards, and, although opposed by the Christian church, nevertheless became popular in Great Britain, the Low Countries, Italy, Germany, Spain and her colonies. On account of adverse legislation cocking has practically died out everywhere excepting in Spain, countries of Spanish origin and the Orient, where it is still legal and extremely popular. It was probably introduced into England by the Romans before Caesar's time. William Fitz-Stephen first speaks of it in the time of Henry II. as a sport for school-boys on holidays, and particularly on Shrove Tuesday, the masters themselves directing the fights, or mains, from which they derived a material advantage, as the dead birds fell to them. It became very popular throughout England and Wales, as well as in Scotland, where it was introduced in 1681. Occasionally the authorities tried to repress it, especially Cromwell, who put an almost complete stop to it for a brief period, but the Restoration re-established it among the national pastimes. Contemporary apologists do not, in the 17th century, consider its cruelty at all, but concern themselves solely with its justification as a source of pleasure. "If Leviathan took his sport in the waters, how much more may Man take his sport upon the land?" From the time of Henry VIII., who added the famous Royal Cock-pit to his palace of Whitehall, cocking was called the "royal diversion," and the Stuarts, particularly James I. and Charles II., were among its most enthusiastic devotees, their example being followed by the gentry down to the 19th century. Gervase Markham in his *Pleasures of Princes* (1614) wrote "Of the Choyce, Ordring, Breeding and Dyeting of the fighting-Cocke for Battell," his quaint directions being of the most explicit nature. When a cock is to be trained for the pit he must be fed "three or foure daies only with old Maunchet (fine white bread) and spring water." He is then set to spar with another cock, "putting a payre of hots upon each of their heeles, which Hots are soft, bumbasted roules of Leather, covering their spurs, so that they cannot hurt each other. . . . Let them fight and buffet one another a good space." After exercise the bird must be put into a basket, covered with hay and set near the fire. "Then let him sweate, for the nature of this scowring is to bring away his grease, and to breed breath, and strength." If not killed in the fight, "the first thing you doe, you shall search his wounds, and as many as you can find you shall with your mouth sucke the blood out of them, then wash them with the warm salt water, . . . give him a roule or two, and so stove him up as hot as you can."

Cocking-mains usually consisted of fights between an agreed number of pairs of birds, the majority of victories deciding the main; but there were two other varieties that aroused the particular ire of moralists. These were the "battle royal," in which a number of birds were "set," *i.e.* placed in the pit, at the same time, and allowed to remain until all but one, the victor, were killed or disabled; and the "Welsh main," in which eight pairs were matched, the eight victors being again paired, then four, and finally the last surviving pair. Among London cock-pits were those at Westminster, in Drury Lane, Jewin Street and Birdcage Walk (depicted by Hogarth). Over the royal pit at Whitehall presided the king's cockmaster. The pits were circular in shape with a matted stage about 20 ft. in diameter and surrounded by a barrier to keep the birds from falling off. Upon this barrier the first row of the audience leaned. Hardly a town in the kingdom was without its cockpit, which offered the sporting classes opportunities for betting not as yet sufficiently supplied by horse-racing. With the growth of the latter sport and the increased facilities for reaching the racing centres, cocking gradually declined, especially after parliament passed laws against it, so that gentlemen risked arrest by attending a main.

Among the best-known devotees of the sport was a Colonel Mordaunt, who, about 1780, took a number of the best English gamecocks to India. There he found the sport in high favour with the native rulers and his birds were beaten. Perhaps the most famous

main in England took place at Lincoln in 1830 between the birds of
Joseph Gilliver, the most celebrated breeder, or "feeder," of his day,
and those of the earl of Derby. The conditions called for seven birds
a side, and the stakes were 5000 guineas the main and 1000 guineas
each match. The main was won by Gilliver by five matches to two.
His grandson was also a breeder, and the blood of his cocks still runs
in the best breeds of Great Britain and America. Another famous
breeder was Dr Bellyse of Audlem, the principal figure in the great
mains fought at Chester during race-week at the beginning of the
19th century. His favourite breed was the white pile, and "Cheshire
piles" are still much-fancied birds. Others were Irish brown-reds,
Lancashire black-reds and Staffordshire duns.

In Wales, as well as some parts of England, cocking-mains took
place regularly in churchyards, and in many instances even inside the
churches themselves. Sundays, wakes and church festivals were favourite occasions for them. The habit of holding mains in schools
was common from the 12th to about the middle of the 19th century.
When cocking was at its height, the pupils of many schools were made
a special allowance for purchasing fighting-cocks, and parents were
expected to contribute to the expenses of the annual main on Shrove
Tuesday, this money being called "cockpence." Cock-fighting was prohibited by law in Great Britain in 1849.

Cocking was early introduced into America, though it was always
frowned upon in New England. Some of the older states, as Massachusetts, forbade it by passing laws against cruelty as early as 1836,
and it is now expressly prohibited in Canada and in most states of
the Union, or is repressed by general laws for the prevention of
cruelty to animals.

Cocks are fought at an age of from one to two years. "Heeling,"
or the proper fastening of the spurs, and "cutting out," trimming
the wings at a slope, and cutting the tail down by one-third of its
length and shortening the hackle and rump feathers, are arts acquired by experience. The comb is cut down close, so as to offer the
least possible mark for the hostile bird's bill. The cock is then provided
with either "short heels," spurs 1½ in. or less in length, or with "long
heels," from 2 to 2½ in. in length. The training of a cock for the pit
lasts from ten days to a month or more, during which time the bird
is subjected to a rigid diet and exercise in running and sparring. The
birds may not be touched after being set down in the pit, unless to
extricate them from the matting. Whenever a bird refuses to fight
longer he is set breast to breast with his adversary in the middle of
the pit, and if he then still refuses to fight he is regarded as defeated.

Among the favourite breeds may be mentioned the "Irish gilders," "Irish Grays," "Shawlnecks," "Gordons," "Eslin Red-Quills," "Baltimore Topknots," "Dominiques," "Warhorses" and "Claibornes."

⟨◈⟩ **MOUNTAINEERING,** the art of moving about safely in mountain regions, avoiding the dangers incidental to them, and attaining high points difficult of access. It consists of two main divisions, rock-craft and snow-craft. Rock-craft consists in the intelligent selection of a line of route and in gymnastic skill to follow the line chosen. In snow-craft the choice of route is the result of a full understanding of the behaviour of snow under a multitude of varying conditions; it depends largely upon experience, and much less upon gymnastic skill. The dangers which the craft of climbing has been developed to avoid are of two main kinds: the danger of things falling on the traveller and the danger of his falling himself. The things that may fall are rocks, ice and snow; the traveller may fall from rocks, ice or snow, or into crevasses in ice or snow. There are also dangers from weather. Thus in all there are eight chief dangers: falling rocks, falling ice, snow-avalanches, falls from difficult rocks, falls from ice slopes, falls down snow slopes, falls into crevasses, dangers from weather. To select and follow a route avoiding these dangers is to exercise the climber's craft.

Falling Rocks.—Every rock mountain is falling to pieces, the process being specially rapid above the snow-line. Rock-faces are constantly swept by falling stones, which it is generally possible to dodge. Falling rocks tend to form furrows in a mountain face, and these furrows (*couloirs*) have to be ascended with caution, their sides being often safe when the middle is stone-swept. Stones fall more frequently on some days than on others, according to the recent weather. Local experience is a valuable help on such a question. The direction of the dip of rock strata often determines whether a particular face is safe or dangerous; the character of the rock must also be considered. Where stones fall frequently débris will be found below, whilst on snow slopes falling stones cut furrows visible from a great distance. In planning an ascent of a new peak such traces must be looked for. When falling stones get mixed in considerable quantity with slushy snow or water a mud avalanche is formed (common in the Himalaya). It is necessary to avoid camping in their possible line of fall.

Falling Ice.—The places where ice may fall can always be determined beforehand. It falls in the broken parts of glaciers (*seracs*) and from overhanging cornices formed on the crests of narrow ridges. Large icicles are often formed on steep rock-faces, and these fall frequently in fine weather following cold and stormy days. They have to be avoided like falling stones. Seracs are slow in formation, and slow in arriving (by glacier motion) at a condition of unstable equilibrium. They generally fall in or just after the hottest part of the day, and their débris seldom goes far. A skilful and experienced ice-man will usually devise a safe route through a most intricate ice-fall, but such places should be avoided in the afternoon of a hot day. Hanging glaciers (*i.e.* glaciers perched on steep slopes) often discharge themselves over steep rock-faces, the snout breaking off at intervals. They can always be detected by their débris below. Their track should be avoided.

Snow Avalanches.—These mainly occur on steep slopes when the snow is in bad condition, early in the year, or after a recent fresh fall. Days when snow is in bad condition are easily recognized; on such days it may be inadvisable to traverse snow-slopes which at another time may be as safe as a high-road. Beds of snow collected on rock-ledges in bad weather fall off when a thaw comes, and are dangerous to rock-climbers. Snow that has recently fallen upon ice slopes is always liable to slip off bodily. Such falling masses generally make the lower part of their descent by couloirs. Snow avalanches never fall in unexpected places, but have their easily recognizable routes, which can be avoided in times of danger by experienced mountaineers.

Falls from Rocks.—The skill of a rock-climber is shown by his choice of handhold and foothold, and his adhesion to those he has chosen. Much depends on a correct estimate of the firmness of the rock where weight is to be thrown upon it. Many loose rocks are quite firm enough to bear a man's weight, but experience is needed to know which can be trusted, and skill is required in transferring the weight to them without jerking. On all difficult rocks the rope is the greatest safeguard for all except the first man in the ascent, the last in the descent. In such places a party of three or four men roped together, with a distance of 15 to 20 ft. between one and another, will be able to hold up one of their number (except the top man) if one only moves at a time and the others are firmly placed and keep the rope tight between them, so that a falling individual may be arrested before his velocity has been accelerated. In very difficult places help may be obtained by throwing a loose rope round a projection above and pulling on it; this method is specially valuable in a difficult descent. The rope usually employed is a strong Manila cord called Alpine Club rope, but some prefer a thinner rope used double. On rotten rocks the rope must be handled with special care, lest it should start loose stones on to the heads of those below. Similar care must be given to hand-holds and footholds, for the same reason. When a horizontal traverse has to be made across very difficult rocks, a dangerous situation may arise unless at both ends of the traverse there be firm positions. Even then the end men gain little from the rope. Mutual assistance on hard rocks takes all manner of forms: two, or even three, men climb-ing on one another's shoulders, or using for foothold an ice-axe propped up by others. The great principle is that of co-operation, all the members of the party climbing with reference to the others, and not as independent units; each when moving must know what the man in front and the man behind are doing. After bad weather steep rocks are often found covered with a veneer of ice (*verglas*), which may even render them inaccessible. Climbing-irons (crampons, *steigeisen*) are useful on such occasions.

Ice Slopes.—Climbing-irons are also most useful on ice or hard snow, as by them step-cutting can sometimes be avoided, and the footing at all times rendered more secure. True ice slopes are rare in Europe, though common in tropical mountains, where newly-fallen snow quickly thaws on the surface and becomes sodden below, so that the next night's frost turns the whole into a mass of solid ice. An ice slope can only be surmounted by step-cutting. For this an ice-axe is needed, the common form being a small pick-axe on the end of a pole as long as from the elbow of a man to the ground. This pole is used also as a walking-stick, and is furnished with a spike at the foot.

Snow Slopes—are very common, and usually easy to ascend. At the foot of a snow or ice slope is generally a big crevasse, called a *berg-schrund,* where the final slope of the mountain rises from a snow-field or glacier. Such *bergschrunds* are generally too wide to be strided, and must be crossed by a snow bridge, which needs careful testing and a painstaking use of the rope. A steep snow slope in bad condition may be dangerous, as the whole body of snow may start as an ava-lanche. Such slopes are less dangerous if ascended directly than obliquely, for an oblique or horizontal track cuts them across and facilitates movement of the mass. New snow lying on ice is specially dangerous. Experience is needful for deciding on the advisability of advancing over snow in doubtful condition. Snow on rocks is usually rotten unless it be thick; snow on snow is likely to be sound. A day or two of fine weather will usually bring new snow into sound con-dition. Snow cannot lie at a very steep angle, though it often deceives the eye as to its slope. Snow slopes seldom exceed 40°. Ice slopes may be much steeper. Snow slopes in early morning are usually hard and safe, but the same in the afternoon are quite soft and possibly dangerous; hence the advantage of an early start.

Crevasses.—These are the slits or deep chasms formed in the substance of a glacier as it passes over an uneven bed. They may be open or hidden. In the lower part of a glacier the crevasses are open. Above the snow-line they are frequently hidden by arched-over accumulations of winter snow. The detection of hidden crevasses requires care and experience. After a fresh fall of snow they can only be detected by sounding with the pole of the ice-axe, or by looking to right and left where the open extension of a partially hidden crevasse may be obvious. The safeguard against accident is the rope, and no one should ever cross a snow-covered glacier unless roped to one, or better to two, companions.

Weather.—The main group of dangers caused by bad weather centre round the change it effects in the condition of snow and rock, making ascents suddenly perilous which before were easy, and so altering the aspect of things as to make it hard to find the way or retrace a route. In storm the man who is wont to rely on a compass has great advantage over a merely empirical follower of his eyes. In large snow-fields it is, of course, easier to go wrong than on rocks, but a trained intelligence is the best companion and the surest guide. (W.M.C.)

PUGILISM (from Lat. *pugil,* boxer), the practice or sport of fighting with the fists. The first mention of such fighting in literature is found in the 23rd book of the *Iliad,* and shows that in Homer's time the art was already highly developed. The occasion was the games at the funeral of Patroclus, the champions engaged being Epeus, the builder of the wooden horse, and Euryalus. Each combatant seems to have been naked except for a belt, and to have worn the cestus. The fight ends with the defeat of Euryalus. According to Virgil (*Aeneid,* v.) similar games took place within the walls of Troy at the funeral of Hector, the principal boxers being Dares, the winner, and the gigantic Butex, a pupil of Amycus, Paris, the Trojan champion, abstaining from the contests. Further on we find the account of the games on the occasion of the funeral of Anchises, in the course of which Dares, the Trojan, receiving no answer to his challenge from the Sicilians, who stood aghast at his mighty proportions, claims the prize; but, just as it is about to be awarded him, Entellus, an aged but huge and sinewy Sicilian, arises and casts into the arena as a sign of his acceptance of the combat the massive cesti, all stained with blood and brains, which he has inherited from King

Eryx, his master in the art of boxing. The Trojans are now appalled in their turn, and Dares, aghast at the fearful implements, refused the battle, which, however, is at length begun after Aeneas has furnished the heroes with equally matched cesti. For some time the young and lusty Dares circles about his gigantic but old and stiff opponent, upon whom he rains a torrent of blows which are avoided by the clever guarding and dodging of the Sicilian hero. At last Entellus, having got his opponent into a favourable position, raises his tremendous right hand on high and aims a terrible blow at the Trojan's head; but the wary Dares deftly steps aside, and Entellus, missing his adversary altogether, falls headlong by the impetus of his own blow, with a crash like that of a falling pine. Shouts of mingled exultation and dismay break from the multitude, and the friends of the aged Sicilian rush forward to raise their fallen champion and bear him from the arena; but, greatly to the astonishment of all, Entellus motions them away and returns to the fight more keenly than before. The old man's blood is stirred, and he attacks his youthful enemy with such furious and headlong rushes, buffeting him grievously with both hands, that Aeneas puts an end to the battle, though barely in time to save the discomfited Trojan from being beaten into insensibility.

Although fist-fighting was supposed by the Greeks of the classic period to have been a feature of the mythological games at Olympia, it was not actually introduced into the historical Olympic contests until the 23rd Olympiad after the re-establishment of the famous games by Iphitus (about 880 B.C.). Onomastos was the first Olympic victor. In heroic times the boxers are supposed to have worn the belt, but in the Greek games the contestants, except for the cestus, fought entirely naked, since the custom had been introduced in the 15th Olympiad, and was copied by the contestants at the Pythian, Nemean, Isthmian and Panathenaic games. At Olympia the boxers were rubbed with oil to make them supple and limit the flow of perspiration, a precaution the more necessary as the Olympic games were held during the hottest part of the year. The cesti, of which there were several varieties, were bound on the boxers' hands and wrists by attendants or teachers acting as seconds. On account of the weight of the gloves worn, the style of boxing differed from that now in vogue, the modern straight-from-the-shoulder blow having been little used. Both Homer and Virgil speak of "falling blows," and this was the common method of attack, consisting more in swinging and hammering than in punching. The statue of a Greek boxer in the Louvre shows the right foot forward, the left hand raised as if to ward off a blow from above, and the right hand held opposite the breast, the whole attitude more resembling that of a warrior with sword and shield than of a modern boxer. The pugilists of Rome, who were in many cases Greeks and employed Greek methods, exaggerated the brutality of the fist-fight to please the Roman taste, and the sanguinary contest between Dares and Entellus, described above, although in some respects an anachronism as an account of a pugilistic battle in primitive times, was doubtless an exact portrayal of the encounters to be seen in Virgil's day in the circuses of Rome. Nevertheless it must not be understood that the boxing matches at the Greek games were not themselves severe to the point of brutality, in spite of the fact that style and grace of movement were sedulously taught by the masters of the time. The Greek champions trained for months before the games, but encounters between athletes armed with such terrible weapons as the loaded cestus were bound to result in very serious bruises and even disfigurement. Pluck was as highly thought of as at the present day, and it was related of a certain Eurydamas that, when his teeth were battered in, he swallowed them rather than show that he was hurt, whereupon his antagonist, in despair at seeing his most furious blows devoid of effect, gave up the battle. As, on account of the swinging style of blows, the ears were particularly liable to injury ear-protectors were generally used in practice, though not in serious combats. The so-called "pancratist's ear," swollen and mis-shapen, was a characteristic feature of the Greek boxer. The satirists of the time flung their grim jests at the champion bruisers. Lucilius writing of a Greek boxer of Etruria says, "Aulos, the pugilist, consecrates to the God of Pisa all the bones of his cranium, gathering up one by one. Let him but return alive from the Nemean Games, O mighty Jupiter, and he will also offer thee, without doubt, the vertebrae of his neck, which is all he has left!"

The rules of Greek boxing were strict. No wrestling, grappling, kicking nor biting were allowed, and the contest ended when one combatant owned himself beaten. On this account pugilism and the *pancratium* (see below) were forbidden by Lycurgus, lest the Spartans should become accustomed to an acknowledgment of defeat (Plutarch, *Lycurgus*). In spite of the terrible injuries which often resulted from these contests it was strictly forbidden to kill an adversary, on pain of losing the prize. Rhodes, Aegina, Arcadia and Elis produced most of the Olympic victors in boxing, which was considered as an excellent training for war. According to Lucan (*Anach. 3*) Solon recommended it for pedagogic purposes, and the contest with the *sphairai,* or studded cesti, was added by Plato to his list of warlike exercises as being the nearest approach to actual battle.

The Greek athletic contest called *pancratium* (complete, or all-round, contest), which was introduced into the Olympic games in the 38th Olympiad, was a combination of boxing and wrestling in which the contestants, who fought naked, not wearing even the cestus, were allowed to employ any means except biting to wring from each other the acknowledgment of defeat. Boxing, wrestling, kicking, dislocation of joints, breaking of bones, pulling of hair and strangling were freely indulged in. The fight began with sparring for openings and was continued on the ground when the contestants fell. Many pancratists excelled in obtaining quick holds of their opponents' fingers, which they crushed and dislocated so completely that all effective opposition ceased. Sudden attacks resulting in the dislocation of an arm or leg were also taught, reminding one of the Japanese jiu-jitsu. The *pancratium* was considered by the Greeks the greatest of all athletic contests and, needless to say, only the most powerful athletes attempted it. It became popular in Rome during the Empire and remained so until the time of Justinian.

From the fall of the Roman Empire to the beginning of the 19th century pugilism seems to have been unknown among civilized nations with the single exception of the English.

The first references to boxing in England as a regular sport occur towards the end of the 17th century, but little mention is made of it before the time of George I., when "prize-fighters" engaged in public encounters for money, with the backsword, falchion, foil, quarterstaff and single-stick, and, to a less extent, with bare fists, the last gradually gaining in popularity with the decline of fencing. The most celebrated of these fighters and the one who is generally considered to have been the first champion of England, fighting with the bare fists, was James Figg, who was supreme from 1719 to 1730. Figg was succeeded by Pipes and Gretting, both of whom made way in 1734 for Jack Broughton, who built the amphitheatre for public displays near Tottenham Court Road and who was undisputed champion until 1750. Broughton seems to have been a man of intelligence, and to him is ascribed the scientific development of the art of boxing. During his time the sport became truly national and the prize-fighter the companion of the greatest in the land. Among Broughton's successors were Slack, "Big Ben" Brain, Daniel Mendoza (a Jew who flourished about 1790 and was the proprietor of the Lyceum in the Strand), J. Jackson, Tom Cribb, Jem Belcher, Pearce (called the "Game

Chicken"), and John Gully, who afterwards represented Pontefract in Parliament.

To Broughton is ascribed the invention of boxing-gloves for use in practice. All prize-fights, however, took place with bare knuckles in roped-off spaces called rings, usually in the open air. Pugilists toughened their hands by "pickling" them in a powerful astringent solution. A fight ended when one of the "bruisers," as they were called, was unable to "come to the scratch," *i.e.* the middle of the ring, at the call of the referee at the beginning of a new round. Each round ended when one fighter fell or was knocked or thrown to the ground, but a pugilist "going down to avoid punishment," *i.e.* without being struck by the opponent, was liable to forfeit the fight. Wrestling played an important role in the old prize-ring, and a favourite method of weakening an adversary was to throw him heavily and then fall upon him, seemingly by accident, as the manoeuvre, if done intentionally, was foul. The fighting was of the roughest description, low tricks of all kinds being practised when the referee's attention was diverted, gouging out an adversary's eye being by no means unknown. Until 1795 pugilists wore long hair, but during a fight in that year Jackson caught Mendoza by his long locks and held him down helpless while he hit him. This was adjudged fair by the referee, with the result that prize-fighters have ever since cropped their head. Nevertheless there were rules which no fighter dared to overstep, such as those against kicking, hitting below the belt, and striking a man when he had fallen.

What is still the most celebrated prize-fight of modern times took place at Farnborough in April 1860, between Tom Sayers and the huge youthful American pugilist J. C. Heenan, the "Benicia Boy," who had been defeated in America by Morrissey, but had succeeded to the championship upon the latter's retirement. The English champion was a much smaller and lighter man than his challenger, a fact which increased the popular interest in the fight. Although the local English authorities endeavoured to prevent it taking place, Heenan complaining that he had "been chased out of eight counties," the ring at Farnborough was surrounded by a company containing representatives of the highest classes, and the exaggerated statement was made that "Parliament had been emptied to patronize a prize-fight." The battle lasted for 2 hours and 20 minutes, during which Heenan, owing to his superiority in weight and reach, seemed to have the advantage, although nearly blinded by Sayers's hard straight punches. During one of the opening rounds a tendon in Sayers's right forearm was ruptured in guarding, and he fought the rest of the battle with a pluck which roused the enthusiasm of the spectators. Heenan had neglected to harden his hands properly, with the result that they soon swelled to unnatural proportions, rendering his blows no more effective than if he had worn boxing-gloves. Nevertheless towards the close of the fight Heenan repeatedly threw Sayers violently, and held him on the ropes enclosing the ring, which, just as the police interfered, were cut by persons who asserted that Heenan was on the point of strangling Sayers. In spite of the indecisive outcome of the battle both fighters claimed the victory, but the match was officially adjudged a draw. This was the last great prize-fight with bare fists on English soil, as public opinion was aroused, and orders were given to the police thenceforth to regard prize-fights as illegal, as tending to a "breach of the peace." Several surreptitious prize-fights did indeed occur within a few years after the Sayers-Heenan battle; but more than once, notably in the fight between Heenan and Tom King, one of the participants was "doctored," *i.e.* drugged, and this lack of fairplay, added to the brutality of fist-fights, gave the death-blow to pugilism of the old kind. In its place came fighting and boxing with padded gloves, small ones weighing about 4 oz. being used by professionals, while amateurs, who boxed and sparred rather than fought, made use of larger and softer gloves.

An added impetus was given to boxing as well as pugilism in 1866 by the founding of the "Amateur Athletic Club" by John C. Chambers, who, assisted by the marquess of Queensberry, drew up the code of rules for competitions still in vogue and called after that nobleman, who, in 1867, presented cups for the amateur championships at the different weights. These rules prohibit all rough and unfair fighting, as well as wrestling, and divide a match into rounds of three (or two) minutes each, with half a minute rest between the rounds. It is a matter of agreement in professional battles whether in "breaking away" after a clinch blows may be struck or not. When a contestant is knocked down (a man on one knee is technically down) he is allowed ten seconds, usually counted aloud by the referee, in which to rise and renew the fight. Should he be unable to do so he is "counted out" and loses the match.

RIDING, the art or practice of locomotion on the back of an animal or in a vehicle (the verb *to ride* originally meant "to travel," or "go," as the derived noun *road* means "a way"). Where no vehicle is specified (*e.g.* "riding a bicycle"), the word is associated with horseback riding, for exercise or pleasure.

The origin of the use of the horse as a means of transport goes back to prehistoric times. The fable of the centaurs would indicate the early existence of pastoral peoples living on horseback, like the modern cowboys (cp. "cow-punchers") or *gauchos* of North and South America. Archaeological discoveries in India, Persia, Assyria and Egypt show that in the polished stone age quaternary man had domesticated the horse, while a Chinese treatise, the *Goei-leaotse,* the fifth book of the Vouking, a sort of military code dating from the reign of the emperor Hoang-Ti (2637 years B.C.), places the cavalry on the wings of the army. The Hebrews understood the use of the horse in war (Job xxxix. 18–25), as did the Persians (Cyrus at the battle of Thymbra), Greeks and Romans. The Greeks and Romans, especially the former, were skilled horsemen, and feats on horseback were a feature of their games. They used no stirrup, but had both bridle and bit. They rode bareback, or on a cloth or skin strapped to the horse.

When roads were poor and vehicles cumbersome horseback was almost the only method of travel for both sexes. With the introduction of steam-locomotion and the improvement of roads, however, riding has become a large extent a sport, rather than a necessity. There are different styles of riding adapted to the different purposes for which horses are ridden—on the road, in the school, hunting, racing, steeple-chasing and in the cavalry service—just as there are different horses more suitable by conformation, breeding and training for each.

In western civilization there is a traditional difference between the riding of men and women, in this particular, that men ride astride and women on a side-saddle. But in the following observations we deal generally with the more important features of riding as practised astride.

After securing an animal of the right height, weight and disposition, with a saddle of a length of tree and a breadth of seat that fits the rider and that is lined to fit the back of the horse, with a bridle bitted to his mouth, the first step is to mount. Having taken up the reins, the rider should stand at his horse's near (left) shoulder, facing towards the tail, and in that position hold the stirrup with his right hand for the reception of his left foot. By standing at the shoulder the rider is out of harm's way in the event of the horse kicking while he mounts. Ladies generally have the aid of a block or a groom's or escort's hand beneath the left foot. But a woman should be able to mount without aid, by lowering her stirrup, so that she can reach it from the ground, and then raising it again when she is seated in the saddle. Riding astride is sometimes recommended for women. The chief argument in its favour—symmetrical development of the figure—is, however, lost if the growing girl be taught to ride on a side-saddle of which the pommels can be shifted to the off side on alternate days.

Having gained the saddle, the necessity arises for *seat* and *hands*. Here good instruction is imperative at the outset. The great desideratum in a seat on horseback is that it should be firm. A rider with an insecure seat is apt to be thrown by any unexpected movement the horse may make; and, without a firm seat, the acquirement of good hands is well-nigh hopeless, because, when the balance is once disturbed the insecure rider will have to depend on something else for the maintenance of his seat, and this generally takes the shape of "riding on the horse's mouth," a practice as cruel as it is ugly.

Having gained the saddle, the rider should adjust the stirrups to the proper length, depending on the kind of riding, the length of his leg and the roughness of the horse's trot. Sitting well in the middle of the saddle, the thighs turned in, and the heels drawn somewhat back, the stirrup leathers may be let out or taken up until the tread of the stirrup is on a level with the inner ankle bone, and at this length, when the rider stands up, his fork will easily clear the pommel of the saddle. For maintaining his seat the horseman should depend upon his thighs and knees only, and not upon the knee and calf; a proper seat should be a mixture of balance and grip; a man riding by balance only is sure to be thrown, while to grip with all one's might during an hour's ride is to undertake as much exertion as should last for a whole day. The position of the foot exercises much influence on the security of the seat; it should be opposite the girth, parallel with the barrel of the horse, with the heels depressed. A good seat on a horse should not be strong merely; it should be graceful; above the loins the body should be loose, so as readily to adapt itself to every motion of the horse, but it should be upright.

Beginners are advised to practise riding with and without stirrups; thus, let the pupil who has ridden half an hour in a saddle with stirrups have a cloth substituted for the saddle for about ten minutes, care being taken to observe the rules already laid down for the position of the legs; in this way the proper seat will be strengthened.

The proper adjustment of the reins is the next thing to be attended to, and as the management of these depends so much upon the seat being firm and independent of the bridle the acquisition of a firm seat is certainly half-way towards the acquirement of good hands. An excellent way to start a pupil is on a sure-footed horse without bridle,

the master governing him by a leading rein until the pupil has acquired a firm seat and can be trusted with reins. Assuming that a
double-reined bridle is used, the third finger of the left hand should
be first inserted between the snaffle reins; then the little, third and
second fingers should be between the curb reins, the two outside
reins being the curb, and the two inside ones the snaffle. In this
manner of holding the reins the snaffle is not so likely to slip, while
the curb can be easily slackened or drawn tighter. As military riders
use the curb only the position of snaffle and curb as just explained
is reversed in the cavalry service. The snaffle reins should be drawn
up gently until the rider feels that he has an equal and light hold of
his horse's mouth on both sides, with just so much pressure that the
slightest movement of the left or right rein would cause him to turn
to the left or right respectively. The arms from the shoulder to the
elbow should hang naturally, close to the sides, and the arms from
elbow to wrist should be about parallel to the ground, the wrist being
kept loose, so as to yield gently with every motion of the horse. The
rider sitting in the position described, square to the front, with his
shoulders well back, will be riding with fairly long reins, one of the
secrets of good hands.

When the horse is in motion the hands should not be held rigid,
as the horse's mouth would thereby become dead, and the horse
would lean unpleasantly on the hand; but the rider should give and
take, without, however, entirely relaxing the hold.

In order to encourage the horse to walk the head must not be
confined, but a light feeling of the horse's mouth must be kept up.
Should the horse, unasked, break into a trot, never snatch at his
mouth, but restrain him gently. To trot, press the legs to the saddle,
and raise the bridle hand a little, and, after a moment's sitting close,
begin to rise ("pose") in cadence with the action of the horse. The
rising to the trot should be performed easily; the legs must not swing
backwards and forwards, nor should the hands be jerked up and
down. To start the canter, which should always be done from the walk
and not the trot, take up the curb rein a little and turn the horse's
head slightly to the right, at the same time pressing the left leg behind
the girth; the horse will then lead with the off (right) fore leg, which
is generally preferred; but a well-broken hack should lead with either
leg at command, and if he be cantered in a circle to the left he must
lead with the near leg, as otherwise an ugly fall is likely to result from
the leg being crossed. Galloping is a pace not to be generally indulged
in by road or park riders; when it is, the hands should be kept low,

the body thrown back, and an extra grip taken with the knees, as nearly all horses pull more or less when extended.

༄ **STILTS,** poles provided at a certain distance above the ground with steps or stirrups for the feet, for the purpose of walking on them. As a means of amusement stilts have been used by all peoples in all ages, as well as by the inhabitants of marshy or flooded districts. The city of Namur in Belgium, which formerly suffered from the overflowing of the rivers Sambre and Meuse, has been celebrated for its stilt-walkers for many centuries. Not only the towns-people but also the soldiers used stilts, and stilt-fights were indulged in, in which parties of a hundred or more attacked each other, the object being to overset as many of the enemy as possible. The governor of Namur having promised the archduke Albert (about 1600) a company of soldiers that should neither ride nor walk, sent a detachment on stilts, which so pleased the archduke that he conferred upon the city perpetual exemption from the beer-tax, no small privilege at that time.

The home of stilt-walking at the present day is the department of Landes in Gascony, where, owing to the impermeability of the subsoil, all low-lying districts are converted into marshes, compelling the shepherds, farmers and marketmen to spend the greater part of their lives on stilts. These are strapped to the leg below the knee, the foot resting in a stirrup about five feet from the ground. Their wearers, who are called *tchangues* (long-legs) in the Gascon dialect, also carry long staves, which are often provided with a narrow piece of board, used as a seat in case of fatigue. In the last quarter of the 19th century stilt-races, for women as well as men, became very popular in the Landes district, and still form an important feature of every provincial festivity. One winner of the annual championship races accomplished 490 kilometers (more than 304 m.) in 103 hours, 36 minutes. Silvain Dornon, a baker of the Landes, walked on stilts from Paris to Moscow in 58 days in the spring of 1891. The rapids of the Niagara have been waded on stilts. In many of the Pacific islands, particularly the Marquesas, stilts are used during the rainy season. Stilts used by children are very long, the upper half being held under the arms; they are not strapped to the leg. Stilts play an important part in the Italian masquerades, and are used for mounting the gigantic figures in the grotesque processions of Lisle, Dunkirk, Louvain and other cities.

〰️ **SWIMMING** (from "swim," A.S. *swimman,* the root being common in Teutonic languages), the action of self-support and self-propulsion on or in water; though used by analogy of inanimate objects, the term is generally connected with animal progression and specially with the art of self-propulsion on water as practised by man. Natation (the synonym derived from Lat. *natare*) is one of the most useful of the physical acquirements of man. There have been cases in which beginners have demonstrated some ability in the art upon their first immersion in deep water, but generally speaking it is an art which has to be acquired.

One of the most useful accomplishments for a swimmer is that of *floating,* but curiously enough many of them cannot acquire a knowledge of it. It is purely a matter of buoyancy, and requires constant practice before one can become perfect in it. In learning to float the beginner experiences great difficulty in overcoming the tendency of the legs to sink, and if after frequent trials they are still found to sink he should get some one to hold them up or else place them on the steps or behind the rail of the bath, and thus assisted learn to balance the body on the surface. Before doing so he should completely fill his lungs, spread his legs wide, and then lie backwards with the arms extended in a line with the body and beyond the head, with the palms upwards, care being taken to throw as much weight beyond the head as possible. Furthermore he must lie perfectly still and take care not to hollow the back or raise the abdomen above water. One may sink for an instant, but if the breath be held the lips will come above the surface, when easy breathing may be indulged in. Only the face, chest and toes should appear above the surface of the water. If the feet still have a tendency to sink after they have been gently released from the step or rail, more weight should be thrown beyond the head by turning it well back and lifting the hands out of the water, which will raise the feet. A knowledge of floating is of good service to those attempting to save life and is also essential to those desirous of making a study of the many tricks and scientific feats which are performed by swimmers.

The usual method of entering the water is by what is known as *diving;* some think that it should be termed "springing." The best method of learning to dive is to stand on the side of the bath or on the bank of the river, and then stoop down until the body is nearly double, stretch out the arms in front of the head, sink the head between them and gradually fall over into the water. The ability to enter the water head first will then soon be acquired. To begin, the legs should be placed together and the body kept erect, then a few short inspirations should be made and the lungs cleared and inflated, the arms should be swung from the front and a spring made from the diving base. As the feet leave the base they should be thrown upwards, the body straightened and the head placed between the arms, which should be kept at full stretch beyond the head, with the hands palm downwards and the thumbs touching so as to act as a cut-water. Immediately the body has entered the water, the hands should be turned upwards and the body will then come to the surface at once. In *high diving* a leap is made into midair, the body straightened almost to horizontal level, the arms and head then declined towards the water and the legs brought up. This action causes the body to shoot towards the water at a proper angle and the dive is thereby made clean and effective. A useful accomplishment is that known as *surface diving*, because it enables you to find and bring an object to the surface. The correct method of performing it is to first swim a few yards on the surface with the breast stroke, take a breath, then suddenly depress the head, look downwards, elevate the body at the hips, and at the same time make a powerful stroke with the legs and an upward stroke with the hands. The impetus thus obtained will suffice to take the swimmer to the bottom in 10 ft. of water. Once under the surface it is only necessary to keep the head depressed and swim by means of the breast stroke in order to find the object of search. When about to rise to the surface, the head should be turned backwards with the eyes upwards, and a vigorous stroke made with arms and legs. *Plunging* is not very generally practised, though there is a championship for it. A plunge is a standing dive made head first from a firm take off, free from spring. The body must be kept motionless face downwards, no progressive movement must be imparted other than the action of the dive. The plunge terminates when the plunger raises his face above the surface of the water. (W.Hy.)

WRESTLING (O. Eng. *wræstlian*), a sport in which two persons strive to throw each other to the ground. It is one of the most primitive and universal of sports. Upon the walls of the temple-tombs of Beni Hasan, near the Nile, are sculptured many hundred scenes from wrestling matches, depicting practically all the holds and falls known at the present day, thus proving that wrestling was a highly developed sport at least 3000 years before the Christian era. As the description of the bout between Odysseus and Ajax in the 23rd book of the *Iliad,* and the evolutions of the classic Greek wrestlers, tally with the sculptures of Beni Hasan and Nineveh, the sport may have been introduced into Greece from Egypt or Asia. In Homer's celebrated description of the match between Ajax and Odysseus the two champions wore only a girdle, which was, however, not used in the classic Greek games. Neither Homer nor Eustathius, who also minutely depicted the battle between Ajax and Odysseus, mentions the use of oil, which, however, was invariable at the Olympic games, where wrestling was introduced during the 18th Olympiad. The Greek wrestlers were, after the application of the oil, rubbed with fine sand, to afford a better hold.

In Great Britain wrestling was cultivated at a very early age, both Saxons and Celts having always been addicted to it, and English literature is full of references to the sport. On St James's and St Bartholomew's days special matches took place throughout England, those in London being held in St Giles's Field, whence they were afterwards transferred to Clerkenwell. The lord mayor and his sheriffs were often present on these occasions, but the frequent brawls among the spectators eventually brought public matches into disrepute. English monarchs have not disdained to patronize the sport, and Henry VIII. is known to have been a powerful wrestler.

It was inevitable, in a country where the sport was so ancient and so universal, that different methods of wrestling should grow up. It is likely that the "loose" style, in which the contestants took any hold they could obtain, generally prevailed throughout Great Britain until the close of the 18th century, when the several local fashions became gradually coherent; but it was not until well into the 19th that their several rules were codified. Of these the "Cumberland and Westmorland" style, which prevails principally in the N. of England (except Lancashire) and the S. of Scotland, is the most important. In this the wrestlers stand chest to chest, each grasping the other with locked hands round the body with his chin on the other's right shoulder. The right arm is below and the left above the adversary's. When this hold has been firmly taken the umpire gives the word and the bout proceeds until one man touches the ground with any part of his person except his feet, or he fails to retain his hold, in either of which cases he loses. When both fall together the one who is underneath, or first touches the ground, loses. If both fall simultaneously side by side, it is a "dog-fall," and the bout begins anew. The different maneuvers used in British wrestling to throw the adversary are called "chips," those most important in the "Cumberland and Westmorland" or "North Country" style being the "back-heel," in which a wrestler gets a leg behind his opponent's heel on the outside; the "outside stroke," in which after a sudden twist of his body to the left the opponent is struck with the left foot on the outside of his ankle; the "hank," or lifting the opponent off the ground after a sudden turn, so that both fall together, but with the opponent underneath; the "inside click," a hank applied after jerking the opponent forward, the pressure then being straight back; the "outside click," a back-heel applied by a wrestler as he is on the point of being lifted from the ground—it prevents this and often results in oversetting the opponent; the "cross-buttock," executed by getting one's hip underneath the opponent's, throwing one's leg across both his, lifting and throwing him; the "buttock," in which one's hip is worked still further under that of the opponent, who is then thrown right over one's back; the "hipe" or "hype," executed by lifting the opponent, and, while swinging him to the right, placing the left knee under his right leg and carrying it as high as posssible before the throw; the "swinging hipe," in which the opponent is swung nearly or quite round before the hipe is applied; and the "breast-stroke," which is a sudden double twist, first to one side and then to the other, followed by a throw.

In the "Cornwall and Devon" or "West Country" style the men wrestle in stout, loosely cut linen jackets, the hold being anywhere above the waist or on any part of the jacket. A bout is won by throwing the opponent on his back so that two shoulders and a hip, or two hips and a shoulder (three points), shall touch the ground simultaneously. This is a difficult matter, since ground wrestling is forbidden, and a man, when he feels himself falling, will usually turn and land on his side or face. Many of the "chips" common to other styles are used here, the most celebrated being the "flying mare," in which the opponent's left wrist is seized with one's right, one's back turned on him, his left elbow grasped with the left hand and he is then thrown over one's back, as in the buttock. Until comparatively recently there was a difference between the styles of Cornwall and Devon, the wrestlers of the latter county having worn heavily-soled shoes, with which it was legitimate to belabour the adversary's shins. In 1826 a memorable match took place between Polkinhorne, the Cornish champion, and the best wrestler of Devon, Abraham Cann, who wore "kicking-boots of an appalling pattern." Polkinhorne, however, encased his shins in leather, and the match was eventually drawn.

THE INVISIBLE WORLD

We here refer to all manner of psychic phenomena, "primitive" belief, superstition, altered states of being, and parapsychology. It should be kept in mind that editor Hugh Chisholm was relatively indifferent to advances in the realm of cure and therapy for the mind and body, and that a valued collaborator who worked closely with him recalled after publication of the eleventh that "on Medicine he had very decided and somewhat old-fashioned views. Bringing up to date some branches of it meant a hard fight." Chisholm's squeamishness extended also to the fields of psychology and psychoanalysis. By 1910 Freud had published his *Studies on Hysteria, The Interpretation of Dreams, The Psychopathology of Everyday Life,* and *Three Contributions to Sexual Theory.* Furthermore, Freud's lectures at Clark University in Worcester, Massachusetts, had been publicized, and by 1910 the International Psychoanalytical Association had been formed with C. G. Jung as its first president. The gap was criticized by a professor from Cornell two years after the publication of the eleventh; he noted that "a twentieth century encyclopaedia that has no psychologist either upon its advisory board or upon its editorial staff is an anachronism." As our selections suggest, the articles commissioned generally tended to explore the world of spiritualism and occult phenomena rather than attempting to project a still experimental field into an identifiable body of knowledge.

ABIOGENESIS, in biology, the term, equivalent to the older terms "spontaneous generation," *Generatio aequivoca, Generatio primaria,* and of more recent terms such as archegenesis and archebiosis, for the theory according to which fully formed living organisms sometimes arise from not-living matter. Aristotle explicitly taught abiogenesis, and laid it down as an observed fact that some animals spring from putrid matter, that plant-lice arise from the dew which falls on plants, that fleas are developed from putrid matter, and so forth. T. J. Parker (*Elementary Biology*) cites a passage from Alexander Ross, who, commenting on Sir Thomas Browne's doubt as to "whether mice may be bred by putrefaction," gives a clear statement of the common opinion on abiogenesis held until about two centuries ago. Ross wrote: "So may he (Sir Thomas Browne) doubt whether in cheese and timber worms are generated; or if beetles and wasps in cows' dung; or if butterflies, locusts, grasshoppers, shellfish, snails, eels, and such like, be procreated of putrefied matter, which is apt to receive the form of that creature to which it is by formative power disposed. To question this is to question reason, sense and experience. If he doubts of this let him go to Egypt, and there he will find the fields swarming with mice, begot of the mud of Nylus, to the great calamity of the inhabitants."

The first step in the scientific refutation of the theory of abiogenesis was taken by the Italian Redi, who, in 1668, proved that no maggots were "bred" in meat on which flies were prevented by wire screens from laying their eggs. From the 17th century onwards it was gradually shown that, at least in the case of all the higher and readily visible organisms, abiogenesis did not occur, but that *omne vivum e vivo*, every living thing came from a pre-existing living thing.

The discovery of the microscope carried the refutation further. In 1683 A. van Leeuwenhoek discovered bacteria, and it was soon found that however carefully organic matter might be protected by screens, or by being placed in stoppered receptacles, putrefaction set in, and was invariably accompanied by the appearance of myriads of bacteria and other low organisms. As knowledge of microscopic forms of life increased, so the apparent possibilities of abiogenesis increased, and it became a tempting hypothesis that whilst the higher forms of life arose only by generation from their kind, there was a perpetual abiogenetic fount by which the first steps in the evolution of living organisms continued to arise, under suitable conditions, from inorganic matter. It was due chiefly to L. Pasteur that the occurrence of abiogenesis in the microscopic world was disproved as much as its occurrence in the macroscopic world.

ABRACADABRA, a word analogous to Abraxas, used as a magical formula by the Gnostics of the sect of Basilides in invoking the aid of beneficent spirits against disease and misfortune. It is found on Abraxas stones which were worn as amulets. Subsequently its use spread beyond the Gnostics, and in modern times it is applied contemptuously (*e.g.* by the early opponents of the evolution theory) to a conception or hypothesis which purports to be a simple solution of apparently insoluble phenomena. The Gnostic physician Serenus Samonicus gave precise instructions as to its mystical use in averting or curing agues and fevers generally. The paper on which the word was written had to be folded in the form of a cross, suspended from the neck by a strip of linen so as to rest on the pit of the stomach, worn in this way for nine days, and then, before sunrise, cast behind the wearer into a stream running to the east. The letters were usually arranged as a triangle in one of the following ways:—

```
    ABRACADABRA              ABRACADABRA
    ABRACADABR               BRACADABR
    ABRACADAB                RACADAB
    ABRACADA                 ACADA
    ABRACAD                  CAD
    ABRACA                   A
    ABRAC
    ABRA
    ABR
    AB
    A
```

❧ ANIMAL WORSHIP.

Bear.—The bear enjoys a large measure of respect from all savage races that come in contact with it, which shows itself in apologies and in festivals in its honour. The most important developments of the cult are in East Asia among the Siberian tribes; among the Ainu of Sakhalin a young bear is caught at the end of winter and fed for some nine months; then after receiving honours it is killed, and the people, who previously show marks of grief at its approaching fate, dance merrily and feast on its body. Among the Gilyaks a similar festival is found, but here it takes the form of a celebration in honour of a recently dead kinsman, to whom the spirit of the bear is sent. Whether this feature or a cult of the hunting type was the primary form, is so far an open question. There is a good deal of evidence to connect the Greek goddess Artemis with a cult of the bear; girls danced as "bears" in her honour, and might not marry before undergoing this ceremony. The bear is traditionally associated with Bern in Switzerland, and in 1832 a statue of Artio, a bear goddess, was dug up there.

Buffalo.—The Todas of S. India abstain from the flesh of their domestic animal, the buffalo; but once a year they sacrifice a bull calf, which is eaten in the forest by the adult males.

Cattle.—Cattle are respected by many pastoral peoples; they live on milk or game, and the killing of an ox is a sacrificial function. Conspicuous among Egyptian animal cults was that of the bull, Apis. It was distinguished by certain marks, and when the old Apis died a new one was sought; the finder was rewarded, and the bull underwent four months' education at Nilopolis. Its birthday was celebrated once a year; oxen, which had to be pure white, were sacrificed to it; women were forbidden to approach it when once its education was finished.

Oracles were obtained from it in various ways. After death it was mummified and buried in a rock-tomb. Less widespread was the cult of the Mnevis, also consecrated to Osiris. Similar observances are found in our own day on the Upper Nile; the Nuba and Nuer worship the bull; the Angoni of Central Africa and the Sakalava of Madagascar keep sacred bulls. In India respect for the cow is widespread, but is of post-Vedic origin; there is little actual worship, but the products of the cow are important in magic.

Crow.—The crow is the chief deity of the Thlinkit Indians of N. W. America; and all over that region it is the chief figure in a group of myths, fulfilling the office of a culture hero who brings the light, gives fire to mankind, &c. Together with the eagle-hawk the crow plays a great part in the mythology of S.E. Australia.

Dog.—Actual dog-worship is uncommon; the Nosarii of western Asia are said to worship a dog; the Kalangs of Java had a cult of the red dog, each family keeping one in the house; according to one authority the dogs are images of wood which are worshipped after the death of a member of the family and burnt after a thousand days. In Nepal it is said that dogs are worshipped at the festival called Khicha Puja. Among the Harranians dogs were sacred, but this was rather as brothers of the mystae.

Elephant.—In Siam it is believed that a white elephant may contain the soul of a dead person, perhaps a Buddha; when one is taken the capturer is rewarded and the animal brought to the king to be kept ever afterwards; it cannot be bought or sold. It is baptized and fêted and mourned for like a human being at its death. In some parts of Indo-China the belief is that the soul of the elephant may injure people after death; it is therefore fêted by a whole village. In Cambodia it is held to bring luck to the kingdom. In Sumatra the elephant is regarded as a tutelary spirit. The cult of the white elephant is also found at Ennarea, southern Abyssinia.

Fish.—Dagon seems to have been a fish-god with human head and hands; his worshippers wore fish-skins. In the temples of Apollo and Aphrodite were sacred fish, which may point to a fish cult. Atargatis is said to have had sacred fish at Askelon, and from Xenophon we read that the fish of the Chalus were regarded as gods.

Goat.—Dionysus was believed to take the form of a goat, probably as a divinity of vegetation. Pan, Silenus, the Satyrs and the Fauns were either capriform or had some part of their bodies shaped like that of a goat. In northern Europe the wood spirit, Ljesche, is believed to have a goat's horns, ears and legs. In Africa the Bijagos are said to have a goat as their principal divinity.

Hare.—In North America the Algonquin tribes had as their chief deity a "mighty great hare" to whom they went at death. According to one account he lived in the east, according to another in the north. In his anthropomorphized form he was known as Menabosho or Michabo.

Hawk.—In North Borneo we seem to see the evolution of a god in the three stages of the cult of the hawk among the Kenyahs, the Kayans and the sea Dyaks. The Kenyahs will not kill it, address to it thanks for assistance, and formally consult it before leaving home on an expdition; it seems, however, to be regarded as the messenger of the supreme god Balli Penyalong. The Kayans have a hawk-god, Laki Neho, but seem to regard the hawk as the servant of the chief god, Laki Tenangan. Singalang Burong, the hawk-god of the Dyaks, is completely anthropomorphized. He is god of omens and ruler of the omen birds; but the hawk is not his messenger, for he never leaves his house; stories are, however, told of his attending feasts in human form and flying away in hawk form when all was over.

Horse.—There is some reason to believe that Poseidon, like other water gods, was originally conceived under the form of a horse. In the cave of Phigalia Demeter was, according to popular tradition, represented with the head and mane of a horse, possibly a relic of the time when a non-specialized corn-spirit bore this form. Her priests were called Poloi (colts) in Laconia. In Gaul we find a horse-goddess, Epona; there are also traces of a horse-god, Rudiobus. The Gonds in India worship a horse-god, Koda Pen, in the form of a shapeless stone; but it is not clear that the horse is regarded as divine. The horse or mare is a common form of the corn-spirit in Europe.

Leopard.—The cult of the leopard is widely found in West Africa. Among the Ewe a man who kills one is liable to be put to death; no leopard skin may be exposed to view, but a stuffed leopard is worshipped. On the Gold Coast a leopard hunter who has killed his victim is carried round the town behind the body of the leopard; he may not speak, must besmear himself so as to look like a leopard and imitate its movements. In Loango a prince's cap is put upon the head of a dead leopard, and dances are held in its honour.

Lion.—The lion was associated with the Egyptian gods Rē and Horus; there was a lion-god at Baalbek and a lion-headed goddess Sekhet. The Arabs had a lion-god, Yaghuth. In modern Africa we find a lion-idol among the Balonda.

Serpent.—The cult of the serpent is found in many parts of the Old World; it is also not unknown in America; in Australia, on the other hand, though many species of serpent are found, there does not appear to be any species of cult unless we include the Warramunga cult of the mythical Wollunqua totem animal, whom they seek to placate by rites. In Africa the chief centre of serpent worship was Dahomey; but the cult of the python seems to have been of exotic origin, dating back to the first quarter of the 17th century. By the conquest of Whydah the Dahomeyans were brought in contact with a people of serpent worshippers, and ended by adopting from them the cult which they at first despised. At Whydah, the chief centre, there is a serpent temple, tenanted by some fifty snakes; every python of the danh-gbi kind must be treated with respect, and death is the penalty for killing one, even by accident. Danh-gbi has numerous wives, who until 1857 took part in a public procession from which the profane crowd was excluded; a python was carried round the town in a hammock, perhaps as a ceremony for the expulsion of evils. The rainbow-god of the Ewe was also conceived to have the form of a snake; his messenger was said to be a small variety of boa; but only certain individuals, not the whole species, were sacred. In many parts of Africa the serpent is looked upon as the incarnation of deceased relatives; among the Amazulu, as among the Betsileo of Madagascar, certain species are assigned as the abode of certain classes; the Masai, on the other hand, regard each species as the habitat of a particular family of the tribe.

In America some of the Amerindian tribes reverence the rattle-snake as grandfather and king of snakes who is able to give fair winds or cause tempest. Among the Hopi (Moqui) of Arizona the serpent figures largely in one of the dances. The rattlesnake was worshipped in the Natchez temple of the sun; and the Aztec deity Quetzalcoatl was a serpent-god. The tribes of Peru are said to have adored great snakes in the pre-Inca days; and in Chile the Araucanians made a serpent figure in their deluge myth.

Over a large part of India there are carved representations of cobras (Nāgas) or stones as substitutes; to these human food and flowers are offered and lights are burned before the shrines. Among the Dravidians a cobra which is accidentally killed is burned like a human being; no one would kill one intentionally; the serpent-god's image is carried in an annual procession by a celibate priestess.

Serpent cults were well known in ancient Europe; there does not, it is true, appear to be much ground for supposing that Aesculapius was a serpent-god in spite of his connexion with serpents. On the other hand, we learn from Herodotus of the great serpent which defended the citadel of Athens; the Roman *genius loci* took the form of a serpent; a snake was kept and fed with milk in the temple of

Potrimpos, an old Slavonic god. To this day there are numerous traces in popular belief, especially in Germany, of respect for the snake, which seems to be a survival of ancestor worship, such as still exists among the Zulus and other savage tribes; the "house-snake," as it is called, cares for the cows and the children, and its appearance is an omen of death, and the life of a pair of house-snakes is often held to be bound up with that of the master and mistress themselves. Tradition says that one of the Gnostic sects known as the Ophites caused a tame serpent to coil round the sacramental bread and worshipped it as the representative of the Saviour.

Sheep.—Only in Africa do we find a sheep-god proper; Ammon was the god of Thebes; he was represented as ram-headed; his worshippers held the ram to be sacred; it was, however, sacrificed once a year, and its fleece formed the clothing of the idol.

Tiger.—The tiger is associated with Siva and Durga, but its cult is confined to the wilder tribes; in Nepal the tiger festival is known as Bagh Jatra, and the worshippers dance disguised as tigers. The Waralis worship Waghia the lord of tigers in the form of a shapeless stone. In Hanoi and Manchuria tiger-gods are also found.

Wolf.—Both Zeus and Apollo were associated with the wolf by the Greeks; but it is not clear that this implies a previous cult of the wolf. It is frequently found among the tutelary deities of North American dancing or secret societies. The Thlinkits had a god, Khanukh, whose name means "wolf," and worshipped a wolf-headed image. (N.W.T.)

AUTOMATIC WRITING, the name given by students of psychical research to writing performed without the volition of the agent. The writing may also take place without any consciousness of the words written; but some automatists are aware of the word which they are actually writing, and perhaps of two or three words on either side, though there is rarely any clear perception of the meaning of the whole. Automatic writing may take place when the agent is in a state of trance, spontaneous or induced, in hystero-epilepsy or other morbid states; or in a condition not distinguishable from normal wakefulness. Automatic writing has played an important part in the history of modern spiritualism. The phenomenon first appeared on a large scale in the early days (*c.* 1850–1860) of the movement in America. Numerous writings are reported at that period, many of considerable length, which purported for the most part to have been produced under spirit guidance. Some of these were written in "unknown tongues." Of those which were published the most notable are Andrew J. Davis's *Great Harmonia,* Charles Linton's *The Healing of the Nations,* and J. Murray Spear's *Messages from the Spirit Life.*

In England also the early spiritualist newspapers were filled with "inspirational" writing,—*Pages of the Paraclete,* &c. The most notable series of English automatic writings are the *Spirit Teachings* of the Rev. W. Stainton Moses. The phenomenon, of course, lends itself to deception, but there seems no reason to doubt that in the great majority of the cases recorded the writing was in reality produced without deliberate volition. In the earlier years of the spiritualist movement, a "planchette," a little heart-shaped board running on wheels, was employed to facilitate the process of writing.

Of late years, whilst the theory of external inspiration as the cause of the phenomenon has been generally discredited, automatic writing has been largely employed as a method of experimentally investigating subconscious mental processes. Knowledge which had lapsed from the primary consciousness is frequently revealed by this means; *e.g.* forgotten fragments of poetry or foreign languages are occasionally given. An experimental parallel to this reproduction of forgotten knowledge was devised by Edmund Gurney. He showed that information communicated to a subject in the hypnotic trance could be subsequently reproduced through the handwriting, whilst the attention of the subject was fully employed in conversing or reading aloud; or an arithmetical problem which had been set during the trance could be worked out under similar conditions without the apparent consciousness of the subject.

Automatic writing for the most part, no doubt, brings to the surface only the debris of lapsed memories and half-formed impressions which have never reached the focus of consciousness—the stuff that dreams are made of. But there are indications in some cases of something more than this. In some spontaneous instances the writing produces anagrams, puns, nonsense verses and occasional blasphemies or obscenities; and otherwise exhibits characteristics markedly divergent from those of the normal consciousness. In the well-known case recorded by Th. Flournoy (*Des Indes à la planète Mars*) the automatist produced writing in an unknown character, which purported to be the Martian language. The writing generally resembles the ordinary handwriting of the agent, but there are sometimes marked differences, and the same automatist may employ two or three distinct handwritings. Occasionally imitations are produced of the handwriting of other persons, living or dead. Not infrequently the writing is reversed, so that it can be read only in a looking-glass (*Spiegelschrift*);

the ability to produce such writing is often associated with the liability to spontaneous somnambulism. The hand and arm are often insensible in the act of writing. There are some cases on record in which the automatist has seemed to guide his hand not by sight, but by some special extension of the muscular sense.

Automatic writing frequently exhibits indications of telepathy. The most remarkable series of automatic writings recorded in this connexion are those executed by the American medium, Mrs Piper, in a state of trance. These writings appear to exhibit remarkable telepathic powers, and are thought by some to indicate communication with the spirits of the dead.

The opportunities afforded by automatic writing for communicating with subconscious strata of the personality have been made use of by Pierre Janet and others in cases of hysteroepilepsy, and other forms of dissociation of consciousness. A patient in an attack of hysterical convulsions, to whom oral appeals are made in vain, can sometimes be induced to answer in writing questions addressed to the hand, and thus to reveal the secret of the malady or to accept therapeutic suggestions. (F.P.)

COCK LANE GHOST, a supposed apparition, the vagaries of which attracted extraordinary public attention in London during 1762. At a house in Cock Lane, Smithfield, tenanted by one Parsons, knockings and other noises were said to occur at night varied by the appearance of a luminous figure, alleged to be the ghost of a Mrs Kent who had died in the house some two years before. A thorough investigation revealed that Parsons' daughter, a child of eleven, was the source of the disturbance. The object of the Parsons family seems to have been to accuse the husband of the deceased woman of murdering her, with a view to blackmail. Parsons was prosecuted and condemned to the pillory. Among the crowds who visited the house was Dr Johnson, who was in consequence made the object of a scurrilous attack by the poet Charles Churchill in "The Ghost."

CONJURING. In all ages a very popular magical effect has been the apparent floating of a person in empty space. An endless variety of ingenious apparatus has been invented for the purpose of producing such effects, and the present article would be incomplete without some reference to one or two of the more modern

examples. A very pretty illusion of this kind is that originally produced under the title of "Astarte." A lady is brought forward, and
after making her bow to the audience she retires to the back of the
stage, the whole of which is draped with black velvet and kept in
deep shadow. There she is caused to rise in the air, to move from
side to side, to advance and retire, and to revolve in all directions.
The secret consists in an iron lever, covered with velvet to match the
background, and therefore invisible to the audience. This lever is
passed through an opening in the back curtain and attached to a
socket upon the metal girdle worn by the performer. The girdle
consists of two rings, one inside the other, the inner one being capable
of turning about its axis. By means of this main lever and a spindle
passing through it and gearing into the inner ring of the girdle, the
various movements are produced. A hoop is passed over the performer with a view to demonstrate her complete isolation, but the
audience is not allowed to examine it. It has a spring joint which
allows it to pass the supporting lever. Among illusions of this class
there is probably none that will bear comparison with the "levitation"
mystery produced by Mr Maskelyne. A performer, in a recumbent
position, is caused to rise several feet from the stage, and to remain
suspended in space while an intensely brilliant light is thrown upon
him, illuminating the entire surroundings. Persons walk completely
round him, and a solid steel hoop, examined by the audience, is
passed over him, backwards and forwards, to prove the absence of
any tangible connexion.

CROSS-ROADS, BURIAL AT, in former
times the method of disposing of executed criminals and suicides. At
the cross-roads a rude cross usually stood, and this gave rise to the
belief that these spots were selected as the next best burying-places
to consecrated ground. The real explanation is that the ancient Teutonic peoples often built their altars at the cross-roads, and as human
sacrifices, especially of criminals, formed part of the ritual, these spots
came to be regarded as execution grounds. Hence after the introduction of Christianity, criminals and suicides were buried at the
cross-roads during the night, in order to assimilate as far as possible
their funeral to that of the pagans. An example of a cross-road
execution-ground was the famous Tyburn in London, which stood
on the spot where the Oxford, Edgware and London roads met.

◯◠◠◯ **DEATH-WARNING,** a term used in psychical research for an intimation of the death of another person received by other than the ordinary sensory channels, *i.e.* by (1) a sensory hallucination or (2) a massive sensation, both being of telepathic origin. Both among civilized and uncivilized peoples there is a widespread belief that the apparition of a living person is an omen of death; but until the Society of Psychical Research undertook the statistical examination of the question, there were no data for estimating the value of the belief. In 1885 a collection of spontaneous cases and a discussion of the evidence was published under the title *Phantasms of the Living,* and though the standard of evidence was lower than at the present time, a substantial body of testimony, including many striking cases, was there put forward. In 1889 a further inquiry was undertaken, known as the "Census of Hallucinations," which provided information as to the percentage of individuals in the general population who, at some period of their lives, while they were in a normal state of health, had had "a vivid impression of seeing or being touched by a living being or inanimate object, or of hearing a voice; which impression, so far as they could discover, was not due to any external cause." To the census question about 17,000 answers were received, and after making all deductions it appeared that death coincidences numbered about 30 in 1300 cases of recognized apparitions; or about 1 in 43, whereas if chance alone operated the coincidences would have been in the proportion of 1 to 19,000. As a result of the inquiry the committee held it to be proved that "between deaths and apparitions of the dying person a connexion exists which is not due to chance alone." From an evidential point of view the apparition is the most valuable class of death-warning, inasmuch as recognition is more difficult in the case of an auditory hallucination, even where it takes the form of spoken words; moreover, auditory hallucinations coinciding with deaths may be mere knocks, ringing of bells, &c.; tactile hallucinations are still more difficult of recognition; and the hallucinations of smell which are sometimes found as death-warnings rarely have anything to associate them specially with the dead person. Occasionally the death-warning is in the form of an apparition of some other person; it may also take the form of a temporary feeling of intense depression or other massive sensation.

◯◠◠◯ **EVIL EYE.** The terror of the arts of "fascination," *i.e.* that certain persons can bewitch, injure and even kill with a glance, has been and is still very widely spread. The power was not

thought to be always maliciously cultivated. It was as often supposed
to be involuntary (cf. Deuteronomy xxviii. 54); and a story is told of
a Slav who, afflicted with the evil eye, at last blinded himself in order
that he might not be the means of injuring his children (Woyciki,
Polish Folklore, p. 25). Few of the old classic writers fail to refer to the
dread power. In Rome the "evil eye" was so well recognized that Pliny
states that special laws were enacted against injury to crops by incan-
tation, excantation or fascination. The power was styled βασκανια
by the Greeks and *fascinatio* by the Latins. Children and young animals
of all kinds were thought to be specially susceptible. Charms were
worn against the evil eye both by man and beast, and in Judges viii.
21 it is thought there is a reference to this custom in the allusion to
the "ornaments" on the necks of camels. In classic times the wearing
of amulets was universal. They were of three classes: (1) those the
intention of which was to attract on to themselves, as the lightning-
rod the lightning, the malignant glance; (2) charms hidden in the
bosom of the dress; (3) written words from sacred writings. Of these
three types the first was most numerous. They were oftenest of a
grotesque and generally grossly obscene nature. They were also made
in the form of frogs, beetles and so on. But the ancients did not
wholly rely on amulets. Spitting was among the Greeks and Romans
a most common antidote to the poison of the evil eye. According to
Theocritus it is necessary to spit three times into the breast of the
person who fears fascination. Gestures, too, often intentionally obscene, were regarded as prophylactics on meeting the dreaded individual. The evil eye was believed to have its impulse in envy, and
thus it came to be regarded as unlucky to have any of your possessions
praised. Among the Romans, therefore, it was customary when prais-
ing anything to add *Praefiscini dixerim* (Fain Evil! I should say). This
custom survives in modern Italy, where in like circumstances is said
Si mal occhio non ci fosse (May the evil eye not strike it). The object of
these conventional phrases was to prove that the speaker was sincere
and had no evil designs in his praise. Though there is no set formula,
traces of the custom are found in English rural sayings, *e.g.* the Som-
ersetshire "I don't wish ee no harm, so I on't zay no more." This is
what the Scots call "forespeaking," when praise beyond measure is
likely to be followed by disease or accident. A Manxman will never
say he is very well: he usually admits that he is "middling," or qualifies
his admission of good health by adding "now" or "just now." The
belief led in many countries to the saying, when one heard anybody
or anything praised superabundantly, "God preserve him or it." So
in Ireland, to avoid being suspected of having the evil eye, it is ad-

visable when looking at a child to say "God bless it"; and when passing a farm-yard where cows are collected at milking time it is usual for the peasant to say, "The blessing of God be on you and all your labour." Bacon writes: "It seems some have been so curious as to note that the times when the stroke . . . of an envious eye does most hurt are particularly when the party envied is beheld in glory and triumph."

The powers of the evil eye seem indeed to have been most feared by the prosperous. Its powers are often quoted as almost limitless. Thus one record solemnly declares that in a town of Africa a fascinator called Elzanar killed by his evil art no less than 80 people in two years (W. W. Story, *Castle St. Angelo*, 1877, p. 149). The belief as affecting cattle was universal in the Scottish Highlands as late as the 18th century and still lingers. Thus if a stranger looks admiringly on a cow the peasants still think she will waste away, and they offer the visitor some of her milk to drink in the belief that in this manner the spell is broken. The modern Turks and Arabs also think that their horses and camels are subject to the evil eye. But the people of Italy, especially the Neapolitans, are the best modern instances of implicit believers. The *jettatore*, as the owner of the evil eye is called, is so feared that at his approach it is scarcely an exaggeration to say that a street will clear: everybody will rush into doorways or up alleys to avoid the dreaded glance. The *jettatore di bambini* (fascinator of children) is the most dreaded of all. The evil eye is still much feared for horses in India, China, Turkey, Greece and almost everywhere where horses are found. In rural England the pig is of all animals oftenest "overlooked." While the Italians are perhaps the greatest believers in the evil eye as affecting persons, the superstition is rife in the East. In India the belief is universal. In Bombay the blast of the evil eye is supposed to be a form of spirit-possession. In western India all witches and wizards are said to be evil-eyed. Modern Egyptian mothers thus account for the sickly appearance of their babies. In Turkey passages from the Koran are painted on the outside of houses to save the inmates, and texts as amulets are worn upon the person, or hung upon camels and horses by Arabs, Abyssinians and other peoples. The superstition is universal among savage races.

HYSTERIA, a term applied to an affection which may manifest itself by a variety of symptoms, and which depends upon a disordered condition of the highest nervous centres. It is characterized by psychical peculiarities, while in addition there is often derangement of the functions subserved by the lower cerebral and spinal centres. Histological examination of the nervous system has failed to disclose associated structural alterations.

The causes of hysteria may be divided into (*a*) the predisposing, such as hereditary predisposition to nervous disease, sex, age and national idiosyncrasy; and (*b*) the immediate, such as mental and physical exhaustion, fright and other emotional influences, pregnancy, the puerperal condition, diseases of the uterus and its appendages, and the depressing influence of injury or general disease. Perhaps, taken over all, hereditary predisposition to nerve-instability may be asserted as the most prolific cause. There is frequently direct inheritance, and cases of epilepsy and insanity or other form of nervous disease are rarely wanting when the family history is carefully enquired into. As regards age, the condition is apt to appear at the evolution periods of life—puberty, pregnancy and the climacteric—without any further assignable cause except that first spoken of. It is rare in young children, but very frequent in girls between the ages of fifteen and twenty-five, while it sometimes manifests itself in women at the menopause. It is much more common in the female than in the male—in the proportion of 20 to 1. Certain races are more liable to the disease than others; thus the Latin races are much more prone to hysteria than are those who come of a Teutonic stock, and in more aggravated and complex forms. In England it has been asserted that an undue proportion of cases occur among Jews. Occupation, or be it rather said want of occupation, is a prolific cause. This is noticeable more especially in the higher classes of society.

An hysterical attack may occur as an immediate sequel to an epileptic fit. If the patient suffers only from *petit mal* unaccompanied by true epileptic fits, the significance of the hysterical seizure, which is really a post-epileptic phenomenon, may remain unrecognized.

It is convenient to group the very varied symptoms of hysteria into paroxysmal and chronic. The popular term "hysterics" is applied to an explosion of emotionalism, generally the result of mental excitement, on which convulsive fits may supervene. The characters of these vary, and may closely resemble epilepsy. The hysterical fit is generally preceded by an aura or warning. This sometimes takes the form of a sensation as of a lump in the throat (*globus hystericus*). The patient may fall, but very rarely is injured in so doing. The eyes are often tightly closed, the body and limbs become rigid, and the back may become so arched that the patient rests on her heels and head (*opisthotonos*). This stage is usually followed by violent struggling movements. There is no loss of consciousness. The attack may last for half-an-hour or even longer. Hysterical fits in their fully developed form are rarely seen in England, though common in France. In the chronic condition we find an extraordinary complexity of symptoms, both physical and mental. The physical symptoms are extremely diverse. There may be a paralysis of one or more limbs associated with rigidity, which may persist for weeks, months or years. In some cases, the patient is unable to walk; in others there are peculiarities of the gait quite unlike anything met with in organic disease. Perversions of sensation are usually present; a common instance is the sensation of a nail being driven through the vertex of the head (*clavus hystericus*). The region of the spine is a very frequent seat of hysterical pain. Loss of sensation (*anaesthesia*), of which the patient may be unaware, is of common occurrence. Very often this sensory loss is limited exactly to one-half of the body, including the leg, arm and face on that side (*hemianaesthesia*). Sensation to touch, pain, heat and cold, and electrical stimuli may have completely disappeared in the anaesthetic region. In other cases, the anaesthesia is relative or it may be partial, certain forms of sensation remaining intact. Anaesthesia is almost always accompanied by an inability to recognize the exact position of the affected limb when the eyes are closed. When hemianaesthesia is present, sight, hearing, taste and smell are usually impaired on that side of the body. Often there is loss of voice (hysterical aphonia). It is to such cases of hysterical paralysis and sensory disturbance that the wonderful cures effected by quacks and charlatans may be referred. The mental symptoms have not the same tendency to pass away suddenly. They may be spoken of as interparoxysmal and paroxysmal. The chief characteristics of the former are extreme emotionalism combined with obstructiveness, a desire to be an object of interest and a constant craving for sympathy which is often procured at an immense sacrifice of personal comfort. Obstructiveness is the invariable symptom. Hysteria may pass into absolute insanity.

The treatment of hysteria demands great tact and firmness on the part of the physician. The affection is a definite entity and has to be clearly distinguished from malingering, with which it is so often erroneously regarded as synonymous. Drugs are of little value. The moral treatment is all important. In severe cases, removal from home surroundings and isolation, either in a hospital ward or nursing home, are essential, in order that full benefit may be derived from psychotherapeutic measures. (J.B.T.; E.Bra.)

CRS> **LYCANTHROPY,** a name employed (1) in folk-lore for the liability or power of a human being to undergo transformation into an animal; (2) in pathology for a form of insanity in which the patient believes that he is transformed into an animal and behaves accordingly.

I. Although the term lycanthropy properly speaking refers to metamorphosis into a wolf, it is in practice used of transformation into any animal. The Greeks also spoke of kynanthropy; in India and the Asiatic islands the tiger is the commonest form, in North Europe the bear, in Japan the fox, in Africa the leopard or hyena, sometimes also the lion, in South America the jaguar; but though there is a tendency for the most important carnivorous animal of the area to take the first place in stories and beliefs as to transformation, the less important beasts of prey and even harmless animals like the deer also figure among the wer-animals.

Lycanthropy is often confused with transmigration; but the essential feature of the wer-animal is that it is the alternative form or the double of a living human being, while the soul-animal is the vehicle, temporary or permanent, of the spirit of a dead human being. The vampire is sometimes regarded as an example of lycanthropy; but it is in human form, sometimes only a head, sometimes a whole body, sometimes that of a living person, at others of a dead man who issues nightly from the grave to prey upon the living.

Even if the denotation of lycanthropy be limited to the animal-metamorphosis of living human beings, the beliefs classed together under this head are far from uniform, and the term is somewhat capriciously applied. The transformation may be voluntary or involuntary, temporary or permanent; the wer-animal may be the man himself metamorphosed, it may be his double whose activity leaves the real man to all appearance unchanged, it may be his soul, which goes forth seeking whom it may devour and leaving its body in a state of trance; or it may be no more than the messenger of the human being, a real animal or a familiar spirit, whose intimate connexion with its owner is shown by the fact that any injury to it is believed, by a phenomenon known as repercussion, to cause a corresponding injury to the human being.

The phenomenon of repercussion, the power of animal meta-morphosis, or of sending out a familiar, real or spiritual, as a messenger, and the supernormal powers conferred by association with such a familiar, are also attributed to the magician, male and female, all the world over; and witch superstitions are closely parallel to, if not identical with, lycanthrophic beliefs, the occasional involuntary character of lycanthropy being almost the sole distinguishing feature. In another direction the phenomenon of repercussion is asserted to manifest itself in connexion with the bush-soul of the West African and the *nagual* of Central America; but though there is no line of demarcation to be drawn on logical grounds, the assumed power of the magician and the intimate association of the bush-soul or the *nagual* with a human being are not termed lycanthropy. Nevertheless it will be well to touch on both these beliefs here.

In North and Central America, and to some extent in West Africa, Australia and other parts of the world, every male acquires at puberty a tutelary spirit; in some tribes of Indians the youth kills the animal of which he dreams in his initiation fast; its claw, skin or feathers are put into a little bag and become his "medicine" and must be carefully retained, for a "medicine" once lost can never be replaced. In West Africa this relation is said to be entered into by means of the blood bond, and it is so close that the death of the animal causes the man to die and vice versa. Elsewhere the possession of a tutelary spirit in animal form is the privilege of the magician. In Alaska the candidate for magical powers has to leave the abodes of men; the chief of the gods sends an otter to meet him, which he kills by saying "O" four times; he then cuts out its tongue and thereby secures the powers which he seeks. The Malays believe that the office of *pawang* (priest) is only hereditary if the soul of the dead priest, in the form of a tiger, passes into the body of his son. While the familiar is often regarded as the alternative form of the magician, the *nagual* or bush-soul is commonly regarded as wholly distinct from the human being. Transitional beliefs, however, are found, especially in Africa, in which the power of transformation is attributed to the whole of the population of certain areas. The people of Banana are said to change themselves by magical means, composed of human embryos and other ingredients, but in their leopard form they may do no hurt to mankind under pain of retaining for ever the beast shape. In other cases the change is supposed to be made for the purposes of evil magic and human victims are not prohibited. We can, therefore, draw no line of demarcation, and this makes it probable that lycanthropy is connected with nagualism and the belief in familiar spirits, rather than with metempsychosis, as Dr Tylor argues, or with totemism, as suggested by J. F. M'Lennan. A further link is supplied by the Zulu belief that the magician's familiar is really a transformed human being; when he finds a dead body on which he can work his spells without fear of discovery, the wizard breathes a sort of life into it, which enables it to move and speak, it being thought that some dead wizard has taken possession of it. He then burns a hole in the head and through the aperture extracts the tongue. Further spells have the effect of changing the revivified body into the form of some animal, hyena, owl or wild cat, the latter being most in favour. This creature then becomes the wizard's servant and obeys him in all things; its chief use is, however, to inflict sickness and death upon persons who are disliked by its master.

MEDIUM, primarily a person through whom, as an intermediate, communication is deemed to be carried on between living men and spirits of the departed, according to the spiritistic hypothesis; such a person is better termed sensitive or automatist. The phenomena of mediumship fall into two classes, (1) "physical phenomena" and (2) trance and automatic phenomena (utterances, script, &c.); both these may be manifested by the same person, as in the case of D. D. Home and Stainton Moses, but are often independent.

I. No sufficient mass of observations is to hand to enable us to distinguish between the results of trickery or hallucination on the one hand, and genuine supernormal phenomena on the other; but the evidence for raps and lights is good; competent observers have witnessed supposed materializations and there is respectable evidence for movements of objects.

Mediumship in the modern sense of the term may be said to have originated with the Rochester rappings of 1848; but similar phenomena had been reported by such authors as Apollonius of Tyana; they figure frequently in the lives of the saints; and the magician in the lower stages of culture is in many respects a counterpart of the white medium. Among physical mediums who have attained celebrity may be mentioned D. D. Home, Stainton Moses and Eusapia Palladino; the last has admittedly been fraudulent at times, but no deceit was ever proved of Home; Stainton Moses sat in a private circle and no suspicion of his good faith was ever aroused.

W. Stainton Moses (1839–1892) was a man of university education, a clergyman and a schoolmaster. In 1872 he became interested in spiritualism and soon began to manifest mediumistic phenomena, which continued for some ten years. These included, besides trance communications, raps, telekinesis, levitation, production of lights, perfumes and musical sounds, apports and materialized hands. But the conditions under which the experiments were tried were not sufficiently rigid to exclude the possibility of normal causes being at work; for no amount of evidence that the normal life is marked by no lapse from rectitude affords a presumption that uprightness will characterize states of secondary personality.

Eusapia Palladino has been observed by Sir O. Lodge, Professor Richet, F. W. H. Myers, and other eminent investigators; the first named reported that none of the phenomena in his presence went beyond what could be accomplished in a normal manner by a free and uncontrolled person; but he was convinced that movements were produced without apparent contact. Among other phenomena asserted to characterize the mediumship of Eusapia are the production of temporary prolongations from the medium's body; these have been seen in a good light by competent witnesses. It was shown in some sittings held at Cambridge in 1895 that Eusapia produced phenomena by fraudulent means: but though the evidence of this is conclusive it has not been shown that her mediumship is entirely fraudulent. Automatic records of seances can alone solve the problems raised by physical mediumship. It has been shown in the Davey-Hodgson experiments that continuous observation, even for a short period, is impossible, and that in the process of recording the observations many omissions and errors are inevitable. Even were it otherwise, no care could provide against the possibility of hallucination.

II. The genuineness of trance mediumship can no longer be called in question. The problem for solution is the source of the information. The best observed case is that of Mrs Piper of Boston; at the outset of her career, in 1884, she did not differ from the ordinary American trance medium. In 1885 the attention of Professor William James of Harvard was attracted to her; and for twenty years she remained under the supervision of the Society for Psychical Research. During that period three phases may be distinguished: (1) 1884–1891, trance utterances of a "control" calling himself Dr Phinuit, a French physician, of whose existence in the body no trace can be found; (2) 1892–1896, automatic writing by a "control" known as "George Pelham," the pseudonym of a young American author; (3) 1896 onwards, supervision by "controls" purporting to be identical with those associated with Stainton Moses. There is no evidence for regarding Mrs Piper as anything but absolutely honest. Much of the Piper material remains unpublished, partly on account of its intimate character. Many of those to whom the communications were made have been convinced that the "controls" are none other than discarnate spirits. Probably no absolute proof of identity can be given, though the reading of sealed letters would come near it; these have been left by more than one prominent psychical researcher, but so far the "controls" who claim to be the writers of them have failed to give their contents, even approximately.

Professor Flournoy has investigated a medium of very different type, known as Hélène Smith; against her good faith nothing can be urged, but her phenomena—trance utterance and glossolalia—have undoubtedly been produced by her own mind. These represent her to be the reincarnation of a Hindu princess, and of Marie Antoinette among others, but no evidence of identity has been produced. The most striking phenomenon of her trance was the so-called Martian language, eventually shown by analysis to be a derivative of French, comparable to the languages invented by children in the nursery, but more elaborate. (N.W.T.)

METEMPSYCHOSIS or Transmigration of the Soul, the doctrine that at death the soul passes into another living creature, man, animal, or even plant. This doctrine, famous in antiquity and still held as a religious tenet by certain sects of the civilized world, has its roots far back in primitive culture. It is developed out of three universal savage beliefs: (1) that man has a soul, connected in some vague way with the breath, which can be separated from his material body, temporarily in sleep, permanently at death; (2) that animals and even plants have souls, and are possessed to a large extent of human powers and passions; (3) that souls can be transferred from one organism to another. Innumerable examples might be mentioned of the notion that a new-born child is the reincarnation of someone departed, as in Tibet the soul of the Dalai-Lama is supposed to pass into an infant born nine months after his decease. Transmigration of human souls into non-human bodies is implied in totemism, for, as Professor Frazer says, "it is an article of faith that as the clan sprang from the totem, so each clansman at death reassumes the totem form." All these savage notions are to be regarded as presuppositions of metempsychosis, rather than identified with that doctrine itself as a reasoned theory.

Till full investigation of Egyptian records put us in possession of the facts, it was supposed that the Egyptians believed in metempsychosis, and Herodotus (ii. 123) explicitly credits them with it. We now know that he was wrong. All that they believed was that certain privileged souls might in the other world be able to assume certain forms at pleasure, those of a sparrow-hawk, lily, &c. Herodotus misunderstood the Egyptians to hold beliefs identical with those which were current in his day in Greece. In India, on the contrary, the doctrine was thoroughly established from ancient times; not from the most ancient, as it is not in the Vedas; but onwards from the Upanishads. In them it is used for moral retribution: he who kills a Brahman is, after a long progress through dreadful hells, to be reborn as a dog, pig, ass, camel, &c. This we always find in metempsychosis as a reasoned theory. It is formed by combination of two sets of ideas which belong to different planes of culture: the ideas of judgment and punishment after death elaborated in a relatively cultured society by a priestly class are combined with ideas, like that of totem-transmigration, proper to a savage society. In India we may explain the whole phenomenon as an infusion of the lower beliefs of the non-Aryan conquered races into the higher religious system of their Aryan conquerors. In later Hinduism metempsychosis reached a monstrous development; according to Monier-Williams it was believed that there were 8,400,000 forms of existence through which all souls were liable to pass before returning to their source in the Deity. Buddhism appeared as a reaction against all this, and sought by a subtle modification to harmonize the theory with its own pessimistic view of the world. According to Buddhism there is no soul, and consequently no metempsychosis in the strict sense. Something, however, is transmitted, *i.e. Karma* (character), which passes from individual to individual, till in the perfectly righteous man the will to live is extinguished and that particular chain of lives is brought to an end.

We do not know exactly how the doctrine of metempsychosis arose in Greece; it cannot, as was once supposed, have been borrowed from Egypt and is not likely to have come from India. It is easiest to assume that savage ideas which had never been extinguished were utilized for religious and philosophic purposes. The Orphic religion, which held it, first appeared in Thrace upon the semi-barbarous north-eastern frontier. Orpheus, its legendary founder, is said to have taught that "soul and body are united by a compact unequally binding on either; the soul is divine, immortal and aspires to freedom, while the body holds it in fetters as a prisoner. Death dissolves this compact, but only to re-imprison the liberated soul after a short time: for the wheel of birth revolves inexorably. Thus the soul continues its journey, alternating between a separate unrestrained existence and fresh reincarnation, round the wide circle of necessity, as the companion of many bodies of men and animals. To these unfortunate prisoners Orpheus proclaims the message of liberation, that they stand in need of the grace of redeeming gods and of Dionysus in particular, and calls them to turn to God by ascetic piety of life and self-purification: the purer their lives the higher will be their next reincarnation, until the soul has completed the spiral ascent of destiny to live for ever as God from whom it comes." Such was the teaching of Orphism which appeared in Greece about the 6th century B.C., organized itself into private and public mysteries at Eleusis and elsewhere, and produced a copious literature.

The earliest Greek thinker with whom metempsychosis is connected is Pherecydes; but Pythagoras, who is said to have been his pupil, is its first famous philosophic exponent. Pythagoras probably neither invented the doctrine nor imported it from Egypt, but made his reputation by bringing Orphic doctrine from North-Eastern Hellas to Magna Graecia and by instituting societies for its diffusion.

The real weight and importance of metempsychosis is due to its adoption by Plato. Had he not embodied it in some of his greatest works it would be merely a matter of curious investigaiton for the anthropologist and student of folk-lore. In the eschatological myth which closes the *Republic* he tells the story how Er, the son of Armenius, miraculously returned to life on the twelfth day after death and recounted the secrets of the other world. After death, he said, he went with others to the place of Judgment and saw the souls returning from heaven and from purgatory, and proceeded with them to a place where they chose new lives, human and animal. "He saw the soul of Orpheus changing into a swan, Thamyras becoming a nightingale, musical birds choosing to be men, the soul of Atalanta choosing the honours of an athlete. Men were seen passing into animals and wild and tame animals changing into each other." After their choice the souls drank of Lethe and then shot away like stars to their birth. There are myths and theories to the same effect in other dialogues, the *Phaedrus, Meno, Phaedo, Timaeus* and *Laws*. In Plato's view the number of souls was fixed; birth therefore is never the creation of a soul, but only a transmigration from one body to another. Plato's acceptance of the doctrine is characteristic of his sympathy with popular beliefs and desire to incorporate them in a purified form into his system. Aristotle, a far less emotional and sympathetic mind, has a doctrine of immortality totally inconsistent with it. (H.St.)

PREMONITION, an impression relating to a future event. Strictly the word should mean a warning proceeding from an external source. Its modern extension to all forms of impression supposed to convey information as to the future is justified on the assumption that such intimations commonly originate in the subliminal consciousness of the percipient and are thence transferred to the ordinary consciousness. In modern times the best attested premonitions are those relating to events about to occur in the subject's own organism. It was observed by the animal magnetists at the beginning of the 19th century in France and Germany, that certain of their subjects, when in the "magnetic" trance, could foretell accurately the course of their diseases, the date of the occurrence of a crisis and the length of time needed to effect a cure. Similar observations were subsequently recorded in Great Britain and in America (see, for instance, the case of Anna Winsor, 1860–1863, reported by Dr Ira Barrows). The power of prediction possessed by the subject in such cases may be explained in two ways: (1) As due to an abnormal power of perception possessed by certain persons, when in the hypnotic trance, of the working of their own pathological processes; or (2) more probably, as the result of self-suggestion; the organism is "set" to explode at a given date in a crisis, or to develop the fore-ordained symptoms.

Apart from these cases there are two types of alleged premonitions. (1) The future event may be foreshadowed by a symbol. Amongst the best known of these symbolic impressions are banshees, corpse lights, phantom funeral processions, ominous animals or sounds and symbolic dreams (*e.g.* of teeth falling out). Of all such cases it is enough to say that it is impossible for the serious inquirer to establish any causal connexion between the omen and the event which it is presumed to foreshadow. (2) There are many instances, recorded by educated witnesses, of dreams, visions, warning voices, &c., giving precise information as to coming events. In some of these cases, where the dream, &c., has been put on record before its "fulfilment" is known, chance is sufficient to explain the coincidence, as in the recorded cases of dreams foretelling the winner of the Derby or the death of a crowned head. In cases where such an explanation is precluded by the nature of the details foreshadowed, the evidence is found to be defective, generally from the absence of contemporary documents. The persistent belief on the part of the narrators in the genuineness of their previsions indicates that in some cases there may be a hallucination of memory, analogous to the well known feeling of "false recognition." Prof. Josiah Royce has suggested for this supposed form of hallucination the term "pseudo-presentiment." (F.P.)

⟨⟩⟩⟩ **SLEEP,** a normal condition of the body, occurring periodically, in which there is a greater or less degree of unconsciousness due to inactivity of the nervous system and more especially of the brain and spinal cord.

The coincidence of the time of sleep with the occurrence of the great terrestrial phenomena that cause night is more apparent than real. The oscillations of vital activity are not correlated to the terrestrial revolutions as effect and cause, but the occurrence of sleep, in the majority of cases, on the advent of night is largely the result of habit. Whilst the darkness and stillness of night are favourable to sleep, the state of physiological repose is determined more by the condition of the body itself. Fatigue will normally cause sleep at any time of the twenty-four hours. Thus many of the lower animals habitually sleep during the day and prowl in search of food in the night; some hibernate during the winter season, passing into long periods of sleep during both day and night; and men whose avocations require them to work during the night find that they can maintain health and activity by sleeping the requisite time during the day.

The approach of sleep is usually marked by a desire for sleep, or sleepiness, embracing an obscure and complicated group of sensations, resembling such bodily states of feeling as hunger, thirst, the necessity of breathing, &c. All of these bodily states, although on the whole ill-defined, are referred with some precision to special organs. Thus hunger, although due to a general bodily want, is referred to the stomach, thirst to the fauces, and breathing to the chest; and in like manner the desire for sleep is referred chiefly to the region of the head and neck. There is a sensation of weight in the upper eyelids, intermittent spasm of the sub-hyoid muscles causing yawning, and drooping of the head. Along with these signs there is obscuration of the intelligence, depression both of general sensibility and of the special senses, and relaxation of the muscular system. The half-closed eyelids tend more and more to close; the inspirations become slower and deeper; the muscles supporting the lower jaw become relaxed, so that the mouth opens; the muscles of the back of the neck that tend to support the head also relax and the chin droops on the breast; and the limbs relax and tend to fall into a line with the body. At the same time the hesitating utterances of the sleepy man indicate vagueness of thought, and external objects gradually cease to make an impression on the senses. These are the chief phenomena of the advent of sleep. After it has supervened there are many gradations in its depth and character. In some cases the sleep may be so light that the individual is partially conscious of external impressions and of the disordered trains of thought and feeling that pass through his mind, constituting dreams, and these may be more or less vivid, according to the degree of consciousness remaining. On the other hand, the sleep may be so profound as to abolish all psychical phenomena: there are no dreams, and when the sleeper awakes the time passed in this unconscious state is a blank. The first period of sleep is the most profound. After a variable period, usually from five to six hours of deep sleep, the faculties awaken, not simultaneously but often fitfully, so that there are transient periods of consciousness. This is the time of dreaming. As the period of waking approaches the sensibility becomes more acute, so that external impressions are faintly perceived. These impressions may influence and mould the flow of images in the mind of the sleeper, frequently altering the nature of his dreams or making them more vivid. The moment of waking is usually not instantaneous, but is preceded by an intermediate state of partial consciousness, and a strange play of the mental faculties that has more of the character of an "intellectual mirage" than of consecutive thought. (J.G.M.)

〇◯◯◯◯ **SOMNAMBULISM** (from Lat. *somnus,* sleep, and *ambulare,* to walk), or sleep-walking, the condition under which people are known to walk along while asleep, apparently unconscious of external impressions, return to bed, and when they awake have no recollection of any of these occurrences. Sometimes the actions performed are of a complicated character and bear some relation to the daily life of the sleeper. Thus a cook has been known to rise out of bed, carry a pitcher to a well in the garden, fill it, go back to the house, fill various vessels carefully and without spilling a drop of water, then return to bed, and have no recollection of what had transpired. Again, somnambulists have been observed to write letters or reports, execute drawings, and play upon musical instruments. Frequently they have gone along dangerous paths, executing delicate movements with precision.

Four types of somnambulists may be noticed: (1) those who speak without acting, a common variety often observed in children and not usually considered somnambulistic; (2) those who act without speaking, also well known and the most common type; (3) those who both act and speak, more exceptional; and (4) those who both act and speak and who have not merely the sense of touch active but also the senses of sight and hearing. The fourth class is the most extreme type and merges into the physiological condition of mesmerism or hypnotism, and it is necessary here only to notice it in connexion with the subject of sleep. Many observations indicate that, at all events in some cases, the somnambulist engaged, for example, in writing, has a mental picture of the page before him and of the words he has written. He does not see what he really writes. This has been proved by causing persons to write on a sheet of paper lying on the top of other sheets. After he had been allowed to write a few sentences, the sheet was carefully withdrawn and he continued his writing on the next sheet, beginning on the new sheet at the corresponding point where he left off on the first one. Moreover, the somnambulist, by force of habit, stroked t's and dotted i's at the exact places where the t's and i's would have been had he written continuously on one sheet, showing that what he was conscious of was not what was before him, but the mental picture of what he had done.

NATURAL
SELECTIONS

The eleventh lavished much
care and affection on the description of the animal world,
birds in particular. Well over two hundred species are given
copious descriptions in elegant and precise language, but

it should be said that equally studious treatment is given to less poetic creatures such as the electric eel, the boa, the bug, and the cockroach, the last receiving a handy prescription directed at the reader for quick extermination of the pest in the home. Also note the scrupulous accounts of the processes of "Migration of Birds" and "Nidification," and take special note of the charm and eloquence of the excerpt we have entitled "The Song of Birds." Most of it was written by Alfred Newton, professor of zoology at Cambridge, whose numerous descriptions of birds, their habits and their habitat were happily taken over by editor Hugh Chisholm from their original appearance in the ninth edition of the *Encyclopaedia,* one of the instances in which abundant material from the ninth was brought forth into the eleventh without much retouching.

ALBATROSS (from the Port. *Alcatras,* a pelican), the name of a genus of aquatic birds (*Diomedea*), closely allied to the petrels, and belonging, like them, to the order *Tubinares.* In the name *Diomedea,* assigned to them by Linnaeus, there is a reference to the mythical metamorphosis of the companions of the Greek warrior Diomedes into birds. The beak is large, strong and sharp-edged, the upper mandible terminating in a large hook, the wings are narrow and very long; the feet have no hind toe, and the three anterior toes are completely webbed. The best known is the common or wandering albatross, which occurs in all parts of the Southern Ocean. It is the largest and strongest of all sea-birds. The length of the body is stated at 4 ft., and the weight at from 15 to 25 lb. It sometimes measures as much as 17 ft. between the tips of the extended wings, averaging probably from 10 to 12 ft. Its strength of wing is very great. It often accompanies a ship for days—not merely following it, but wheeling in wide circles around it—without ever being observed to alight on the water, and continues its flight, apparently untired, in tempestuous as well as in moderate weather. It has even been said to sleep on the wing, and Moore alludes to this fanciful "cloud-rocked slumbering" in his *Fire Worshippers.* It feeds on small fish and on the animal refuse that floats on the sea, eating to such excess at times that it is unable to fly and rests helplessly on the water. The colour of the bird is white, the back being streaked transversely with black or brown bands, and the wings dark. Sailors capture the bird for its long wing-bones, which they manufacture into tobacco-pipe stems. The albatross lays one egg; it is white, with a few spots, and is about 4 in. long. In breeding-time the bird resorts to solitary island groups, like the Crozet Islands and the elevated Tristan da Cunha, where it has its nest—a natural hollow or a circle of earth roughly scraped together—on the open ground. The early explorers of the great Southern Sea cheered themselves with the companionship of the albatross in its dreary solitudes; and the evil hap of him who shot with his cross-bow the bird of good omen is familiar to readers of Coleridge's *Rime of the Ancient Mariner*.

BITTERN, a genus of wading birds, belonging to the family *Ardeidae*, comprising several species closely allied to the herons, from which they differ chiefly in their shorter neck, the back of which is covered with down, and the front with long feathers, which can be raised at pleasure. They are solitary birds, frequenting countries possessing extensive swamps and marshy grounds, remaining at rest by day, concealed among the reeds and bushes of their haunts, and seeking their food, which consists of fish, reptiles, insects and small quadrupeds, in the twilight. The common bittern (*Botaurus stellaris*) is nearly as large as the heron, and is widely distributed over the eastern hemisphere. Formerly it was common in Britain, but extensive drainage and persecution have greatly diminished its numbers and it is now only an uncertain visitor. Not a winter passes without its appearing in some numbers, when its uncommon aspect, its large size, and beautifully pencilled plumage cause it to be regarded as a great prize by the lucky gun-bearer to whom it falls a victim. Its value as a delicacy for the table, once so highly esteemed, has long vanished. The old fable of this bird inserting its beak into a reed or plunging it into the ground, and so causing the booming sound with which its name will be always associated, is also exploded, and nowadays indeed so few people in Britain have ever heard its loud and awful voice, which seems to be uttered only in the breeding-season, and is therefore unknown in a country where it no longer breeds, that incredulity as to its booming at all has in some quarters succeeded the old belief in this as in other reputed peculiarities of the species. The bittern in the days of falconry was strictly preserved, and afforded excellent sport. It sits crouching on the ground during the day, with its bill pointing in the air, a position from which it is not easily roused, and even when it takes wing, its flight is neither swift nor long sustained. When wounded it requires to be approached with caution, as it will then attack either man or dog with its long sharp bill and its acute claws. It builds a rude nest among the reeds and flags, out of the materials which surround it, and the female lays four or five eggs of a brownish olive. During the breeding season it utters a booming noise, from which it probably derives its generic name, *Botaurus*, and which has made it in many places an object of superstitious dread. Its plumage for the most part is of a pale buff colour, rayed and speckled with black and reddish brown. The American bittern (*Botaurus lenliginosus*) is somewhat smaller than the European species, and is found throughout the central and southern portions of North America. It also occurs in Britain as an occasional straggler. It is distinguishable by its uniform greyish-brown primaries, which want the tawny bars that characterize *B. stellaris*. Both species are good eating.

⧈ **BLACKCOCK** (*Tetrao tetrix*), the English name given to a bird of the family *Tetraonidae* or grouse, the female of which is known as the grey hen and the young as poults. In size and plumage the two sexes offer a striking contrast, the male weighing about 4 lb, its plumage for the most part of a rich glossy black shot with blue and purple, the lateral tail features curved outwards so as to form, when raised, a fan-like crescent, and the eyebrows destitute of feathers and of a bright vermilion red. The female, on the other hand, weighs only 2 lb, its plumage is of a russet brown colour irregularly barred with black, and its tail features are but slightly forked. The males are polygamous, and during autumn and winter associate together, feeding in flocks apart from the females; but with the approach of spring they separate, each selecting a locality for itself, from which it drives off all intruders, and where morning and evening it seeks to attract the other sex by a display of its beautiful plumage, which at this season attains its greatest perfection, and by a peculiar cry, which Selby describes as "a crowing note, and another similar to the noise made by the whetting of a scythe." The nest, composed of a few stalks of grass, is built on the ground, usually beneath the shadow of a low bush or a tuft of tall grass, and here the female lays from six to ten eggs of a dirty-yellow colour speckled with dark brown. The blackcock then rejoins his male associates, and the female is left to perform the labours of hatching and rearing her young brood. The plumage of both sexes is at first like that of the female, but after moulting the young males gradually assume the more brilliant plumage of their sex. There are also many cases on record, and specimens may be seen in the principal museums, of old female birds assuming, to a greater or less extent, the plumage of the male. The blackcock is very generally distributed over the highland districts of northern and central Europe, and in some parts of Asia. It is found on the principal heaths in the south of England, but is specially abundant in the Highlands of Scotland.

〜〜〜 **BOA,** a name formerly applied to all large serpents which, devoid of poison fangs, kill their prey by constriction; but now confined to that subfamily of the *Boidae* which are devoid of teeth in the praemaxilla and are without supraorbital bones. The others are known as pythons. The true boas comprise some forty species; most of them are American, but the genus *Eryx* inhabits North Africa, Greece and south-western Asia; the genus *Enygrus* ranges from New Guinea to the Fiji; *Casarea dussumieri* is restricted to Round Island, near Mauritius; and two species of *Boa* and one of *Corallus* represent this subfamily in Madagascar, while all the other boas live in America, chiefly in tropical parts. All *Boidae* possess vestiges of pelvis and hind limbs, appearing externally as claw-like spurs on each side of the vent, but they are so small that they are practically without function in climbing. The usually short tail is prehensile.

One of the commonest species of the genus *Boa* is the *Boa constrictor,* which has a wide range from tropical Mexico to Brazil. The head is covered with small scales, only one of the preoculars being enlarged. The general colour is a delicate pale brown, with about a dozen and a half darker cross-bars, which are often connected by a still darker dorso-lateral streak, enclosing large oval spots. On each side is a series of large dark brown spots with light centres. On the tail the markings become bolder, brick red with black and yellow. The under parts are yellowish with black dots. This species rarely reaches a length of more than 10 ft. It climbs well, prefers open forest in the neighbourhood of water, is often found in plantations where it retires into a hole in the ground, and lives chiefly on birds and small mammals. Like most true boas, it is of a very gentle disposition and easily domesticates itself in the palm or reed thatched huts of the natives, where it hunts the rats during the night.

The term "boa" is applied by analogy to a long article of women's dress wound round the neck.

〜〜〜 **BUG,** the common name for hemipterous insects of the family *Cimicidae*, of which the best-known example is the house bug or bed bug (*Cimex lectularius*). This disgusting insect is of an oval

shape, of a rusty red colour, and, in common with the whole tribe
to which it belongs, gives off an offensive odour when touched; unlike
the others, however, it is wingless. The bug is provided with a pro-
boscis, which when at rest lies along the inferior side of the thorax,
and through which it sucks the blood of man, the sole food of this
species. It is nocturnal in its habits, remaining concealed by day in
crevices of bed furniture, among the hangings, or behind the wall
paper, and shows considerable activity in its nightly raids in search
of food. The female deposits her eggs at the beginning of summer
in crevices of wood and other retired situations, and in three weeks
the young emerge as small, white, and almost transparent larvae.
These change their skin very frequently during growth, and attain
full development in about eleven weeks. Two centuries ago the bed
bug was a rare insect in Britain, and probably owes its name, which
is derived from a Celtic word signifying "ghost" or "goblin," to the
terror which its attacks at first inspired. An allied species, the dove-
cote bug (*Cimex columbaria*), attacks domestic fowls and pigeons.

 CANARY (*Serinus canarius*), a well-known species
of passerine bird, belonging to the family *Fringillidae* or finches. It is
a native of the Canary Islands and Madeira, where it occurs abundantly in the wild state, and is of a greyish-brown colour, slightly
varied with brighter hues, although never attaining the beautiful
plumage of the domestic bird. It was first domesticated in Italy during
the 16th century, and soon spread over Europe, where it is now the
most common of cage-birds. During the years of its domestication,
the canary has been the subject of careful artificial selection, the result
being the production of a bird differing widely in the colour of its
plumage, and in a few of its varieties even in size and form, from the
original wild species. The prevailing colour of the most admired
varieties of the canary is yellow, approaching in some cases to orange,
and in others to white; while the most robust birds are those which,
in the dusky green of the upper surface of their plumage, show a
distinct approach to the wild forms. The least prized are those in
which the plumage is irregularly spotted and speckled. In one of the
most esteemed varieties, the wing and tail feathers are at first black—
a peculiarity, however, which disappears after the first moulting. Size
and form have also been modified by domestication, the wild canary
being not more than 5½ in. in length, while a well-known Belgian
variety usually measures 8 in. There are also hooped or bowed canaries, feather-footed forms and top-knots, the latter having a distinct

crest on the head; but the offspring of two such top-knotted canaries, instead of showing an increased development of crest, as might be expected, are apt to be bald on the crown. Most of the varieties, however, of which no fewer than twenty-seven were recognized by French breeders so early as the beginning of the 18th century, differ merely in the colour and the markings of the plumage. Hybrids are also common, the canary breeding freely with the siskin, goldfinch, citril, greenfinch and linnet. The hybrids thus produced are almost invariably sterile. It is the female canary which is almost invariably employed in crossing, as it is difficult to get the females of the allied species to sit on the artificial nest used by breeders. In a state of nature canaries pair, but under domestication the male bird has been rendered polygamous, being often put with four or five females; still he is said to show a distinct preference for the female with which he was first mated. It is from the others, however, that the best birds are usually obtained. The canary is very prolific, producing eggs, not exceeding six in number, three or four times a year; and in a state of nature it is said to breed still oftener. The work of building the nest, and of incubation, falls chiefly on the female, while the duty of feeding the young rests mainly with the cock bird. The natural song of the canary is loud and clear; and in their native groves the males, especially during the pairing season, pour forth their song with such ardour as sometimes to burst the delicate vessels of the throat. The males appear to compete with each other in the brilliancy of their melody, in order to attract the females, which, according to the German naturalist Johann Matthaüs Bechstein (1757–1822) always select the best singers for their mates. The canary readily imitates the notes of other birds, and in Germany and especially Tirol, where the breeding of canaries gives employment to a large number of people, they are usually placed for this purpose beside the nightingale. (A.N.)

CHAMELEON, the common name of one of the three suborders of Lacertilia or lizards. The common chameleon is the most typical. The head is raised into a pyramidal crest far beyond the occiput, there is no outer ear, nor a drum-cavity. The limbs are very long and slender, and the digits form stout grasping bundles; on the hand the first three form an inner bundle, opposed to the remaining two; on the foot the inner bundle is formed by the first and second toe, the outer by the other three toes. The tail is prehensile, by being rolled downwards; it is not brittle and cannot be renewed. The eyeballs are large, but the lids are united into one concentric fold, leaving only the small pupil visible. The right and left eyes are incessantly moved separately from each other and literally in every direction, up and down, forwards and straight backwards, producing the most terrible squinting. Chameleons alone of all reptiles can focus their eyes upon one spot, and conformably they alone possess a retinal *macula centralis,* or spot of acutest, binocular vision. The tongue has attained an extraordinary development. It is club-shaped, covered with a sticky secretion, and based upon a very narrow root, which is composed of extremely elastic fibres and telescoped over the much elongated, style-shaped copular piece of the hyoid. The whole apparatus is kept in a contracted state like a spring in a tube. When the spring is released, so to speak, by filling the apparatus with blood and by the play of the hyoid muscles, the heavy thick end shoots out upon the insect prey and is withdrawn by its own elasticity. The whole act is like a flash. An ordinary chameleon can shoot a fly at the distance of fully 6 in., and it can manage even a big sphinx moth.

Another remarkable feature is their changing of colour. This proverbial power is greatly exaggerated. They cannot assume in succession all the colours of the rainbow, nor are the changes quick. The common chameleon may be said to be greenish grey, changing to grass-green or to dull black, with or without maroon red, or brown, lateral series of patches. At night the same specimen assumes as a rule a more or less uniform pale straw-colour. After it has been watched for several months, when all its possibilities seem exhausted, it will probably surprise us by a totally new combination, for instance, a black garb with many small yellow specks, or green with many black specks. Pure red and blue are not in the register of this species, but they are rather the rule upon the dark green ground colour of the South African dwarf chameleon. The changes are partly under control of the will, partly complicated reflex actions, intentionally adaptive to the physical and psychical surroundings. The mechanism is as follows. The cutis contains several kinds of specialized cells in many layers, each filled with minute granules of guanine. The upper cells are the smallest, most densely filled with crystals, and cause the white colour by diffusion of direct light; near the Malpighian layer the cells are charged with yellow oil drops; the deeper cells are the largest, tinged light brown, and acting as a turbid medium they cause a blue colour, which, owing to the superimposed yellow drops, reaches our eye as green; provided always that there is an effective screen at the back, and this is formed by large chromatophores which lie at the bottom and send their black pigment half-way up, or on to the top of the layers of guanine and oil containing cells. When all the pigment is shifted towards the surface, as near the epidermis as possible, the creature looks black; when the black pigment is withdrawn into the basal portions of the chromatophores the skin appears yellow.

Chameleons are insectivorous. They prefer locusts, grasshoppers and lepidoptera, but are also fond of flies and mealworms. They are notoriously difficult to keep in good health. They want not only warmth, but sunshine, and they must have water, which they lick up in drops from the edges of wet leaves whenever they have a chance. The silliness of the fable that they live on air is shown by the fact that they usually die in an absolutely emaciated and parched condition after three or four months' starvation. (H.F.G.)

⚬ **CICADA** (*Cicadidae*), insects of the homopterous division of the Hemiptera, generally of large size, with the femora of the anterior legs toothed below, two pairs of large clear wings, and prominent compound eyes. Cicadas are chiefly remarkable for the shrill song of the males, which in some cases may be heard in concert at a distance of a quarter of a mile or more. The vocal organs, of which there is a pair in the thorax, protected by an opercular plate, are quite unlike the sounding organs of other insects. Each consists in essence of a tightly stretched membrane or drum which is thrown into a state of rapid vibration by a powerful muscle attached to its inner surface and passing thence downwards to the floor of the thoracic cavity. Although no auditory organs have been found in the females, the song of the males is believed to serve as a sexual call. Cicadas are also noteworthy for their longevity, which so far as is known surpasses that of all other insects. By means of a saw-like ovipositor the female lays her eggs in the branches of trees. Upon hatching, the young, which differ from the adult in possessing long antennae and a pair of powerful fossorial anterior legs, fall to the ground, burrow below the surface, and spend a prolonged subterranean larval existence feeding upon the roots of vegetation. After many years the larva is transformed into the pupa or nymph, which is distinguishable principally by the shortness of its antennae and the presence of wing pads. After a brief existence the pupa emerges from the ground, and, holding on to a plant stem by means of its powerful front legs, sets free the perfect insect through a slit along the median dorsal line of the thorax. In some cases the pupa upon emerging constructs a chimney of soil, the use of which is not known. In one of the best-known species, *Cicada septemdecim*, from North

America, the life-cycle is said to extend over seventeen years. Cicadas are particularly abundant in the tropics, where the largest forms are found. They also occur in temperate countries, and were well known to the ancient Greeks and Romans. One species only is found in England, where it is restricted to the southern counties but is an insect not commonly met with.

〜〜〜 **CIVET,** or properly CIVET-CAT, the designation of the more typical representatives of the mammalian family *Viverridae*. Civets are characterized by the possession of a deep pouch in the neighbourhood of the genital organs, into which the substance known as civet is poured from the glands by which it is secreted. This fatty substance is at first semifluid and yellow, but afterwards acquires the consistency of pomade and becomes darker. It has a strong musky odour, exceedingly disagreeable to those unaccustomed to it, but "when properly diluted and combined with other scents it produces a very pleasing effect, and possesses a much more floral fragrance than musk, indeed it would be impossible to imitate some flowers without it." The African civet (*Viverra civetta*) is from 2 to 3 ft. in length, exclusive of the tail, which is half the length of the body, and stands from 10 to 12 in. high. It is covered with long hair, longest on the middle line of the back, where it is capable of being raised or depressed at will, of a dark-grey colour, with numerous transverse black bands and spots. In habits it is chiefly nocturnal, and by preference carnivorous, feeding on birds and the smaller quadrupeds, in pursuit of which it climbs trees, but it is said also to eat fruits, roots and other vegetable matters. In a state of captivity the civet is never completely tamed, and only kept for the sake of its perfume, which is obtained in largest quantity from the male, especially when in good condition and subjected to irritation, being scraped from the pouch with a small spoon usually twice a week. The zibeth (*Viverra zibetha*) is a widely distributed species extending from Arabia to Malabar, and throughout several of the larger islands of the Indian Archipelago. It is smaller than the true civet, and wants the dorsal crest. In the wild state it does great damage among poultry, and frequently makes off with the young of swine and sheep. When hunted it makes a determined resistance, and emits a scent so strong as even to sicken the dogs, who nevertheless are exceedingly fond of the sport, and cannot be got to pursue any other game while the stench of the zibeth is in their nostrils. In confinement, it becomes comparatively tame, and yields civet in considerable quantity. In preparing this for the market it is usually spread out on the leaves of the pepper plant in order to free it from the hairs that have become detached from the pouch. On the Malabar coast this species is replaced by *V. civettina*. The small Indian civet or rasse (*Viverricula malaccensis*) ranges from Madagascar through India to China, the Malay Peninsula, and the islands of the Archipelago. It is almost 3 ft. long including the tail, and prettily marked with dark longitudinal stripes, and spots which have a distinctly linear arrangement. The perfume, which is extracted in the same way as in the two preceding species, is highly valued and much used by the Javanese. Although this animal is said to be an expert climber it usually inhabits holes in the ground. It is frequently kept in captivity in the East, and becomes tame. Fossil remains of extinct civets are found in the Miocene strata of Europe.

COCKATRICE, a fabulous monster, the existence of which was firmly believed in throughout ancient and medieval times,—descriptions and figures of it appearing in the natural history works of such writers as Pliny and Aldrovandus, those of the latter published so late as the beginning of the 17th century. Produced from a cock's egg hatched by a serpent, it was believed to possess the most deadly powers, plants withering at its touch, and men and animals dying poisoned by its look. It stood in awe, however, of the cock, the sound of whose crowing killed it, and consequently travelers were wont to take this bird with them in travelling over regions supposed to abound in cockatrices. The weasel alone among mammals was unaffected by the glance of its evil eye, and attacked it at all times successfully; for when wounded by the monster's teeth it found a ready remedy in rue—the only plant which the cockatrice could not wither. This myth reminds one of the real contests between the weasel-like mungoos of India and the deadly cobra, in which the latter is generally killed. The term "cockatrice" is employed on four occasions in the English translation of the Bible, in all of which it denotes nothing more than an exceedingly venomous reptile; it seems also to be synonymous with "basilisk," the mythical king of serpents.

COCKROACH, a family of orthopterous insects, distinguished by their flattened bodies, long thread-like antennae, and shining leathery integuments. Cockroaches are nocturnal creatures, secreting themselves in chinks and crevices about houses, issuing from their retreats when the lights are extinguished, and moving about with extraodinary rapidity in seach of food. They are voracious and omnivorous, devouring, or at least damaging, whatever comes in their way, for all the species emit a disagreeable odour, which they communicate to whatever article of food or clothing they may touch.

The common cockroach (*Stilopyga orientalis*) is not indigenous to Europe, but is believed to have been introduced from the Levant in the cargoes of trading vessels. The wings in the male are shorter than the body; in the female they are rudimentary. The eggs, which are 16 in number, are deposited in a leathery capsule fixed by a gum-like substance to the abdomen of the female, and thus carried about till the young are ready to escape, when the capsule becomes softened by the emission of a fluid substance. The larvae are perfectly white at first and wingless, although in other respects not unlike their parents, but they are not mature insects until after the sixth casting of the skin.

The American cockroach (*Periplaneta americana*) is larger than the former, and is not uncommon in European seaports trading with America, being conveyed in cargoes of grain and other food produce. It is very abundant in the Zoological Gardens in London, where it occurs in conjunction with a much smaller imported species *Phyllodromia germanica*, which may also be seen in some of the cheaper restaurants.

In both of these species the females, as well as the males, are winged.

In addition to these noxious and obtrustive forms, England has a few indigenous species belonging to the genus *Ectobia*, which live under stones or fallen trees in fields and woods. The largest known species is the drummer of the West Indies (*Blabera gigantea*), so called from the tapping noise it makes on wood, sufficient, when joined in by several individuals, as usually happens, to break the slumbers of a household. It is about 2 in. long, with wings 3 in. in expanse, and forms one of the most noisome and injurious of insect pests. Wingless females of many tropical species present a close superficial resemblance to woodlice; and one interesting apterous form known as *Pseudoglomeris*, from the East Indies, is able to roll up like a millipede.

The best mode of destroying cockroaches is, when the fire and lights are extinguished at night, to lay some treacle on a piece of wood afloat on a broad basin of water. This proves a temptation to the vermin too great to be resisted. The chinks and holes from which they issue should also be filled up with unslaked lime, or painted with a mixture of borax and heated turpentine.

CO&S CONDOR (*Sarcorhamphus gryphus*), an American vulture, and almost the largest of existing birds of flight, although by no means attaining the dimensions attributed to it by early writers. It usually measures about 4 ft. from the point of the beak to the extremity of the tail, and 9 ft. between the tips of its wings, while it is probable that the expanse of wing never exceeds 12 ft. The head and neck are destitute of feathers, and the former, which is much flattened above, is in the male crowned with a caruncle or comb, while the skin of the latter in the same sex lies in folds, forming a wattle. The adult plumage is of a uniform black, with the exception of a frill of white feathers nearly surrounding the base of the neck, and certain wing feathers which, especially in the male, have large patches of white. The middle toe is greatly elongated, and the hinder one but slightly developed, while the talons of all the toes are comparatively straight and blunt, and are thus of little use as organs of prehension. The female, contrary to the usual rule among birds of prey, is smaller than the male.

The condor is a native of South America, where it is confined to the region of the Andes, from the Straits of Magellan to 4° north latitude,—the largest examples, it is said, being found about the volcano of Cayambi, situated on the equator. It is often seen on the shores of the Pacific, especially during the rainy season, but its favourite haunts for roosting and breeding are at elevations of 10,000 to 16,000 ft. There, during the months of February and March, on inaccessible ledges of rock, it deposits two white eggs, from 3 to 4 in. in length, its nest consisting merely of a few sticks placed around the eggs. The period of incubation lasts for seven weeks, and the young are covered with a whitish down until almost as large as their parents. They are unable to fly till nearly two years old, and continue for a considerable time after taking wing to roost and hunt with their parents. The white ruff on the neck, and the similarly coloured feathers of the wing, do not appear until the completion of the first moulting. By preference the condor feeds on carrion, but it does not hesitate to attack sheep, goats, and deer, and for this reason it is hunted down by the shepherds, who, it is said, train their dogs to look up and bark at the condors as they fly overhead. They are exceedingly voracious, a single condor of moderate size having been known, according to Orton, to devour a calf, a sheep and a dog in a single week. When thus gorged with food, they are exceedingly stupid, and may then be readily caught. For this purpose a horse or mule is killed, and the carcass surrounded with palisades to which the condors are soon attracted by the prospect of food, for the weight of evidence seems to favour the opinion that those vultures owe their knowledge of the presence of carrion more to sight than to scent. Having feasted themselves to excess, they are set upon by the hunters with sticks, and being unable, owing to the want of space within the pen, to take the run without which they are unable to rise on wing, they are readily killed or captured. They sleep during the greater part of the day, searching for food in the clearer light of morning and evening. They are remarkably heavy sleepers, and are readily captured by the inhabitants ascending the trees on which they roost, and noosing them before they awaken. Great numbers of condors are thus taken alive, and these, in certain districts, are employed in a variety of bull-fighting. They are exceedingly tenacious of life, and can exist, it is said, without food for over forty days. Although the favourite haunts of the condor are at the level of perpetual snow, yet it rises to a much greater height, Humboldt having observed it flying over Chimborazo at a height of over 23,000 ft. On wing the movements of the condor, as it wheels in majestic circles, are remarkably graceful. The birds flap their wings on rising from the ground, but after attaining a moderate elevation they seem to sail on the air, Charles Darwin having watched them for half an hour without once observing a flap of their wings.

ELECTRIC EEL, a member of the family of fishes known as *Gymnotidae*. In spite of their external similarity the *Gymnotidae* having nothing to do with the eels (*Anguilla*). They resemble the latter in the elongation of the body, the large number of vertebrae, and the absence of pelvic fins; but they differ in all the more important characters of internal structure. They are in fact allied to the carps or *Cyprinidae* and the cat-fishes or *Siluridae*. In common with these two families and the *Characinidae* of Africa and South America, the *Gymnotidae* possess the peculiar structures called *ossicula auditus* or Weberian ossicles. These are a chain of small bones belonging to the first four vertebrae, which are much modified, and connecting the air-bladder with the auditory organs. Such an agreement in the structure of so complicated and specialized an apparatus can only be the result of a community of descent of the families possessing it. Accordingly these families are now placed together in a distinct sub-order, the Ostariophysi. The *Gymnotidae* are strongly modified and degraded *Characinidae*. In them the dorsal and caudal fins are very rudimentary or absent, and the anal is very long, extending from the anus, which is under the head or throat, to the end of the body.

Gymnotus is the only genus of the family which possesses electric organs. These extend the whole length of the tail, which is four-fifths of the body. They are modifications of the lateral muscles and are supplied with numerous branches of the spinal nerves. They consist of longitudinal columns, each composed of an immense number of "electric plates." The posterior end of the organ is positive, the anterior negative, and the current passes from the tail to the head. The maximum shock is given when the head and tail of the *Gymnotus* are in contact with different points in the surface of some other animal. *Gymnotus electricus* attains a length of 3 ft. and the thickness of a man's thigh, and frequents the marshes of Brazil and the Guianas, where it is regarded with terror, owing to the formidable electrical apparatus with which it is provided. When this natural battery is discharged in a favourable position, it is sufficiently powerful to stun the largest animal; and according to A. von Humboldt, it has been found necessary to change the line of certain roads passing through the pools frequented by the electric eels. These fish are eaten by the Indians, who, before attempting to capture them, seek to exhaust their electrical power by driving horses into the ponds. By repeated discharges upon these they gradually expend this marvellous force; after which, being defenceless, they become timid, and approach the edge for shelter, when they fall an easy prey to the harpoon. It is only after long rest and abundance of food that the fish is able to resume the use of its subtle weapon. Humboldt's description of this method of capturing the fish has not, however, been verified by recent travellers.

JACKDAW, or simply DAW, one of the smallest species of the genus *Corvus*, and a very well known inhabitant of Europe, the *C. monedula* of ornithologists. In some of its habits it much resembles its congener the rook, with which it constantly associates during a great part of the year; but, while the rook only exceptionally places its nest elsewhere than on the boughs of trees and open to the sky, the daw almost invariably chooses holes, whether in rocks, hollow trees, rabbit-burrows or buildings. Nearly every church-tower and castle, ruined or not, is more or less numerously occupied by daws. Chimneys frequently give them the accommodation they desire, much to the annoyance of the householder, who finds the funnel choked by the quantity of sticks brought together by the birds, since their industry in collecting materials for their nests is as marvellous as it often is futile. In some cases the stack of loose sticks piled up by daws in a belfry or tower has been known to form a structure 10 or 12 ft. in height, and hence this species may be accounted one of the greatest nest-builders in the world. The style of architecture practised by the daw thus brings it more than the rook into contact with man, and its familiarity is increased by the boldness of its disposition which, though tempered by discreet cunning, is hardly surpassed among birds. Its small size, in comparison with most of its congeners, alone incapacitates it from inflicting the serious injuries of which some of them are often the authors, yet its pilferings are not to be denied, though on the whole its services to the agriculturist are great, for in the destruction of injurious insects it is hardly inferior to the rook, and it has the useful habit of ridding sheep, on whose backs it may be frequently seen perched, of some of their parasites. (A.N.)

MIGRATION OF BIRDS, THE. How do

birds manage to find their way, thousands and thousands of miles across land and water? This question has been extolled as a mystery of mysteries. It has been stated that the old birds show the way to the young, a speculation which does not apply to those many cases in which old and young notoriously travel at different times. It has been assumed that they travel by sight, taking advantage of certain landmarks; another untenable idea, since—experience having to be excluded in a flock of birds which made the journey for the first time—it implies that the young must have inherited the reminiscence of those landmarks! Others have likened the bird to a kind of compass, because in eastern Siberia E. von Middendorff found some migration routes to coincide with the direction of the magnetic pole. The whole question reduces itself to a sense of direction, a faculty which is possessed by nearly all animals; in some it is present to an astonishing extent; but the manifestations of this sense vary only in degree. The cat which escapes out of the bag finds its way back, directly or after many adventures. The bee, after having loaded itself with pollen, returns by the proverbial line to the hive which may be a mile away, but, move the small entrance hole in the meantime an inch to the right or left, and the bee will knock its head against the hive and blunder about; move the hive a few yards and bee after bee returning will be puzzled to find its hive again. They, maybe with the help of landmarks, have accustomed themselves to steer a course. Such instances need not be multiplied. The principle is the same whether the journey be one of a few yards or of many miles. Given the sense of direction, it is no more difficult to steer a course due north than it is to lay on south-east by east, provided always the impetus to be on the move. There is no mystery, except that we, the most intellectual of mankind, should so well nigh have lost this sense, and even this fact is simply an instance of the loss of a faculty through long-continued disuse. (H.F.G.)

NIDIFICATION (from Lat. *nidus*), the process of making a nest. Nidification is with most birds the beginning of the breeding season, but with many it is a labour that is scamped if not shirked. Some of the auk tribe place their single egg on a bare ledge of rock, where its peculiar conical shape is but a precarious safeguard when rocked by the wind or stirred by the thronging crowd of its parents' fellows. The stone-curlew and the goatsucker deposit their eggs without the slightest preparation of the soil on which they rest; yet this is not done at haphazard, for no birds can be more constant in selecting, almost to an inch, the very same spot which year after year they choose for their procreant cradle. In marked contrast to such artless care stand the wonderful structures which others, such as the tailor-bird, the bottle-titmouse or the fantail-warbler, build for the comfort or safety of their young. But every variety of disposition may be found in the class. The apteryx seems to entrust its abnormally big egg to an excavation among the roots of a tree-fern; while a band of female ostriches scrape holes in the desert-sand and therein promiscuously drop their eggs and leave the task of incubation to the male. Some megapodes bury their eggs in sand, leaving them to come to maturity by the mere warmth of the ground, while others raise a huge hotbed of dead leaves wherein they deposit theirs, and the young are hatched without further care on the part of either parent. Some of the grebes and rails seem to avail themselves in a less degree of the heat generated by vegetable decay and, dragging from the bottom or sides of the waters they frequent fragments of aquatic plants, form of them a rude half-floating mass which is piled on some growing water-weed—but these birds do not spurn the duties of maternity.

Many of the gulls, sandpipers and plovers lay their eggs in a shallow pit which they hollow out in the soil, and then as incubation proceeds add thererto a low breastwork of haulm. The ringed plover commonly places its eggs on shingle, which they so much resemble in colour, but when breeding on grassy uplands it paves the nest-hole with small stones. Pigeons mostly make an artless platform of sticks so loosely laid together that their pearly treasures may be perceived from beneath by the inquisitive observer. The magpie, as though self-conscious that its own thieving habits may be imitated by its neighbours, surrounds its nest with a hedge of thorns. Very many birds of almost every group bore holes in some sandy cliff, and at the end of their tunnel deposit their eggs with or without bedding. Such bedding, too, is very various in character; thus, while the sheldduck and the sand-martin supply the softest of materials—the one of down from her own body, the other of feathers collected by dint of diligent search—the kingfisher forms a couch of the undigested spiny fish bones which she ejects in pellets from her own stomach. Other birds, such as the woodpeckers, hew holes in living trees, even when the timber is of considerable hardness, and therein establish their nursery. Some of the swifts secrete from their salivary glands a fluid which rapidly hardens as it dries on exposure to the air into a substance resembling isinglass, and thus furnish the "edible birds' nests" that are the delight of Chinese epicures. In the architecture of nearly all the passerine birds, too, some salivary secretion seems to play an important part. By its aid they are enabled to moisten and bend the otherwise refractory twigs and straws, and glue them to their place. Spiders' webs also are employed with great advantage for the purpose last mentioned, but perhaps chiefly to attach fragments of moss and lichen so as to render the whole structure less obvious to the eye of the spoiler. The tailor-bird deliberately spins a thread of cotton and therewith stitches together the edges of a pair of leaves to make a receptacle for its nest. Beautiful, too, is the felt fabricated of fur or hairs by the various species of titmouse, while many birds ingeniously weave into a compact mass both animal and vegetable fibres, forming an admirable non-conducting medium which guards the eggs from the extremes of temperature outside. Such a structure may be open and cup-shaped, supported from below as that of the chaffinch and goldfinch, domed like that of the wren and bottle-titmouse, slung hammock-wise as in the case of the golden-crested wren and the orioles, or suspended by a single cord as with certain grosbeaks and humming-birds.

Certain warblers (*Aedon* and *Thamnobia*) invariably lay a piece of snake's slough in their nests—to repel, it has been suggested, marauding lizards who may thereby fear the neighbourhood of a deadly enemy. The clay-built edifices of the swallow and martin are known to everybody, and the nuthatch plasters up the gaping mouth of its nest-hole till only a postern large enough for entrance and exit, but easy of defence, is left. In South America the oven-birds (*Furnariidae*) construct on the branches of trees globular ovens, so to speak, of mud, wherein the eggs are laid and the young hatched. The flamingo erects in the marshes it frequents a mound of earth sometimes 2 ft. in height, with a cavity atop. The females of the hornbills submit to incarceration during this interesting period, the males immuring them by a barrier of mud, leaving only a small window to admit air and food.

But though in a general way the dictates of hereditary instinct are rigidly observed by birds, in many species a remarkable degree of elasticity is exhibited, or the rule of habit is rudely broken. Thus the falcon, whose ordinary eyry is on the beetling cliff, will for the convenience of procuring prey condescend to lay its eggs on the ground in a marsh, or appropriate the nest of some other bird in a tree. The golden eagle, too, remarkably adapts itself to circumstances, now rearing its young on a precipitous ledge, now on the arm of an ancient monarch of the forest and again on a treeless plain, making a humble home amid grass and herbage. Herons will breed according to circumstances in an open fen, on sea-banks or (as is most usual) on lofty trees. Such changes are easy to understand. The instinct of finding food for the family is predominant, and where most food is there will the feeders be gathered together. This explains, in all likelihood, the associated bands of ospreys or fish-hawks, which in North America breed (or used to breed) in large companies where sustenance is plentiful, though in the Old World the same species brooks not the society of aught but its mate. Birds there are of eminently social predilections. In Europe, apart from sea-fowls—whose congregations are universal and known to all—only the heron, the fieldfare and the rook habitually flock during the breeding season; but in other parts of the world many birds unite in company at that time, and in none possibly is this habit so strongly developed as in the anis of the neotropical region, the republican swallow of North America and the sociable grosbeak of South Africa, which last joins nest to nest until the tree is said to break down under the accumulated weight of the common edifice.

In the strongest contrast to these amiable qualities is the parasitic nature of the cuckoos of the Old World and the cow-birds of the New. The egg of the parasite is introduced into the nest of the dupe, and after the necessary incubation by the fond fool of a foster-mother the interloper successfully counterfeits the heirs, who perish miserably, victims of his superior strength. The whole process has been often watched, but the reflective naturalist will pause to ask how such a state of things came about, and there is not much to satisfy his inquiry. Certain it is that some birds whether by mistake or stupidity do not infrequently lay their eggs in the nests of others. It is within the knowledge of many that pheasants' eggs and partridges' eggs are often laid in the same nest, and gulls' eggs have been found in the nests of eider-ducks and vice versa; a redstart and a pied flycatcher will lay their eggs in the same convenient hole—the forest being rather deficient in such accommodation; an owl and a duck will resort to the same nest-box, set up by a scheming woodsman for his own advantage; and the starling, which constantly dispossesses the green woodpecker, sometimes discovers that the rightful heir of the domicile has to be brought up by the intruding tenant. In all such cases it is not possible to say which species is so constituted as to obtain the mastery, but it is not difficult to conceive that in the course of ages that which was driven from its home might thrive through the fostering of its young by the invader, and thus the abandonment of domestic habits and duties might become a direct gain to the evicted householder. (A.N.)

PIGEON POST. The use of homing pigeons to carry messages is as old as Solomon, and the ancient Greeks, to whom the art of training the birds came probably from the Persians, conveyed the names of Olympic victors to their various cities by this means. Before the electric telegraph this method of communication had a considerable vogue amongst stockbrokers and financiers. The Dutch government established a civil and military pigeon system in Java and Sumatra early in the 19th century, the birds being obtained from Bagdad. Numerous private societies were established for keeping pigeons of this class in all important European countries; and, in time, various governments established systems of communication for military purposes by pigeon post. When the possibility of using the birds between military fortresses had been thoroughly tested attention was turned to their use for naval purposes, to send messages between coast stations and ships at sea. They are also found of great use by news agencies and private individuals. Governments have in several countries established lofts of their own. Laws have been passed making the destruction of such pigeons a serious offence; premiums to stimulate efficiency have been offered to private societies, and rewards given for destruction of birds of prey. Pigeons have been used by newspapers to report yacht races, and some yachts have actually been fitted with lofts. It has also been found of great importance to establish registration of all birds. In order to hinder the efficiency of the systems of foreign countries, difficulties have been placed in the way of the importation of their birds for training, and in a few cases falcons have been specially trained to interrupt the service in war-time, the Germans having set the example by employing hawks against the Paris pigeons in 1870–71. No satisfactory method of protecting the weaker birds seems to have been evolved, though the Chinese formerly provided their pigeons with whistles and bells to scare away birds of prey.

In view of the development of wireless telegraphy the modern tendency is to consider fortress warfare as the only sphere in which homing pigeons can be expected to render really valuable services. Consequently, the British Admiralty has discontinued its pigeon service, which had attained a high standard of efficiency, and other powers will no doubt follow the example. Nevertheless, large numbers of birds are, and will presumably continue to be, kept at the great inland fortresses of France, Germany and Russia.

REDBREAST, or ROBIN, perhaps the favourite among English birds because of its pleasing colour, its sagacity and fearlessness of man, and its cheerful song, even in winter. In July and August the hedgerows of the southern counties of England are beset with redbreasts, not in flocks, but each individual keeping its own distance from the next—all, however, on their way to cross the Channel. On the European continent the migration is still more marked, and the redbreast on its autumnal and vernal passages is the object of bird-catchers, since its value as a delicacy has long been recognized. Even those redbreasts which stay in Britain during the winter are subject to a migratory movement. The first sharp frost makes them change their habitation, and a heavy fall of snow drives them towards the homesteads for food. The redbreast exhibits a curious uncertainty of temperament in regard to its nesting habits. At times it will place the utmost confidence in man, and at times show the greatest jealousy. The nest is usually built of moss and dead leaves, with a moderate lining of hair. In this are laid from five to seven white eggs, sprinkled or blotched with light red.

SONG OF BIRDS, THE. The characteristic modulated voice of birds is the outstanding example of natural "song" in the animal world. The essential requirements of a vocal organ, the pressure of vibratory membranes or chord, are found in the bird's *syrinx,* but how these membranes act in particular, and how their tension is modified by the often numerous syringeal muscles, we do not know. The voice of birds is produced entirely by the syrinx; the larynx no doubt modifies it, but the tongue seems to play no part in it. The "loosening of the tongue" by cutting its *frenum,* in order to assist a bird in talking &c., is an absolutely silly operation. The possession of the most elaborate syrinx is not enough to enable a bird to sing. In this respect they are like ourselves: special mental faculties are required to control the apparatus. Anatomically the raven has the same elaborate syrinx as the thrush or the nightingale, and yet the raven cannot "sing" although it can modulate its voice and can even learn to talk. As a rule the faculty of singing is restricted to the males, although the females possess the same organs; moreover, birds vary individually. Some learn to sing marvellously well, while others remain tyros in spite of the best education. But given all the necessary mental faculties, birds sing only when they are in such a healthy condition that there is a surplus of energy. This, of course, is greatest during the time of propagation, when much of the surplus of the general metabolism comes out—to use homely words—in unwonted functions, such as dancing, posing, spreading of feathers and giving voice. Every one of these muscular exertions is a spasm, releasing some energy, and—again in homely parlance—relieving the mind. In many cases these antics and other manifestations become rhythmical, and music consists of rhythmical sounds. Of course, birds, like other creatures, are to a certain extent reflex machines, and they often sing because they cannot help it, just as male frogs continue to croak long after the pairing season, and not necessarily because they or their mates appreciate those sounds. But birds stand mentally on such a high level that we can scarcely doubt that in many cases they enjoy, and therefore sing their song. Many a tame bird, a canary, starling, magpie, will repay its keeper with its song, out of season, for any kindness shown to it, or for his mere presence.

If we regard any sound made by a bird under the all-powerful influence of love or lust as its "song," then probably every bird is possessed of this faculty, but in the ordinary acceptance of the term very few, besides the oscines, can sing, and even this group contains many which, like the ravens and the crows, are decidedly not songsters. On the other hand, it seems unfair not to call the charming series of notes of the dove its song.

D. Barrington in a very remarkable paper ("Experiments and Observations on the Singing of Birds," *Phil. Trans.,* 1773, pp. 249–291) defines a bird's song "to be a succession of three or more different notes, which are continued without interruption during the same interval with a musical bar of four crotchets in an adagio movement, or whilst a pendulum swings four seconds." The late A. Newton (*Encyl. Brit.*, 9th ed., iii. 771; see also *Dict. Birds*, s.v. "Song," pp. 892–894), taking a much wider view of "song," proceeds as follows:—

"It seems impossible to draw any but an arbitrary line between the deep booming of the emeu, the harsh cry of the guillemot (which, when proceeding from a hundred or a thousand throats, strikes the distant ear in a confused murmur like the roar of a tumultuous crowd), the plaintive wail of the plover, the melodious whistle of the wigeon, 'the cock's shrill clarion,' the scream of the eagle, the hoot of the owl, the solemn chime of the bell-bird, the whip-cracking of the manakin, the chaffinch's joyous burst, or the hoarse croak of the raven, on the one hand, and the bleating of the snipe or the drumming of the ruffled grouse, on the other. Innumerable are the forms which such utterances take. In many birds the sounds are due to a combination of vocal and instrumental powers, or, as in the cases last mentioned, to the latter only. But, however produced—and of the machinery whereby they are accomplished there is not room here to speak—all have the same cause and the same effect. The former has been already indicated, and the latter is its consummation. Almost coinstantaneously with the hatching of the nightingale's brood the song of the sire is hushed, and the notes to which we have for weeks hearkened with rapt admiration are changed to a guttural croak, expressive of alarm and anxiety, inspiring a sentiment of the most opposite character. No greater contrast can be imagined, and no instance can be cited which more completely points out the purpose which 'song' fulfils in the economy of the bird, for if the nightingale's nest at this early time be destroyed or its contents removed, the cock speedily recovers his voice, and his favourite haunts again resound to his bewitching strains. For them his mate is content again to undergo the wearisome round of nest-building and incubation. But should some days elapse before disaster befalls their callow care, his constitution undergoes a change and no second attempt to rear a family is made. It would seem as though a mild temperature, and the abundance of food by which it is generally accompanied, prompt the physiological alteration which inspires the males of most birds to indulge in the 'song' peculiar to them. Thus after the annual moult is accomplished, and this is believed to be the most critical epoch in the life of any bird, cock thrushes, skylarks, and others begin to sing, not indeed with the jubilant voice of spring but in an uncertain cadence which is quickly silenced by the supervention of cold weather. Yet some birds we have which, except during the season of moult, hard frost, and time of snow, sing almost all the year round. Of these the redbreast and the wren are familiar examples, and the chiffchaff repeats its two-noted cry, almost to weariness, during the whole period of its residence in this country.

"Akin to the 'song of birds,' and undoubtedly proceeding from the same cause, are the peculiar gestures which the males of many perform under the influence of the approaching season of pairing, but these again are far too numerous here to describe with particularity. It must suffice to mention a few cases. The ruff on his hillock in a marsh holds a war-dance. The snipe and some of his allies mount aloft and wildly execute unlooked-for evolutions almost in the clouds. The woodcock and many of the goatsuckers beat evening after evening the same aerial path with its sudden and sharp turnings. The ring-dove rises above the neighbouring trees and then with motionless wings slides down to the leafy retreat they afford. The capercally and blackcock, perched on a commanding eminence, throw themselves into postures that defy the skill of the caricaturist—other species of the grouse-tribe assume the strangest attitudes and run in circles till the turf is worn bare. The peacock in pride spreads his train so as to show how nearly akin are the majestic and the ludicrous. The bower-bird, not content with its own splendour, builds an arcade, decked with bright feathers and shining shells, through and around which he paces with his gay companions. The larks and pipits never deliver their song so well as when seeking the upper air. Rooks rise one after the other to a great height and, turning on their back, wantonly precipitate themselves many yards towards the ground, while the solemn raven does not scorn a similar feat, and, with the tenderest of croaks, glides supinely alongside or in front of his mate."

THE LITERARY LIFE

A few words to present a collection of articles on literature—authors, mostly, with Cinderella, Merlin, and Tristan included as mythic variations. Although we were tempted to include articles and commentary by authors that might be readily recognized by the reader, Swinburne, for instance, we were dissuaded from doing so by the humdrum quality of the work, the sense that someone was functioning more on his reputation than doing the kind of job that editor Hugh Chisholm generally expected and received from his contributors. Our preferences went to the shorter entries or extracts from longer pieces, which more accurately reflected the best of the contributions, well known or less well known. To this end, we have included five pieces by Edmund Gosse ("Hans Christian Anderson," "Bouts-Rimés," "Diary," "Robert Louis Stevenson," and "Robert Herrick"). To the majestic Lord Thomas Babington Macaulay we owe the acid portrait of the last days of Oliver Goldsmith, to E. V. Lucas the short sketch on Jane Austen, to Arthur Symons the evocation of Mallarmé. To students of the work of T. S. Eliot, we offer a good portion of the article on the Tristan legend, written by Jessie L. Weston, whose *From Ritual to Romance* had, if we are to believe the poet, such a seminal effect upon the making of "The Waste Land."

ANDERSEN, HANS CHRISTIAN (1805–

1875), Danish poet and fabulist, was born at Odense, in Fünen, on the 2nd of April 1805. He was the son of a sickly young shoemaker of twenty-two, and his still younger wife: the whole family lived and slept in one little room. Andersen very early showed signs of imaginative temperament, which was fostered by the indulgence and superstition of his parents. In 1816 the shoemaker died and the child was left entirely to his own devices. He ceased to go to school; he built himself a little toy-theatre and sat at home making clothes for his puppets, and reading all the plays that he could borrow; among them were those of Holberg and Shakespeare. At Easter 1819 he was confirmed at the church of St Kund, Odense, and began to turn his thoughts to the future. It was thought that he was best fitted to be a tailor; but as nothing was settled, and as Andersen wished to be an opera-singer, he took matters into his own hand and started for Copenhagen in September 1819. There he was taken for a lunatic, snubbed at the theatres, and nearly reduced to starvation, but he was befriended by the musicians Christoph Weyse and Siboni, and afterwards by the poet Frederik Hoëgh Guldberg (1771–1852). His voice failed, but he was admitted as a dancing pupil at the Royal

Theatre. He grew idle, and lost the favour of Guldberg, but a new patron appeared in the person of Jonas Collin, the director of the Royal Theatre, who became Andersen's life-long friend. King Frederick VI. was interested in the strange boy and sent him for some years, free of charge, to the great grammar-school at Slagelse. Before he started for school he published his first volume, *The Ghost at Palnatoke's Grave* (1822). Andersen, a very backward and unwilling pupil, actually remained at Slagelse and at another school in Elsinore until 1827; these years, he says, were the darkest and bitterest in his life. Collin at length consented to consider him educated, and Andersen came to Copenhagen. In 1829 he made a considerable success with a fantastic volume entitled *A Journey on Foot from Holman's Canal to the East Point of Amager,* and he published in the same season a farce and a book of poems. He thus suddenly came into request at the moment when his friends had decided that no good thing would ever come out of his early eccentricity and vivacity. He made little further progress, however, until 1833, when he received a small travelling stipend from the king, and made the first of his long European journeys. At Le Locle, in the Jura, he wrote *Agnate and the Merman;* and in October 1834 he arrived in Rome. Early in 1835 Andersen's novel, *The Improvisatore,* appeared, and achieved a real success; the poet's troubles were at an end at last. In the same year, 1835, the earliest instalment of Andersen's immortal *Fairy Tales* (Eventyr) was published in Copenhagen. Other parts, completing the first volume, appeared in 1836 and 1837. The value of these stories was not at first perceived, and they sold slowly. Andersen was more successful for the time being with a novel, *O. T.,* and a volume of sketches, *In Sweden;* in 1837 he produced the best of his romances, *Only a Fiddler.* He now turned his attention, with but ephemeral success, to the theatre, but was recalled to his true genius in the charming miscellanies of 1840 and 1842, the *Picture-Book without Pictures,* and *A Poet's Bazaar.* Meanwhile the fame of his *Fairy Tales* had been steadily rising; a second series began in 1838, a third in 1845. Andersen was now celebrated throughout Europe, although in Denmark itself there was still some resistance to his pretensions. In June 1847 he paid his first visit to England, and enjoyed a triumphal social success; when he left, Charles Dickens saw him off from Ramsgate pier. After this Andersen continued to publish much; he still desired to excel as a novelist and a dramatist, which he could not do, and he still disdained the enchanting *Fairy Tales,* in the composition of which his unique genius lay. Nevertheless he continued to write them, and in 1847 and 1848 two fresh volumes appeared. After a long silence Andersen published in 1857 another romance, *To be or not to be*. In 1863, after a very interesting journey, he issued one of the best of his travel-books, *In Spain*. His *Fairy Tales* continued to appear, in instalments, until 1872, when, at Christmas, the last stories were published. In the spring of that year Andersen had an awkward accident, falling out of bed and severely hurting himself. He was never again quite well, but he lived till the 4th of August 1875, when he died very peacefully in the house called Rolighed, near Copenhagen. (E.G.)

AUSTEN, JANE (1775–1817), English novelist, was born on the 16th of December 1775 at the parsonage of Steventon, in Hampshire, a village of which her father, the Rev. George Austen, was rector. She was the youngest of seven children. Her mother was Cassandra Leigh, niece of Theophilus Leigh, a dry humorist, and for fifty years master of Balliol, Oxford. The life of no woman of genius could have been more uneventful than Miss Austen's. She did not marry, and she never left home except on short visits, chiefly to Bath. Her first sixteen years were spent in the rectory at Steventon, where she began early to trifle with her pen, always jestingly, for family entertainment. In 1801 the Austens moved to Bath, where Mr Austen died in 1805, leaving only Mrs Austen, Jane and her sister Cassandra, to whom she was always deeply attached, to keep up the home; his sons were out in the world, the two in the navy, Francis William and Charles, subsequently rising to admiral's rank. In 1805 the Austen ladies moved to Southampton, and in 1809 to Chawton, near Alton, in Hampshire, and there Jane Austen remained till 1817, the year of her death, which occurred at Winchester, on July 18th, as a memorial window in the cathedral testifies.

During her placid life Miss Austen never allowed her literary work to interfere with her domestic duties: sewing much and admirably, keeping house, writing many letters and reading aloud. Though, however, her days were quiet and her area circumscribed, she saw enough of middle-class provincial society to find a basis on which her dramatic and humorous faculties might build, and such was her power of searching observation and her sympathetic imagination that there are not in English fiction more faithful representations of the life she knew than we possess in her novels. She had no predecessors in this genre. Miss Austen's "little bit (two inches wide) of ivory" on which she worked "with so fine a brush"—her own phrases—was her own invention.

Her best-known, if not her best work, *Pride and Prejudice*, was also her first. It was written between October 1796 and August 1797, although, such was the blindness of publishers, not issued until 1813, two years after *Sense and Sensibility*, which was written, on an old scenario called "Eleanor and Marianne," in 1797 and 1798. Miss Austen's inability to find a publisher for these stories, and for *Northanger Abbey*, written in 1798 (although it is true that she sold that MS. in 1803 for £10 to a Bath bookseller, only, however, to see it locked away in a safe for some years, to be gladly resold to her later), seems to have damped her ardour; for there is no evidence that between 1798 and 1809 she wrote anything but the fragment called "The Watsons," after which year she began to revise her early work for the press. Her other three books belong to a later date—*Mansfield Park, Emma* and *Persuasion* being written between 1811 and 1816. The years of publication were *Sense and Sensibility*, 1811; *Pride and Prejudice*, 1813; *Mansfield Park*, 1814; and *Emma*, 1816—all in their author's lifetime. *Persuasion* and *Northanger Abbey* were published posthumously in 1818. All were anonymous, agreeably to their author's retiring disposition.

Although *Pride and Prejudice* is the novel which in the mind of the public is most intimately associated with Miss Austen's name, both *Mansfield Park* and *Emma* are finer achievements—at once riper and richer and more elaborate. But the fact that *Pride and Prejudice* is more single-minded, that the love story of Elizabeth Bennet and D'Arcy is not only *of* the book but *is* the book (whereas the love story of Emma and Mr Knightley and Fanny Price and Edmund Bertram have parallel streams), has given *Pride and Prejudice* its popularity above the others among readers who are more interested by the course of romance than by the exposition of character. Entirely satisfactory as is *Pride and Prejudice* so far as it goes, it is, however, thin beside the niceness of analysis of motives in *Emma* and the wonderful management of two housefuls of young lovers that is exhibited in *Mansfield Park*.

It has been generally agreed by the best critics that Miss Austen has never been approached in her own domain. No one indeed has attempted any close rivalry. No other novelist has so concerned herself or himself with the trivial daily comedy of small provincial family life, disdaining equally the assistance offered by passion, crime and religion. Whatever Miss Austen may have thought privately of these favourite ingredients of fiction, she disregarded all alike when she took her pen in hand. Her interest was in life's little perplexities of emotion and conduct; her gaze was steadily ironical. The most untoward event in any of her books is Louisa's fall from the Cobb at

Lyme Regis, in *Persuasion;* the most abandoned, Maria's elopement with Crawford, in *Mansfield Park*. In pure ironical humour Miss Austen's only peer among novelists is George Meredith, and indeed *Emma* may be said to be her *Egoist*, or the *Egoist* his *Emma*. But irony and fidelity to the fact alone would not have carried her down the ages. To these gifts she allied a perfect sense of dramatic progression and an admirably lucid and flowing prose style which makes her stories the easiest reading.

Recognition came to Miss Austen slowly. It was not until quite recent times that to read her became a necessity of culture. But she is now firmly established as an English classic, standing far above Miss Burney (Madame d'Arblay) and Miss Edgeworth, who in her day were the popular women novelists of real life, while Mrs Radcliffe and "Monk" Lewis, whose supernatural fancies *Northanger Abbey* was written in part to ridicule, are no longer anything but names. Although, however, she has become only lately a household word, Miss Austen had always her panegyrists among the best intellects—such as Coleridge, Tennyson, Macaulay, Scott, Sydney Smith, Disraeli and Archbishop Whately, the last of whom may be said to have been her discoverer. Macaulay, whose adoration of Miss Austen's genius was almost idolatrous, considered *Mansfield Park* her greatest feat; but many critics give the palm to *Emma*. Disraeli read *Pride and Prejudice* seventeen times. Scott's testimony is often quoted: "That young lady had a talent for describing the involvements, feelings and characters of ordinary life which is to me the most wonderful I have ever met with. The big bow-wow I can do myself like any one going; but the exquisite touch which renders commonplace things and characters interesting from the truth of the description and the sentiment is denied to me." (E.V.L.)

⟨✦⟩ **BOUTS-RIMÉS,** literally (from the French) "rhymed ends," the name given in all literatures to a kind of verses of which no better definition can be found than was made by Addison, in the *Spectator*, when he described them as "lists of words that rhyme to one another, drawn up by another hand, and given to a poet, who was to make a poem to the rhymes in the same order that they were placed upon the list." The more odd and perplexing the rhymes are, the more ingenuity is required to give a semblance of common-sense to the production. For instance, the rhymes *breeze, elephant, squeeze, pant, scant, please, hope, pope* are submitted, and the following stanza is the result:—

Escaping from the Indian *breeze,*
The vast, sententious *elephant*
Through groves of sandal loves to *squeeze*
And in their fragrant shade to *pant;*
Although the shelter there be *scant,*
The vivid odours soothe and *please,*
And while he yields to dreams of *hope,*
Adoring beasts surround their *Pope.*

The invention of bouts-rimés is attributed to a minor French poet of the 17th century, Dulot, of whom little else is remembered. According to the *Menagiana,* about the year 1648, Dulot was complaining one day that he had been robbed of a number of valuable papers, and, in particular, of three hundred sonnets. Surprise being expressed at his having written so many, Dulot explained that they were all "blank sonnets," that is to say, that he had put down the rhymes and nothing else. The idea struck every one as amusing, and what Dulot had done seriously was taken up as a jest. Bouts-rimés became the fashion, and in 1654 no less a person than Sarrasin composed a satire against them, entitled *La Défaite des bouts-rimés,* which enjoyed a great success. Nevertheless, they continued to be abundantly composed in France throughout the 17th century and a great part of the 18th century. In 1701 Etienne Mallemans (d. 1716) published a collection of serious sonnets, all written to rhymes selected for him by the duchess of Maine. Neither Piron, nor Marmontel, nor La Motte disdained this ingenious exercise, and early in the 19th century the fashion was revived. The most curious incident, however, in the history of bouts-rimés is the fact that the elder Alexandre Dumas, in 1864, took them under his protection. He issued an invitation to all the poets of France to display their skill by composing to sets of rhymes selected for the purpose by the poet, Joseph Méry (1798–1866). No fewer than 350 writers responded to the appeal, and Dumas published the result, as a volume, in 1865.

W. M. Rossetti, in the memoir of his brother prefixed to D. G. Rossetti's *Collected Works* (1886), mentions that, especially in 1848 and 1849, he and Dante Gabriel Rossetti constantly practised their pens in writing sonnets to *bouts-rimés,* each giving the other the rhymes for a sonnet, and Dante Gabriel writing off these exercises in verse-making at the rate of a sonnet in five or eight minutes. Most of W. M. Rossetti's poems in *The Germ* were *bouts-rimés* experiments. Many of Dante Gabriel's, a little touched up, remained in his brother's possession, but were not included in the *Collected Works.* (E.G.)

〜〜〜 **LORD BYRON** (George Gordon Byron, 6th Baron; 1788–1824). In his own lifetime Byron stood higher on the continent of Europe than in England or even in America. His works as they came out were translated into French, into German, into Italian, into Russian, and the stream of translation has never ceased to flow. The *Bride of Abydos* has been translated into ten, *Cain* into nine languages. Of *Manfred* there is one Bohemian translation, two Danish, two Dutch, two French, nine German, three Hungarian, three Italian, two Polish, one Romaic, one Rumanian, four Russian and three Spanish translations. The dictum or verdict of Goethe that "the English may think of Byron as they please, but this is certain that they show no poet who is to be compared with him" was and is the keynote of continental European criticism. A survey of European literature is a testimony to the universality of his influence. Victor Hugo, Lamartine, Delavigne, Alfred de Musset, in France; Börne, Müller and Heine in Germany; the Italian poets Leopardi and Giusti; Pushkin and Lermontov among the Russians; Mickiewicz and Slowacki among the Poles—more or less, as eulogists or imitators or disciples—were of the following of Byron. This fact is beyond dispute, that after the first outburst of popularity he has touched and swayed other nations rather than his own. The part he played or seemed to play in revolutionary politics endeared him to those who were struggling to be free. He stood for freedom of thought and of life. He made himself the mouthpiece of an impassioned and welcome protest against the hypocrisy and arrogance of his order and his race. He lived on the continent and was known to many men in many cities. It has been argued that foreigners are insensible to his defects as a writer, and that this may account for an astonishing and perplexing preference. The cause is rather to be sought in the quality of his art. It was as the creator of new types, "forms more real than living man," that Byron appealed to the artistic sense and to the imagination of Latin, Teuton or Slav. That "he taught us little" of the things of the spirit, that he knew no cure for the sickness of the soul, were considerations which lay outside the province of literary criticism. "It is a mark," says Goethe (*Aus meinem Leben: Dichtung und Wahrheit*, 1876, iii. 125), "of true poetry, that as a secular gospel it knows how to free us from the earthly burdens which press upon us, by inward serenity, by outward charm." Now of this "secular gospel" the redemption from "real woes" by the exhibition of imaginary glory, and imaginary delights, Byron was both prophet and evangelist.

Byron was 5 ft. 8 in. in height, and strongly built; only with difficulty and varying success did he prevent himself from growing fat.

At five-and-thirty he was extremely thin. He was "very slightly lame," but he was painfully conscious of his deformity and walked as little and as seldom as he could. He had a small head covered and fringed with dark brown or auburn curls. His forehead was high and narrow, of a marble whiteness. His eyes were of a light grey colour, clear and luminous. His nose was straight and well-shaped, but "from being a little too thick, it looked better in profile than in front face." Moore says that it was in "the mouth and chin that the great beauty as well as expression of his fine countenance lay." The upper lip was of a Grecian shortness and the corners descending. His complexion was pale and colourless. Scott speaks of "his beautiful pale face—like a spirit's good or evil." Charles Matthews said that "he was the only man to whom he could apply the word beautiful." Coleridge said that "if you had seen him you could scarce disbelieve him . . . his eyes the open portals of the sun—things of light and for light." He was likened to "the god of the Vatican," the Apollo Belvedere. (E.H.C.)

⟨⟩ CHASTELARD, PIERRE DE BOCSO-ZEL DE (1540–1563), French poet, was born in Dauphiné, a scion

of the house of Bayard. His name is inseparably connected with Mary, queen of Scots. From the service of the Constable Montmorency, Chastelard, then a page, passed to the household of Marshal Damville, whom he accompanied in his journey to Scotland in escort of Mary (1561). He returned to Paris in the marshal's train, but left for Scotland again shortly afterward, bearing letters of recommendation to Mary from his old protector, Montmorency, and the *Regrets* addressed to the ex-queen of France by Pierre Ronsard, his master in the art of song. He undertook to transmit to the poet the service of plate with which Mary rewarded him. But he had fallen in love with the queen, who is said to have encouraged his passion. Copies of verse passed between them; she lost no occasion of showing herself partial to his person and conversation. The young man hid himself under her bed, where he was discovered by her maids of honour. Mary pardoned the offence, and the old familiar terms between them were resumed. Chastelard was so rash as again to violate her privacy. He was discovered a second time, seized, sentenced and hanged the next morning. He met his fate valiantly and consistently, reading, on his way to the scaffold, his master's noble *Hymne de la mort,* and turning at the instant of doom towards the palace of Holyrood, to address to his unseen mistress the famous farewell—"Adieu, toi si belle et si cruelle, qui me tues et que je ne puis cesser d'aimer." This at least is the version of the *Mémoires* of Brantôme, who is, however, notoriously untrustworthy. But for his madness of love, it is possible that Chastelard would have left no shadow or shred of himself behind. As it is, his life and death are of interest as illustrating the wild days in which his lot was cast.

CHOISY, FRANÇOIS TIMOLÉON,

ABBÉ DE (1644–1724), French author, was born in Paris on the 16th of August 1644, and died in Paris on the 2nd of October 1724. His father was attached to the household of the duke of Orleans, and his mother, who was on intimate terms with Anne of Austria, was regularly called upon to amuse Louis XIV. By a whim of his mother, the boy was dressed like a girl until he was eighteen, and, after appearing for a short time in man's costume, he resumed woman's dress on the advice—doubtless satirical—of Madame de La Fayette. He delighted in the most extravagant toilettes until he was publicly rebuked by the duc de Montausier, when he retired for some time to the provinces, using his disguise to assist his numerous intrigues. He had been made an abbé in his childhood, and poverty, induced by his extravagance, drove him to live on his benefice at Sainte-Seine in Burgundy, where he found among his neighbours a kindred spirit in Bussy-Rabutin. He visited Rome in the suite of the cardinal de Bouillon in 1676, and shortly afterwards a serious illness brought about a sudden and rather frivolous conversion to religion. In 1685 he accompanied the chevalier de Chaumont on a mission to Siam. He was ordained priest, and received various ecclesiastical preferments. He was admitted to the Academy in 1687, and wrote a number of historical and religious works, of which the most notable were the following:—*Quatre dialogues sur l'immortalité de l'âme* . . . (1684), written with the Abbé Dangeau and explaining his conversion; *Traduction de l'Imitation de Jésus-Christ* (1692), *Histoire de France sous les règnes de Saint Louis . . . de Charles V et Charles VI* (5 vols., 1688–1695); and *Histoire de l'Église* (II vols., 1703–1723) He is remembered, however, by his gossiping *Mémoires* (1737), which contain striking and accurate pictures of his time and remarkably exact portraits of his contemporaries, although he has otherwise small pretensions to historical accuracy.

CINDERELLA (*i.e.* little cinder girl), the heroine of an almost universal fairy-tale. Its essential features are (1) the persecuted maiden whose youth and beauty bring upon her the jeal-

ousy of her step-mother and sisters, (2) the intervention of a fairy or other supernatural instrument on her behalf, (3) the prince who falls in love with and marries her. In the English version, a translation of Perrault's *Cendrillon,* the *glass* slipper which she drops on the palace stairs is due to a mistranslation of *pantoufle en vair* (a *fur* slipper), mistaken for *en verre.* It has been suggested that the story originated in a nature-myth, Cinderella being the dawn, oppressed by the night-clouds (cruel relatives) and finally rescued by the sun (prince).

CRUDEN, ALEXANDER (1701–1770), author of the well-known concordance to the English Bible, was born at Aberdeen on the 31st of May 1701. He was educated at the grammar school, Aberdeen, and studied at Marischal College, intending to enter the ministry. He took the degree of master of arts, but soon after began to show signs of insanity owing to a disappointment in love. After a term of confinement he recovered and removed to London. In 1722 he had an engagement as private tutor to the son of a country squire living at Eton Hall, Southgate, and also held a similar post at Ware. Years afterwards, in an application for the title of bookseller to the queen, he stated that he had been for some years corrector for the press in Wild Court. This probably refers to this time. In 1729 he was employed by the 10th earl of Derby as a reader and secretary, but was discharged on the 7th of July for his ignorance of French pronunciation. He then lodged in a house in Soho frequented exclusively by Frenchmen, and took lessons in the language in the hope of getting back his post with the earl, but when he went to Knowsley in Lancashire, the earl would not see him. He returned to London and opened a bookseller's shop in the Royal Exchange. In April 1735 he obtained the title of book-seller to the queen by recommendation of the lord mayor and most of the Whig aldermen. The post was an unremunerative sinecure. In 1737 he finished his concordance, which, he says, was the work of several years. It was presented to the queen on the 3rd of November 1737, a fortnight before her death.

Although Cruden's biblical labours have made his name a household word among English-speaking people, he was disappointed in his hopes of immediate profit, and his mind again became unhinged. In spite of his earnest and self-denying piety, and his exceptional intellectual powers, he developed idiosyncrasies, and his life was marred by a harmless but ridiculous egotism, which so nearly bordered on insanity that his friends sometimes thought it necessary to

have him confined. He paid unwelcome addresses to a widow, and
was confined in a madhouse in Bethnal Green. On his release he
published a pamphlet dedicated to Lord H. (probably Harrington,
secretary of state) entitled *The London Citizen exceedingly injured, or a
British Inquisition Displayed.* He also published an account of his trial,
dedicated to the king. In December 1740 he writes to Sir H. Sloane
saying he has been employed since July as Latin usher in a boarding-
school at Enfield. He then found work as a proof-reader, and several
editions of Greek and Latin classics are said to have owed their accuracy to his care. He superintended the printing of one of Matthew
Henry's commentaries, and in 1750 printed a small *Compendium of
the Holy Bible* (an abstract of the contents of each chapter), and also
reprinted a larger edition of the *Concordance.*

About this time he adopted the title of "Alexander the Corrector,"
and assumed the office of correcting the morals of the nation, especially with regard to swearing and Sunday observance. For this
office he believed himself divinely commissioned, but he petitioned
parliament for a formal appointment in this capacity. In April 1755
he printed a letter to the speaker and other members of the House
of Commons, and about the same time an "Address to the King and
Parliament." He was in the habit of carrying a sponge, with which
he effaced all inscriptions which he thought contrary to good morals.
In September 1753, through being involved in a street brawl, he was
confined in an asylum in Chelsea for seventeen days at the instance
of his sister, Mrs Wild. He brought an unsuccessful action against his
friends, and seriously proposed that they should go into confinement
as an atonement. He published an account of this second restraint
in "The Adventures of Alexander the Corrector." He made attempts
to present to the king in person an account of his trial, and to obtain
the honour of knighthood, one of his predicted honours. In 1754
he was nominated as parliamentary candidate for the city of London,
but did not go to the poll. In 1755 he paid unwelcome addresses to
the daughter of Sir Thomas Abney, of Newington (1640–1722), and
then published his letters and the history of his repulse in the third
part of his "Adventures." In June and July 1755 he visited Oxford
and Cambridge. He was treated with the respect due to his learning
by officials and residents in both universities, but experienced some
boisterous fooling at the hands of the undergraduates. At Cambridge
he was knighted with mock ceremonies. There he appointed "deputy
correctors" to represent him in the university. He also visited Eton,
Windsor, Tonbridge and Westminster schools, where he appointed
four boys to be his deputies. (An *Admonition to Cambridge* is preserved

among letters from J. Neville of Emmanuel to Dr Cox Macro, in the British Museum.) *The Corrector's Earnest Address to the Inhabitants of Great Britain,* published in 1756, was occasioned by the earthquake at Lisbon. In 1762 he saved an ignorant seaman, Richard Potter, from the gallows, and in 1763 published a pamphlet recording the history of the case. Against John Wilkes, whom he hated, he wrote a small pamphlet, and used to delete with his sponge the number 45 wherever he found it, this being the offensive number of the *North Briton.* In 1769 he lectured in Aberdeen as "Corrector," and distributed copies of the fourth commandment and various religious tracts. The wit that made his eccentricites palatable is illustrated by the story of how he gave to a conceited young minister whose appearance displeased him *A Mother's Catechism dedicated to the young and ignorant.* The *Scripture Dictionary,* compiled about this time, was printed in Aberdeen in two volumes shortly after his death. Alexander Chalmers, who in his boyhood heard Cruden lecture in Aberdeen and wrote his biography, says that a verbal index to Milton, which accompanied the edition of Thomas Newton, bishop of Bristol, in 1769, was Cruden's.

The second edition of the Bible *Concordance* was published in 1761, and presented to the king in person on the 21st of December. The third appeared in 1769. Both contain a pleasing portrait of the author. He is said to have gained £800 by these two editions. He returned to London from Aberdeen, and died suddenly while praying in his lodgings in Camden Passage, Islington, on the 1st of November 1770. He was buried in the ground of a Protestant dissenting congregation in Dead Man's Place, Southwark. He bequeathed a portion of his savings for a £5 bursary at Aberdeen, which preserves his name on the list of benefactors of the university. (D.Mn.)

DARWIN, CHARLES (Daily Routine of). In

a deeply interesting chapter of the *Life and Letters* Francis Darwin has given us his reminiscences of his father's everyday life. Rising early, he took a short walk before breakfasting alone at 7.45, and then at once set to work, "considering the 1½ hours between 8.0 and 9.30 one of his best working times." He then read his letters and listened to reading aloud, returning to work at about 10.30. At 12 or 12.15 "he considered his day's work over," and went for a walk, whether wet or fine. For a time he rode, but after accidents had occurred twice, was advised to give it up. After lunch he read the newspaper and wrote his letters or the MS. of his books. At about 3.0 he rested and smoked for an hour while being read to, often going to sleep.

He then went for a short walk, and returning about 4.30, worked for an hour. After this he rested and smoked, and listened to reading until tea at 7.30, a meal which he came to prefer to late dinner. He then played two games of backgammon, read to himself, and listened to music and to reading aloud. He went to bed, generally very much tired, at 10.30, and was often much troubled by wakefulness and the activity of his thoughts. It is thus apparent that the number of hours devoted to work in each day was comparatively few. The immense amount he achieved was due to concentration during these hours, also to the unfailing and, because of his health, the necessary regularity of his life. (E.B.P.)

DIARY, the Lat. *diarium* (from *dies*, a day), the book in which are preserved the daily memoranda regarding events and actions which come under the writer's personal observation, or are related to him by others. The person who keeps this record is called a diarist. It is not necessary that the entries in a diary should be made each day, since every life, however full, must contain absolutely empty intervals. But it is essential that the entry should be made during the course of the day to which it refers. When this has evidently not been done, as in the case of Evelyn's diary, there is nevertheless an effort made to give the memoranda the effect of being so recorded, and in point of fact, even in a case like that of Evelyn, it is probable that what we now read is an enlargement of brief notes jotted down on the day cited. When this is not approximately the case, the diary is a fraud, for its whole value depends on its instantaneous transcript of impressions.

In its primitive form, the diary must always have existed; as soon as writing was invented, men and women must have wished to note down, in some almanac or journal, memoranda respecting their business, their engagements or their adventures. but the literary value of these would be extremely insignificant until the spirit of individualism had crept in, and human beings began to be interesting to other human beings for their own sake. It is not, therefore, until the close of the Renaissance that we find diaries beginning to have literary value, although, as the study of sociology extends, every scrap of genuine and unaffected record of early history possesses an ethical interest. In the 17th century, diaries began to be largely written in England, although in most cases without any idea of even eventual publication. Sir William Dugdale (1605–1686) had certainly no expectation that his slight diary would ever see the light. There is no surviving record of a journal kept by Clarendon, Richard Baxter, Lucy Hutchinson and other autobiographical writers of the middle of the century, but we may take it for granted that they possessed some such record, kept from day to day. Bulstrode Whitelocke (1605–1675), whose *Memorials of the English Affairs* covers the ground from 1625 to 1660, was a genuine diarist. So was the elder George Fox (1624–1690), who kept not merely "a great journal," but "the little journal books," and whose work was published in 1694. The famous diary of John Evelyn (1620–1706) professes to be the record of seventy years, and, although large tracts of it are covered in a very perfunctory manner, while in others many of the entries have the air of having been written in long after the event, this is a very interesting and amusing work; it was not published until 1818. In spite of all its imperfections there is a great charm about the diary of Evelyn, and it would hold a still higher position in the history of literature than it does if it were not overshadowed by what is unquestionably the most illustrious of the diaries of the world, that of Samuel Pepys (1633–1703). This was begun on the 1st of January 1660 and was carried on until the 29th of May 1669. The extraordinary value of Pepys' diary consists in its fidelity to the portraiture of its author's character. He feigns nothing, conceals nothing, sets nothing down in malice or insincerity. He wrote in a form of shorthand intelligible to no one but himself, and not a phrase betrays the smallest expectation that any eye but his own would ever investigate the pages of his confession. The importance of this wonderful document, in fact, lay unsuspected until 1819, when the Rev. John Smith of Baldock began to decipher the MS. in Magdalene College, Cambridge. It was not until 1825 that Lord Braybrooke published part of what was only fully edited, under the care of Mr Wheatley, in 1893–1896. In the age which succeeded that of Pepys, a diary of extarordinary emotional interest was kept by Swift from 1710 to 1713, and was sent to Ireland in the form of a "Journal to Stella"; it is a surprising amalgam of ambition, affection, wit and freakishness. John Byrom (1692–1763), the Manchester poet, kept a journal, which was published in 1854. The diary of the celebrated dissenting divine, Philip Doddridge (1702–1751), was printed in 1829. Of far greater interest are the admirably composed and vigorously written journals of John Wesley (1703–1791). But the most celebrated work of this kind produced in the latter half of the 18th century was the diary of Fanny Burney (Madame D'Arblay), published in 1842–1846. It will be perceived that, without exception, these works were posthumously published, and the whole conception of the diary has been that it should be written for the writer alone, or, if for the public, for the public when all prejudice shall have passed away and all passion cooled down. Thus, and thus only, can the diary be written so as to impress upon its eventual readers a sense of its author's perfect sincerity and courage.

Many of the diaries described above were first published in the opening years of the 19th century, and it is unquestionable that the interest which they awakened in the public led to their imitation. Diaries ceased to be rare, but as a rule the specimens which have hitherto appeared have not presented much literary interest. Exception must be made in favour of the journals of two minor politicians, Charles Greville (1794–1865) and Thomas Creevey (1768–1838), whose indiscretions have added much to the gaiety of nations; the papers of the former appeared in 1874–1887, those of the latter in 1903. The diary of Henry Crabb Robinson (1775–1867), printed in 1869, contains excellent biographical material. Tom Moore's journal, published in 1856 by Lord John Russell, disappointed its readers. But it is probable, if we reason by the analogy of the past, that the most curious and original diaries of the 19th century are still unknown to us, and lie jealously guarded under lock and key by the descendants of those who compiled them.

It was natural that the form of the diary should appeal to a people so sensitive to social peculiarities and so keen in the observation of them as the French. A medieval document of immense value is the diary kept by an anonymous *curé* during the reigns of Charles VI. and Charles VII. This *Journal d'un bourgeois de Paris* was kept from 1409 to 1431, and was continued by another hand down to 1449. The marquis de Dangeau (1638–1720) kept a diary from 1684 till the year of his death; this although dull, and as Saint-Simon said "of an insipidity to make you sick," is an inexhaustible storehouse of facts about the reign of Louis XIV. Saint-Simon's own brilliant memoirs, written from 1691 to 1723, may be considered as a sort of diary. The lawyer, Edmond Barbier (1689–1771), wrote a journal of the anecdotes and little facts which came to his knowledge from 1718 to 1762. The studious care which he took to be correct, and his manifest candour, give a singular value to Barbier's record; his diary was not printed at all until 1847, nor, in its entirety, until 1857. The songwriter Charles Collé (1709–1783), kept a *journal historique* from 1758 to 1782; it is full of vivactiy, but very scandalous and spiteful. It saw the light in 1805, and surprised those to whom Collé, in his lifetime, had seemed the most placid and good-natured of men. Petit de Bachaumont (1690–1770) had access to remarkable sources of information, and his *Mémoires secrets* (a diary the publication of which began in 1762 and was continued after Bachaumont's death, until 1787, by other persons) contains a valuable mass of documents. The marquis d'Argenson (1694–1757) kept a diary, of which a comparatively full text was first published in 1859. In recent times the posthumous publication of the diaries of the Russian artist, Marie Bashkirtseff (1860–1884), produced a great sensation in 1887, and revealed a most remarkable temperament. The brothers Jules and Edmond de Goncourt kept a very minute diary of all that occurred around them in artistic and literary Paris; after the death of Jules, in 1870, this was continued by Edmond, who published the three first volumes in 1888. The publication of this work was continued, and it produced no little scandal. It is excessively ill-natured in parts, but of its vivid picturesqueness, and of its general accuracy as a transcript of conversation, there can be no two opinions. (E.G.)

GIBBON, EDWARD (1737–1794), (as he finishes *The Decline and Fall of the Roman Empire*). When once fairly reseated at his task, he proceeded in this delightful retreat leisurely, yet rapidly, to its completion. The fourth volume, partly written in 1782, was completed in June 1784; the preparation of the fifth volume occupied less than two years; while the sixth and last, begun 18th May 1786, was finished in thirteen months. The feelings with which he brought his labours to a close must be described in his own inimitable words: "It was on the day, or rather night, of the 27th of June 1787, between the hours of eleven and twelve, that I wrote the last lines of the last page in a summer house in my garden. After laying down my pen, I took several turns in a *berceau* or covered walk of acacias, which commands a prospect of the country, the lake, and the mountains. The air was temperate, the sky was serene, the silver orb of the moon was reflected from the waters, and all nature was silent. I will not dissemble the first emotions of joy on the recovery of my freedom, and, perhaps, the establishment of my fame. But my pride was soon humbled, and a sober melancholy was spread over my mind by the idea that I had taken an everlasting leave of an old and agreeable companion, and that whatsoever might be the future date of my *History*, the life of the historian must be short and precarious."

Taking the manuscript with him, Gibbon, after an absence of four years, once more visited London in 1787; and the 51st anniversary of the author's birthday (27th April 1788) witnessed the publication

of the last three volumes of *The Decline and Fall.* They met with a
quick and easy sale, were very extensively read, and very liberally
and deservedly praised for the unflagging industry and vigour they
displayed, though just exception, if only on the score of good taste,
was taken to the scoffing tone he continued to maintain in all passages
where the Christian religion was specially concerned, and much fault
was found with the indecency of some of his notes. (J.B.B.)

GOLDSMITH, OLIVER (1728–1774), (Character of). His associates seem to have regarded him with kindness,
which, in spite of their admiration of his writings, was not unmixed
with contempt. In truth, there was in his character much to love, but
very little to respect. His heart was soft even to weakness; he was so
generous that he quite forgot to be just; he forgave injuries so readily
that he might be said to invite them, and was so liberal to beggars
that he had nothing left for his tailor and his butcher. He was vain,
sensual, frivolous, profuse, improvident. One vice of a darker shade
was imputed to him, envy. But there is not the least reason to believe
that this bad passion, though it sometimes made him wince and utter
fretful exclamations, ever impelled him to injure by wicked arts the
reputation of any of his rivals. The truth probably is that he was not
more envious, but merely less prudent, than his neighbours. His heart
was on his lips. All those small jealousies, which are but too common
among men of letters, but which a man of letters who is also a man
of the world does his best to conceal, Goldsmith avowed with the
simplicity of a child. When he was envious, instead of affecting indifference, instead of damning with faint praise, instead of doing
injuries slyly and in the dark, he told everybody that he was envious.
"Do not, pray, do not, talk of Johnson in such terms," he said to
Boswell; "you harrow up my very soul." George Steevens and Cumberland were men far too cunning to say such a thing. They would
have echoed the praises of the man whom they envied, and then have
sent to the newspapers anonymous libels upon him. Both what was
good and what was bad in Goldsmith's character was to his associates
a perfect security that he would never commit such villainy. He was
neither ill-natured enough, nor long-headed enough, to be guilty of
any malicious act which required contrivance and disguise.

Goldsmith has sometimes been represented as a man of genius,
cruelly treated by the world, and doomed to struggle with difficulties,
which at last broke his heart. But no representation can be more
remote from the truth. He did, indeed, go through much sharp

misery before he had done anything considerable in literature. But after his name had appeared on the title-page of the *Traveller*, he had none but himself to blame for his distresses. His average income, during the last seven years of his life, certainly exceeded £400 a year, and £400 a year ranked, among the incomes of that day, at least as high as £800 a year would rank at present. A single man living in the Temple, with £400 a year, might then be called opulent. Not one in ten of the young gentlemen of good families who were studying the law there had so much. But all the wealth which Lord Clive had brought from Bengal and Sir Lawrence Dundas from Germany, joined together, would not have sufficed for Goldsmith. He spent twice as much as he had. He wore fine clothes, gave dinners of several courses, paid court to venal beauties. He had also, it should be remembered, to the honour of his heart, though not of his head, a guinea, or five, or ten, according to the state of his purse, ready for any tale of distress, true or false. But it was not in dress or feasting, in promiscuous amours or promiscuous charities, that his chief expense lay. He had been from boyhood a gambler, and at once the most sanguine and the most unskilful of gamblers. For a time he put off the day of inevitable ruin by temporary expedients. He obtained advances from booksellers by promising to execute works which he never began. But at length this course of supply failed. He owed more than £2000; and he saw no hope of extrication from his embarrassments. His spirits and health gave way. He was attacked by a nervous fever, which he thought himself competent to treat. It would have been happy for him if his medical skill had been appreciated as justly by himself as by others. Notwithstanding the degree which he pretended to have received on the continent, he could procure no patients. "I do not practise," he once said; "I make it a rule to prescribe only for my friends." "Pray, dear Doctor," said Beauclerk, "alter your rule; and prescribe only for your enemies." Goldsmith, now, in spite of this excellent advice, prescribed for himself. The remedy aggravated the malady. The sick man was induced to call in real physicians; and they at one time imagined that they had cured the disease. Still his weakness and restlessness continued. He could get no sleep. He could take no food. "You are worse," said one of his medical attendants, "than you should be from the degree of fever which you have. Is your mind at ease?" "No; it is not," were the last recorded words of Oliver Goldsmith. He died on the 4th of April 1774, in his forty-sixth year. He was laid in the churchyard of the Temple; but the spot was not marked by any inscription and is now forgotten. The coffin was followed by Burke and Reynolds. Both these great men were sincere mourners. Burke, when he heard of Goldsmith's death, had burst into a flood of tears. Reynolds had been so much moved by the news that he had flung aside his brush and palette for the day. (M.)

⟨⟨⟨∽⟩ HERRICK, ROBERT (1591–1674), English

poet, was born at Cheapside, London, and baptized on the 24th of August 1591. He belonged to an old Leicestershire family which had settled in London. He was the seventh child of Nicholas Herrick, goldsmith, of the city of London, who died in 1592, under suspicion of suicide. The children were brought up by their uncle, Sir William Herrick, one of the richest goldsmiths of the day, to whom in 1607 Robert was bound apprentice. He had probably been educated at Westminster school, and in 1614 he proceeded to Cambridge; and it was no doubt during his apprenticeship that the young poet was introduced to that circle of wits which he was afterwards to adorn. He seems to have been present at the first performance of *The Alchemist* in 1610, and it was probably about this time that Ben Jonson adopted him as his poetical "son." He entered the university as fellow-commoner of St John's College, and he remained there until, in 1616, upon taking his degree, he removed to Trinity Hall. A lively series of fourteen letters to his uncle, mainly begging for money, exists at Beaumanoir, and shows that Herrick suffered much from poverty at the university. He took his B.A. in 1617, and in 1620 he became master of arts. From this date until 1627 we entirely lose sight of him; it has been variously conjectured that he spent these years preparing for the ministry at Cambridge, or in much looser pursuits in London. In 1629 (September 30) he was presented by the king to the vicarage of Dean Prior, not far from Totnes in Devonshire. At Dean Prior he resided quietly until 1648, when he was ejected by the Puritans. The solitude there oppressed him at first; the village was dull and remote, and he felt very bitterly that he was cut off from all literary and social associations; but soon the quiet existence in Devonshire soothed and delighted him. He was pleased with the rural and semi-pagan customs that survived in the village, and in some of his most charming verses he has immortalized the morris-dances, wakes and quintains, the Christmas mummers and the Twelfth Night revellings, that diversified the quiet of Dean Prior. Herrick never married, but lived at the vicarage surrounded by a happy family of pets, and tended by an excellent old servant named Prudence Baldwin. His first appearance in print was in some verses he contributed to *A Description of the King and Queen of Fairies*, in 1635. In 1650 a volume of *Wit's Recreations* contained sixty-two small poems afterwards acknowledged by Herrick in the *Hesperides,* and one not reprinted until our own day. These partial appearances make it probable that he visited London from time to time. We have few hints of his life as a clergyman. Anthony Wood says that Herrick's sermons were florid and witty, and that he was "beloved by the neighbouring gentry." A very aged woman, one Dorothy King, stated that the poet once threw his sermon at his congregation, cursing them for their inattention. The same old woman recollected his favourite pig, which he taught to drink out of a tankard. He was a devotedly loyal supporter of the king during the Civil War, and immediately upon his ejection in 1648 he published his celebrated collection of lyrical poems, entitled *Hesperides; or the Works both Human and Divine of Robert Herrick.* The "divine works" bore the title of *Noble Numbers* and the date 1647. That he was reduced to great poverty in London has been stated, but there is no evidence of the fact. In August 1662 Herrick returned to Dean Prior, supplanting his own supplanter, Dr John Syms. He died in his eighty-fourth year, and was buried at Dean Prior, October 15, 1674. A monument was erected to his memory in the parish church in 1857, by Mr Perry Herrick, a descendant of a collateral branch of the family. The *Hesperides* (and *Noble Numbers*) is the only volume which Herrick published, but he contributed poems to *Lachrymae Musarum* (1649) and to *Wit's Recreations.*

As a pastoral lyrist Herrick stands first among English poets. His genius is limited in scope, and comparatively unambitious, but in its own field it is unrivalled. His tiny poems—and of the thirteen hundred that he has left behind him not one is long—are like jewels of various value, heaped together in a casket. Some are of the purest water, radiant with light and colour, some were originally set in false metal that has tarnished, some were rude and repulsive from the first. Out of the unarranged, heterogeneous mass the student has to select what is not worth reading, but, after he has cast aside all the rubbish, he is astonished at the amount of excellent and exquisite work that remains. Herrick has himself summed up, very correctly, the themes of his sylvan muse when he says:—

> I sing of brooks, of blossoms, birds and bowers,
> Of April, May, of June and July flowers,
> I sing of May-poles, hock-carts, wassails, wakes,
> Of bridegrooms, brides and of their bridal-cakes.

He saw the picturesqueness of English homely life as no one before him had seen it, and he described it in his verse with a certain purple

James, Henry

glow of Arcadian romance over it, in tones of immortal vigour and freshness. His love poems are still more beautiful; the best of them have an ardour and tender sweetness which give them a place in the forefront of modern lyrical poetry, and remind us of what was best in Horace and in the poets of the Greek anthology. (E.G.)

JAMES, HENRY (1843–[1916]), American author, was born in New York on the 15th of April 1843. His father was Henry James (1811–1882), a theological writer of great originality, from whom both he and his brother Professor William James derived their psychological subtlety and their idiomatic, picturesque English. Most of Henry's boyhood was spent in Europe, where he studied under tutors in England, France and Switzerland. In 1860 he returned to America, and began reading law at Harvard, only to find speedily that literature, not law, was what he most cared for. His earliest short tale, "The Story of a Year," appeared in 1865, in the *Atlantic Monthly,* and frequent stories and sketches followed. In 1869 he again went to Europe, where he subsequently made his home, for the most part living in London, or at Rye in Sussex. Among his specially noteworthy works are the following: *Watch and Ward* (1871); *Roderick Hudson* (1875); *The American* (1877); *Daisy Miller* (1878); *French Poets and Novelists* (1878); *A Life of Hawthorne* (1879); *The Portrait of a Lady* (1881); *Portraits of Places* (1884); *The Bostonians* (1886); *Partial Portraits* (1888); *The Tragic Muse* (1890); *Essays in London* (1893); *The Two Magics* (1898); *The Awkward Age* (1898); *The Wings of the Dove* (1902); *The Ambassadors* (1903); *The Golden Bowl* (1904); *English Hours* (1905); *The American Scene* (1907); *The High Bid* (1909); *Italian Hours* (1909).

As a novelist, Henry James is a modern of the moderns both in subject matter and in method. He is entirely loyal to contemporary life and reverentially exact in his transcription of the phase. His characters are for the most part people of the world who conceive of life as a fine art and have the leisure to carry out their theories. Rarely are they at close quarters with any ugly practical task. They are subtle and complex with the subtlety and the complexity that come from conscious preoccupation with themselves. They are specialists in conduct and past masters in casuistry, and are full of variations and shadows of turning. Moreover, they are finely expressive of *milieu;* each belongs unmistakably to his class and his race; each is true to inherited moral traditions and delicately illustrative of some social code. To reveal the power and the tragedy of life through so many minutely limiting and apparently artificial conditions, and by means of characters who are somewhat self-conscious and are apt to make of life only a pleasant pastime, might well seem an impossible task. Yet it is precisely in this that Henry James is pre-eminently successful. The essentially human is what he really cares for, however much he may at times seem preoccupied with the *technique* of his art or with the mask of conventions through which he makes the essentially human reveal itself. Nor has "the vista of the spiritual been denied him." No more poignant spiritual tragedy has been recounted in recent fiction than the story of Isabel Archer in *The Portrait of a Lady*. His method, too, is as modern as his subject matter. He early fell in love with the "point of view," and the good and the bad qualities of his work all follow from this literary passion. He is a very sensitive impressionist, with a technique that can fix the most elusive phase of character and render the most baffling surface. The skill is unending with which he places his characters in such relations and under such lights that they flash out in due succession their continuously varying facets. At times he may seem to forget that a character is something incalculably more than the sum of all its phases; and then his characters tend to have their existence, as Positivists expect to have their immortality, simply and solely in the minds of other people. But when his method is at its best, the delicate phases of character that he transcribes coalesce perfectly into clearly defined and suggestive images of living, acting men and women. Doubtless, there is a certain initiation necessary for the enjoyment of Mr James. He presupposes a cosmopolitan outlook, a certain interest in art and in social artifice, and no little abstract curiosity about the workings of the human mechanism. But for speculative readers, for readers who care for art in life as well as for life in art, and for readers above all who want to encounter and comprehend a great variety of very modern and finely modulated characters, Mr James holds a place of his own, unrivalled as an interpreter of the world of to-day.

LEAR, EDWARD (1812–1888), English artist and humorist, was born in London on the 12th of May 1812. His earliest drawings were ornithological. When he was twenty years old he published a brilliantly coloured selection of the rarer Psittacidae. Its power attracted the attention of the 13th earl of Derby, who employed Lear to draw his Knowsley menagerie. He became a permanent favourite with the Stanley family; and Edward, 15th earl, was the child for whose amusement the first *Book of Nonsense* was composed. From birds Lear turned to landscape, his earlier efforts in which recall the manner of J. D. Harding; but he quickly acquired a more individual style. About 1837 he set up a studio at Rome, where he lived for ten years, with summer tours in Italy and Sicily, and occasional visits to England. During this period he began to publish his *Illustrated Journals of a Landscape Painter:* charmingly written reminiscences of wandering, which ultimately embraced Calabria, the Abruzzi, Albania, Corsica, &c. From 1848–1849 he explored Greece, Constantinople, the Ionian Islands, Lower Egypt, the wildest recesses of Albania, and the desert of Sinai. He returned to London, but the climate did not suit him. In 1854–1855 he wintered on the Nile, and migrated successively to Corfu, Malta and Rome, finally building himself a villa at San Remo. From Corfu Lear visited Mount Athos, Syria, Palestine, and Petra; and when over sixty, by the assistance of Lord Northbrook, then Governor-General, he saw the cities and scenery of greatest interest within a large area of India. From first to last he was, in whatever circumstances of difficulty or ill-health, an indomitable traveller. Before visiting new lands he studied their geography and literature, and then went straight for the mark; and wherever he went he drew most indefatigably and most accurately. His sketches are not only the basis of more finished works, but an exhaustive record in themselves. Some defect of technique or eyesight occasionally left his larger oil painting, though nobly conceived, crude or deficient in harmony; but his smaller pictures and more elaborate sketches abound in beauty, delicacy, and truth. Lear modestly called himself a topographical artist; but he included in the term the perfect rendering of all characteristic graces of form, colour, and atmosphere. The last task he set himself was to prepare for popular circulation a set of some 200 drawings, illustrating from his travels the scenic touches of Tennyson's poetry; but he did not live to complete the scheme, dying at San Remo on the 30th of January 1888. Until sobered by age, his conversation was brimful of humorous fun. The paradoxical originality and ostentatiously uneducated draughtmanship of his numerous nonsense books won him a more universal fame than his serious work. He had a true artist's sympathy with art under all forms, and might have become a skilled musician had he not been a painter. Swainson, the naturalist, praised young Lear's great red and yellow macaw as "equalling any figure ever painted by Audubon in grace of design, perspective, and anatomical accuracy." Murchison, examining his sketches, complimented them as rigorously embodying geological truth. Tennyson's lines "To E.L. on his Travels in Greece," mark the poet's genuine admiration of a cognate spirit in classical art. Ruskin placed the *Book of Nonsense* first in the list of a hundred delectable volumes of contemporary literature, a judgment endorsed by English-speaking children all over the world. (F.L.)

⟨⟩⟩ **MALLARMÉ, STÉPHANE** (1842–1898), French poet and theorist, was born at Paris, on the 18th of March 1842. His life was simple and without event. His small income as professor of English in a French college was sufficient for his needs, and, with his wife and daughter, he divided the year between a fourth-floor flat in Paris and a cottage on the banks of the Seine. His Tuesday evening receptions, which did so much to form the thought of the more interesting of the younger French men of letters, were almost as important a part of his career as the few carefully elaborated books which he produced at long intervals. *L' Après-midi d'un faune* (1876) and other fragments of his verse and prose had been known to a few people long before the publication of the *Poésies complètes* of 1887, in a facsimile of his clear and elegant handwriting, and of the *Pages* of 1891 and the *Vers et prose* of 1893. His remarkable translation of poems of Poe appeared in 1888, "The Raven" having been published as early as 1875, with illustrations by Manet. *Divagations*, his own final edition of his prose, was published in 1897, and a more or less complete edition of the *Poésies*, posthumously, in 1899. He died at Valvins, Fontainebleau, on the 9th of September 1898. All his life Mallarmé was in search of a new aesthetics, and his discoveries by the way were often admirable. But he was too critical ever to create freely, and too limited ever to create abundantly. His great achievement remains unfinished, and all that he left towards it is not of equal value. There are a few poems and a few pieces of imaginative prose which have the haunting quality of Gustave Moreau's pictures, with the same jewelled magnificence, mysterious and yet definite. His later work became more and more obscure, as he seemed to himself to have abolished limit after limit which holds back speech from the expression of the absolute. Finally, he abandoned punctuation in verse, and invented a new punctuation, along with a new construction, for prose. Patience in the study of so difficult an author has its reward. No one in our time has vindicated with more pride the self-sufficiency of the artist in his struggle with the material world. To those who knew him only by his writings his conversation was startling in its clearness; it was always, like all his work, at the service of a few dignified and misunderstood ideas. (A.Sy.)

⟨∾⟩ **MELVILLE, HERMAN** (1819–1891), American author, was born in New York City on the 1st of August 1819. He shipped as a cabin-boy at the age of eighteen, thus being enabled to make his first visit to England, and at twenty-two sailed for a long whaling cruise in the Pacific. After a year and a half he deserted his ship at the Marquesas Islands, on account of the cruelty of the captain; was captured by cannibals on the island of Nukahiva, and detained, without hardship, four months; was rescued by the crew of an Australian vessel, which he joined, and two years later reached New York. Thereafter, with the exception of a passenger voyage around the world in 1860, Melville remained in the United States, devoting himself to literature—though for a considerable period (1866–1885) he held a post in the New York custom-house—and being perhaps Hawthorne's most intimate friend among the literary men of America. His writings are numerous, and of varying merit; his verse, patriotic and other, is forgotten; and his works of fiction and of travel are of irregular execution. Nevertheless, few authors have been enabled so freely to introduce romantic personal experiences into their books: in his first work, *Typee: A Peep at Polynesian Life, or Four Months' Residence in a Valley of the Marquesas* (1846), he described his escape from the cannibals; while in *Omoo, a Narrative of Adventures in the South Seas* (1847), *White Jacket, or The World in a Man-of-War* (1850), and especially *Moby Dick, or The Whale* (1851), he portrayed seafaring life and character with vigour and originality, and from a personal knowledge equal to that of Cooper, Marryat or Clark Russell. But these records of adventure were followed by other tales so turgid, eccentric, opinionative, and loosely written as to seem the work of another author. Melville was the product of a period in American literature when the fiction written by writers below Irving, Poe and Hawthorne was measured by humble artistic standards. He died in New York on the 28th of September 1891.

⟨∾⟩ **MERLIN** (Welsh, *Myrddhin*), the famous bard of Welsh tradition, and enchanter of Arthurian romance. His history as related in this latter may be summarized as follows. The infernal powers, aghast at the blow to their influence dealt by the Incarnation, determine to counteract it, if possible, by the birth of an Antichrist, the offspring of a woman and a devil. As in the book of Job, a special family is singled out as subjects of the diabolic experiment, their property is destroyed, one after the other perishes miserably, till one daughter, who has placed herself under the special protection of the

Church, is left alone. The demon takes advantage of an unguarded moment of despair, and Merlin is engendered. Thanks, however, to the prompt action of the mother's confessor, Blayse, in at once baptizing the child of this abnormal birth, the mother truly protesting that she has had intercourse with no man, Merlin is claimed for Christianity, but remains dowered with demoniac powers of insight and prophecy. An infant in arms, he saves his mother's life and confounds her accusers by his knowledge of their family secrets. Meanwhile Vortigern, king of the Britons, is in despair at the failure of his efforts to build a tower in a certain spot; however high it may be reared in a day, it falls again during the night. He consults his diviners, who tell him that the foundations must be watered with the blood of a child who has never had a father; the king accordingly sends messengers through the land in search of such a prodigy. They come to the city where Merlin and his mother dwell at the moment when the boy is cast out from the companionship of the other lads on the ground that he has had no father. The messengers take him to the king, and on the way he astonishes them by certain prophecies which are fulfilled to their knowledge. Arrived in Vortigern's presence, he at once announces that he is aware alike of the fate destined for him and of the reason, hidden from the magicians, of the fall of the tower. It is built over a lake, and beneath the waters of the lake in a subterranean cavern lie two dragons, a white and a red; when they turn over the tower falls. The lake is drained, the correctness of the statement proved, and Merlin's position as court prophet assured. Henceforward he acts as adviser to Vortigern's successors, the princes Ambrosius and Uther (subsequently Uther-Pendragon). As a monument to the Britons fallen on Salisbury Plain he brings from Ireland, by magic means, the stones now forming Stonehenge. He aids Uther in his passion for Yguerne, wife to the duke of Cornwall, by Merlin's spells Uther assumes the form of the husband, and on the night of the duke's death Arthur is engendered. At his birth the child is committed to Merlin's care, and by him given to Antor, who brings him up as his own son. On Arthur's successful achievement of the test of the sword in the "perron," Merlin reveals the truth of his parentage and the fact that he is by hereditary right, as well as by divine selection, king of the Britons. During the earlier part of Arthur's reign Merlin acts as counsellor; then he disappears mysteriously from the scene. According to one account he is betrayed by a maiden, Nimue or Niniane (a king's daughter, or a water-fairy, both figure in different versions), of whom he is enamoured, and who having beguiled from him a knowledge of magic spells, casts him into a slumber and imprisons him living in a rocky tomb. This version, with the great cry, or *Brait,* which the magician uttered before his death, appears to have been the most popular. Another represents his prison as one of air; he is invisible to all, but can see and hear, and occasionally speak to passers by; thus he holds converse with Gawain. In the prose *Perceval* he retires voluntarily to an "Esplumeor" erected by himself, and is seen no more of man. (J.L.W.)

PALIMPSEST. The custom of removing writing from the surface of the material on which it had been inscribed, and thus preparing that surface for the reception of another text, has been practised from early times. The term palimpsest (from Gr. πάλιν, again, and ψάω, I scrape) is used by Catullus, apparently with reference to papyrus; by Cicero, in a passage wherein he is evidently speaking of waxen tablets; and by Plutarch, when he narrates that Plato compared Dionysius to a βιβλίον παλίμψηστον, in that his tyrant nature, being δυσέκπλυτος, showed itself like the imperfectly erased writing of a palimpsest MS. In this passage reference is clearly made to the washing off of writing from papyrus. The word πα- λίμψηστος can only in its first use have been applied to MSS. which were actually scraped or rubbed, and which were, therefore, composed of a material of sufficient strength to bear the process. In the first instance, then, it might be applied to waxen tablets; secondly, to vellum books. There are still to be seen, among the surviving waxen tablets, some which contain traces of an earlier writing under a fresh layer of wax. Papyrus could not be scraped or rubbed; the writing was washed from it with the sponge. This, however, could not be so thoroughly done as to leave a perfectly clean surface, and the material was accordingly only used a second time for documents of an ephemeral or common nature. To apply, therefore, the title of palimpsest to a MS. of this substance was not strictly correct; the fact that it was so applied proves that the term was a common expression. Traces of earlier writing are very rarely to be detected in extant papyri. Indeed, the supply of that material must have been so abundant that it was hardly necessary to go to the trouble of preparing a papyrus, already used, for a second writing.

In the early period of palimpsests, vellum MSS. were no doubt also washed rather than scraped. The original surface of the material, at all events, was not so thoroughly defaced as was afterwards the case. In course of time, by atmospheric action or other chemical causes, the original writing would to some extent reappear; and it is thus

that so many of the capital and uncial palimpsests have been successfully deciphered. In the later middle ages the surface of the vellum
was scraped away and the writing with it. The reading of the later
examples is therefore very difficult or altogether impossible. Besides
actual erasure, various recipes for effacing the writing have been
found, such as to soften the surface with milk and meal, and then
to rub with pumice. In the case of such a process being used, total
obliteration must almost inevitably have been the result. To intensify
the traces of the original writing, when such exist, various chemical
reagents have been tried with more or less success. The old method
of smearing the vellum with tincture of gall restored the writing, but
did irreparable damage by blackening the surface, and, as the stain
grew darker in course of time, by rendering the text altogether il-
legible. Of modern reagents the most harmless appears to be hydro-
sulphate of ammonia; but this also must be used with caution.

The primary cause of the destruction of vellum MSS. by wilful
obliteration was, it need hardly be said, the dearth of material. In
the case of Greek MSS., so great was the consumption of old codices
for the sake of the material, that a synodal decree of the year 691
forbade the destruction of MSS. of the Scriptures or the church
fathers—imperfect or injured volumes excepted. The decline of the
vellum trade also on the introduction of paper caused a scarcity which
was only to be made good by recourse to material already once used.
Vast destruction of the broad quartos of the early centuries of our
era took place in the period which followed the fall of the Roman
Empire. The most valuable Latin palimpsests are accordingly found
in the volumes which were remade from the 7th to the 9th centuries,
a period during which the large volumes referred to must have been
still fairly numerous. Late Latin palimpsests rarely yield anything of
value. It has been remarked that no entire work has been found in
any instance in the original text of a palimpsest, but that portions of
many works have been taken to make up a single volume. These facts
prove that scribes were indiscriminate in supplying themselves with
material from any old volumes that happened to be at hand. (E.M.T.)

PEPYS, SAMUEL (1633–1703), (Diary of).

The other Pepys, whom Sir Walter Scott called "that curious fellow,"
was revealed in 1825, when his secret diary was partly published.
The first entry was made on the 1st of January 1660, the last on the
31st of May 1669, when the increasing weakness of his eyes, which
had given him trouble since 1664, compelled him to cease writing in

the conditions he imposed upon himself. If there is in all the literature of the world a book which can be called "unique" with strict propriety it is this. Confessions, diaries, journals, autobiographies abound, but such a revelation of a man's self has not yet been discovered. The diary is a thing apart by virtue of three qualities which are rarely found in perfection when separate and nowhere else in combination. It was secret; it was full; and it was honest. That Pepys meant it for his own eye alone is clear. He wrote it in Shelton's system of tachygraphy published in 1641, which he complicated by using foreign languages or by varieties of his own invention whenever he had to record the passages least fit to be seen by his servants or by "all the world." Relying on his cypher he put down whatever he saw, heard, felt or imagined, every motion of his mind, every action of his body. And he noted all this, not as he desired it to appear to others, but as it was to his seeing. The result is "a human document" of amazing vitality. The man who displays himself to himself in the diary is often odious, greedy, cowardly, casuistical, brutal. He tells how he kicked his cook, and blacked his wife's eye, and was annoyed when others saw what he had done. He notes how he compelled the wives of unfortunate men who came to draw their husband's pay at the navy office to prostitute themselves; how he took "compliments," that is to say gifts, from all who had business to do with the navy office; how he got tipsy and suffered from sick headache; how he repented, made vows of sobriety, and found casuistical excuses for breaking them. The style is as peculiar as the matter—colloquial, garrulous, racy from simplicity of language, and full of the unconscious humour which is never absent from a truthful account of the workings of nature in the average sensual man. His position enabled him to see much. His complete harmony with the animalism and vulgarity of the Restoration makes him a valuable witness for his time. To his credit must be put the facts that he knew the animalism and vulgarity to be what they were; that he had a real love of music and gave help to musicians, Cesare Morelli for instance; that though he made money out of his places he never allowed bad work to be done for the navy if he could help it; that he was a hard worker; and that he had a capacity for such acts of kindness and generosity as are compatible with a gross temperament and a pedestrian ambition.

◈ STEVENSON, ROBERT LOUIS (1850–1894), (Character of).

The charm of the personal character of Stevenson and the romantic vicissitudes of his life are so predominant in the minds of all who knew him, or lived within earshot of his legend, that they made the ultimate position which he will take in the history of English literature somewhat difficult to decide. That he was the most attractive figure of a man of letters in his generation is admitted; and the acknowledged fascination of his character was deepened, and was extended over an extremely wide circle of readers, by the publication in 1899 of his *Letters,* which have subdued even those who were rebellious to the entertainment of his books. It is therefore from the point of view of its "charm" that the genius of Stevenson must be approached, and in this respect there was between himself and his books, his manners and his style, his practice and his theory, a very unusual harmony. Very few authors of so high a class have been so consistent, or have made their conduct so close a reflection of their philosophy. This unity of the man in his work makes it difficult, for one who knew him, to be sure that one rightly gauges the purely literary significance of the latter. There are some living who still hear in every page of Stevenson the voice of the man himself, and see in every turn of his language his flashing smile. So far, however, as it is possible to disengage one's self from this captivation, it may be said that the mingling of distinct and original vision with a singularly conscientious handling of the English language, in the sincere and wholesome self-consciousness of the strenuous artist, seems to be the central feature of Stevenson as a writer by profession. He was always assiduously graceful, always desiring to present his idea, his image, his rhapsody, in as persuasive a light as possible and, particularly, with as much harmony as possible. He had mastered his manner and, as one may say, learned his trade, in the exercise of criticism and the reflective parts of literature, before he surrendered himself to that powerful creative impulse which had long been tempting him, so that when, in mature life, he essayed the portraiture of invented character he came to it unhampered by any imperfection of language. This distinguished mastery of style, and love of it for its own sake within the bounds of good sense and literary decorum, gave him a pre-eminence among the story-tellers of his time. No doubt it is still by his romances that Stevenson keeps the wider circle of his readers. But many hold that his letters and essays are finer contributions to pure literature, and that on these exquisite mixtures of wisdom, pathos, melody and humour his fame is likely to be ultimately based. In verse he had a touch far less sure than in prose. Here we find less evidence of sedulous workmanship, yet not infrequently a piercing sweetness, a depth of emotion, a sincere and spontaneous lovableness, which are irresistibly touching and inspiring.

The personal appearance of Stevenson has often been described: he was tall, extremely thin, dark-haired, restless, compelling attention with the lustre of his wonderful brown eyes. In the existing portraits of him those who never saw him are apt to discover a strangeness which seems to them sinister or even affected. This is a consequence of the false stability of portraiture, since in life the unceasing movement of light in the eyes, the mobility of the mouth, and the sympathy and sweetness which radiated from all the features, precluded the faintest notion of want of sincerity. Whatever may be the ultimate order of reputation among his various books, or whatever posterity may ultimately see fit to ordain as regards the popularity of any of them, it is difficult to believe that the time will ever come in which Stevenson will not be remembered as the most beloved of the writers of that age which he did so much to cheer and stimulate by his example. (E.G.)

∾ THOREAU, HENRY DAVID (1817–1862),

American recluse, naturalist and writer, was born at Concord, Massachusetts, on the 12th of July 1817. To Thoreau this Concord country contained all of beauty and even grandeur that was necessary to the worshipper of nature: he once journeyed to Canada; he went west on one occasion; he sailed and explored a few rivers; for the rest, he haunted Concord and its neighbourhood as faithfully as the stork does its ancestral nest. John Thoreau, his father, who married the daughter of a New England clergyman, was the son of a John Thoreau of the isle of Jersey, who, in Boston, married a Scottish lady of the name of Burns. This last-named John was the son of Philippe Thoreau and his wife Marie le Gallais, persons of pure French blood, settled at St Helier, in Jersey. From his New England Puritan mother, from his Scottish grandmother, from his Jersey-American grandfather and from his remoter French ancestry Thoreau inherited distinctive traits: the Saxon element perhaps predominated, but the "hauntings of Celtism" were prevalent and potent. The stock of the Thoreaus was a robust one; and in Concord the family, though never wealthy nor officially influential, was ever held in peculiar respect. As a boy, Henry drove his mother's cow to the pastures, and thus early became enamoured of certain aspects of nature and of certain delights of solitude. At school and at Harvard University he in nowise distinguished himself, though he as an intelligently receptive student; he became, however, proficient enough in Greek, Latin, and the more general acquirements to enable him to act for a time as a master. But long before this he had become apprenticed to the learning of nature in preference to that of man: when only twelve years of age he had made collections for Agassiz, who had then just arrived in America, and already the meadows and the hedges and the stream-sides had become cabinets of rare knowledge to him. On the desertion of schoolmastering as a profession, Thoreau became a lecturer and author, though it was the labour of his hands which mainly supported him through many years of his life: professionally he was a surveyor. In the effort to reduce the practice of economy to a fine art he arrived at the conviction that the less labour a man did, over and above the positive demands of necessity, the better for him and for the community at large; he would have had the order of the week reversed— six days of rest for one of labour. It was in 1845 he made the now famous experiment of Walden. Desirous of proving to himself and others that man could be as independent of this kind as the nest-building bird, Thoreau retired to a hut of his own construction on the pine-slope over against the shores of Walden Pond—a hut which he built, furnished and kept in order entirely by the labour of his own hands. During the two years of his residence in Walden woods he lived by the exercise of a little surveying, a little job-work and the tillage of a few acres of ground which produced him his beans and potatoes. His absolute independence was as little gained as if he had camped out in Hyde Park; relatively he lived the life of a recluse. He read considerably, wrote abundantly, thought actively if not widely, and came to know beasts, birds and fishes with an intimacy more extraordinary than was the case with St Francis of Assisi. Birds came at his call, and forgot their hereditary fear of man; beasts lipped and caressed him; the very fish in lake and stream would glide, unfearful, between his hands. This exquisite familiarity with bird and beast would make us love the memory of Thoreau if his egotism were triply as arrogant, if his often meaningless paradoxes were even more absurd, if his sympathies were even less humanitarian than we know them to have been. His *Walden,* the record of this fascinating two years' experience, must always remain a production of great interest and considerable psychological value. Some years before Thoreau took to Walden woods he made the chief friendship of his life, that with Emerson. He became one of the famous circle of the transcendentalists, always keenly preserving his own individuality amongst such more or less potent natures as Emerson, Hawthorne and Margaret Fuller. From Emerson he gained more than from any man, alive or dead; and, though the older philosopher both enjoyed and learned from the association with the younger, it cannot be said that the gain was equal. There was nothing electrical in Thoreau's intercourse with his fellow men; he gave off no spiritual sparks. He absorbed intensely, but when called upon to illuminate in turn was found wanting. It is with a sense of relief that we read of his having really been stirred into active enthusiasm anent the wrongs done the ill-fated John Brown. With children he was affectionate and gentle, with old people and strangers considerate. In a word, he loved his kind as animals, but did not seem to find them as interesting as those furred and feathered. In 1847 Thoreau left Walden Lake abruptly, and for a time occupied himself with lead-pencil making, the parental trade. He never married, thus further fulfilling his policy of what one of his essayist-biographers has termed "indulgence in fine renouncements." At the comparatively early age of forty-five he died, on the 6th of May 1862. His grave is in the Sleepy Hollow cemetery at Concord, beside those of Hawthorne and Emerson.

Thoreau's fame will rest on *Walden; or, Life in the Woods* (Boston, 1854), and the *Excursions* (Boston, 1863), though he wrote nothing which is not deserving of notice. Up till his thirtieth year he dabbled in verse, but he had little ear for metrical music, and he lacked the spiritual impulsiveness of the true poet. His weakness as a philosopher is his tendency to base the laws of the universe on the experience-born, thought-produced convictions of one man—himself. His weakness as a writer is the too frequent striving after antithesis and paradox. If he had had all his own originality without the itch of appearing original, he would have made his fascination irresistible. As it is, Thoreau holds a unique place. He was a naturalist, but absolutely devoid of the pedantry of science; a keen observer, but no retailer of disjointed facts. He thus holds sway over two domains: he had the adherence of the lovers of fact and of the children of fancy. He must always be read, whether lovingly or interestedly, for he has all the variable charm, the strange saturninity, the contradictions, austerities and delightful surprises, of Nature herself.

TRISTAN, or TRISTRAM, one of the most famous heroes of medieval romance. In the earlier versions of his story he is the son of Rivalîn, a prince of North West Britain, and Blancheflor, sister to King Mark of Cornwall. Rivalîn is killed in battle, and Blancheflor, after giving birth to a son, dies of grief. The boy is brought up as his own by Roâld, or Rual, seneschal of the kingdom, who has him carefully trained in all chivalric and courtly arts. With the possible exception of Horn, Tristan is by far the most accomplished hero in the whole range of knightly romance; a finished musician, linguist and chess-player, no one can rival him in more knightly arts, in horse-manship or fencing. He has, besides, the whole science of "venérie" at his finger-tips; in fact Tristan is the "Admirable Crichton" of me-dieval romance, there is nothing he cannot do, and that superlatively well—it must be regretfully admitted that he is also a most accom-plished liar! Attracted by his gifts, pirates from the North Sea kidnap the boy, but terrified by the storms which subsequently beset them, put him ashore on the coast of Cornwall, whence he finds his way to the court of his uncle King Mark. Here we have a first proof of his talent for romancing; for alike to two pilgrims who show him the road and to the huntsmen of Mark's court (whom he instructs in the rightful method of cutting up and disposing the quarry), Tristan invents different, and most detailed, fictions of his land and parent-age. He becomes a great favourite at court, and when Roâld, who has sought his young lord far and wide, at last reaches Tintagel, Mark welcomes the revelation of Tristan's identity with joy. Cornwall is at this time in subjection to the king of Ireland, Gormond, and every third year must pay tribute; the Irish champion, Morôlt, brother to the queen, arrives to claim his toll of thirty youths and as many maidens. The Cornish knights (who in Arthurian romance are always represented as hopeless cowards), dare not contest his claim but Tris-tan challenges him to single combat, slays him and frees Cornwall from tribute. Unfortunately he himself has been wounded in the fight, and that by a poisoned weapon; and none but the queen of Ireland, Isôlt, or Iseult, possessed the secret of healing. Tristan causes himself to be placed in a boat with his harp, and committed to the waves, which carry him to the shores of Ireland. There he gives himself out for a minstrel, Tantris, and as such is tended and healed by Queen Iseult and her daughter of the same name. When recovered he makes a plausible excuse for leaving Ireland (pretending he has left a wife in his native land) and returns to Cornwall. His uncle receives him with joy, but the barons of the court are bitterly jealous and plot his destruction. They persuade Mark that he should marry, and Tristan, who has sung the praises of the princess Iseult, is des-patched to Ireland to demand her hand, a most dangerous errand, as Gormond, incensed at the death of Morôlt, has sworn to slay any Cornish knight who sets foot in Ireland. Tristan undertakes the mis-sion, though he stipulates that he shall be accompanied by twenty of the barons, greatly to their disgust. His good fortune, however, does not forsake him; he lands in Ireland just as a fierce dragon is dev-astating the country, and the king has promised the hand of the princess to the slayer of the monster. Tristan achieves this feat, but, overcome by the venom exhaled from the dragon's tongue, which he has cut out, falls in a swoon. The seneschal of the court, a coward who has been watching for such an opportunity, cuts off the dragon's head, and, presenting it to the king, claims the reward, much to the dismay of Iseult and her mother. Suspecting that the seneschal is not really the slayer of the dragon, mother and daughter go secretly to the scene of the combat, find Tristan, whom they recognize as the minstrel, Tantris, and bring him back to the palace. They tend him in secret, but one day, through the medium of a splinter from his sword, which had remained fixed in Morôlt's skull, and been preserved by the queen, the identity of Tantris and Tristan is made clear. The princess would slay him, but is withheld by her mother, who sees they have need of Tristan's aid to unmask the seneschal. This is done in the presence of the court; Tristan is pardoned, formally declares his errand, and receives the hand of Iseult for his uncle King Mark.

Tristan and Iseult set sail for Cornwall, Iseult accompanied by her waiting-woman, Brangaene (who, in some versions, is also a kinswoman), to whose care the queen, skilled in magic arts, confides a love-potion. This is intended to be drunk by king and queen on their bridal night and will ensure their undying love for each other. Unhappily, on the voyage, by some mistake (accounted for in different ways), Tristan and Iseult drink the love drink, and are forthwith seized with a fatal passion each for the other. From this moment begins a long-drawn-out series of tricks and subterfuges, undertaken with the view of deceiving Mark, whose suspicions, excited by sundry of his courtiers, from time to time get beyond his control, and are as often laid to rest by some clever ruse on the part of his nephew, or his wife, ably seconded by Brangaene. In the poems, Mark is, as a rule, represented in a favourable light, a gentle, kindly man, deeply attached to both Tristan and Iseult, and only too ready to allow his suspicions to be dispelled by any plausible explanation they may choose to offer. At the same time the fact that the lovers are the helpless victims of the fatal force of a magic spell is insisted upon, in order that their career of falsehood and deception may not deprive them of sympathy.

One episode, in especial, has been most charmingly treated by the poets. Mark, in one of his fits of jealousy, banishes Tristan and Iseult from the court; the two fly to the woods, where they lead an idyllic life, blissfully happy in each other's company. Mark, hunting in the forest, comes upon them sleeping in a cave, and as Tristan, who knows that the king is in the neighbourhood, has placed his sword between them, is convinced of their innocence. Through a cleft in the rock a ray of light falls upon Iseult's face, Mark stops up the crevice with his glove (or with grass and flowers), and goes his way, determined to recall his wife and nephew. He does so, and the same drama of plot and counter-plot is resumed. Eventually Mark surprises the two under circumstances which leave no possible room for doubt as to their mutual relation; Tristan flies for his life and takes refuge with Hoel, duke of Britanny. After some time, hearing nothing of Queen Iseult, and believing himself forgotten, he weds the duke's daughter, Iseult of the white hand, but weds her only in name, remaining otherwise faithful to Iseult of Ireland. Later on he returns to Cornwall in disguise, and has more than one interview with his mistress. Ultimately, while assisting his brother-in-law in an intrigue with the wife of a neighbouring knight, Tristan is wounded by a poisoned arrow; unable to find healing, and being near to death, he sends a messenger to bring Queen Iseult to his aid; if successful the ship which brings her is to have a white sail, if she refuses to come, a black. Iseult of the white hand overhears this, and when the ship returns, bringing Iseult to her lover's aid, either through jealousy or by pure inadvertence (both versions are given), she tells Tristan that the sail is black, whereon, despairing of seeing his love again, the hero turns his face to the wall and dies. Iseult of Ireland lands to find the city in mourning for its lord; hastening to the bier, she lays herself down beside Tristan, and with one last embrace expires. (One dramatic version represents her as finding the wife seated by the bier, and ordering her away, "Why sit ye there, ye who have slain him? Arise, and begone!") The bodies are sent to Cornwall, and Mark, learning the truth, has a fair chapel erected and lays them in tombs, one at each side of the building, when a sapling springs from the heart of Tristan, and reaching its boughs across the chapel, makes its way into the grave of Iseult. However often the tree may be cut down it never fails to grow again. (In some versions it is respectively a vine and a rose which grow from either tomb and interlace midway.)

We need have little wonder that this beautiful love-story was extremely popular throughout the middle ages. Medieval literature abounds in references to Tristan and Iseult, and their adventures were translated into many tongues and are found depicted in carvings and tapestries. (J.L.W.)

VOLTAIRE (Character of). In person Voltaire was not engaging, even as a young man. His extraordinary thinness is commemorated, among other things, by the very poor but well-known epigram attributed to Young, and identifying him at once with "Satan, Death and Sin." In old age he was a mere skeleton, with a long nose and eyes of preternatural brilliancy peering out of his wig. He never seems to have been addicted to any manly sport, and took little exercise. He was sober enough (for his day and society) in eating and drinking generally; but drank coffee, as his contemporary, counterpart and enemy, Johnson, drank tea, in a hardened and inveterate manner. It may be presumed with some certainty that his attentions to women were for the most part platonic; indeed, both on the good and the bad side of him, he was all brain. He appears to have had no great sense of natural beauty, in which point he resembled his generation (though one remarkable story is told of his being deeply affected by Alpine scenery); and, except in his passion for the stage, he does not seem to have cared much for any of the arts. Conversation and literature were, again as in Johnson's case, the sole gods of his idolatry. As for his moral character, the wholly intellectual cast of mind just referred to makes it difficult to judge that. His beliefs or absence of beliefs emancipated him from conventional scruples; and he is not a good subject for those who maintain that a nice morality may exist independently of religion. He was good-natured when not crossed, generous to dependents who made themselves useful to him, and indefatigable in defending the cause of those who were oppressed by the systems with which he was at war. But he was inordinately vain, and totally unscrupulous in gaining money, in attacking an enemy, or in protecting himself when he was threatened with danger. His peculiar fashion of attacking the popular beliefs of his time has also failed to secure the approval of some who had very little sympathy with those beliefs. The only excuse made for the alternate cringing and insult, the alternate abuse and lying, which marked his course in this matter, has been the very weak plea that a man cannot fight with a system—a plea which is sufficiently answered by the retort that a great many men have so fought and have won. Voltaire's works, and especially his private letters, constantly contain the word "l'infâme" and the expression (in full or abbreviated) "écrasez l'infâme." This has been misunderstood in many ways—the mistake going so far as in some cases to suppose that Voltaire meant Christ by this opprobrious expression. No careful and competent student of his works has ever failed to correct this gross misapprehension. "L'infâme" is not God; it is not Christ; it is not Christianity; it is not even Catholicism. Its briefest equivalent may be given as "persecuting and privileged orthodoxy" in general, and, more particularly, it is the particular system which Voltaire saw around him. (G.Sa.)

PEOPLES

Characterizations of collective behavior and customs of a people surely came to be a conversational habit born out of the British colonial experience. In the eleventh edition, such descriptions, done in a more formalized manner, were not at all a consistent feature. There are no attempts to "sum up" the national character, say, of France, Germany, Italy, or England itself. These centers of cultural authority were the standard by which the rest of the world was being measured in the eleventh edition, and thus hardly needed detailed description or summation. But geographical distance in space brought this same sense of authority—the ruler—into contact with peoples wholly different, even alien—the ruled. These were *distinct* peoples, and thus needed presentation, a kind of collective thumbnail sketch. The eleventh is full of passages where far-off races, tribes, and nations are traced out in a summary way. Wherever a criticism is voiced, it is usually founded on a perceived lack of "civilization"— civic disorder, dubious individual morality, general unreliability—in comparison to the solid values represented by the observer. As one critic of this process recently put it, ". . . cultures were ranked on an evolutionary ladder, and the upward struggle along it endowed life and history with meaning." This brand of writing is now unthinkable in our age, and indeed all of the material chosen as examples reflecting this prejudicial attitude should be taken as such— the point of view of the empire, looking out and *down* at the world. Still, there are degrees of nuance in all this, and it is not easy to readily explain or justify why such Eurocentric attitudes vary so widely within themselves. Some African tribes are here described in a comprehensive and objective manner; the careful treatment accorded Egyptian life and customs surely owes much to an illustrious predecessor in English travel literature—E. W. Lane's *Manners and Customs of the Modern Egyptians*—first published in 1836. On the other hand, the collective character of the Afghans, the Gipsies [sic], and most certainly the Greek people fall victim to the most demeaning stereotyping; it is the individual contributor's way of dealing with what he did not understand.

In this regard, the most notorious is the article on "Negro," an article which displays a prejudice worth comment and rebuttal. Its author, Thomas Athol Joyce, was an assistant in the Department of Ethnography at the British Museum, and author of numerous works on the archaeology of the Maya; he had coedited a curious two-volume anthology entitled *Women of All Nations, A Record of Their Characteristics, Habits, Manners, Customs and Influence* (1909). Just from this alone, it is difficult to understand why editor Hugh Chisholm thought him the man for the job. Joyce's article takes over much material on the "negro" from the ninth edition (equally inexplicably, written by a professor of Hindustani), and most particularly a passage describing the alleged decline of intelligence in the negro after the onset of puberty. This was written by one F. Manetta, who, according to the ninth and now T. A. Joyce in the eleventh, had made "a long study of the negro in America." Manetta is thus invoked as an expert, a scientist of human intelligence and behavior, and what he says "may be taken as generally true of the whole race."

It is nowhere indicated that Filippo Manetta was an Italian adventurer and traveler who, after five years of residence in Boston, Providence, and New York in the mid-1850s, and intrigued by the "odd tales" ("storielle disordinate") told him by Abolitionists, traveled to Virginia. There he became a tutor to the only child of a rich plantation owner who also had holdings in Louisiana; he went on to similar duties with two other "respectable and rich (plantation) families" for a total of six years just prior to the outbreak of the Civil War. Manetta's pamphlet of observations and opinions, *The Negro Race in Its Savage State in Africa and Its Double Condition of Freedman and Slave in America,* was published in Turin in 1864. His memories and vision of life in the antebellum South are crystalline—the plantation owners were well educated, multilingual, cultured, "affable, hospitable and jovial, *generosi come Cesari.*" Their slaves were always well treated, better indeed than any working class in Europe. Moreover, the slaves should consider themselves a "privileged caste" among the working peoples of the world, such is the solicitude about their well-being shown by their owner. Conditions are humane; the work day is from dawn to dusk, it is true, but two hours are generously permitted by the *padrone* at noon, three in the hottest summer months. Older and "weaker" slaves are never forced to hoe. Relations between master and slave were admirably benevolent (Manetta speaks of "reciproco sentimento d'affeto"). In six years of living in the Old South, he saw only two beatings, one for theft, the other for sodomy. He delights in telling us of his ten-year-old companion on fishing expeditions, Sam, who addresses Manetta as "Sah!"

In short, Joyce was relying on an antiquated and strongly polemical source for his declarations, to say the least. Manetta was a servant of the aristocracy of the Confederacy; in other pages of his pamphlet he excoriates Lincoln and condemns the Emancipation Proclamation, priding himself on being a propagandist in Europe for the "peculiar institution" of slavery. That an "authority" such as Manetta could have been cited in both the ninth and eleventh editions, and that a person so oddly prepared as was Thomas Athol Joyce be asked to write about such a subject remains a blemish on the book as a whole and a grave editorial lapse on the part of Hugh Chisholm. Perhaps the only accurate aspect of the article is that it gives evidence, even as late as 1910, of a lingering nostalgia and admiration in England for the Confederate cause.

In any case, when whole nations and races are portrayed in the manner so often displayed in the pages of the eleventh edition, eccentricities have to be expected. In this regard, we offer a more lengthy excerpt taken from the patronizingly whimsical article on Japan, with its fundamental argument that "the most prominent trait of Japanese disposition is gaiety of heart."

ABYSSINIANS. The Abyssinian character reflects the country's history. Murders and executions are frequent, yet cruelty is not a marked feature of their character; and in war they seldom kill their prisoners. When a man is convicted of murder, he is handed over to the relatives of the deceased, who may either put him to death or accept a ransom. When the murdered person has no relatives, the priests take upon themselves the office of avengers. The natural indolence of the people has been fostered by the constant wars, which have discouraged peaceful occupations. The soldiers live by plunder, the monks by alms. The haughtiest Abyssinian is not above begging, excusing himself with the remark, "God has given us speech for the purpose of begging." The Abyssinians are vain and selfish, irritable but easily appeased; and are an intelligent bright people, fond of gaiety. On every festive occasion, as a saint's day, birth, marriage, &c., it is customary for a rich man to collect his friends and neighbours, and kill a cow and one or two sheep. The principal parts of the cow are eaten raw while yet warm and quivering, the remainder being cut into small pieces and cooked with the favourite sauce of butter and red pepper paste. The raw meat eaten in this way is considered to be very superior in taste and much more tender than when cold. The statement by James Bruce respecting the cutting of steaks from a live cow has frequently been called in question, but there can be no doubt that Bruce actually saw what he narrates. Mutton and goat's flesh are the meats most eaten: pork is avoided on religious grounds, and the hare is never touched, possibly, as in other countries, from superstition. Many forms of game are forbidden; for example, all water-fowl. The principal drinks are *mēse*, a kind of mead, and *bousa*, a sort of beer made from fermented cakes. The Abyssinians are heavy eaters and drinkers, and any occasion is seized as an excuse for a carouse. Old and young, of both sexes, pass days and nights in these *symposia*, at which special customs and rules prevail. Little bread is eaten, the Abyssinian preferring a thin cake of durra meal or *teff*, kneaded with water and exposed to the sun till the dough begins to rise, when it is baked. Salt is a luxury; "he eats salt" being said of a spend-thrift. Bars of rock-salt, after serving as coins, are, when broken up, used as food. There is a general looseness of morals: marriage is a very slight tie, which can be dissolved at any time by either husband or wife. Polygamy is by no means uncommon. Hence there is little family affection, and what exists is only between children of the same father and mother. Children of the same father, but of different mothers, are said to be "always enemies of each other." (Samuel Gobat's *Journal of a Three Years' Residence in Abyssinia,* 1834.)

The dress of the Abyssinians is much like that of the Arabs. It consists of close-fitting drawers reaching below the knees, with a sash to hold them, and a large white robe. The Abyssinian, however, is beginning to adopt European clothes on the upper part of the body, and European hats are becoming common. The Christian Abyssinians usually go barehead and barefoot, in contrast to the Mahommedans, who wear turbans and leather sandals. The women's dress is a smock with sleeves loose to the wrist, where they fit tightly. The priests wear a white jacket with loose sleeves, a head-cloth like a turban and a special type of shoe with turned-up toes and soles projecting at the heel. In the Woldeba district hermits dress in ochre-yellow clothes, while the priests of some sects wear hides dyed red. Clothes are made of cotton, though the nobles and great people wear silk robes presented by the emperor as a mark of honour. The possessor of one of these is allowed to appear in the royal presence wearing it instead of having one shoulder bared, as is the usual Abyssinian method of showing respect. A high-born man covers himself to the mouth in the presence of inferiors. The men either cut their hair short or plait it; married women plait their hair and wind round the head a black or part-coloured silk handkerchief; girls wear their hair short. In the hot season no Abyssinian goes without a flag-shaped fan of plaited rushes. The Christain Abyssinians, men and women, wear a blue silk cord round the neck, to which is often attached a crucifix. For ornament women wear silver ankle-rings with bells, silver necklaces and silver or gold rosettes in the ears. Silver rings on fingers and also on toes are common. The women are very fond of strong scents, which are generally oils imported from India and Ceylon. The men scarcely ever appear without a long curved knife, generally they carry shield and spear as well. Although the army has been equipped with modern rifles, the common weapon of the people is the match-lock, and slings are still in use. The original arms were a sickle-shaped sword, spear and shield. The Abyssinians are great hunters and are also clever at taming wild beasts. The nobles hunt antelopes with leopards, and giraffes and ostriches with horse and greyhound. In elephant-hunting iron bullets weighing a quarter of a pound are used; throwing-clubs are employed for small game, and lions are hunted with the spear. Lion skins belong to the emperor, but the slayer keeps a strip to decorate his shield. (G.)

AFGHANS. The Afghans, inured to bloodshed from childhood, are familiar with death, and audacious in attack, but easily discouraged by failure; excessively turbulent and unsubmissive to law or discipline; apparently frank and affable in manner, espe-cially when they hope to gain some object, but capable of the grossest brutality when that hope ceases. They are unscrupulous in perjury, treacherous, vain and insatiable, passionate in vindictiveness, which they will satisfy at the cost of their own lives and in the most cruel manner. Nowhere is crime committed on such trifling grounds, or with such general impunity, though when it is punished the punish-ment is atrocious. Among themselves the Afghans are quarrelsome, intriguing and distrustful; estrangements and affrays are of constant occurrence; the traveller conceals and misrepresents the time and direction of his journey. The Afghan is by breed and nature a bird of prey. If from habit and tradition he respects a stranger within his threshold, he yet considers it legitimate to warn a neighbour of the prey that is afoot, or even to overtake and plunder his guest after he has quitted his roof. The repression of crime and the demand of taxation he regards alike as tyranny. The Afghans are eternally boasting of their lineage, their independence and their prowess. They look on the Afghans as the first of nations, and each man looks on himself as the equal of any Afghan.

They are capable of enduring great privation, and make excellent soldiers under British discipline, though there are but few in the Indian army. Sobriety and hardiness characterize the bulk of the people, though the higher classes are too often stained with deep and degrading debauchery. The first impression made by the Afghan is favourable. The European, especially if he comes from India, is charmed by their apparently frank, open-hearted, hospitable and manly manners; but the charm is not of long duration, and he finds that the Afghan is as cruel and crafty as he is independent. No trustworthy statistics exist showing either present numbers or fluctuations in the population of Afghanistan. Within the amir's dominions there are probably from four to five millions of people, and of these the vast majority are agriculturists. (T.H.H.)

AKKA (TIKKI-TIKKI), a race of African pygmies first seen by the traveller G. A. Schweinfurth in 1870, when he was in the Mangbettu country, N.W. of Albert Nyanza. The home of the Akka is the dense forest zone of the Aruwimi district of the Congo State. They form a branch of the primitive pygmy negroid race, and appear to be divided into groups, each with its own chief. Of all African "dwarfs" the Akka are believed the best representatives of the "little people" mentioned by Herodotus. Giovanni Miani, the Italian explorer who followed Schweinfurth, obtained two young Akka in exchange for a dog and a calf. These, sent to Italy in 1873, were respectively 4 ft. 4 in. and 4 ft. 8 in. high, while the tallest seen by Schweinfurth did not reach 5 ft. None of the four Akka brought to Europe in 1874 and 1876 exceeded 3 ft. 4 in. The average height of the race would seem to be somewhat under 4 ft., but sufficient measurements have not been taken to allow of a conclusive statement. Schweinfurth says the Akka have very large and almost spherical skulls (this last detail proves to be an exaggeration). They are of the colour of coffee slightly roasted, with hair almost the same colour, woolly and tufted; they have very projecting jaws, flat noses and protruding lips, which give them an "ape-like" appearance. Marked physical features are an abdominal protuberance which makes all

Akka look like pot-bellied children, and a remarkable hollowing of
the spine into a curve like an **S**. Investigation has shown that these
are not true racial characteristics, but tend to disappear, the abdominal enlargement subsiding after some weeks of regular and wholesome diet. The upper limbs are long, and the hands, according to
Schweinfurth, are singularly delicate. The lower limbs are short, relatively to the trunk, and curve in somewhat, the feet being bent in
too, which gives the Akka a topheavy, tottering gait. There is a tendency to steatopygia among the women. The Akka are nomads, living
in the forests, where they hunt game with poisoned arrows, with
pitfalls and springs set everywhere, and with traps built like huts, the
roofs of which, hung by tendrils only, fall in on the animal. They
collect ivory and honey, manufacture poison, and bring these to market to exchange for cereals, tobacco and iron weapons. They are
courageous hunters, and do not hesitate to attack even elephants,
both sexes joining in the chase. They are very agile, and are said by
the neighbouring negroes to leap about in the high grasses like grasshoppers. They are timid as children before strangers, but are declared to be malevolent and treacherous fighters. In dress, weapons
and utensils they are as the surrounding negroes. They build round
huts of branches and leaves in the forest clearings. They seem in no
way a degenerate race, but rather a people arrested in development
by the forest environment.

ARABS. Physically the Arabs are one of the
strongest and noblest races of the world. Baron de Larrey, surgeon-
general to Napoleon on his expedition to Egypt and Syria, writes:
"Their physical structure is in all respects more perfect than that of
Europeans; their organs of sense exquisitely acute, their size above
the average of men in general, their figure robust and elegant, their
colour brown; their intelligence proportionate to their physical perfection and without doubt superior, other things being equal, to that
of other nations." The typical Arab face is of an oval form, lean-
featured; the eyes a brilliant black, deep-set under bushy eyebrows;
nose aquiline, forehead straight but not high. In body the Arab is
muscular and long-limbed, but lean. Deformed individuals or dwarfs
are rare among Arabs; nor, except leprosy, which is common, does
any disease seem to be hereditary among them. They often suffer
from ophthalmia, though not in the virulent Egyptian form. They
are scrupulously clean in their persons, and take special care of their
teeth, which are generally white and even. Simple and abstemious in

their habits, they often reach an extreme yet healthy old age; nor is it common among them for the faculties of the mind to give way sooner than those of the body.

Thus, physically, they yield to few races, if any, of mankind; mentally, they surpass most, and are only kept back in the march of progress by the remarkable defect of organizing power and incapacity for combined action. Lax and imperfect as are their forms of government, it is with impatience that even these are borne; of the four caliphs who alone reigned—if reign theirs could be called—in Arabia proper, three died a violent death; and of the Wahhābi princes, the most genuine representatives in later times of pure Arab rule, almost all have met the same fate. The Arab face, which is not unkindly, but never smiling, expresses that dignity and gravity which are typical of the race. While the Arab is always polite, good-natured, manly and brave, he is also revengeful, cruel, untruthful and superstitious. Of the Arab nature Burkhardt (other authorities, *e.g.* Barth and Rohlfs, are far less complimentary) wrote: "The Arab displays his manly character when he defends his guest at the peril of his own life, and submits to the reverses of fortune, to disappointment and distress, with the most patient resignation. He is distinguished from a Turk by the virtues of pity and gratitude. The Turk is cruel, the Arab of a more kind temper; he pities and supports the wretched, and never forgets the generosity shown to him even by an enemy." The Arab will lie and cheat and swear false oaths, but once his word is pledged he may be trusted to the last. There are some oaths such as *Wallah* (by Allah) which mean nothing, but such an oath as the threefold one with *wa, bi* and *ta* as particles of swearing the meanest thief will not break. In temper, or at least in the manifestation of it, the Arab is studiously calm; and he rarely so much as raises his voice in a dispute. But this outward tranquillity covers feelings alike keen and permanent; and the remembrance of a rash jest or injurious word, uttered years before, leads only too often to that blood-revenge which is a sacred duty everywhere in Arabia.

There exist, however, marked tribal or almost semi-national diversities of character among the Arabs. Thus, the inhabitants of Hejaz are noted for courtesy and blamed for fickleness; those of Nejd are distinguished by their stern tenacity and dignity of deportment; the nations of Yemen are gentle and pliant, but revengeful; those of Hasa and Oman cheerful and fond of sport, though at the same time turbulent and unsteady. Anything approaching to a game is rare in Nejd, and in the Hejaz religion and the yearly occurrence of the pilgrim ceremonies almost exclude all public diversions; but in Yemen the well-known game of the "jerīd," or palm-stick, with dances and music is not rare. In Oman such amusements are still more frequent. Again in Yemen and Oman, coffee-houses, where people resort for conversation, and where public recitals, songs and other amusements are indulged in, stand open all day; while nothing of the sort is tolerated in Nejd. So too the ceremonies of circumcision or marriage are occasions of gaiety and pastime on the coast, but not in the central provinces.

An Arab town, or even village, except it be the merest hamlet, is invariably walled round; but seldom is a stronger material than dried earth used; the walls are occasionally flanked by towers of like construction. A dry ditch often surrounds the whole. The streets are irregular and seldom parallel. The Arab, indeed, lacks an eye for the straight. The Arab carpenter cannot form a right angle; an Arab servant cannot place a cloth square on a table. The Ka'ba at Mecca has none of its sides or angles equal. The houses are of one or two storeys, rarely of three, with flat mud roofs, little windows and no external ornament. If the town be large, the expansion of one or two streets becomes a market-place, where are ranged a few shops of eatables, drugs, coffee, cottons or other goods. Many of these shops are kept by women. The chief mosque is always near the market-place; so is also the governor's residence, which, except in size and in being more or less fortified Arab fashion, does not differ from a private house. Drainage is unthought of; but the extreme dryness of the air obviates the inconvenience and disease that under other skies could not fail to ensue, and which in the damper climates of the coast make themselves seriously felt. But the streets are roughly swept every day, each householder taking care of the roadway that lies before his own door. Whitewash and colour are occasionally used in Yemen, Hejaz and Oman; elsewhere a light ochre tint, the colour of the sun-dried bricks, predominates, and gives an Arab town the appearance at a distance of a large dust-heap in the centre of the bright green ring of gardens and palm-groves. Baked bricks are unknown in Arabia, and stone buildings are rare, especially in Nejd. Palm branches and the like, woven in wattles, form the dwellings of the poorer classes in the southern districts. Many Arab towns possess watch-towers, like huge round factory chimneys in appearance, built of sun-dried bricks, and varying in height from 50 to 100 ft. or even more. Indeed, two of these constructions at the town of Birkat-el-Mauj, in Oman, are said to be each of 170 ft. in height, and that of Nezwah, in the same province, is reckoned at 140; but these are of stone.

The principal feature in the interior of an Arab house is the "kahwah" or coffee-room. It is a large apartment spread with mats, and sometimes furnished with carpets and a few cushions. At one end is a small furnace or fireplace for preparing coffee. In this room the men congregate; here guests are received, and even lodged; women rarely enter it, except at times when strangers are unlikely to be present. Some of these apartments are very spacious and supported by pillars; one wall is usually built transversely to the compass direction of the Ka'ba; it serves to facilitate the performance of prayer by those who may happen to be in the kahwah at the appointed times. The other rooms are ordinarily small.

The Arabs are proverbially hospitable. A stranger's arrival is often the occasion of an amicable dispute among the wealthier inhabitants as to who shall have the privilege of receiving him. Arab cookery is of the simplest. Roughly-ground wheat cooked with butter; bread in thin cakes, prepared on a heated iron plate or against the walls of an open oven; a few vegetables, generally of the leguminous kinds; boiled mutton or camel's flesh, among the wealthy; dates and fruits— this is the *menu* of an ordinary meal. Rice is eaten by the rich and fish is common on the coasts. Tea, introduced only a few decades back, is now largely drunk. A food of which the Arabs are fond is locusts boiled in salt and water and then dried in the sun. They taste like stale shrimps, but there is a great sale for them. Spices are freely employed; butter much too largely for a European taste.

After eating, the hands are always washed, soap or the ashes of an alkaline plant being used. A covered censer with burning incense is then passed round, and each guest perfumes his hands, face, and sometimes his clothes; this censer serves also on first receptions and whenever special honour is intended. In Yemen and Oman scented water often does duty for it. Coffee, without milk or sugar, but flavoured with an aromatic seed brought from India, is served to all. This, too, is done on the occasion of a first welcome, when the cups often make two or three successive rounds; but, in fact, coffee is made and drunk at any time, as frequently as the desire for it may suggest itself; and each time fresh grains are sifted, roasted, pounded and boiled—a very laborious process, and one that requires in the better sort of establishments a special servant or slave for the work. Arabs generally make but one solid meal a day—that of supper, soon after sunset. Even then they do not each much, gluttony being rare among them, and even daintiness esteemed disgraceful. Wine, like other fermented drinks, is prohibited by the Koran, and is, in fact, very rarely taken, though the inhabitants of the mountains of Oman are said to indulge in it. On the coast spirits of the worst quality are sometimes procured; opium and hashish are sparingly indulged in. On the other hand, wherever Wahhābiism has left freedom of action, tobacco-smoking prevails; short pipes of clay, long pipes with large open bowls, or most frequently the water-pipe or "narghileh," being used. The tobacco smoked is generally strong and is either brought from the neighbourhood of Bagdad or grown in the country itself. The strongest quality is that of Oman; the leaf is broad and coarse, and retains its green colour even when dried; a few whiffs have been known to produce absolute stupor. The aversion of the Wahhābis to tobacco is well known; they entitle it "mukhzi" or "the shameful," and its use is punished with blows, as the public use of wine would be elsewhere.

ARMENIANS. The original inhabitants of Armenia are unknown, but, about the middle of the 9th century B.C., the mass of the people belonged to that great family of tribes which seems to have been spread over western Asia and to have had a common non-Aryan language. Mixed with these proto-Armenians, there was an important Semitic element of Assyrian and Hebrew origin. In the 7th century B.C., between 640 and 600, the country was conquered by an Aryan people, who imposed their language, and possibly their name, upon the vanquished, and formed a military aristocracy that was constantly recruited from Persia and Parthia. Politically the two races soon amalgamated, but, except in the towns, there was apparently little intermarriage, for the peasants in certain districts closely resemble the proto-Armenians, as depicted on their monuments. After the Arab and Seljuk invasions, there was a large emigration of Aryan and Semitic Armenians to Constantinople and Cilicia; and all that remained of the aristocracy was swept away by the Mongols and Tartars. This perhaps explains the diversity of type and characteristics amongst the modern Armenians. In the recesses of Mount Taurus the peasants are tall, handsome, though somewhat sharp-featured, agile and brave. In Armenia and Asia Minor they are robust, thick-set and coarse-featured, with straight black hair and large hooked noses. They are good cultivators of the soil, but are poor, superstitious, ignorant and unambitious, and they live in semi-subterranean houses as their ancestors did 800 years B.C. The townsmen, especially in the large towns, have more regular features—often of the Persian type. They are skilled artisans, bankers and merchants, and are remarkable for their industry, their quick intelligence, their aptitude for business, and for that enterprising spirit which led their ancestors, in Roman times, to trade with Scythia, China and India. The upper classes are polished and well educated, and many have occupied high positions in the public service in Turkey, Russia, Persia and Egypt. The Armenians are essentially an Oriental people, possessing, like the Jews, whom they resemble in their exclusiveness and widespread dispersion, a remarkable tenacity of race and faculty of adaptation to circumstances. They are frugal, sober, industrious and intelligent, and their sturdiness of character has enabled them to preserve their nationality and religion under the sorest trials. They are strongly attached to old manners and customs, but have also a real desire for progress which is full of promise. On the other hand they are greedy of gain, quarrelsome in small matters, self-seeking and wanting in stability; and they are gifted with a tendency to exaggeration and a love of intrigue which has had an unfortunate influence on their history. They are deeply separated by religious differences, and their mutual jealousies, their inordinate vanity, their versatility and their cosmopolitan character must always be an obstacle to the realization of the dreams of the nationalists. The want of courage and self-reliance, the deficiency in truth and honesty sometimes noticed in connexion with them, are doubtless due to long servitude under an unsympathetic government. (C.W.W.)

AUSTRALIAN, ABORIGINAL. Physically the typical Australian is the equal of the average European in height, but is inferior in muscular development, the legs and arms being of a leanness which is often emphasized by an abnormal corpulence. The bones are delicately formed, and there is the lack of calf usual in black races. The skull is abnormally thick and the cerebral capacity small. The head is long and somewhat narrow, the forehead broad and receding, with overhanging brows, the eyes sunken, large and black, the nose thick and very broad at the nostrils. The mouth is large and the lips thick but not protuberant. The teeth are large, white and strong. In old age they appear much ground down; particularly is this the case with women, who chew the different kinds of fibres, of which they make nets and bags. The lower jaw is heavy; the cheekbones somewhat high, and the chin small and receding. The neck is thicker and shorter than that of most Europeans. The colour of the skin is a deep copper or chocolate, never sooty black. When born, the Australian baby is of a much lighter colour than its parents and remains so for about a week. The hair is long, black or very dark auburn, wavy and sometimes curly, but never woolly, and the men have luxuriant beards and whiskers, often of an auburn tint, while the whole body inclines to hairiness. On the Balonne river, Queensland, Baron Mikluho Maclay found a group of hairless natives. The head hair is usually matted with grease and dirt, but when clean is fine and glossy. The skin gives out an objectionable odour, owing to the habit of anointing the body with fish-oils, but the true fetor of the negro is lacking in the Australian. The voices of the blackfellows are musical. Their mental faculties, though inferior to those of the Polynesian race, are not contemptible. They have much acuteness of perception for the relations of individual objects, but little power of generalization. No word exists in their language for such general terms as tree, bird or fish; yet they have invented a name for every species of vegetable and animal they know. The grammatical structure of some north Australian languages has a considerable degree of refinement. The verb presents a variety of conjugations, expressing nearly all the moods and tenses of the Greek. There is a dual, as well as a plural form in the declension of verbs, nouns, pronouns and adjectives. The distinction of genders is not marked, except in proper names of men and women. All parts of speech, except adverbs, are declined by terminational inflections. There are words for the elementary numbers, one, two, three; but "four" is usually expressed by "two-two." They have no idea of decimals. The number and diversity of separate languages is bewildering.

In disposition the Australians are a bright, laughter-loving folk, but they are treacherous, untruthful and hold human life cheaply. They have no great physical courage. They are mentally in the condition of children. None of them has an idea of what the West calls morality, except the simple one of right or wrong arising out of property. A wife will be beaten without mercy for unfaithfulness to her husband, but the same wife will have had to submit to the first-night promiscuity, a widespread revel which Roth shows is a regular custom in north-west-central Queensland. A husband claims his wife as his absolute property, but he has no scruple in handing her over for a time to another man. There is, however, no proof that anything like community of women or unlimited promiscuity exists anywhere. It would be wrong, however, to conclude that moral considerations have led up to this state of things. Of sexual morality, in the everyday sense of the word, there is none. In his treatment of women the aboriginal may be ranked lower than even the Fuegians. Yet the Australian is capable of strong affections, and the blind (of whom there have always been a great number) are cared for, and are often the best fed in a tribe.

The Australians when first discovered were found to be living in almost a prehistoric simplicity. Their food was the meat they killed in the chase, or seeds and roots, grubs or reptiles. They never, in any situation, cultivated the soil for any kind of food-crop. They never reared any kind of cattle, or kept any domesticated animal except the dog, which probably came over with them in their canoes. They nowhere built permanent dwellings, but contented themselves with mere hovels for temporary shelter. They neither manufactured nor possessed any chattels beyond such articles of clothing, weapons, ornaments and utensils as they might carry on their persons, or in the family store-bag for daily use. In most districts both sexes are entirely nude. Sometimes in the south during the cold season they wear a cloak of skin or matting, fastened with a skewer, but open on the right-hand side.

When going through the bush they sometimes wear an apron of skins, for protection merely. No headgear is worn, except sometimes a net to confine the hair, a bunch of feathers, or the tails of small animals. The breast or back, of both sexes, is usually tattooed, or rather, scored with rows of hideous raised scars, produced by deep gashes made at puberty. Their dwellings for the most part are either bowers, formed of the branches of trees, or hovels of piled logs, loosely covered with grass or bark, which they can erect in an hour, wherever they encamp. But some huts of a more substantial form were seen by Captain Matthew Flinders on the south-east coast in 1799, and by Captain King and Sir T. Mitchell on the north-east, where they no longer appear. The ingenuity of the race is mostly exhibited in the manufacture of their weapons of warfare and the chase. While the use of the bow and arrow does not seem to have occurred to them, the spear and axe are in general use, commonly made of hard-wood; the hatchets of stone, and the javelins pointed with stone or bone. The characteristic weapon of the Australian is the boomerang. Their nets, made by women, either of the tendons of animals or the fibres of plants, will catch and hold the kangaroo or the emu, or the very large fish of Australian rivers. Canoes of bent bark, for the inland waters, are hastily prepared at need; but the inlets and straits of the north-eastern sea-coast are navigated by larger canoes and rafts of a better construction. As to food, they are omnivorous. In central Queensland and elsewhere, snakes, both venomous and harmless, are eaten, the head being first carefully smashed to pulp with a stone.

∽ **BONGO** (DOR OR DERAN), a tribe of Nilotic negroes, probably related to the Zandeh tribes of the Welle district,
inhabiting the south-west portion of the Bahr-el-Ghazal province,
Anglo-Egyptian Sudan. G. A. Schweinfurth, who lived two years
among them, declares that before the advent of the slave-raiders, c.
1850, they numbered at least 300,000. Slave-raiders, and later the
dervishes, greatly reduced their numbers, and it was not until the
establishment of effective control by the Sudan government (1904–
1906) that recuperation was possible. The Bongo formerly lived in
countless little independent and peaceful communities, and under
the Sudan government they again manage their own affairs. Their
huts are well built, and sometimes 24 ft. high. The Bongo are a race
of medium height, inclined to be thick-set, with a red-brown complexion—"like the soil upon which they reside"—and black hair.
Schweinfurth declares their heads to be nearly round, no other African race, to his knowledge, possessing a higher cephalic index. The
women incline to steatopygia in later life, and this deposit of fat,
together with the tail of bast which they wore, gave them, as they
walked, Schweinfurth says, the appearance of "dancing baboons."
The Bongo men formerly wore only a loin-cloth, and many dozen
iron rings on the arms (arranged to form a sort of armour), while
the women had simply a girdle, to which was attached a tuft of grass.
Both sexes now largely use cotton cloths as dresses. The tribal ornaments consist of nails or plugs which are passed through the lower
lip. The women often wear a disk several inches in diameter in this
fashion, together with a ring or a bit of straw in the upper lip, straws
in the *alae* of the nostrils, and a ring in the *septum*. The Bongo, unlike
other of the upper Nile Negroes, are not great cattle-breeders, but
employ their time in agriculture. The crops mostly cultivated are
sorghum, tobacco, sesame and durra. The Bongo eat the fruits, tubers
and fungi in which the country is rich. They also eat almost every
creature—bird, beast, insect and reptile, with the exception of the
dog. They despise no flesh, fresh or putrid. They drive the vulture
from carrion, and eat with relish the intestinal worms of the ox. Earth-
eating, too, is common among them. They are particularly skilled in
the smelting and working of iron. Iron forms the currency of the
country, and is extensively employed for all kinds of useful and ornamental purposes. Bongo spears, knives, rings, and other articles
are frequently fashioned with great artistic elaboration. They have a
variety of musical instruments—drums, stringed instruments, and
horns—in the practice of which they take great delight; and they
indulge in a vocal recitative which seems intended to imitate a succes-

sion of natural sounds. Schweinfurth says that Bongo music is like the raging of the elements. Marriage is by purchase; and a man is allowed to acquire three wives, but not more. Tattooing is partially practised. As regards burial, the corpse is bound in a crouching position with the knees drawn up to the chin; men are placed in the grave with the face to the north, and women with the face to the south. The form of the grave is peculiar, consisting of a niche in a vertical shaft, recalling the mastaba graves of the ancient Egyptians. The tombs are frequently ornamented with rough wooden figures intended to represent the deceased. Of the immortality of the soul they have no defined notion; and their only approach to a knowledge of a beneficent deity consists in a vague idea of luck. They have, however, a most intense belief in a great variety of petty goblins and witches, which are essentially malignant. Arrows, spears and clubs form their weapons, the first two distinguished by a multiplicity of barbs. Euphorbia juice is used as a poison for the arrows. Shields are rare. Their language is musical, and abounds in the vowels *o* and *a;* its vocabulary of concrete terms is very rich, but the same word has often a great variety of meanings. The grammatical structure is simple. As a race the Bongo are gentle and industrious, and exhibit strong family affection.

DINKA (called by the Arabs *Jange*), a widely spread negro people dwelling on the right bank of the White Nile to about 12°N., around the mouth of the Bahr-el-Ghazal, along the right bank of that river and on the banks of the lower Sobat. Like the Shilluk, they were greatly harried from the north by Nuba-Arabic tribes, but remained comparatively free owing to the vast extent of their country, estimated to cover 40,000 sq. m., and their energy in defending themselves. They are a tall race with skins of almost blue black. The men wear practically no clothes, married women having a short apron, and unmarried girls a fringe of iron cones round the waist. They tattoo themselves with tribal marks, and extract the lower incisors; they also pierce the ears and lip for the attachment of ornaments, and wear a variety of feather, iron, ivory and brass ornaments. Nearly all shave the head, but some give the hair a reddish colour by moistening it with animal matter. Polygamy is general; some headmen have as many as thirty or more wives; but six is the average number. They are great cattle and sheep breeders; the men tend their beasts with great devotion, despising agriculture, which is left to the women; the cattle are called by means of drums. Save under stress of famine cattle are never killed for food, the people subsisting largely on durra. The Dinkas reverence the cow, and snakes, which they call "brothers." Their folklore recognizes a good and evil deity; one of the two wives of the good deity created man, and the dead go to live with him in a great park filled with animals of enormous size. The evil deity created cripples. The Dinka came, in 1899, under the control of the Sudan government, justice being administered as far as possible in accord with tribal custom. A compendium of Dinka laws was compiled by Captain H. D. E. O'Sullivan.

⟨∾⟩ EGYPTIANS.

It remains here to describe characteristics and customs common to the Moslem Egyptians and particularly to those of the cities. In some respects the manner of life of the natives has been modified by contact with Europeans, and what follows depicts in general the habits of the people little affected by western culture. With regard to physical characteristics the Egyptians are of full average height (the men are mostly 5 ft. 8 in. or 5 ft. 9 in), and both sexes are remarkably well proportioned and of strong physique. The Cairenes and the inhabitants of Lower Egypt generally have a clear complexion and soft skin of a light yellowish colour; those of Middle Egypt have a tawny skin, and the dwellers in Upper Egypt a deep bronze or brown complexion. The face of the men is of a fine oval, forehead prominent but seldom high, straight nose, eyes deep set, black and brilliant, mouth well formed, but with rather full lips, regular teeth beautifully made, and beard usually black and curly but scanty. Moustaches are worn, while the head is shaved save for a small tuft (called *shusheh*) upon the crown. As to the women, "from the age of about fourteen to that of eighteen or twenty, they are generally models of beauty in body and limbs; and in countenance most of them are pleasing, and many exceedingly lovely; but soon after they have attained their perfect growth, they rapidly decline." There are few Egyptian women over forty who retain either good looks or good figures. "The forms of womanhood begin to develop themselves about the ninth and tenth year: at the age of fifteen or sixteen they generally attain their highest degree of perfection. With regard to their complexions, the same remarks apply to them as to the men, with only this difference that their faces, being generally veiled when they go abroad, are not quite so much tanned as those of the men. They are characterized, like the men, by a fine oval countenance, though in some instances it is rather broad. The eyes, with very few exceptions, are black, large and of a long almond-form, with long and beautiful lashes, and an exquisitely soft, bewitching expression—eyes more beautiful can hardly be conceived: their charming effect is much heightened by the concealment of the other features (however pleasing the latter may be), and is rendered still more striking by a practice universal among the females of the higher and middle classes, and very common among those of the lower orders, which is that of blackening the edge of the eyelids both above and below the eye, with a black powder called 'kohl' " (Lane, *Modern Egyptians*). Both sexes, but especially the women, tattoo several parts of the person, and the women stain their hands and feet with the red dye of the henna.

The dress of the men of the upper and middle classes who have not adopted European clothing—a practice increasingly common—consists of cotton drawers, and a cotton or silk shirt with very wide sleeves. Above these are generally worn a waistcoat without sleeves, and a long vest of silk, called kaftan, which has hanging sleeves, and reaches nearly to the ankles. The kaftan is confined by the girdle, which is a silk scarf, or cashmere or other woollen shawl. Over all is worn a long cloth robe, the gibbeh (or jibbeh) somewhat resembling the kaftan in shape, but having shorter sleeves, and being open in front. The dress of the lower orders is the shirt and drawers, and waistcoat, with an outer shirt of blue cotton or brown woollen stuff; some wear a kaftan. The head-dress is the red cloth fez or tarbush round which a turban is usually worn. Men who have otherwise adopted European costume retain the tarbush. Many professions and religions, &c., are distinguished by the shape and colour of the turban, and various classes, and particularly servants, are marked by the form and colour of their shoes; but the poor go usually barefoot. Many ladies of the upper classes now dress in European style, with certain modifications, such as the head-veil. Those who retain native costume wear a very full pair of silk trousers, bright coloured stockings (usually pink), and a close-fitting vest with hanging sleeves and skirts, open down the front and at the sides, and long enough to turn up and fasten into the girdle, which is generally a cashmere shawl; a cloth jacket, richly embroidered with gold, and having short sleeves, is commonly worn over the vest. The hair in front is combed down over the forehead and cut across in a straight line; behind it is divided into very many small plaits, which hang down the back, and are lengthened by silken cords, and often adorned with gold coins and ornaments. A small tarbush is worn on the back of the head, sometimes having a plate of gold fixed on the crown, and a handkerchief is tastefully bound round the temples. The women of the lower orders

have trousers of printed or dyed cotton, and a close waistcoat. All
wear the long and elegant head-veil. This is a simple "breadth" of
muslin, which passes over the head and hangs down behind, one side,
being drawn forward over the face in the presence of a man. A lady's
veil is of white muslin, embroidered at the ends in gold and colours;
that of a person of the lower class is simply dyed blue. In going abroad
the ladies wear above their indoor dress a loose robe of coloured silk
without sleeves, and nearly open at the sides, and above it a large
enveloping piece of black silk, which is brought over the head, and
gathered round the person by the arms and hands on each side. A
face-veil entirely conceals the features, except the eyes; it is a long
and narrow piece of thick white muslin, reaching to a little below the
knees. The women of the lower orders have the same out-door dress
of different materials and colour. Ladies use slippers of yellow morocco, and abroad, inner boots of the same material, above which
they wear, in either case, thick shoes, having only toes. The poor wear
red shoes, very like those of the men. The women, especially in Upper
Egypt, not infrequently wear nose-rings.

Children, though often neglected, are not unkindly treated, and
reverence for their parents and the aged is early inculcated. They
are also well grounded in the leading doctrines of Islam. Boys are
circumcised at the age of five or six years, when the boy is paraded,
generally with a bridal procession, on a gaily caparisoned horse and
dressed in woman's clothes. Most parents send their boys to school
where a knowledge of reading and writing Arabic—the common
tongue of the Egyptians—is obtainable, and from the closing years
of the 19th century a great desire for the education of girls has arisen.

It is deemed disreputable for a young man not to marry when he
has attained a sufficient age; there are, therefore, few unmarried
men. Girls, in like manner, marry very young, some at ten years of
age, and few remain single beyond the age of sixteen; they are generally very prolific. The bridegroom never sees his future wife before
the wedding night, a custom rendered more tolerable than it otherwise might be by the facility of divorce. A dowry is always given,
and a simple marriage ceremony performed by a *fiki* (a school-master,
or one who recites the Koran, properly one learned in *fiqh*, Mahommedan law) in the presence of two witnesses. The bridal of a virgin
is attended with great festivity and rejoicing, a grandee's wedding
sometimes continuing eleven days and nights. On the last day, which
should be that terminating with the eve of Friday, or of Monday, the
bride is taken in procession to the bridegroom's house, accompanied
by her female friends, and a band of musicians, jugglers, wrestlers,

&c. As before stated, a boy about to be circumcised joins in such a procession, or, frequently, a succession of such boys. Though allowed by his religion four wives, most Egyptians are monogamists. A man may, however, possess any number of concubines, who, though objects of jealousy to the legal wife, are tolerated by her in consideration of her superior position and power over them, a power which she often uses with great tyranny; but certain privileges are possessed by concubines, especially if they have borne sons to their master. A divorce is rendered obligatory by the simple words "Thou art divorced." Repudiation may take place twice without being final, but if the husband repeats thrice "Thou art divorced" the separation is absolute. In that case the dowry must be returned to the wife.

Elaborate ceremonies are observed at funerals. Immediately on death the corpse is turned towards Mecca, and the women of the household, assisted by hired mourners, commence their peculiar wailing, while fikis recite portions of the Koran. The funeral takes place on the day of the death, if that happen in the morning; otherwise on the next day. The corpse, having been washed and shrouded, is placed in an open bier, covered with a cashmere shawl, in the case of a man; or in a closed bier, having a post in front, on which are placed feminine ornaments, in that of a woman or child. The funeral procession is headed by a number of poor, and generally blind, men, chanting the profession of the faith, followed by male friends of the deceased, and a party of schoolboys, also chanting, generally from a poem descriptive of the state of the soul after death. Then follows the bier, borne on the shoulders of friends, who are relieved by the passers-by, such an act being deemed highly meritorious. Behind come the women relatives and the hired wailers. On the way to the cemetery the corpse is generally carried to some revered mosque. Here the funeral service is performed by the imam, and the procession then proceeds to the tomb. In the burials of the rich, water and bread are distributed to the poor at the grave; and sometimes a buffalo or several buffaloes are slaughtered there, and the flesh given away. The tomb is a vault, surmounted by an oblong stone monument, with a stele at the head and feet; and a cupola, supported by four walls, covers the whole in the case of sheikhs' tombs and those of the wealthy. During the night following the interment, called the Night of Desolation, or that of Solitude, the soul being believed to remain with the body that one night, fikis are engaged at the house of the deceased to recite various portions of the Koran, and, commonly, to repeat the first clause of the profession of the faith, "There is no God but God," three thousand times. The women alone put on mourning attire, by dyeing their veils, shirts, &c., dark blue, with indigo; and they stain their hands, and smear the walls, with the same colour. Everything in the house is also turned upside down. The latter customs are not, however, observed on the death of an old man. At certain periods after the burial, a khatmeh, or recitation of the whole of the Koran, is performed, and the tomb is visited by the women relations and friends of the deceased. The women of the peasants of Upper Egypt perform strange dances, &c., at funerals, which are regarded partly as relics of ancient Egyptian customs.

The harem system of appointing separate apartments to the women, and secluding them from the gaze of men, is observed in Egypt as in other Moslem countries, but less strictly. The women of an Egyptian household in which old customs are maintained never sit in the presence of the master, but attend him at his meals, and are treated in every respect as inferiors. The mother, however, forms a remarkable exception to this rule; in rare instances, also, a wife becomes a companion to her husband. On the other hand, if a pair of women's shoes are placed outside the door of the harem apartments, they are understood to signify that female visitors are within, and a man is sometimes thus excluded from the upper portion of his own house for many days. Ladies of the upper or middle class lead a life of extreme inactivity, spending their time at the bath, which is the general place of gossip, or in receiving visits, embroidering, and the like, and in absolute *dolce far niente*. Both sexes are given to licentiousness.

The principal meals are breakfast, about an hour after sunrise; dinner, or the mid-day meal, at noon; and supper, which is the chief meal of the day, a little after sunset. Pastry, sweetmeats and fruit are highly esteemed. Coffee is taken at all hours, and is, with a pipe, presented at least once to each guest. Tobacco is the great luxury of the men of all classes in Egypt, who begin and end the day with it, and generally smoke all day with little intermission. Many women, also, especially among the rich, adopt the habit. The smoking of hashish, though illegal, is indulged in by considerable numbers of people. Men who can afford to keep a horse, mule or ass are very seldom seen to walk. Ladies ride asses and sit astride. The poorer classes cannot fully observe the harem system, but the women are in general carefully veiled. Some of them keep small shops, and all fetch water, make fuel, and cook for their households. Domestic slavery lingers but is moribund. The majority of the slaves are negresses employed in household duties.

In social intercourse the Egyptians observe many forms of salutation and much etiquette; they are very affable, and readily enter into conversation with strangers. Their courtesy and dignity of manner are very striking, and are combined with ease and a fluency of discourse. They have a remarkable quickness of apprehension, a ready wit, a retentive memory, combined, however, with religious pride and hypocrisy, and a disregard for the truth. Their common discourse is full of asserations and expressions respecting sacred things. They entertain reverence for their Prophet; and the Koran is treated with the utmost respect—never, for example, being placed in a low situation—and this is the case with everything they esteem holy. They are fatalists, and bear calamities with surprising resignation. Their filial piety and respect for the aged have been mentioned, and benevolence and charity are conspicuous in their character. Humanity to animals is another virtue, and cruelty is openly discountenanced in the streets. Their affability, cheerfulness and hospitality are remarkable, as well as frugality and temperance in food and drink, and honesty in the payment of debt. Their cupidity is mitigated by generosity; their natural indolence by the necessity, especially among the peasantry, to work hard to gain a livelihood. Egyptians, however, are as a rule suspicious of all not of their own creed and country. Murders and other grave crimes are rare, but petty larcenies are very common.

The amusements of the people are generally not of a violent kind, being in keeping with their sedentary habits and the heat of the climate. The bath is a favourite resort of both sexes and all classes. They are acquainted with chess, draughts, backgammon, and other games, among which is one peculiar to themselves, called Mankalah, and played with cowries. Notwithstanding its condemnation by Mahomet, music is the most favourite recreation of the people; the songs of the boatmen, the religious chants, and the cries in the streets are all musical. There are male and female musical performers; the former are both instrumental and vocal, the latter (called 'Almeh, pl. 'Awālim) generally vocal. The 'Awālim are, as their name ("learned") implies, generally accomplished women, and should not be confounded with the Ghawāzi, or dancing-girls. There are many kinds of musical instruments. The music, vocal and instrumental, is generally of little compass, and in the minor key; it is therefore plaintive, and strikes a European ear as somewhat monotonous, though often possessing a simple beauty, and the charm of antiquity, for there is little doubt that the favourite airs have been handed down from remote ages. The Ghawāzi (sing. Ghāzīa) form a separate class, very similar to the gipsies. They intermarry among themselves only, and their women are professional dancers. Their performances are often objectionable and are so regarded by many Egyptians. They dance in public, at fairs and religious festivals, and at private festivities, but, it is said, not in respectable houses. Mehemet Ali banished them to Esna, in Upper Egypt; and the few that remained in Cairo called themselves 'Awālim, to avoid punishment. Many of the dancing-girls of Cairo to-day are neither 'Awālim nor Ghawāzi, but women of the very lowest class whose performances are both ungraceful and indecent. A most objectionable class of male dancers also exists, who imitate the dances of the Ghawāzi, and dress in a kind of nondescript female attire. Not the least curious of the public performances are those of the serpent-charmers, who are generally Rifā'iā (Saadia) dervishes. Their power over serpents has been doubted, yet their performances remain unexplained; they, however, always extract the fangs of venomous serpents. Jugglers, rope-dancers and farce-players must also be mentioned. In the principal coffee-shops of Cairo are to be found reciters of romances, surrounded by interested audiences. (F.R.C.)

ESKIMO. The Eskimo are not a tall race, their height varying from 5 ft. 4 in. to 5 ft. 10 in., but men of 6 ft. are met. Both men and women are muscular and active, the former often inclining to fat. The faces of both have a pleasing, good-humoured expression, and not infrequently are even handsome. The typical face is broadly oval, flat, with fat cheeks; forehead not high, and rather retreating; teeth good, though, owing to the character of the food, worn down to the gums in old age; nose very flat; eyes rather obliquely set, small, black and bright; head largish, and covered with coarse black hair, which the women fasten up into a knot on the top, and the men clip in front and allow to hang loose and unkempt behind. Their skulls are of the mesocephalic type, the height being greater than the breadth; according to Davis, 75 is the index of the latter and 77 of the former. Some of the tribes slightly compress the skulls of their new-born children laterally (Hall), but this practice is a very local one.

The men have usually a slight moustache, but no whiskers, and rarely any beard. The skin has generally a "bacony" feel, and when cleaned of the smoke, grease and other dirt—the accumulation of which varies according to the age of the individual—is only so slightly brown that red shows in the cheeks of the children and young women. The hands and feet are small and well formed. The Eskimo dress entirely in skins of the seal, reindeer, bear, dog, or even fox, the first two being, however, the most common. The men's and women's dress is much the same, a jacket suit, the trousers tucked into seal-skin boots. The jacket has a hood, which in cold weather is used to cover the head, leaving only the face exposed. The women's jacket has a large hood for carrying a child and an absurd-looking tail behind, which is, however, usually tucked up. The women's trousers are usually ornamented with eider-duck neck feathers or embroidery of native dyed leather; their boots, which are of white leather, or (in Greenland) dyed of various colours, reach over the knees, and in some tribes are very wide at the top, thus giving them an awkward appearance and a clumsy waddling walk. In winter two suits are worn, one with their hair inside, the other with it outside. They also sometimes wear shirts of bird-skins, and stockings of dog or young reindeer skins. Their clothes are very neatly made, fit beautifully, and are sewn with "sinew-thread," with a bone needle if a steel one cannot be had. In person the Eskimo are usually filthy, and never wash. Infants are, however, sometimes cleaned by being licked by their mother before being put into the bag of feathers which serves as their bed, cradle and blankets.

In summer the Eskimo live in conical skin tents, and in winter usually in half-underground huts of stone, turf, earth and bones, entered by a long tunnel-like passage, which can only be traversed on all fours. Sometimes, if residing temporarily at a place, they will erect neat round huts of blocks of snow with a sheet of ice for a window. In the roof are deposited their spare harpoons, &c; and from it is suspended the steatite basin-like lamp, the flame of which, the wick being of moss, serves as fire and light. On one side of the hut is the bench which is used as sofa, seats and common sleeping place. The floor is usually very filthy, a pool of blood or a dead seal being often to be seen there. Ventilation is almost non-existent; and after the lamp has blazed for some time, the heat is all but unbearable. In the summer the wolfish-looking dogs lie outside on the roof of the huts, in the winter in the tunnel-like passage just outside the family apartment. The Western Eskimo build their houses chiefly of planks, merely covered on the outside with green turf. The same Eskimo have, in the more populous places, a public room for meetings. "Council chambers" are also said to exist in Labrador, but are only known in Greenland by tradition. Sometimes in south Greenland and in the Western Eskimo country the houses are made to accommodate several families, but as a rule each family has a house to itself.

The Eskimo are solely hunters and fishers, and derive most of their food from the sea. Their country allows of no cultivation; and beyond a few berries, roots, &c., they use no vegetable food. The seal, the reindeer and the whale supply the bulk of their food, as well as their clothing, light, fuel, and frequently also, when driftwood is scarce or unavailable, the material for various articles of domestic economy. Thus the Eskimo canoe is made of seal-skin stretched on a wooden or whalebone frame, with a hole in the centre for the paddler. It is driven by a bone-tipped doubled-bladed paddle. A waterproof skin or entrail dress is tightly fastened round the mouth of the hole so that, should the canoe overturn, no water can enter. A skilful paddler can turn a complete somersault, boat and all, through the water. The Eskimo women use a flat-bottomed skin luggage-boat. The Eskimo sledge is made of two runners of wood or bone—even, in one case on record, of frozen salmon (Maclure)—united by cross bars tied to the runners by hide thongs, and drawn by from 4 to 8 dogs harnessed abreast. Some of their weapons are ingenious—in particular, the harpoon, with its detachable point to which an inflated sealskin is fastened. When the quarry is struck, the floating skin serves to tire it out, marks its course, and buoys it up when dead. The bird-spears, too, have a bladder attached, and points at the sides which strike the creature should the spear-head fail to wound. An effective bow is made out of whale's rib. Altogether, with meagre material the Eskimo show great skill in the manufacture of their weapons. Meat is sometimes boiled, but, when it is frozen, it is often eaten raw. Blood, and the half-digested contents of the reindeer's paunch, are also eaten; and sometimes, but not habitually, blubber. As a rule this latter is too precious: it must be kept for winter fuel and light. The Eskimo are enormous eaters; two will easily dispose of a seal at a sitting; and in Greenland, for instance, each individual has for his daily consumption, on an average, 2½ lb of flesh with blubber, and 1 lb of fish, besides mussels, berries, sea-weed, &c., to which in the Danish settlements may be added 2 oz. of imported food. Ten pounds of flesh, in addition to other food, is not uncommonly consumed in a day in time of plenty. A man will lie on his back and allow his wife to feed him with tit-bits of blubber and flesh until he is unable to move.

FALASHAS (*i.e.* exiles; Ethiopic *falas*, a stranger), or "Jews of Abyssinia," a tribe of Hamitic stock, akin to Galla, Somali and Beja, though they profess the Jewish religion. They claim to be descended from the ten tribes banished from the Holy

Land. Another tradition assigns them as ancestor Menelek, Solomon's alleged son by the queen of Sheba. There is little or no physical difference between them and the typical Abyssinians, except perhaps that their eyes are a little more oblique; and they may certainly be regarded as Hamitic. It is uncertain when they became Jews: one account suggests in Solomon's time; another, at the Babylonian captivity; a third, during the 1st century of the Christian era. That one of the earlier dates is correct seems probable from the fact that the Falashas know nothing of either the Babylonian or Jerusalem Talmud, make no use of phylacteries *(tefillin)*, and observe neither the feast of Purim nor the dedication of the temple. They possess—not in Hebrew, of which they are altogether ignorant, but in Ethiopic (or Geez)—the canonical and apocryphal books of the Old Testament; a volume of extracts from the Pentateuch, with comments given to Moses by God on Mount Sinai; the Te-e-sa-sa Sanbat, or laws of the Sabbath; the Ardit, a book of secrets revealed to twelve saints, which is used as a charm against disease; lives of Abraham, Moses, &c.; and a translation of Josephus called Sana Aihud. A copy of the Orit or Mosaic law is kept in the holy of holies in every synagogue. Various pagan observances are mingled in their ritual: every newly-built house is considered uninhabitable till the blood of a sheep or fowl has been spilt in it; a woman guilty of a breach of chastity has to undergo purification by leaping into a flaming fire; the Sabbath has been deified, and, as the goddess Sanbat, receives adoration and sacrifice and is said to have ten thousand times ten thousand angels to wait on her commands. There is a monastic system, introduced it is said in the 4th century A.D. by Aba Zebra, a pious man who retired from the world and lived in the cave of Hoharewa, in the province of Armatshoho. The monks must prepare all their food with their own hands, and no lay person, male or female, may enter their houses. Celibacy is not practised by the priests, but they are not allowed to marry a second time, and no one is admitted into the order who has eaten bread with a Christian, or is the son or grandson of a man thus contaminated. Belief in the evil eye or shadow is universal, and spirit-raisers, soothsayers and rain-doctors are in repute. Education is in the hands of the monks and priests, and is confined to boys. Fasts, obligatory on all above seven years of age, are held on every Monday and Thursday, on every new moon, and at the passover (the 21st or 22nd of April). The annual festivals are the passover, the harvest feast, the Baala Mazalat or feast of tabernacles (during which, however, no booths are built), the day of covenant or assembly and Abraham's day. It is believed that after death the soul remains in a place of darkness till the third day, when the first sacrifice for the dead is offered; prayers are read in the synagogue for the repose of the departed, and for seven days a formal lament takes place every morning in his house. No coffins are used, and a stone vault is built over the corpse so that it may not come into direct contact with the earth.

The Falashas are an industrious people, living for the most part in villages of their own, or, if they settle in a Christian or Mahommedan town, occupying a separate quarter. They had their own kings, who, they pretend, were descended from David, from the 10th century until 1800, when the royal race became extinct, and they then became subject to the Abyssinian kingdom of Tigré. They do not mix with the Abyssinians, and never marry women of alien religions. They are even forbidden to enter the houses of Christians, and from such a pollution have to be purified before entering their own houses. Polygamy is not practised; early marriages are rare, and their morals are generally better than those of their Christian masters. Unlike most Jews, they have no liking for trade, but are skilled in agriculture, in the manufacture of pottery, ironware and cloth, and are good masons. Their numbers are variously estimated at from one hundred to one hundred and fifty thousand.

GIPSIES. Those who have lived among the Gipsies will readily testify that their religious views are a strange medley of the local faith, which they everywhere embrace, and some old-world superstitions which they have in common with many nations. Among the Greeks they belong to the Greek Church, among the Mahommedans they are Mahommedans, in Rumania they belong to the National Church. In Hungary they are mostly Catholics, according to the faith of the inhabitants of that country. They have no ethical principles and they do not recognize the obligations of the Ten Commandments. There is extreme moral laxity in the relation of the two sexes, and on the whole they take life easily, and are complete fatalists. At the same time they are great cowards, and they play the role of the fool or the jester in the popular anecdotes of eastern Europe. There the poltroon is always a Gipsy, but he is good-humoured and not so malicious as those Gipsies who had endured the hardships of outlawry in the west of Europe. Although they love their children, it sometimes happens that a Gipsy mother will hold her child by the legs and beat the father with it. In Rumania and Turkey among the settled Gipsies a good number are carriers and bricklayers; and the women take their full share in every kind of work, no matter how hard it may be. The nomadic Gipsies carry on the ancient craft of coppersmiths, or workers in metal; they also make sieves and traps, but in the East they are seldom farriers or horse-dealers. They are far-famed for their music, in which art they are unsurpassed. The Gipsy musicians belong mostly to the class who originally were serfs. They were retained at the courts of the boyars for their special talent in reciting old ballads and love songs and their deftness in playing, notably the guitar and the fiddle. The former was used as an accompaniment to the singing of either love ditties and popular songs or more especially in recital or heroic ballads and epic songs; the latter for dances and other amusements. They were the troubadours and minstrels of eastern Europe; the largest collection of Rumanian popular ballads and songs was gathered by G. Dem. Teodorescu from a Gipsy minstrel, Petre Sholkan; and not a few of the songs of the guslars among the Servians and other Slavonic nations in the Balkans come also from the Gipsies. They have also retained the ancient tunes and aires from the dreamy "doina" of the Rumanian to the fiery "czardas" of the Hungarian or the stately "hora" of the Bulgarian. Liszt went so far as to ascribe to the Gipsies the origin of the Hungarian national music. This is an exaggeration, as seen by the comparison of the Gipsy music in other parts of southeast Europe; but they undoubtedly have given the most faithful expression to the national temperament. Equally famous is the Gipsy woman for her knowledge of occult practices. She is the real witch; she knows charms to injure the enemy or to help a friend. She can break the charm if made by others. But neither in the one case nor in the other, and in fact as little as in their songs, do they use the Gipsy language. It is either the local language of the natives as in the case of charms, or a slightly Romanized form of Greek, Rumanian or Slavonic. The old Gipsy woman is also known for her skill in palmistry and fortune-telling by means of a special set of cards, the well-known Tarok of the Gipsies.

As a race they are of small stature, varying in colour from the dark tan of the Arab to the whitish hue of the Servian and the Pole. In fact there are some white-coloured Gipsies, especially in Servia and Dalmatia, and these are often not easily distinguishable from the native peoples, except that they are more lithe and sinewy, better proportioned and more agile in their movements than the thick-set Slavs and the mixed race of the Rumanians. By one feature, however, they are easily distinguishable and recognize one another, viz. by the lustre of their eyes and the whiteness of their teeth. Some are well built; others have the features of a mongrel race, due no doubt to intermarriage with outcasts of other races. The women age very quickly and the mortality among the Gipsies is great, especially among children; among adults it is chiefly due to pulmonary diseases. They love display and Oriental showiness, bright-coloured dresses, ornaments, bangles, &c.; red and green are the colours mostly favoured by the Gipsies in the East. Along with a showy handkerchief or some shining gold coins round their necks, they will wear torn petticoats and no covering on their feet. And even after they have been assimilated and have forgotten their own language they still retain some of the prominent features of their character, such as the love of inordinate display and gorgeous dress; and their moral defects not only remain for a long time as glaring as among those who live the life of vagrants, but even become more pronounced. The Gipsy of to-day is no longer what his forefathers have been. The assimilation with the nations in the near East and the steps taken for the suppression of vagrancy in the West, combine to denationalize the Gipsy and to make "Romani Chib" a thing of the past.

GREEKS. The Greeks display great intellectual vivacity; they are clever, inquisitive, quick-witted and ingenious, but not profound; sustained mental industry and careful accuracy are distasteful to them, and their aversion to manual labour is still more marked. Even the agricultural class is but moderately industrious; abundant opportunities for relaxation are provided by the numerous church festivals. The desire for instruction is intense even in the lowest ranks of the community; rhetorical and literary accomplishments possess a greater attraction for the majority than the fields of modern science. The number of persons who seek to qualify for the learned professions is excessive; they form a superfluous element in the community, an educated proletariat, attaching themselves to the various political parties in the hope of obtaining state employment and spending an idle existence in the cafés and the streets when their party is out of power. In disposition the Greeks are lively, cheerful, plausible, kind to their servants and dependants, remarkably temperate and frugal in their habits, amiable and united in family life. Drunkenness is almost unknown, thrift is universally practised; the standard of sexual morality is high, especially in the rural districts, where illegitimacy is extremely rare. The faults of the Greeks must in a large degree be attributed to their prolonged subjection to alien races; their cleverness often degenerates into cunning, their ready invention into mendacity, their thrift into avarice, their fertility of resource into trickery and fraud. Dishonesty is not a national vice, but many who would scorn to steal will not hesitate to compass illicit gains by duplicity and misrepresentation; deceit, indeed, is often practised gratuitously for the mere intellectual satisfaction which it affords. In the astuteness of their monetary dealings the Greeks proverbially surpass the Jews, but fall short of the Armenians; their remarkable aptitude for business is sometimes marred by a certain short-sightedness which pursues immediate profits at the cost of ulterior advantages. Their vanity and egoism, which are admitted by even the most favourable observers, render them jealous, exacting, and peculiarly susceptible to flattery. In common with other southern European peoples the Greeks are extremely excitable; their passionate disposition is prone to take offence at slight provocation, and trivial quarrels not infrequently result in homicide. They are religious, but by no means fanatical, except in regard to politico-religious questions affecting their national aims. In general the Greeks may be described as a clever, ambitious and versatile people, capable of great effort and sacrifice, but deficient in some of the more solid qualities which make for national greatness. (T.D.B.)

JAPANESE (Moral characteristics of). The most prominent trait of Japanese disposition is gaiety of heart. Emphatically of a laughter-loving nature, the Japanese passes through the world with a smile on his lips. The petty ills of life do not disturb his equanimity. He takes them as part of the day's work, and though he sometimes grumbles, rarely, if ever, does he repine. Exceptional to this general rule, however, is a mood of pessimism which sometimes overtakes youths on the threshold of manhood. Finding the problem of life insolvable, they abandon the attempt to solve it and take refuge in the grave. It seems as though there were always a number of young men hovering on the brink of such suicidal despair. An example alone is needed finally to destroy the equilibrium. Some one throws himself over a cataract or leaps into the crater of a volcano, and immediately a score or two follow. Apparently the more picturesquely awful the manner of the demise, the greater the attractive force. The thing is not a product of insanity, as the term is usually interpreted; letters always left behind by the victims prove them to have been in full possession of their reasoning faculties up to the last moment. Some observers lay the blame at the door of Buddhism, a creed which promotes pessimism by begetting the anchorite, the ascetic and the shuddering believer in seven hells. But Buddhism did not formerly produce such incidents, and, for the rest, the faith of Shaka has little sway over the student mind in Japan. The phenomenon is modern: it is not an outcome of Japanese nature nor yet of Buddhist teaching, but is due to the stress of endeavouring to reach the standards of Western acquirement with grievously inadequate equipment, opportunities and resources. In order to support himself and pay his academic fees many a Japanese has to fall into the ranks of the physical labourer during a part of each day or night. Ill-nourished, overworked and, it may be, disappointed, he finds the struggle intolerable and so passes out into the darkness. But he is not a normal type. The normal type is light-hearted and buoyant. One naturally expects to find, and one does find, that this moral sunshine is associated with good temper. The Japanese is exceptionally serene. Irascibility is regarded as permissible in sickly children only: grown people are supposed to be superior to displays of impatience. But there is a limit of imperturbability, and when that limit is reached, the subsequent passion is desperately vehement. It has been said that these traits go to make the Japanese soldier what he is. The hardships of a campaign cause him little suffering since he never frets over them, but the hour of combat finds him forgetful of everything save victory. In the case of the military class—and prior to the Restoration of 1867 the term "military class" was synonymous with "educated class"—this spirit of stoicism was built up by precept on a solid basis of heredity. The *samurai* (soldier) learned that his first characteristic must be to suppress all outward displays of emotion. Pain, pleasure, passion and peril must all find him unperturbed. The supreme test, satisfied so frequently as to be commonplace, was a shocking form of suicide performed with a placid mien. This capacity, coupled with readiness to sacrifice life at any moment on the altar of country, fief or honour, made a remarkably heroic character. On the other hand, some observers hold that the education of this stoicism was effected at the cost of the feelings it sought to conceal. In support of that theory it is pointed out that the average Japanese, man or woman, will recount a death or some other calamity in his own family with a perfectly calm, if not a smiling, face. Probably there is a measure of truth in the criticism. Feelings cannot be habitually hidden without being more or less blunted. But here another Japanese trait presents itself— politeness. There is no more polite nation in the world than the Japanese. Whether in real courtesy of heart they excel Occidentals may be open to doubt, but in all the forms of comity they are unrivalled. Now one of the cardinal rules of politeness is to avoid burdening a stranger with the weight of one's own woes. Therefore a mother, passing from the chamber which has just witnessed her paroxysms of grief, will describe calmly to a stranger—especially a foreigner—the death of her only child. The same suppression of emotional display in public is observed in all the affairs of life. Youths and maidens maintain towards each other a demeanour of reserve and even indifference, from which it has been confidently affirmed that love does not exist in Japan. The truth is that in no other country do so many dual suicides occur—suicides of a man and woman who, unable to be united in this world, go to a union beyond the grave. It is true, nevertheless, that love as a prelude to marriage finds only a small place in Japanese ethics. Marriages in the great majority of cases are arranged with little reference to the feelings of the parties concerned. It might be supposed that conjugal fidelity must suffer from such a custom. It does suffer seriously in the case of the husband, but emphatically not in the case of the wife. Even though she be cognisant—as she often is—of her husband's extra-marital relations, she abates nothing of the duty which she has been taught to regard as the first canon of female ethics. From many points of view, indeed, there is no more beautiful type of character than that of the Japanese woman. She is entirely unselfish; exquisitely modest without being anything of a prude; abounding in intelligence which is never obscured by egoism; patient in the hour of suffering; strong in time of affliction; a faithful wife; a loving mother; a good daughter; and capable, as history shows, of heroism rivalling that of the stronger sex. As to the question of sexual virtue and morality in Japan, grounds for a conclusive verdict are hard to find. In the interests of hygiene prostitution is licensed, and that fact is by many critics construed as proof of tolerance. But licensing is associated with strict segregation, and it results that the great cities are conspicuously free from evidences of vice, and that the streets may be traversed by women at all hours of the day and night with perfect impunity and without fear of encountering offensive spectacles. The ratio of marriages is approximately 8.46 per thousand units of the population, and the ratio of divorces if 1.36 per thousand. There are thus about 16 divorces for every hundred marriages. Divorces take place chiefly among the lower orders, who frequently treat marriage merely as a test of a couple's suitability to be helpmates in the struggles of life. If experience develops incompatibility of temper or some other mutually repellent characteristic, separation follows as a matter of course. On the other hand, divorces among persons of the upper classes are comparatively rare, and divorces on account of a wife's unfaithfulness are almost unknown.

Concerning the virtues of truth and probity, extremely conflicting opinions have been expressed. The Japanese *samurai* always prided himself on having "no second word." He never drew his sword without using it; he never gave his word without keeping it. Yet it may be doubted whether the value attached in Japan to the abstract quality, truth, is as high as the value attached to it in England, or whether the consciousness of having told a falsehood weighs as heavily on the heart. Much depends upon the motive. Whatever may be said of the upper class, it is probably true that the average Japanese will not sacrifice expediency on the altar of truth. He will be veracious only so long as the consequences are not seriously injurious. Perhaps no more can be affirmed of any nation. The "white lie" of the Anglo-Saxon and the *hōben no uso* of the Japanese are twins. In the matter of probity, however, it is possible to speak with more assurance. There is undoubtedly in the lower ranks of Japanese tradesmen a comparatively large fringe of persons whose standard of commercial morality is defective. They are descendants of feudal days when the mercantile element, being counted as the dregs of the population, lost its self-respect. Against this blemish—which is in the process of gradual correction—the fact has to be set that the better class of merchants, the whole of the artisans and the labouring classs in general, obey canons of probity fully on a level with the best to be found elsewhere. For the rest, frugality, industry and patience characterize all the bread-winners; courage and burning patriotism are attributes of the whole nation.

There are five qualities possessed by the Japanese in a marked degree. The first is frugality. From time immemorial the great mass of the people have lived in absolute ignorance of luxury in any form and in the perpetual presence of a necessity to economize. Amid these circumstances there has emerged capacity to make a little go a long way and to be content with the most meagre fare. The second quality is endurance. It is born of causes cognate with those which have begotten frugality. The average Japanese may be said to live without artificial heat; his paper doors admit the light but do not exclude the cold. His brazier barely suffices to warm his hands and his face. Equally is he a stranger to methods of artificial cooling. He takes the frost that winter inflicts and the fever that summer brings as unavoidable visitors. The third quality is obedience; the offspring of eight centuries passed under the shadow of military autocracy. Whatever he is authoritatively bidden to do, that the Japanese will do. The fourth quality is altruism. In the upper classes the welfare of the family has been set above the interests of each member. The fifth quality is a genius for detail. Probably this is the outcome of an extraordinarily elaborate system of social etiquette. Each generation has added something to the canons of its predecessor, and for every ten points preserved not more than one has been discarded. An instinctive respect for minutiae has thus been inculcated, and has gradually extended to all the affairs of life. That this accuracy may sometimes degenerate into triviality, and that such absorption in trifles may occasionally hide the broad horizon, is conceivable. (F.By.)

MONTENEGRINS. The Montenegrins present all the characteristics of a primitive race as yet but little affected by modern civilization. Society is still in that early stage at which personal valour is regarded as the highest virtue, and warlike prowess constitutes the principal, if not the only, claim to pre-eminence. The chiefs are distinguished by the splendour of their arms and the richness of their costume; women occupy a subject position; the physically infirm often adopt the profession of minstrels and sing the exploits of their countrymen like the bards of the Homeric age. A race of warriors, the Montenegrins are brave, proud, chivalrous and patriotic; on the other hand, they are vain, lazy, cruel and revengeful. They possess the domestic virtues of sobriety, chastity and frugality, and are well-mannered, affable and hospitable, though somewhat contemptuous of strangers. They are endowed in no small degree with the high-flown poetic temperament of the Serb race, and delight in interminable recitations of their martial deeds, which are sung to the strains of the *gûsla*, a rudimentary one-stringed fiddle. Dancing is a favourite pastime. Two characteristic forms are the slow and stately ring-dance *(kolo)*, in which women sometimes participate, though it is usually performed by a circle of men; and the livelier measure for both sexes *(oro)*, in which the couples face one another, leaping high into the air, while each man encourages his partner by rapid revolver-firing. The *oro* is the traditional dance in the Katunska district. Women chant wild dirges, generally improvised, over the dead; mourners try to excel one another in demonstrations of grief; and funerals are celebrated by an orgy very like an Irish "wake." Like most imaginative peoples, the Montenegrins are extremely superstitious, and belief in the vampire, demons and fairies is almost universal. Among the mountains they can converse fluently at astonishing distances. The physical type contrasts with that of the northern Serbs: the features are more pronounced, the hair is darker, and the stature is greater. The men are tall, often exceeding 6 ft. in height, muscular,

and wonderfully active, displaying a cat-like elasticity of movement
when scaling their native rocks; their bearing is soldier-like and manly,
though somewhat theatrical. The women, though frequently beautiful in youth, age rapidly, and are short and stunted, though strong,
owing to the drudgery imposed on them from childhood; they work
in the fields, carry heavy burdens, and are generally treated as inferior beings. Like the Albanians, the Montenegrins take great pride
in personal adornment. The men wear a red waistcoat, embroidered
with gold or black braid, over which a long plaid is sometimes thrown
in cold weather; a red girdle, in the folds of which pistols and yat-
aghans are placed; loose dark-blue breeches and white stockings,
which are generally covered with gaiters. The *opanka*, a raw-hide
sandal, is worn instead of boots; patent leather long boots are sometimes worn by military officers and a few of the wealthier class. The
headdress is a small cap *(kapa)*, black at the sides, in mourning for
Kossovo; red at the top, it is said, in token of the blood shed then
and afterwards. On the top near the side, five semicircular bars of
gold braid, enclosing the king's initials, are supposed to represent
the five centuries of Montenegrin liberty. There is little authority,
however, for this and other fanciful interpretations of the pattern,
which was adopted in the reign of Peter I.; the red fez, from which
the kapa probably derives its colour, was previously worn. A blue or
green mantle is sometimes worn in addition by the chiefs. The poorer
mountaineers are often dressed in coarse sacking, but all without
exception carry arms. The women, as befits their servile condition,
are generally clothed in black, and wear a black head-dress or veil;
on Sundays and holidays, however, a white embroidered bodice, silver
girdle, and bright silk skirt are worn beneath an open coat. Over this
is placed a short, sleeveless jacket of red, blue, or violet velvet, according to the wearer's age. Unmarried girls are allowed to wear
the red kapa, but without the embroidered badge. The Vasoyevitch
tribe retain the Albanian costume, in which white predominates.
Turkish dress is often seen at Antivari, Dulcigno and Podgoritza. The
dwelling-houses are invariably of stone, except in the eastern districts,
where wooden huts are found. As a rule, only the mansions of cattle-
owners have a second storey: the ground floor, which is dark and
unventilated, is occupied by the animals; the upper chambers, in
which the family reside, are reached by a ladder or stone staircase.
Chimneys are rare, and the smoke of the fireplace escapes through
the windows (if any exist) or the open doorway. The principal food
of the people is rye or maize cake, cheese, potatoes and salted *scoranze;*
their drink is water or sour milk; meat is seldom tasted, except on

festive occasions, when raki and red wine are also enjoyed. The Montenegrins are great smokers, especially of cigarettes; in the districts which formerly belonged to Turkey the men, whose dignity never permits them to carry burdens, may be seen going to market with the *chibûk,* or long pipe, slung across their backs. The mother possesses little influence over her sons, who are trained from the earliest infancy to cultivate warlike pursuits and to despise the weaker sex. Betrothals often take place in early childhood. Young men who are attached to each other are accustomed to swear eternal brotherhood *(pobratimstvo);* the bond, which receives the sanction of the Church, is never dissolved. Marriages between Montenegrins and converted Turkish girls are a common source of blood-feuds. (J.D.B.)

NEGRO. Mentally the negro is inferior to the white. The remark of F. Manetta, made after a long study of the negro in America, may be taken as generally true of the whole race: "the negro children were sharp, intelligent and full of vivacity, but on approaching the adult period a gradual change set in. The intellect seemed to become clouded, animation giving place to a sort of lethargy, briskness yielding to indolence. We must necessarily suppose that the development of the negro and white proceeds on different lines. While with the latter the volume of the brain grows with the expansion of the brainpan, in the former the growth of the brain is on the contrary arrested by the premature closing of the cranial sutures and lateral pressure of the frontal bone. This explanation is reasonable and even probable as a contributing cause; but evidence is lacking on the subject and the arrest or even deterioration in mental development is no doubt very largely due to the fact that after puberty sexual matters take the first place in the negro's life and thoughts. At the same time his environment has not been such as would tend to produce in him the restless energy which has led to the progress of the white race; and the easy conditions of tropical life and the fertility of the soil have reduced the struggle for existence to a minimum. But though the mental inferiority of the negro to the white or yellow races is a fact, it has often been exaggerated; the negro is largely the creature of his environment, and it is not fair to judge of his mental capacity by tests taken directly from the environment of the white man, as for instance tests in mental arithmetic; skill in reckoning is necessary to the white race, and it has cultivated this faculty; but it is not necessary to the negro.

On the other hand negroes far surpass white men in acuteness of

vision, hearing, sense of direction and topography. A native who has
once visited a particular locality will rarely fail to recognize it again.
For the rest, the mental constitution of the negro is very similar to
that of a child, normally good-natured and cheerful, but subject to
sudden fits of emotion and passion during which he is capable of
performing acts of singular atrocity, impressionable, vain, but often
exhibiting in the capacity of servant a dog-like fidelity which has stood
the supreme test. Given suitable training, the negro is capable of
becoming a craftsman of considerable skill, particularly in metal
work, carpentry and carving. The bronze castings by the lost wax
process, and the cups and horns of ivory elaborately carved, which
were produced by the natives of Guinea after their intercourse with
the Portuguese of the 16th century, bear ample witness to this. But
the rapid decline and practical evanescence of both industries, when
that intercourse was interrupted, shows that the native craftsman was
raised for the moment above his normal level by direct foreign inspiration, and was unable to sustain the high quality of his work when
that inspiration failed. (T.A.J.)

WA, a wild tribe inhabiting the north-east frontier
of Upper Burma. Their country lies to the east of the Northern Shan
States, between the Salween river and the state of Kēng-Tūng, extending for about 100 m. along the Salween and for considerably
less than half that distance inland to the watershed between that river
and the Mekong. The boundaries may be roughly said to be the
Salween on the W., the ridge over the Namting valley on the N.,
the hills E. of the Nam Hka on the eastern and southern sides, while
the country ends in a point formed by the junction of the Nam Hka
with the Salween. The Was claim to have inhabited the country where
they now are since the beginning of time; but it appears more probable that they were the aborigines of the greater part of northern
Siam at least, if not of Indo-China, since old records and travellers
(*e.g.* Captain McLeod in 1837) speak of their having been the original
inhabitants with small communities left behind from Kēng Tūng
down to Chiengmai; while the state of Kēng Tūng, just S.E. of the
Wa country, has still scattered villages of Was and traditions that they
were once spread all over the country. Their fortified village sites too
are still to be found covered over with jungle.The people are short
and dark-featured, with negritic features, and some believe that they
are allied to the Andamanese and the Selungs inhabiting the islands
of the Mergui archipelago, who have been driven back, or retreated,

northwards to the wild country they now inhabit; but their language proves them to belong to the Môn-Khmer family. They are popularly divided into Wild Was and Tame Was. The Wild Was are remarkable as the best authenticated instance of head-hunters in the British Empire. They were formerly supposed to be also cannibals; but it is now known that they are not habitual cannibals, though it is possible that human flesh may be eaten as a religious function at the annual harvest feast. Their head-hunting habits have an animistic basis. In the opinion of the Wa the ghost of a dead man goes with his skull and hangs about its neighbourhood, and so many skulls posted up outside his village gate mean so many watch-dog *umbrae* attached to the village, jealous of their own preserves and intolerant of interlopers from the invisible world. Thus every addition to the collection of skulls is an additional safe-guard against ill-affected demons, and a head-hunting expedition is not undertaken, as was once thought, from motives of cannibalism or revenge, but solely to secure the very latest thing in charms as a protection against the powers of darkness. Outside every village is an avenue of human skulls, amid groves conspicuous from long distances. These consist of strips of the primeval jungle, huge forest trees left standing where all the remaining country is cleared for cultivation. The undergrowth is usually cut away, and these avenues are commonly but not always in deep shade. Along one side (which side apparently does not matter) is a line of posts with skulls fitted into niches facing towards the path. The niche is cut sometimes in front, sometimes in the back of the post. In the latter case there is a round hole in front, through which sometimes only the teeth and empty eye-sockets, sometimes the whole skull, grins a ghastly smile. Most villages count their heads by tens or twenties, but some of them have hundreds, especially when the grove lies between several large villages, who combine or run their collections into one another. The largest known avenue is that between Hsüng Ramang and Hsan Htung. Here there must be a couple of hundred or more skulls; but it is not certain that even this is the largest. It is thought necessary to add some skulls to this pathway every year if the crops are to be good. The heads of distinguished and pious men and of strangers are the most efficacious. The head-hunting season lasts through March and April, and it is when the Wa hill fields are being got ready for planting that the roads in the vicinity become dangerous to the neighbouring Shans. The little that is known of the practice seems to hint at the fact that the victim selected was primarily a harvest victim. A Wild Wa village is a very formidable place to attack, except for civilized weapons of offence. All the villages are perched high up on the slope of the hills, usually on a knoll or spine-like spur, or on a narrow ravine near the crest of the ridge. The only entrance is through a long tunnel. There is sometimes only one, though usually there are two, at opposite sides of the village. This tunnelled way is a few inches over 5 ft. high and not quite so wide, so that two persons cannot pass freely in it, and it sometimes winds slightly, so that a gun cannot be fired up it; moreover, the path is frequently studded with pegs in a sort of dice arrangement, to prevent a rush. None of the tunnels is less than 30 yds. long, and some are as much as 100 yds. Round each village is carried an earthen rampart, 6 to 8 ft. high and as many thick, and this is overgrown with a dense covering of shrubs, thin bushes and cactuses, so as to be quite impenetrable. Outside this is a deep ditch which would effectually stop a rush. These preparations indicate the character of the inhabitants, which is so savage and suspicious that the Wa country is still unadministered and naturally does not appear in the 1901 census returns. The total number of the Wa race is estimated at more than 50,000. (J.G.Sc.)

Cicero is echoed only to invite
the reader to scrutinize some of the articles on the nature
and history of rituals, customs, practices, and procedures
of the past and possibly still of the present. Some are of

legal nature, harking back to early English legal custom such as "Beating the Bounds" and "Window Tax," while others such as "Black Veil," "Cemetery," "Heart-Burial," and "Wake" are of a religious nature. One particular entry, "Lynch Law," describes not ancient custom but rather improvised justice deriving from the harshness of frontier life, written by Walter Lynwood Fleming, a professor at Louisiana State University. There are also good insights into Victorian daily life in such articles as "Luncheon," "Sign-Board," and "Tattooing." Of the abundant number of articles related to the monarchy and how it functions, we found of special interest the lengthy piece (here abbreviated) "Precedence," written by William Alexander Lindsay, which gives the most scrupulous and exact attention to the order of protocol for all royal occasions as applied, from the king to the last gentleman, from the queen to the last gentlewoman. On another plane, we have included an intriguing article on the structure and functioning of a typical "Harem."

AMUCK, RUNNING (or more properly Амок), the native term for the homicidal mania which attacks Malays.

A Malay will suddenly and apparently without reason rush into the street armed with a kris or other weapon, and slash and cut at everybody he meets till he is killed. These frenzies were formerly regarded as due to sudden insanity. It is now, however, certain that the typical *amok* is the result of circumstances, such as domestic jealousy or gambling losses, which render a Malay desperate and weary of his life. It is, in fact, the Malay equivalent of suicide. "The act of running *amuck* is probably due to causes over which the culprit has some amount of control, as the custom has now died out in the British possessions in the peninsula, the offenders probably objecting to being caught and tried in cold blood" (W. W. Skeat).

Though so intimately associated with the Malay there is some ground for believing the word to have an Indian origin, and the act is certainly far from unknown in Indian history. Some notable cases have occurred among the Rajputs. Thus, in 1634, the eldest son of the raja of Jodhpur ran amuck at the court of Shah Jahan, failing in his attack on the emperor, but killing five of his officials. During the 18th century, again, at Hyderabad (Sind), two envoys, sent by the Jodhpur chief in regard to a quarrel between the two states, stabbed the prince and twenty-six of his suite before they themselves fell.

In Malabar there were certain professional assassins known to old travellers as *Amouchi* or *Amuco*. The nearest modern equivalent to these words would seem to be the Malayalim *Amarkhan,* "a warrior" (from *amar,* "fight"). The Malayalim term *chaver* applied to these ruffians meant literally those "who devote themselves to death." In Malabar was a custom by which the zamorin or king of Calicut had to cut his throat in public when he had reigned twelve years. In the 17th century a variation in his fate was made. He had to take his seat, after a great feast lasting twelve days, at a national assembly, surrounded by his armed suite, and it was lawful for anyone to attack him, and if he succeeded in killing him the murderer himself became zamorin (see Alex. Hamilton, "A new Account of the East Indies," in Pinkerton's *Voyages and Travels,* viii. 374). In 1600 thirty would-be assassins were killed in their attempts. These men were called *Amarkhan,* and it has been suggested that their action was "running amuck" in the true Malay sense. Another proposed derivation for *amouchi* is Sanskrit *amokshya,* "that cannot be loosed," suggesting that the murderer was bound by a vow, an explanation more than once advanced for the Malay *amuck;* but *amokshya* in such a sense is unknown in Malayalim.

AZĀN (Arabic for "announcement"), the call or summons to public prayers proclaimed by the Muezzin (crier) from the mosque twice daily in all Mahommedan countries. In small mosques the Muezzin at Azān stands at the door or at the side of the building; in large ones he takes up his position in the minaret. The call translated runs: "God is most great!" (four times), "I testify there is no God but God!" (twice), "I testify that Mahomet is the apostle of God!" (twice), "Come to prayer!" (twice), "Come to salvation!" (twice), "God is most great!" (twice), "There is no God but God!" To the morning Azān are added the words, "Prayer is better than sleep!" (twice). The devout Moslem has to make a set response to each phrase of the Muezzin. At first these are mere repetitions of Azān, but to the cry "Come to prayer!" the listener must answer, "I have no power nor strength but from God the most High and Great." To that of "Come to salvation!" the formal response is, "What God willeth will be: what He willeth not will not be." The recital of the Azān must be listened to with the utmost reverence. The passers in the streets must stand still, all those at work must cease from their labours, and those in bed must sit up.

The Muezzin, who is a paid servant of the mosque, must stand with his face towards Mecca and with the points of his forefingers in his ears while reciting Aẓān. He is specially chosen for good character, and Aẓān must not be recited by any one unclean, by a drunkard, by the insane, or by a woman. The summons to prayers was at first simply "Come to prayer!" Mahomet, anxious to invest the call with the dignity of a ceremony, took counsel of his followers. Some sugegsted the Jewish trumpet, others the Christian bell, but according to legend the matter was finally settled by a dream:—"While the matter was under discussion, Abdallah, a Khazrajite, dreamed that he met a man clad in green raiment, carrying a bell. Abdallah sought to buy it, saying that it would do well for bringing together the assembly of the faithful. 'I will show thee a better way,' replied the stranger; 'let a crier cry aloud. "God is most great, &c." ' On awaking, Abdallah went to Mahomet and told him his dream," and Aẓān was thereupon instituted.

BLACK VEIL, in the Roman Catholic Church, the symbol of the most complete renunciation of the world and adoption of a nun's life. On the appointed day the nun goes through all the ritual of the marriage ceremony, after a solemn mass at which all the inmates of the convent assist. She is dressed in bridal white with wreath and veil, and receives a wedding-ring, as spouse of the Church. Afterwards she presides at a wedding-breakfast, at which a bride-cake is cut. She thus bids adieu to all her friends, and having previously taken the white veil, the betrothal, she now assumes the black, and for ever forswears the world and its pleasures. Her hair is cut short, and her bridal robes are exchanged for the sombre religious habit. Her wedding-ring, however, she continues to wear, and it is buried with her.

BOUNDS, BEATING THE, an ancient custom still observed in many English parishes. In former times when maps were rare it was usual to make a formal perambulation of the parish boundaries on Ascension day or during Rogation week. The latter is in the north of England still called "Gang Week" or "Ganging Days" from this "ganging" or procession. The priest of the parish with the churchwardens and the parochial officials headed a crowd of boys who, armed with green boughs, beat with them the parish border-stones. Sometimes the boys were themselves whipped or even violently bumped on the boundary-stones to make them remember. The object of taking boys was obviously to ensure that witnesses to the boundaries should survive as long as possible. In England the custom is as old as Anglo-Saxon days, as it is mentioned in laws of Alfred and Æthelstan. It is thought that it may have been derived from the Roman Terminalia, a festival celebrated on the 22nd of February in honour of Terminus, the god of landmarks, to whom cakes and wine were offered, sports and dancing taking place at the boundaries. In England a parish-ale or feast was always held after the perambulation, which assured its popularity, and in Henry VIII.'s reign the occasion had become an excuse for so much revelry that it attracted the condemnation of a preacher who declared "these solemne and accustomable processions and supplications be nowe growen into a right foule and detestable abuse." Beating the bounds had a religious side in the practice which originated the term Rogation, the accompanying clergy being supposed to beseech *(rogare)* the divine blessing upon the parish lands for the ensuing harvest. This feature originated in the 5th century, when Mamercus, bishop of Vienne, instituted special prayers and fasting and processions on these days. This clerical side of the parish bounds-beating was one of the religious functions prohibited by the Injunctions of Queen Elizabeth; but it was then ordered that the perambulation should continue to be performed as a quasi-secular function, so that evidence of the boundaries of parishes, &c. might be preserved. Bequests were sometimes made in connexion with bounds-beating. Thus at Leighton Buzzard on Rogation Monday, in accordance with the will of one Edward Wilkes, a London merchant who died in 1646, the trustees of his almshouses accompanied the boys. The will was read and beer and plum rolls distributed. A remarkable feature of the bequest was that while the will is read one of the boys has to stand on his head.

CEMETERY, literally a sleeping-place, the name applied by the early Christians to the places set apart for the burial of their dead. These were generally extra-mural and unconnected with churches, the practice of interment in churches or churchyards being unknown in the first centuries of the Christian era. The term cemetery has, therefore, been appropriately applied in modern times to the burial-grounds, generally extra-mural, which have been substituted for the overcrowded churchyards of populous parishes both urban and rural.

From 1840 to 1855, attention was repeatedly called to the condition of the London churchyards by correspondence in the press and by the reports of parliamentary committees, the first of which, that of Mr Chadwick, appeared in 1843. The vaults under the pavement of the churches, and the small spaces of open ground surrounding them, were crammed with coffins. In many of the buildings the air was so tainted with the products of corruption as to be a direct and palpable source of disease and death to those who frequented them. In the churchyards coffins were placed tier above tier in the graves until they were within a few feet (or sometimes even a few inches) of the surface, and the level of the ground was often raised to that of the lower windows of the church. To make room for fresh interments the sextons had recourse to the surreptitious removal of bones and partially-decayed remains, and in some cases the contents of the graves were systematically transferred to pits adjacent of the site, the grave-diggers appropriating the coffin-plates, handles and nails to be sold as waste metal. The neighbourhood of the churchyards was always unhealthy, the air being vitiated by the gaseous emanations from the graves, and the water, wherever it was obtained from wells, containing organic matter, the source of which could not be mistaken. In all the large towns the evil prevailed in a greater or less degree, but in London, on account of the immense population and the consequent mortality, it forced itself more readily upon public attention, and after more than one partial measure of relief had been passed the churchyards were, with a few exceptions, finally closed by the act of 1855, and the cemeteries which now occupy a large extent of ground to the north, south, east and west became henceforth the burial-places of the metropolis. Several of them had been already established by private enterprise before the passing of the Burial Act of 1855 (Kensal Green cemetery dates from 1832), but that enactment forms the epoch from which the general development of cemeteries in Great Britain and Ireland began. Burial within the limits of cities and towns is now almost everywhere abolished, and where it is still in use it is surrounded by such safeguards as make it practically innocuous. This tendency has been conspicuous both in the United Kingdom and the United States. The increasing practice of cremation has assisted in the movement for disposing of the dead in more sanitary conditions; and the proposals of Sir Seymour Haden and others for burying the dead in more open coffins, and abandoning the old system of family graves, have had considerable effect. The tendency has therefore been, while improving the sanitary aspects of the disposal of the dead, to make the cemeteries themselves as fit as possible for this purpose, and beautiful in arrangement and decoration.

〰〰〰 **CHEERING.** Rhythmical cheering has been developed to its greatest extent in America in the college yells, which may be regarded as a development of the primitive war-cry; this custom has no real analogue at English schools and universities, but the New Zealand football team in 1907 familiarized English crowds at their matches with a similar sort of war-cry adopted from the Maoris. In American schools and colleges there is usually one cheer for the institution as a whole and others for the different classes. The oldest and simplest are those of the New England colleges. The original yells of Harvard and Yale are identical in form, being composed of *rah* (abbreviation of *hurrah*) nine times repeated, shouted in unison with the name of the university at the end. The Yale cheer is given faster than that of Harvard. Many institutions have several different yells, a favourite variation being the name of the college shouted nine times in a slow and prolonged manner. The best known of these variants is the Yale cheer, partly taken from the *Frogs* of Aristophanes, which runs thus:

> Brekekekéx, ko-áx, ko-áx,
> Brekekekéx, ko-áx, ko-áx,
> Oóp, Oóp, parablaoū,
> Yale, Yale, Yale,
> Rah, rah, rah, rah, rah, rah, rah, rah, rah,
> Yale! Yale! Yale!

The regular cheer of Princeton is:

> H'ray, h'ray, h'ray, tiger,
> Siss, boom, ah; Princeton!

This is expanded into the "triple cheer":

> H'ray, h'ray, h'ray,
> Tiger, tiger, tiger,
> Siss, siss, siss,
> Boom, boom, boom,
> Ah, ah, ah
> Princetón, Princetón, Princetón!

The "railroad cheer" is like the foregoing, but begun very slowly and broadly, and gradually accelerated to the end, which is enunciated as fast as possible. Many cheers are formed like that of Toronto University:

> Varsitý, varsitý,
> V-a-r-s-i-t-y (spelled)
> VÁRSÍT-Ý (spelled *staccato*)
> Vár-sí-tý
> Rah, rah, rah!

Another variety of yell is illustrated by that of the School of Practical Science of Toronto University:

> Who are we? Can't you guess?
> We are from the S.P.S.!

The cheer of the United States Naval Academy is an imitation of a nautical syren. The Amherst cheer is:

> Amherst! Amherst! Amherst! Rah! Rah!
> Amherst! Rah! Rah!
> Rah! Rah! Rah! Rah! Rah! Rah! Amherst!

Besides the cheers of individual institutions there are some common to all, generally used to compliment some successful athlete or popular professor. One of the oldest examples of these personal cheers is:

> Who was George Washington?
> First in war,
> First in peace,
> First in the heárts of his countrymén,

followed by a stamping on the floor in the same rhythm.

College yells are used particularly at athletic contests. In any large college there are several leaders, chosen by the students, who stand in front and call for the different songs and cheers, directing with their arms in the fashion of an orchestral conductor. This cheering and singing form one of the distinctive features of inter-collegiate and scholastic athletic contests in America.

CIRCUMCISION. The significance of the rite of circumcision has been much disputed. Some see in it a tribal badge. If this be the true origin of circumcision, it must go back to the time when men went about naked. Mutilations (tattooing, removal of teeth and so forth) were tribal marks; being partly sacrifices and partly means of recognition. Such initiatory rites were often frightful ordeals, in which the neophyte's courage was severely tested (Robertson Smith, *Religion of the Semites*, p. 310). Some regard circumcision as a substitute for far more serious rites, including even human sacrifice. Utilitarian explanations have also been suggested. Sir R. Burton (*Memoirs Anthrop. Soc.* i. 318) held that it was introduced to promote fertility, and the claims of cleanliness have been put forward (following Philo's example, see ed. Mangey, ii. 210). Most probably, however, circumcision (which in many tribes is performed on both sexes) was connected with marriage, and was a preparation for connubium. It was in Robertson Smith's words "originally a preliminary to marriage, and so a ceremony of introduction to the full prerogative of manhood," the transference to infancy among the Jews being a later change. On this view, the decisive Biblical reference would be the Exodus passage (iv. 25), in which Moses is represented as being in danger of his life because he had neglected the proper preliminary to marriage. In Genesis, on the other hand, circumcision is an external sign of God's covenant with Israel, and later Judaism now regards it in this symbolical sense. Barton (*Semitic Origins*, p. 100) declares that "the circumstances under which it is performed in Arabia point to the origin of circumcision as a sacrifice to the goddess of fertility, by which the child was placed under her protection and its reproductive powers consecrated to her service." But Barton admits that initiation to the connubium was the primitive origin of the rite.

As regards the non-ritual use of male circumcision, it may be added that in recent years the medical profession has been responsible for its considerable extension among other than Jewish children, the operation being recommended not merely in cases of malformation, but generally for reasons of health. (I.A.)

FIRE-WALKING, a religious ceremony common to many races. The origin and meaning of the custom is very obscure, but it is shown to have been widespread in all ages. It still survives in Bulgaria, Trinidad, Fiji Islands, Tahiti, India, the Straits Settlements, Mauritius, and it is said Japan. The details of its ritual and its objects vary in different lands, but the essential feature of the rite, the passing of priests, fakirs, and devotees barefoot over heated stones or smouldering ashes is always the same. Fire-walking was usually associated with the spring festivals and was believed to ensure a bountiful harvest. Such was the Chinese vernal festival of fire. In the time of Kublai Khan the Taoist Buddhists held great festivals to the "High Emperor of the Sombre Heavens" and walked through a great fire barefoot, preceded by their priests bearing images of their gods in their arms. Though they were severely burned, these devotees held that they would pass unscathed if they had faith. J. G. Frazer (*Golden Bough*, vol. iii, p. 307) describes the ceremony in the Chinese province of Fo-kien. The chief performers are labourers who must fast for three days and observe chastity for a week. During this time they are taught in the temple how they are to perform their task. On the eve of the festival a huge brazier of charcoal, often twenty feet wide, is prepared in front of the temple of the great god. At sunrise the next morning the brazier is lighted. A Taoist priest throws a mixture of salt and rice into the flames. The two exorcists, barefooted and followed by two peasants, traverse the fire again and again till it is somewhat beaten down. The trained performers then pass through with the image of the god. Frazer suggests that, as the essential feature of the rite is the carrying of the deity through the flames, the whole thing is sympathetic magic designed to give to the coming spring sunshine (the supposed divine emanation), that degree of heat which the image experiences. Frazer quotes Indian fire-walks, notably that of the Dosadhs, a low Indian caste in Behar and Chota Nagpur. On the fifth, tenth, and full moon days of three months of the year, the priest walks over a narrow trench filled with smouldering wood ashes. The Bhuiyas, a Dravidian tribe of Mirzapur, worship their tribal hero Bir by a like performance, and they declare that the walker who is really "possessed" by the hero feels no pain. For fire-walking as observed in the Madras presidency see *Indian Antiquary*, vii. (1878) p. 126; iii. (1874) pp. 6–8; ii. (1873) p. 190 seq. In Fiji the ceremony is called *vilavilarevo*, and according to an eyewitness a number of natives walk unharmed across and among white-hot stones which form the pavement of a huge native oven. In Tahiti priests perform the rite. In April 1899 an Englishman saw a fire-walk in Tokio (see *The Field*, May 20th, 1899). The fire was six yards long by six wide. The rite was in honour of a mountain god. The fire-walkers in Bulgaria are called *Nistinares* and the faculty is regarded as hereditary. They dance in the fire on the 21st of May, the feast of SS. Helena and Constantine. Huge fires of faggots are made, and when these burn down the *Nistinares* (who turn blue in the face) dance on the red-hot embers and utter prophecies, afterwards placing their feet in the muddy ground where libations of water have been poured.

The interesting part of fire-walking is the allged immunity of the performers from burns. On this point authorities and eyewitnesses differ greatly. In a case in Fiji a handkerchief was thrown on to the stones when the first man leapt into the oven, and what remained of it snatched up as the last left the stones. Every fold that touched the stone was charred! In some countries a thick ointment is rubbed on the feet, but this is not usual, and the bulk of the reports certainly leave an impression that there is something still to be explained in the escape of the performers from shocking injuries. S. P. Langley, who witnessed a fire-walk in Tahiti, declares, however, that the whole rite as there practised is a mere symbolic farce (*Nature* for August 22nd, 1901).

HAREM, less frequently HARAM or HARIM (Arab *harīm*—commonly but wrongly pronounced hārĕm—"that which is illegal or prohibited"), the name generally applied to that part of a house in Oriental countries which is set apart for the women. The seclusion of women in the household is fundamental to the Oriental conception of the sex relation, and its origin must, therefore, be sought far earlier than the precepts of Islam as set forth in the Koran, which merely regulate a practically universal Eastern custom. It is inferred from the remains of many ancient Oriental palaces (Babylonian, Persian, &c.) that kings and wealthy nobles devoted a special part of the palace to their womankind. Though in comparatively early times there were not wanting men who regarded polygamy as wrong (*e.g.* the prophets of Israel), nevertheless in the East generally there has never been any real movement against the conception of woman as a chattel of her male relatives. A man may have as many wives and concubines as he can support, but each of these women must be his exclusive property. The object of this insistence upon female chastity is partly the maintenance of the purity of the family with special reference to property, and partly to protect women from marauders, as was the case with the people of India when the Mahommedans invaded the country and sought for women to fill their harems. In Mahommedan countries theoretically a woman must veil her face to all men except her father, her brother and her husband; any violation of this rule is still regarded by strict Mahommedans as the gravest possible offence, though among certain Moslem communities (*e.g.* in parts of Albania) women of the poorer classes may appear in public unveiled. If any other man make his way into a harem he may lose his life; the attempted escape of a harem woman is a capital offence, the husband having absolute power of life and death, to such an extent that, especially in the less civilized parts of the Moslem world, no one would think of questioning a man's right to mutilate or kill a disobedient wife or concubine.

A good deal of misapprehension, due to ignorance combined with strong prejudice against the whole system, exists in regard to the system in Turkey. It is often assumed, for example, that the sultan's seraglio is typical, though on a uniquely large scale, of all Turkish households, and as a consequence that every Turk is a polygamist. This is far from being the case, for though the Koran permits four wives, and etiquette allows the sultan seven, the man of average possessions is perforce content with one, and a small number of female servants. It is, therefore, necessary to take the imperial seraglio separately.

Though the sultan's household in modern times is by no means as numerous as it used to be, it is said that the harem of Abdul Hamid contained about 1000 women, all of whom were of slave origin. This body of women form an elaborately organized community with a complete system of officers, disciplinary and administrative, and strict distinctions of status. The real ruler of this society is the sultan's mother, the *Sultana Validé*, who exercises her authority through a female superintendent, the *Kyahya Khatun*. She has also a large retinue of subordinate officials *(Kalfas)* ranging downwards from the "Lady of the Treasury" to the "Mistress of the Sherbets" and the "Chief Coffee Server." Each of these officials has under her a number of pupil-slaves *(alaiks)*, whom she trains to succeed her if need be, and from whom the service is recruited. After the sultana validé (who frequently enjoys considerable political power and is a mistress of intrigue) ranks the mother of the heir-apparent; she is called the *Bash Kadin Effendi* ("Her excellency the Chief Lady"), and also *hasseki or kasseky*, and is distinguished from the other three chief wives who only bear the title *Kadin Effendi*. Next come the ladies who have borne the younger children of the sultan, the *Hanum Effendis*, and after them the so-called Odalisks or Odalisques (a perversion of *odalik*, from *odah*, chamber). These are subdivided, according to the degree of favour in which they stand with the sultan or padishah, into *Ikbals* ("Favourites") and *Geuzdés* (literally the "Eyed" ones), those whom the sultan has favourably noticed in the course of his visits to the apartments of his wives or his mother. All the women are at the disposal of the sultan, though it is contrary to etiquette for him actually to select recruits for his harem. The numbers are kept up by his female relatives and state officials, the latter of whom present girls annually on the evening before the 15th of Ramadan.

Every odalisk who has been promoted to the royal couch receives a *daïra*, consisting of an allowance of money, a suite of apartments, and a retinue, in proportion to her status. It should be noted that, since all the harem women are slaves, the sultans, with practically no exceptions, have never entered into legal marriage contracts. Any slave, in however menial a position, may be promoted to the position of a kadin effendi. Hence all the slaves who have any pretension to beauty are carefully trained, from the time they enter the harem, in deportment, dancing, music and the arts of the toilette: they are instructed in the Moslem religion and learn the daily prayers *(namaz)*; a certain number are specially trained in reading and writing for secretarial work. Discipline is strict, and continued disobedience leads to corporal punishment by the eunuchs. All the women of the harem are absolutely under the control of the sultana validé (who alone of the harem of her dead husband is not sent away to an older palace when her son succeeds), and owe her the most profound respect, even to the point of having to obtain permission to leave their own apartments. Her financial secretary, the *Haznadar Ousta*, succeeds to her power if she dies. The sultan's foster-mother also is a person of importance, and is known as the *Taia Kadin*.

The security of the harem is in the hands of a body of eunuchs both black and white. The white eunuchs have charge of the outer gates of the seraglio, but they are not allowed to approach the women's apartments, and obtain no posts of distinction. Their chief, however, the *kapu aghasi* ("master of the gates") has part control over the ecclesiastical possessions, and even the vizier cannot enter the royal apartments without his permission. The black eunuchs have the right of entering the gardens and chambers of the harem. Their chief, usually called the *kislar aghasi* ("master of the maidens"), though his true title is *darus skadet aga* ("chief of the abode of felicity"), is an official of high importance. His appointment is for life. If he is deprived of his post he receives his freedom; and if he resigns of his own accord he is generally sent to Egypt with a pension of 100 francs a day. His secretary keeps count of the revenues of the mosques built by the sultans. He is usually succeeded by the second eunuch, who bears the title of treasurer, and has charge of the jewels, &c., of the women. The number of eunuchs is always a large one. The sultana validé and the sultana hasseki have each fifty at their service, and others are assigned to the kadins and the favourite odalisks.

The ordinary middle-class household is naturally on a very different scale. The *selamlik* is on the ground floor with a separate entrance, and there the master of the house receives his male guests;
the rest of the ground floor is occupied by the kitchen and perhaps
the stables. The *haremlik* is generally (in towns at least) on the upper
floor fronting on and slightly overhanging the street; it has a separate
entrance, courtyard and garden. The windows are guarded by lattices
pierced with circular holes through which the women may watch
without being seen. Communication with the *haremlik* is affected by
a locked door, of which the Effendi keeps the key and also by a sort
of revolving cupboard *(dutap)* for the conveyance of meals. The furniture, of the old-fashioned harems at least, is confined to divans,
rugs, carpets and mirrors. For heating purposes the old brass tray of
charcoal and wood ash is giving way to American stoves, and there
is a tendency to import French furniture and decoration without
regard to their suitability.

The presence of a second wife is the exception, and is generally
attributable to the absence of children by the first wife. The expense
of marrying a free woman leads many Turks to prefer a slave woman
who is much more likely to be an amenable partner. If a slave woman
bears a child she is often set free and then the marriage ceremony
is gone through.

The harem system is, of course, wholly inconsistent with any high
ideal of womanhood. Certain misapprehensions, however, should be
noticed. The depravity of the system and the vapid idleness of harem
life are much exaggerated by observers whose sympathies are wholly
against the system. In point of fact much depends on the individuals.
In many households there exists a very high degree of mutual consideration and the standard of conduct is by no means degraded.
Though a woman may not be seen in the streets without the *yashmak*
which covers her face except for her eyes, and does not leave her
house except by her husband's permission, none the less in ordinary
households the harem ladies frequently drive into the country and
visit the shops and public baths. Their seclusion has very considerable
compensations, and legally they stand on a far better basis in relation
to their husbands than do the women of monogamous Christian
communities. From the moment when a woman, free or slave, enters
into any kind of wifely relation with a man, she has a legally enforce-
able right against him both for her own and for her children's maintenance. She has absolute control over her personal property whether
in money, slaves or goods; and, if divorce is far easier in Islam than

in Christendom, still the marriage settlement must be of such amount as will provide suitable maintenance in that event.

On the other hand, of course, the system is open to the gravest abuse, and in countries like Persia, Morocco and India, the life of Moslem women and slaves is often far different from that of middle class women of European Turkey, where law is strict and culture advanced. The early age at which girls are secluded, the dulness of their surroundings, and the low moral standard which the system produces react unfavourably not only upon their moral and intellectual growth but also upon their capacity for motherhood and their general physique. A harem woman is soon passée, and the lot of a woman past her youth, if she is divorced or a widow, is monotonous and empty. This is true especially of child-widows.

Since the middle of the 19th century familiarity with European customs and the direct influence of European administrators has brought about a certain change in the attitude of Orientals to the harem system. This movement is, however, only in its infancy, and the impression is still strong that the time is not ripe for reform. The Oriental women are in general so accustomed to their condition that few have any inclination to change it, while men as a rule are emphatically opposed to any alteration of the system. The Young Turkish party, the upper classes in Egypt, as also the Babists in Persia, have to some extent progressed beyond the orthodox conception of the status of women, but no radical reform has been set on foot.

HEART-BURIAL, the burial of the heart apart from the body. This is a very ancient practice, the special reverence shown towards the heart being doubtless due to its early association with the soul of man, his affections, courage and conscience. In medieval Europe heart-burial was fairly common. Some of the more notable cases are those of Richard I., whose heart, preserved in a casket, was placed in Rouen cathedral; Henry III., buried in Normandy; Eleanor, queen of Edward I., at Lincoln; Edward I., at Jerusalem; Louis IX., Philip III., Louis XIII. and Louis XIV., in Paris. Since the 17th century the hearts of deceased members of the house of Hapsburg have been buried apart from the body in the Loretto chapel in the Augustiner Kirche, Vienna. The most romantic story of heart-burial is that of Robert Bruce. He wished his heart to rest at Jerusalem in the church of the Holy Sepulchre, and on his deathbed entrusted the fulfilment of his wish to Douglas. The latter broke his journey to join the Spaniards in their war with the Moorish king of Granada, and was killed in battle, the heart of Bruce enclosed in a silver casket hanging round his neck. Subsequently the heart was buried at Melrose Abbey. The heart of James, marquess of Montrose, executed by the Scottish Covenanters in 1650, was recovered from his body, which had been buried by the roadside outside Edinburgh, and, enclosed in a steel box, was sent to the duke of Montrose, then in exile. It was lost on its journey, and years afterwards was discovered in a curiosity shop in Flanders. Taken by a member of the Montrose family to India, it was stolen as an amulet by a native chief, was once more regained, and finally lost in France during the Revolution. Of notable 17th-century cases there is that of James II., whose heart was buried in the church of the convent of the Visitation at Chaillot near Paris, and that of Sir William Temple, at Moor Park, Farnham. The last ceremonial burial of a heart in England was that of Paul White-head, secretary to the Monks of Medmenham club, in 1775, the interment taking place in the Le Despenser mausoleum at High Wy-combe, Bucks. Of later cases the most notable are those of Daniel O'Connell, whose heart is at Rome, Shelley at Bournemouth, Louis XVII. at Venice, Kosciusko at the Polish museum at Rapperschwyll, Lake Zürich, and the marquess of Bute, taken by his widow to Je-rusalem for burial in 1900. Sometimes other parts of the body, re-moved in the process of embalming, are given separate and solemn burial. Thus the viscera of the popes from Sixtus V. (1590) onward have been preserved in the parish church of the Quirinal. The custom of heart-burial was forbidden by Pope Boniface VIII.

HUE AND CRY, a phrase employed in English law to signify the old common law process of pursuing a criminal with horn and voice. It was the duty of any person aggrieved, or discovering a felony, to raise the hue and cry, and his neighbours were bound to turn out with him and assist in the discovery of the offender. In the case of a hue and cry, all those joining in the pursuit were justified in arresting the person pursued, even though it turned out that he was innocent. A swift fate awaited any one overtaken by hue and cry, if he still had about him the signs of his guilt. If he resisted he could be cut down, while, if he submitted to capture, his fate was decided. Although brought before a court, he was not al-lowed to say anything in self-defence, nor was there any need for accusation, indictment or appeal. Although regulated from time to time by writs and statutes, the process of hue and cry continued to retain its summary method of procedure, and proof was not required of a culprit's guilt, but merely that he had been taken red-handed by hue and cry. The various statutes relating to hue and cry were repealed in 1827. The Sheriffs Act of 1887 provides that every person in a county must be ready and apparelled at the command of the sheriff and at the cry of the county to arrest a felon, and in default shall on conviction be liable to a fine.

"Hue and cry" has, from its original meaning, come to be applied to a proclamation for the capture of an offender or for the finding of stolen goods, and to an official publication, issued for the information of the authorities interested, in which particulars are given of offenders "wanted," offences committed, &c.

JACTITATION (from Lat. *jactitare*, to throw out publicly), in English law, the maliciously boasting or giving out by one party that he or she is married to the other. In such a case, in order to prevent the common reputation of their marriage that might ensue, the procedure is by suit of jactitation of marriage, in which the petitioner alleges that the respondent boasts that he or she is married to the petitioner, and prays a declaration of nullity and a decree putting the respondent to perpetual silence thereafter. Previously to 1857 such a proceeding took place only in the ecclesiastical courts, but by express terms of the Matrimonial Causes Act of that year it can now be brought in the probate, divorce and admiralty division of the High Court. To the suit there are three defences: (1) denial of the boasting; (2) the truth of the representations; (3) allegation (by way of estoppel) that the petitioner acquiesced in the boasting of the respondent. In *Thompson* v. *Rourke*, 1893, Prob. 70, the court of appeal laid down that the court will not make a decree in a jactitation suit in favour of a petitioner who has at any time acquiesced in the assertion of the respondent that they were actually married. Jactitation of marriage is a suit that is very rare.

LETTRES DE CACHET. Considered solely as French documents, *lettres de cachet* may be defined as letters signed by the king of France, countersigned by one of his ministers, and closed with the royal seal *(cachet)*. They contained an order—in principle, any order whatsoever—emanating directly from the king, and executory by himself. In the case of organized bodies *lettres de cachet* were issued for the purpose of enjoining members to assemble or to accomplish some definite act; the provincial estates were convoked in this manner, and it was by a *lettre de cachet* (called *lettre de jussion*) that the king ordered a parlement to register a law in the teeth of its own remonstrances. The best-known *lettres de cachet*, however, were those which may be called penal, by which the king sentenced a subject without trial and without an opportunity of defence to imprisonment in a state prison or an ordinary goal, confinement in a convent or a hospital, transportation to the colonies, or relegation to a given place within the realm.

The power which the king exercised on these various occasions was a royal privilege recognized by old French law, and can be traced to a maxim which furnished a text of the *Digest* of Justinian: "Rex solutus est a legibus." This signified particularly that when the king intervened directly in the administration proper, or in the administration of justice, by a special act of his will, he could decide without heeding the laws, and even in a sense contrary to the laws. This was an early conception, and in early times the order in question was simply verbal; thus some letters patent of Henry III. of France in 1576 (Isambert, *Anciennes lois françaises*, xiv. 278) state that François de Montmorency was "prisoner in our castle of the Bastille in Paris by verbal command" of the late king Charles IX. But in the 14th century the principle was introduced that the order should be written, and hence arose the *lettre de cachet*. The *lettre de cachet* belonged to the class of *lettres closes*, as opposed to *lettres patentes*, which contained the expression of the legal and permanent will of the king, and had to be furnished with the seal of state affixed by the chancellor. The *lettres de cachet*, on the contrary, were signed simply by a secretary of state (formerly known as *secrétaire des commandements*) for the king; they bore merely the imprint of the king's privy seal, from which circumstance they were often called, in the 14th and 15th centuries, *lettres de petit signet* or *lettres de petit cachet*, and were entirely exempt from the control of the chancellor.

While serving the government as a silent weapon against political adversaries or dangerous writers and as a means of punishing culprits of high birth without the scandal of a suit at law, the *lettres de cachet* had many other uses. They were employed by the police in dealing with prostitutes, and on their authority lunatics were shut up in hospitals and sometimes in prisons. They were also often used by heads of families as a means of correction. *e.g.* for protecting the family honour from the disorderly or criminal conduct of sons; wives, too, took advantage of them to curb the profligacy of husbands and vice versa. They were issued by the intermediary on the advice of the intendants in the provinces and of the lieutenant of police in Paris. In reality, the secretary of state issued them in a completely arbitrary fashion, and in most cases the king was unaware of their issue. In the 18th century it is certain that the letters were often issued blank, *i.e.* without containing the name of the person against whom they were directed; the recipient, or mandatary, filled in the name in order to make the letter effective. (J.P.E.)

     LUNCHEON, in present usage the name given to a meal between breakfast and tea or dinner. When dinner was taken at an early hour, or when it is still the principal midday meal, luncheon was and is still a light repast. The derivation of the word has been obscured, chiefly owing to the attempted connexion with "nuncheon," with which the word has nothing to do etymologically. "Luncheon" is an extended form of "lunch" (another form of "lump," as "hunch" is of "hump"). Lunch and luncheon in the earliest meanings found are applied to a thick piece of bread, bacon, meat, &c.

The word "nuncheon," or "nunchion," with which "luncheon" has been frequently connected, appears as early as the 14th century in the form *noneschenche.* This meant a refreshment or distribution, properly of drink, but also accompanied with some small quantity of meat, taken in the early afternoon. The word means literally "noon-drink," from none or noon, *i.e. nona hora,* the ninth hour, originally 3 o'clock P.M., but later "midday"—the church office of "nones," and also the second meal of the day, having been shifted back—and *schenchen,* to pour out; cf. German *schenken,* which means to retail drink and to give, present. *Schenche* is the same as "shank," the shin-bone, and the sense development appears to be shin-bone, pipe, hence tap for drawing liquor.

     LYNCH LAW, a term loosely applied to various forms of executing rough popular justice, or what is thought to be justice, for the punishment of offenders by a summary procedure, ignoring, or even contrary to, the strict forms of law. The word *lynching* "originally signified a whipping for reformatory purposes with more or less disregard for its legality" (Cutler), or the infliction of minor punishments without recourse to law; but during and after the Reconstruction Period in the United States, it came to mean, generally, the summary infliction of capital punishment. Lynch law is frequently prevalent in sparsely settled or frontier districts where government is weak and officers of the law too few and too powerless to enforce law and preserve order. The practice has been common in all countries when unsettled frontier conditions existed, or in periods of threatened anarchy. In what are considered civilized countries it is now found mainly in Russia, south-eastern Europe and in America, but it is essentially and almost peculiarly an American institution. The origin of the name is obscure; different writers have attempted to trace it to Ireland, to England, to South Carolina, to Pennsylvania and to Virginia. It is certain that the name was first used in America, but it is not certain whether it came from Lynch's Creek, South Carolina, where summary justice was administered to outlaws, or from Virginia and Pennsylvania, where men named Lynch were noted for dealing out summary punishment to offenders. In Europe early examples of a similar phenomenon are found in the proceedings of the Vehmgerichte in medieval Germany, and of Lydford law, gibbet law or Halifax law, Cowper justice and Jeddart justice in the thinly settled and border districts of Great Britain; and since the term "lynch law" came into colloquial use, it is loosely employed to cover any case in which a portion of the community takes the execution of its ideas of justice into its own hands, irrespective of the legal authorities.

In America during the 18th and 19th centuries the population expanded westward faster than well-developed civil institutions could follow, and on the western frontier were always desperadoes who lived by preying on the better classes. To suppress these desperadoes, in the absence of strong legal institutions, resort was continually made to lynch law. There was little necessity for it until the settlement crossed the Allegheny Mountains, but the following instances of lynching in the East may be mentioned: (1) the mistreatment of Indians in New England and the Middle Colonies in disregard of laws protecting them; (2) the custom found in various colonies of administering summary justice to wife-beaters, idlers and other obnoxious persons; (3) the acts of the Regulators of North Carolina, 1767–1771; (4) the popular tribunals of the Revolutionary period, when the disaffection toward Great Britain weakened the authority of the civil governments and the war replaced them by popular governments, at a time when the hostilities between "Patriots" and "Tories" were an incentive to extra-legal violence. In the South, lynching methods were long employed in dealing with agitators, white and black, who were charged with endeavouring to excite the slaves to insurrection or to crime against their masters, and in dealing with anti-slavery agitators generally.

In the West, from the Alleghenies to the Golden Gate, the pioneer settlers resorted to popular justice to get rid of bands of outlaws, and to regulate society during that period when laws were weak or confused, when the laws made in the East did not suit western conditions, and when courts and officials were scarce and distant. The Watauga settlements and the "State" of Franklin furnished examples of lynch law procedure almost reduced to organization. Men trained in the rough school of the wilderness came to have more regard for quick, ready-made, personal justice than for abstract justice and statutes; they were educated to defend themselves, to look to no law for protection or regulation; consequently they became impatient of legal forms and lawyers' technicalities; an appeal to statute law was looked upon with suspicion, and, if some personal matter was involved, was likely to result in deadly private feuds. Thus were formed the habits of thought and action of the western pioneers. Lynch law, not civil law, cleared the western forests, valleys and mountain passes of horse and cattle thieves, and other robbers and outlaws, gamblers and murderers. This was especially true of California, and the states of the far West. H. H. Bancroft, the historian of *Popular Tribunals,* wrote in 1887 that "thus far in the history of these Pacific States far more has been done toward righting wrongs and administering justice outside the pale of law than within it." However, the lack of regard for law fostered by the conditions described led to a survival of the lynching habit after the necessity for it passed away. In parts of the Southern states, where the whites are few and greatly outnumbered by the blacks, certain of the conditions of the West have prevailed, and since emancipation released the blacks from restraint many of the latter have been lawless and turbulent. The Reconstruction, by giving to the blacks temporary political supremacy, increased the friction between the races, and greatly deepened prejudice. The numerous protective societies of whites, 1865–1876, culminating in the Ku Klux movement, may be described as an application of lynch law. With the increase of negro crimes came an increase of lynchings, due to prejudice, to the fact that for some time after Reconstruction the governments were relatively weak, especially in the districts where the blacks outnumber the whites, to the fact that negroes nearly always shield criminals of their own race against the whites, and to the frequent occurrence of the crime of rape by negro men upon white women.

Since 1882 the Chicago *Tribune* has collected statistics of lynching, and some interesting facts may be deduced from these tables. During the twenty-two years from 1882 to 1903 inclusive, the total number of persons lynched in the United States was 3337, the number decreasing during the last decade; of these 2385 were in the South and 752 in the North; of those lynched in the East and West 602 were white and 75 black, and of those in the South 567 were white and 1985 black. Lynchings occur mostly during periods of idleness of the lower classes; in the summer more are lynched for crimes against the person and in the winter (in the West) for crimes against property; the principal causes of lynching in the South are murder and rape, in the North and West, murder and offences against property; more blacks than whites were lynched between 1882 and 1903, the numbers being 2060 negroes, of whom 40 were women, and 1169 whites, of whom 23 were women; of the 707 blacks lynched for rape 675 were in the South; 783 blacks were lynched for murder, and 753 of these were in the South; most of the lynchings of whites were in the West; the lynching of negroes increased somewhat outside of the South and decreased somewhat in the South. Lynching decreases and disappears in a community as the population grows denser and civil institutions grow stronger; as better communications and good police make it harder to commit crime; and as public sentiment is educated to demand legal rather than illegal and irregular infliction of punishment for even the most horrible of crimes. (W.L.F.)

PAWNBROKING. The business of lending money on the security of goods taken in pledge. If we desire to trace with minuteness the history of pawnbroking, we must go back to the earliest ages of the world, since the business of lending money on portable security is one of the most ancient of human occupations. The Mosaic Law struck at the root of pawnbroking as a profitable business, since it forbade the taking of interest from a poor borrower, while no Jew was to pay another for timely accommodation. And it is curious to reflect that, although the Jew was the almost universal usurer and money-lender upon security of the middle ages, it is now very rare in Great Britain to find a Hebrew pawnbroker.

In China the pawnshop was probably as familiar two or three thousand years ago as it is to-day, and its conduct is still regulated quite as strictly as in England. The Chinese conditions, too, are decidedly favourable to the borrower. He may, as a rule, take three years to redeem his property, and he cannot be charged a higher rate than 3% per annum—a regulation which would close every pawnshop in England in a month. Both Rome and Greece were as familiar with the operation of pawning as the modern poor all the world over;

indeed, from the Roman jurisprudence most of the contemporary law on the subject is derived. The chief difference between Roman and English law is that under the former certain things, such as wearing apparel, furniture, and instruments of tillage, could not be pledged, whereas there is no such restriction in English legislation. The emperor Augustus converted the surplus arising to the state from the confiscated property of criminals into a fund from which sums of money were lent, without interest, to those who could pledge valuables equal to double the amount borrowed. It was, indeed, in Italy, and in more modern times, that the pledge system which is now almost universal on the continent of Europe arose. In its origin that system was purely benevolent, the early *monts de piété* established by the authority of the popes lending money to the poor only, without interest, on the sole condition of the advances being covered by the value of the pledges. This was virtually the Augustan system, but it is obvious that an institution which costs money to manage and derives no income from its operations must either limit its usefulness to the extent of the voluntary support it can command, or must come to a speedy end. Thus as early as 1198 something of the kind was started at Freising in Bavaria; while in 1350 a similar endeavour was made at Salins in Franche Comté, where interest at the rate of $7\frac{1}{3}\%$ was charged. Nor was England backward, for in 1361 Michael Northbury, or de Northborough, bishop of London, bequeathed 1000 silver marks for the establishment of a free pawnshop. These primitive efforts, like the later Italian ones, all failed. The Vatican was therefore constrained to allow the Sacri monti di pietà—no satisfactory derivation of the phrase has yet been suggested—to charge sufficient interest to their customers to enable them to defray expenses. Thereupon a learned and tedious controversy arose upon the lawfulness of charging interest, which was only finally set at rest by Pope Leo X., who, in the tenth sitting of the Council of the Lateran, declared that the pawnshop was a lawful and valuable institution, and threatened with excommunication those who should presume to express doubts on the subject. The Council of Trent inferentially confirmed this decision, and at a somewhat later date we find St Charles Borromeo counselling the establishment of state or municipal pawnshops.

Long before this, however, monti di pietà charging interest for their loans had become common in Italy. The date of their establishment was not later than 1464, when the earliest of which there appears to be any record in that country—it was at Orvieto—was confirmed by Pius II. Three years later another was opened at Perugia by the efforts of two Franciscans, Barnabus Interamnensis and Fortunatus de Copolis. They collected the necessary capital by preaching, and the Perugian pawnshop was opened with such success that there was a substantial balance of profit at the end of the first year. The Dominicans endeavoured to preach down the "lending-house," but without avail. Viterbo obtained one of 1469, and Sixtus IV. confirmed another to his native town in Savona in 1479. After the death of Brother Barnabus in 1474, a strong impulse was given to the creation of these establishments by the preaching of another Franciscan, Father Bernandino di Feltre, who was in due course canonized. By his efforts monti di pietà were opened at Assisi, Mantua, Parma, Lucca, Piacenza, Padua, Vicenza, Pavia and a number of places of less importance. At Florence the veiled opposition of the municipality and the open hostility of the Jews prevailed against him, and it was reserved to Savonarola, who was a Dominican, to create the first Florentine pawnshop, after the local theologians had declared that there was "no sin, even venial," in charging interest. The readiness of the popes to give permission for pawnshops all over Italy, makes it the more remarkable that the papal capital possessed nothing of the kind until 1539, and even then owed the convenience to a Franciscan. From Italy the pawnshop spread gradually all over Europe. Augsburg adopted the system in 1591, Nuremberg copied the Augsburg regulations in 1618, and by 1622 it was established at Amsterdam, Brussels, Antwerp and Ghent. Madrid followed suit in 1705, when a priest opened a charitable pawnshop with a capital of fivepence taken from an alms-box.

The institution was, however, very slow in obtaining a footing in France. It was adopted at Avignon in 1577, and at Arras in 1624. The doctors of the once powerful Sorbonne could not reconcile themselves to the lawfulness of interest, and when a pawnshop was opened in Paris in 1626, it had to be closed within a year. Then it was that Jean Boucher published his *Défense des monts de piété*. Marseilles obtained one in 1695; but it was not until 1777 that the first mont de piété was founded in Paris by royal patent. The statistics which have been preserved relative to the business done in the first few years of its existence show that in the twelve years between 1777 and the Revolution, the average value of the pledges was 42 francs 50 centimes, which is double the present average. The interest charged was 10% per annum, and large profits were made upon the sixteen million livres that were lent every year. The National Assembly, in an evil moment, destroyed the monopoly of the mont de piété, but it struggled on until 1795, when the competition of the money-lenders compelled it to close its doors. So great, however, were the extortions of the usurers that the people began to clamour for its reopening, and in July 1797 it recommenced business with a fund of £20,000 found by five private capitalists. At first it charged interest at the rate of 36% per annum, which was gradually reduced, the gradations being 30, 24, 18, 15, and finally 12% in 1804. In 1806 it fell to 9%, and in 1887 to 7%. In 1806 Napoleon I. re-established its monopoly, while Napoleon III., as prince-president, regulated it by new laws that are still in force. In Paris the pledge-shop is, in effect, a department of the administration; in the French provinces it is a municipal monopoly; and this remark holds good, with modifications, for most parts of the continent of Europe.

In England the pawnbroker, like so many other distinguished personages, "came in with the Conqueror." From that time, indeed, to the famous legislation of Edward I., the Jew money-lender was the only pawnbroker. Yet, despite the valuable services which the class rendered, not infrequently to the Crown itself, the usurer was treated with studied cruelty—Sir Walter Scott's Isaac of York was no mere creation of fiction. These barbarities, by diminishing the number of Jews in the country, had, long before Edward's decree of banishment, begun to make it worth the while of the Lombard merchants to settle in England. It is now as well established as anything of the kind can be that the three golden balls, which have for so long been the trade sign of the pawnbroker, were the symbol which these Lombard merchants hung up in front of their houses, and not, as has often been suggested, the arms of the Medici family. It has, indeed, been conjectured that the golden balls were originally three flat yellow effigies of byzants, or gold coins; laid heraldically upon a sable field, but that they were presently converted into balls the better to attract attention. In 1338 Edward III. pawned his jewels to the Lombards to raise money for his war with France. An equally great king—Henry V.—did much the same in 1415.

The Lombards were not a popular class, and Henry VII. harried them a good deal. In the very first year of James I. "An Act against Brokers" was passed and remained on the statute-book until Queen Victoria had been thirty-five years on the throne. It was aimed at "counterfeit brokers," of whom there were then many in London. This type of broker was evidently regarded as a mere receiver of stolen goods, for the act provided that "no sale or pawn of any stolen jewels, plate or other goods to any pawnbroker in London, Westminster or Southwark shall alter the property therein," and that "pawnbrokers refusing to produce goods to their owner from whom stolen shall forfeit double the value."

In the time of Charles I. there was another act which made it quite clear that the pawnbroker was not deemed to be a very respectable or trustworthy person. Nevertheless a plan was mooted for setting that king up in the business. The Civil War was approaching and supplies were badly needed, when a too ingenious Royalist proposed the establishment of a state "pawnhouse." The preamble of the scheme recited how "the intolerable injuries done to the poore subjects by brokers and usurers that take 30, 40, 50, 60, and more in the hundredth, may be remedied and redressed, the poor thereby greatly relieved and eased, and His Majestie much benefited." That the king would have been "much benefited" is obvious, since he was to enjoy two-thirds of the profits, while the working capital of £100,000 was to be found by the city of London. The reform of what Shakespeare calls "broking pawn" was in the air at that time, although nothing ever came of it, and in the early days of the commonwealth it was proposed to establish a kind of mont de piété. The idea was emphasized in a pamphlet of 1651 entitled *Observations manifesting the Conveniency and Commodity of Mount Pieteyes, or Public Bancks for Relief of the Poor or Others in Distress, upon Pawns.* No doubt many a ruined cavalier would have been glad enough of some such means of raising money, but this radical change in the principles of English pawnbroking was never brought about. It is said that the Bank of England, under its charter, has power to establish pawnshops; and we learn from *A Short History of the Bank of England*, published in its very early days, that it was the intention of the directors, "for the ease of the poor," to institute "a Lombard" "for small pawns at a penny a pound interest per month."

Throughout both the 17th and 18th centuries the general suspicion of the pawnbroker appears to have been only too well founded. It would appear from the references Fielding makes to the subject in *Amelia*, which was written when George II. was on the throne, that, taken in the mass, he was not a very scrupulous tradesman. Down to about that time it had been customary for publicans to lend money on pledges that their customers might have the means of drinking, but the practice was at last stopped by act of parliament. Nor was respect for the honesty of the business increased by the attempt of "The Charitable Corporation" to conduct pawnbroking on a large scale. Established by charter in 1707, "this nefarious corporation," as Smollett called it, was a swindle on a large scale. The directors gambled wildly with the shareholders' money and in the end the common council of the city of London petitioned parliament for the dissolution of this dishonest concern, on the ground that "the corporation, by affording an easy method of raising money upon valuables, furnishes the thief and pickpocket with a better opportunity of selling their stolen goods, and enables an intending bankrupt to dispose of the goods he buys on credit for ready money, to the defrauding of his creditors." When the concern collapsed in 1731 its cashier was Mr George Robinson, M.P. for Marlow. In company with another principal official he disappeared, less than £30,300 being left of a capital which had once been twenty times as much.

The pawnbroker in the United States is, generally speaking, subject to considerable legal restriction, but violations of the laws and ordinances are frequent. Each state has its own regulations, but those of New York and Massachusetts may be taken as fairly representative. "Brokers of pawn" are usually licensed by the mayors, or by the mayors and aldermen, but in Boston the police commissioners are the licensing authority. In the state of New York permits are renewable annually on payment of $500, and the pawnbroker must file a bond with the mayor, executed by himself and two responsible sureties, in the sum of $10,000. The business is conducted on much the same lines as in England, and the rate of interest is 3% per month for the first six months, and 2% monthly afterwards. Where, however, the loan exceeds $100 the rates are 2 and 1% respectively. To exact higher rates is a misdemeanour. Unredeemed pledges may be sold at the end of a year. Pawnbrokers are not allowed to engage in any kind of second-hand business. New York contains one pawnshop to every 12,000 inhabitants, and most of the pawnbrokers are Jews. In the state of Massachusetts unredeemed pledges may be sold four months after the date of deposit. The licensing authority may fix the rate of interest, which may vary for different amounts, and in Boston every pawnbroker is bound to furnish to the police daily a list of the pledges taken in during the preceding twenty-four hours, specifying the hour of each transaction and the amount lent. (J.P.B.)

PRECEDENCE (from Lat. *praecedere*, to go before, precede). This word in the sense in which it is here employed means priority of place, or superiority of rank, in the conventional system of arrangement under which the more eminent and dignified orders of the community are classified on occasions of public ceremony and in the intercourse of private life. In the United Kingdom there is no complete and comprehensive code whereby the scheme of social gradation has been defined and settled, once and for all, on a sure and lasting foundation. The principles and rules at present controlling it have been formulated at different periods and have been derived from various sources. The Crown is the fountain of honour, and it is its undoubted prerogative to confer on any of its subjects, in any part of its dominions, such titles and distinctions and such rank and place as to it may seem meet and convenient. Its discretion in this respect is altogether unbounded at common law, and is limited in those cases only wherein it has been submitted to restraint by act of parliament. In the old time all questions of precedence came in the ordinary course of things within the jurisdiction of the court of chivalry, in which the lord high constable and earl marshal presided as judges, and of which the kings of arms, heralds and pursuivants were the assessors and executive officers. When, however, points of unusual moment and magnitude happened to be brought into controversy, they were occasionally considered and decided by the sovereign in person, or by a special commission, or by the privy council, or even by the parliament itself. But it was not until towards the middle of the 16th century that precedence was made the subject of any legislation in the proper meaning of the term.

In 1539 an act "for the placing of the Lords in Parliament" was passed at the instance of the king, and by it the relative rank of the members of the royal family, of the great officers of state and the household, and of the hierarchy and the peerage was definitely and definitively ascertained. In 1563 an act "for declaring the authority of the Lord Keeper of the Great Seal and the Lord Chancellor to be the same" also declared their precedence to be the same. Questions concerning the precedence of peers are mentioned in the Lords Journals, but in the reign of James I. such questions were often referred to the commissioners for executing the office of earl marshal. In the reign of Charles I. the House of Lords considered several questions of precedency and objected in the earl of Banbury's case to warrants overruling the statute of 31 Hen. VIII. In 1689 an act "for enabling Lords Commissioners of the Great Seal to execute the office of Lord Chancellor or Lord Keeper" gave to the commissioners not being peers of the realm place next to the speaker of the House of Commons and to the speaker place next to the peers of the realm. In 1707 the Act of Union with Scotland provided that all peers of Scotland should be peers of Great Britain and should have rank immediately after the peers of the like degrees in England at the time of the union and before all peers of Great Britain of the like degrees created after the union. In 1800 the Act of Union with Ireland provided that the lords spiritual of Ireland should have rank immediately after the lords spiritual of the same degree in Great Britain, and that the lords temporal of Ireland should have rank immediately after the lords temporal of the same degree in Great Britain at the time of the union, and further that "peerages of Ireland created after the union should have precedence with peerages of the United Kingdom created after the union according to the dates of their creation." At different times too during the current century several statutes have been passed for the reform and extension of the judicial organization which have very materially affected the precedence of the judges, more especially the Judicature Act of 1873, under which the lords justices of appeal and the justices of the High Court now receive their appointments. But the statute of Henry VIII. "for the placing of the Lords" still remains the only legislative measure in which it has been attempted to deal directly and systematically with any large and important section of the scale of general precedence; and the law, so far as it relates to the ranking of the sovereign's immediate kindred whether lineal or collateral, the principal ministers of the Crown and court, and both the spiritual and temporal members of the House of Lords, is to all practical intents and purposes what it was made by that statute nearly 350 years ago. Where no act of parliament applies precedence is determined either by the will and pleasure of the sovereign or by what is accepted as "ancient usage and established custom." Of the sovereign's will and pleasure the appropriate method of announcement is by warrant under the sign-manual, or letters patent under the great seal. But, although the Crown has at all periods very frequently conceded special privileges of rank and place to particular persons, its interference with the scale of general precedence has been rare and exceptional. In 1540 it was provided by warrant from Henry VIII. that certain officers of the household therein named should precede the secretaries of state when and if they were under the degree of barons. In 1612 James I. directed by letters patent, not without long and elaborate argument in the Star Chamber, that baronets, then newly created, should be ranked after the younger sons of viscounts and barons, and that a number of political and judicial functionaries should be ranked between knights of the Garter and such knights bannerets as should be made by the sovereign in person "under his standard displayed in an army royal in open war." Four years later he further directed, also by letters patent, that the sons of baronets and their wives and daughters of baronets should be placed before the sons of knights and their wives and the daughters of knights "of what degree or order soever." And again in 1620 the same king commanded by warrant "after solemn argument before his majesty" that the younger sons of earls should precede knights of the privy council and knights of the Garter not being "barons or of a higher degree." If we add to these ordinances the provisions relating to precedence contained in the statutes of several of the orders of knighthood which since then have been instituted or reconstructed, we shall nearly, if not quite, exhaust the catalogue of the interpositions of the sovereign with regard to the rank and place of classes as distinguished from individuals. Of "ancient usage and established custom" the records of the College of Arms furnish the fullest and most trustworthy evidence.

I. General Precedence of Men.

The sovereign; (1) prince of Wales; (2) younger sons of the sovereign; (3) grandsons of the sovereign; (4) brothers of the sovereign; (5) uncles of the sovereign; (6) nephews of the sovereign; (7) ambassadors; (8) archbishop of Canterbury, primate of all England; (9) lord high chancellor of Great Britain or lord keeper of the great seal; (10) archbishop of York, primate of England; (11) prime minister; (12) lord high treasurer of Great Britain; (13) lord president of the privy council; (14) lord keeper of the privy seal; (15) lord great chamberlain of England; (16) lord high constable of England; (17) earl marshal; (18) lord high admiral; (19) lord steward of the household; (20) lord chamberlain of the household; above peers of their own degree; (21) dukes; (22) marquesses; (23) dukes' eldest sons; (24) earls; (25) marquesses' eldest sons; (26) dukes' younger sons; (27) viscounts; (28) earls' eldest sons; (29) marquesses' younger sons; (30) bishops; (31) barons; (32) speaker of the House of Commons; (33) commissioners of the great seal; (34) treasurer of the household; (35) comptroller of the household; (36) master of the horse; (37) vice-chamberlain of the household; (38) secretaries of state; (39) viscounts' eldest sons; (40) earls' younger sons; (41) barons' eldest sons; (42) knights of the Garter; (43) privy councillors; (44) chancellor of the exchequer; (45) chancellor of the duchy of Lancaster; (46) lord chief justice of England; (47) master of the rolls; (48) lords justices of appeal; (49) judges of the High Court of Justice; (50) knights bannerets made by the sovereign in person; (51) viscounts' younger sons; (52) barons' younger sons; (53) sons of lords of appeal; (54) baronets; (55) knights bannerets not made by the sovereign in person; (56) knights of the first class of the Bath, the Star of India, St Michael and St George; (57) the Indian Empire, the Royal Victorian Order; (58) knights of the second class of the Bath, the Star of India, and St Michael and

St George; other orders K.C.I.E., &c.; (59) knights bachelors; (60) sons of commanders of the Royal Victorian Order; (61) judges of county courts; (62) eldest sons of the younger sons of peers; (63) baronets' eldest sons; (64) knights' eldest sons; (65) baronets' younger sons; (66) knights' younger sons; (67) companions of the Bath, the Star of India, St Michael and St George and the Indian Empire; (68) members of the 4th class of the Royal Victorian Order; (69) companions of the Distinguished Service Order; (70) members of the 5th class of the Royal Victorian Order; (71) esquires; (72) gentlemen.

2. General Precedence of Women.

The Queen; (1) queen dowager; (2) princess of Wales; (3) daughters of the sovereign; (4) wives of the sovereign's younger sons; (5) granddaughters of the sovereign; (6) wives of the sovereign's grandsons; (7) sisters of the sovereign; (8) wives of the sovereign's brothers; (9) aunts of the sovereign; (10) wives of the sovereign's uncles; (11) nieces of the sovereign; (12) wives of the sovereign's nephews; (13) wives of dukes of the blood royal; (14) duchesses; (15) wives of eldest sons of dukes of the blood royal; (16) marchionesses; (17) wives of the eldest sons of dukes; (18) dukes' daughters; (19) countesses; (20) wives of younger sons of dukes of the blood royal; (21) wives of the eldest sons of marquesses; (22) marquesses' daughters; (23) wives of the younger sons of dukes; (24) viscountesses; (25) wives of the eldest sons of earls; (26) earls' daughters; (27) wives of the younger sons of marquesses; (28) baronesses; (29) wives of the eldest sons of viscounts; (30) viscounts' daughters; (31) wives of the younger sons of earls; (32) wives of the eldest sons of barons; (33) barons' daughters; (34) maids of honour to the queen; (35) wives of knights of the Garter; (36) wives of knights bannerets made by the sovereign in person; (37) wives of the younger sons of viscounts; (38) wives of the younger sons of barons; (39) baronets' wives; (40) wives of knights bannerets not made by the sovereign in person; (41) wives of knights of the Thistle; (42) wives of knights of St Patrick; (43) wives of knights grand crosses of the Bath, grand commanders of the Star of India, and grand crosses of St Michael and St George; (44) wives of knights commanders of the Bath, the Star of India, and St Michael and St George; (45) knights bachelors' wives; (46) wives of the eldest sons of the younger sons of peers; (47) daughters of the younger sons of peers; (48) wives of the eldest sons of baronets; (49) baronets' daughters; (50) wives of the eldest sons of knights; (51) knights' daughters; (52) wives of the younger sons of baronets; (53) wives of the younger sons of knights; (54) wives of commanders of the Royal Victorian Order, companions of the Bath, the Star of India, St Michael and St

George, and the Indian Empire; (55) wives of members of the 4th class Royal Victorian Order; (56) wives of esquires; (57) gentlewomen. (W.A.L.)

⟨∾⟩ **SEDUCTION** (from Lat. *seducere*, to lead astray), a term generally used in the special sense of wrongfully inducing a woman to consent to sexual intercourse. The action for seduction of an unmarried woman in England stands in a somewhat anomalous position. The theory of English law is that the woman herself has suffered no wrong; the wrong has been suffered by the parent or person *in loco parentis,* who must sue for the damage arising from the loss of service caused by the seduction of the woman. Some evidence of service must be given, but very slight evidence will be sufficient, even making of tea, milking cows, minding children or any small household work. It is no bar if a daughter is out at work during the day time, provided she assists in the household when she comes home in the evening. The relationship of master and servant must, however, exist, and the action must be brought by the person with whom the seduced girl was residing at the time, whether in the capacity of daughter and servant, ward and servant, or servant only. It is so seldom indeed that an action is brought against a seducer when the seduced girl is a servant only, that what Serjeant Manning wrote many years ago is still painfully true: "The *quasi* fiction of *servitium amisit* affords protection to the rich man whose daughter occasionally makes his tea, but leaves without redress the poor man whose child is sent unprotected to earn her bread amongst strangers." This capricious working of the action for seduction is somewhat obviated in Scots law, under which the seduced woman may sue on her own account, but only if deceit has been used, and most often there is a difficulty in showing that the deceit alone was the cause of the injury. Although the action is nominally for loss of service, still exemplary damages are given for the dishonour of the plaintiff's family beyond recompense for the mere loss of service. An action for seduction cannot be brought in the county court except by agreement of the parties. As to seduction of a married woman, the old action for criminal conversation was abolished by the Divorce Act 1857 which substituted for it a claim for damages against the co-respondent in a divorce suit; but if a married woman were living apart from her husband in her father's house, and giving her services to her father in the slightest degree, an action for seduction would lie. Seduction in England is not as a rule a criminal offence. But a conspiracy to seduce is indictable at common law. And the Criminal Law Amendment Act 1885 (which extends to the United Kingdom) makes it felony to seduce a girl under the age of thirteen, and misdemeanour to seduce a girl between thirteen and sixteen. The same act also deals severely with the cognate offences of procuration, abduction and unlawful detention with the intent to seduce a woman of any age. The Children Act 1908 gave a further protection to young people, enacting that if any person having the custody, charge or care of a girl under the age of sixteen causes or encourages the seduction of that girl he shall be guilty of a misdemeanour, and be liable to imprisonment, with or without hard labour, for a term not exceeding two years.

SIGN-BOARD, strictly a board placed or hung before any building to designate its character. The French *enseigne* indicates its essential connexion with what is known in English as a flag, and in France banners not infrequently took the place of sign-boards in the middle ages. Sign-boards, however, are best known in the shape of painted or carved advertisements for shops, inns, &c., they are in fact one of various emblematic methods used from time immemorial for publicly calling attention to the place to which they refer. The ancient Egyptians and Greeks are known to have used signs, and many Roman examples are preserved, among them the widely-recognized bush to indicate a tavern, from which is derived the proverb "Good wine needs no bush." In some cases, such as the bush, or the three balls of pawnbrokers, certain signs became identified with certain trades, but apart from these the emblems employed by traders—evolving often into trade-marks—may in great part be grouped according to their various origins. Thus, at an early period the cross or other sign of a religious character was used to attract Christians, whereas the sign of the sun or the moon would serve the same purpose for pagans. Later, the adaptation of the coats of arms or badges of noble families became common; these would be described by the people without consideration of the language of heraldry, and thus such signs as the Red Lion, the Green Dragon, &c., have become familiar. Another class of sign was that which exhibited merely persons employed in the various trades, or objects typical of them, but in large towns where many practised the same trade, and especially, as was often the case, where these congregated mainly in the same street, such signs did not provide sufficient distinction. Thus a variety of devices came into existence—sometimes the trader used a rebus on his own name (*e.g.* two cocks for the name of Cox); sometimes he adopted any figure of an animal or other object, or portrait of a well-known person, which he considered likely to attract attention. Finally we have the common association of two heterogeneous objects, which (apart from those representing a rebus) were in some cases merely a whimsical combination, but in others arose from a popular misconception of the sign itself (*e.g.* the combination of the "leg and star" may have originated in a representation of the insignia of the garter), or from corruption in popular speech (*e.g.* the combination "goat and compasses" is said by some to be a corruption of "God encompasses"). Whereas the use of signs was generally optional, publicans were on a different footing from other traders in this respect. As early as the 14th century there was a law in England compelling them to exhibit signs, for in 1393 the prosecution of a publican for not doing so is recorded. In France edicts were directed to the same end in 1567 and 1577. Since the object of sign-boards was to attract the public, they were often of an elaborate character. Not only were the signs themselves large and sometimes of great artistic merit (especially in the 16th and 17th centuries, when they reached their greatest vogue) but the posts or metal supports protruding from the houses over the street, from which the signs were swung, were often elaborately worked, and many beautiful examples of wrought-iron supports survive both in England and on the Continent. The signs were a prominent feature of the streets of London at this period. But here and in other large towns they became a danger and a nuisance in the narrow ways. Already in 1669 a royal order had been directed in France against the excessive size of sign-boards and their projection too far over the streets. In Paris in 1761 and in London about 1762–1773 laws were introduced which gradually compelled sign-boards to be removed or fixed flat against the wall. For the most part they only survived in connexion with inns, for which some of the greatest artists of the time painted sign-boards, usually representing the name of the inn. With the gradual abolition of sign-boards the numbering of houses began to be introduced in the 18th century in London. It had been attempted in Paris as early as 1512, and had become almost universal by the close of the 18th century, though not enforced until 1805. It appears to have been first introduced into London early in the 18th century. Pending this development, houses which carried on trade at night (*e.g.* coffee houses, &c.) had various specific arrangements of lights, and these still survive to some extent, as in the case of doctors' dispensaries and chemists' shops.

⟨⟩⟩ **SIN-EATER,** a man who for trifling payment was believed to take upon himself, by means of food and drink, the sins of a deceased person. The custom was once common in many parts of England and in the highlands of Scotland, and survived until recent years in Wales and the counties of Shropshire and Hereford-shire. Usually each village had its official sin-eater to whom notice was given as soon as a death occurred. He at once went to the house, and there, a stool being brought, he sat down in front of the door. A groat, a crust of bread and a bowl of ale were handed him, and after he had eaten and drunk he rose and pronounced the ease and rest of the dead person, for whom he thus pawned his own soul. The earlier form seems to have been more realistic, the sin-eater being taken into the death-chamber, and, a piece of bread and possibly cheese having been placed on the breast of the corpse by a relative, usually a woman, it was afterwards handed to the sin-eater, who ate it in the presence of the dead. He was then handed his fee, and at once hustled and thrust out of the house amid execrations, and a shower of sticks, cinders or whatever other missiles were handy. The custom of sin-eating is generally supposed to be derived from the scapegoat in Leviticus xvi. 21, 22. A symbolic survival of it was witnessed as recently as 1893 at Market Drayton, Shropshire. After a preliminary service had been held over the coffin in the house, a woman poured out a glass of wine for each bearer and handed it to him across the coffin with a "funeral biscuit." In Upper Bavaria sin-eating still survives: a corpse cake is placed on the breast of the dead and then eaten by the nearest relative, while in the Balkan peninsula a small bread image of the deceased is made and eaten by the sur-vivors of the family. The Dutch *doed-koecks* or "dead-cakes," marked with the initials of the deceased, introduced into America in the 17th century, were long given to the attendants at funerals in old New York. The "burial-cakes" which are still made in parts of rural En-gland, for example Lincolnshire and Cumberland, are almost cer-tainly a relic of sin-eating.

⟨⟩⟩ **SUTTEE** (an English corruption of Sanskrit *sati,* "good woman" or true "wife"), the rite of widow-sacrifice, *i.e.* the burning of the living widow on the funeral pyre of her husband, as practised among certain Hindu castes. As early as the *Atharva Veda* the rite is mentioned as an "old custom," but European scholars have shown that the text of the still earlier *Rig Veda* had been corrupted, probably wilfully, by the Hindu priesthood, and that there was no injunction that the rite should be observed. The directions of the *Rig Veda* seem to have involved a merely symbolic suttee: the widow taking her place on the funeral pile, but being recalled to "this world of life" at the last moment by her brother-in-law or adopted child. The practice was sporadically observed in India when the Macedonians reached India late in the 4th century B.C (Diod. Sic. xix. 33–34); but the earlier Indian law books do not enjoin it, and Manu simply commands the widow to lead a life of chastity and asceticism. About the 6th century A.D. a recrudescence of the rite took place, and with the help of corrupted Vedic texts it soon grew to have a full religious sanction. But even so it was not general throughout India. It was rare in the Punjab; and in Malabar, the most primitive part of southern India, it was forbidden. In its medieval form it was essentially a Brahminic rite, and it was where Brahminism was strongest, in Bengal and along the Ganges valley and in Oudh and Rajputana, that it was most usual.

The manner of the sacrifice differed according to the district. In south India the widow jumped or was forced into the fire-pit; in western India she was placed in a grass hut, supporting the corpse's head with her right hand while her left held the torch; in the Ganges valley she lay down upon the already lighted pile; while in Nepal she was placed beside the corpse, and when the pile was lighted the two bodies were held in place by long poles pressed down by relatives. The earliest attempt to stop suttee was made by Akbar (1542–1605), who forbade compulsion, voluntary suttees alone being permitted. Towards the end of the 18th century the British authorities, on the initiative of Sir C. Malet and Jonathan Duncan in Bombay, took up the question, but nothing definite was ventured on till 1829 when Lord William Bentinck, despite fierce opposition, carried in council on the 4th of December a regulation which declared that all who abetted suttee were "guilty of culpable homicide." Though thus illegal, widow-burning continued into modern days in isolated parts of India. In 1905 those who assisted at a suttee in Behar were sentenced to penal servitude.

TATTOOING (Tahitian, *tatu*, from *ta*, mark), the practice of decorating the skin, by cutting or puncturing, with various patterns into which a colouring matter is introduced. Though the word is Polynesian, the custom appears to have been almost universal, but tends to disappear before the spread of civilization. The prohibition to the Jews (Lev. xix. 28) under the Mosaic Law to "print any marks" upon themselves is believed to have reference to tattooing, which is still common in Arabia. The North and South American Indians, the Chinese, Japanese, Burmese, all tattoo. The origin of the custom is disputed. It was probably at first for purely ornamental purposes and with the idea of attracting the opposite sex. The discovery in the caves of Western Europe of hollowed stones which had been apparently used for grinding up ochre and other coloured clays is thought evidence that prehistoric man painted himself, and tattooing for decorative reasons may easily date back to the cave-dwellers. The modern savage paints himself as a protection against cold, against the bites of insects or the sun's rays, and most of all to give himself a ferocious appearance in battle, as Caesar relates of the ancient Britons. Any of these motives may have shared in originating tattooing. Subsequently the practice assumed religious and social significance, varying with the country and according to the age at which it was performed. Thus in Polynesia it is begun in or about the twelfth year, and becomes thus a mark of puberty; while among the Arabs and the Kabyles of Algeria infants are tattooed by their mothers for simple ornament or as a means of recognizing them. The American Indians bore from their initiation at puberty the mark of the personal or tribal *totem,* which at once represented the religious side of their life, and served the practical purpose of enabling them to be known by friendly tribes. Among the Australians tattooing served as a mark of adoption into the family or tribe, the distinctive emblem or *kobong* being scarred on the thighs.

Tattooing is regarded, too, as a mark of courage. A Kaffir who has been a successful warrior has the privilege of making a long incision in his thigh, which is rubbed with cinders until sufficiently discoloured. Elsewhere tattooing is a sign of mourning, deep and numerous cuts being made on face, breast and limbs. Among the Fijians and Eskimos the untattooed were regarded as risking their happiness in the future world. Some of the most remarkable examples of tattooing are those to be found among the Laos, whose stomachs, thighs, legs and breasts are often completely covered with fantastic animal figures like those on Buddhistic monuments.

The rudest form of tattooing is that practised specially by the Australians and some tribes of negroes. It consists in cutting gashes, arranged in patterns, on the skin and filling the wounds with clay so as to form raised scars. This tattooing by scarring as compared with the more common mode of pricking is, as a general rule, confined to the black races. Light-skinned races tattoo, while dark practise scarring. In Polynesia the art of tattooing reached it highest perfection. In the Marquesas group of islands, for example, the men were tattooed all over, even to the fingers and toes and crown of the head, and as each operation took from three to six months, beginning at virility, a man must have been nearly thirty before his body was completely covered. In New Zealand the face was the part most tattooed, and Maori heads so decorated were at one time in much request for European museums, but they are no longer obtainable in the colony. In Japan, where it became a high art, tattooing was neither ceremonial nor symbolical. It was in lieu of clothing, and only on those parts of the body usually covered in civilized countries, and in the case of those only who, like the jinrikisha-men, work half naked. The colours used are black, which appears blue, made from Indian ink, and different tints of red obtained from cinnabar. Fine sewing-needles, eight, twelve, twenty or more, fixed together in a piece of wood, are used. A clever tattooer can cover the stomach or back in a day. As soon as the picture is complete, the patient is bathed in hot water. The Ainus, on the other hand, tattoo only the exposed parts of the body, the women, unlike the Japanese, being frequently patients. The tattooing instruments used in Polynesia consisted of pieces of sharpened bone fastened into a handle, with their edges cut into teeth. These were dipped into a solution of charcoal and then driven into the skin by smart blows with a mallet. During the operation, assistants, usually female relatives, drowned the cries of the sufferer with songs and the beating of drums.

Under the influence of civilization tattooing is losing its ethnological character, and has become, in Europe at least, an eccentricity of soldiers and sailors and of many among the lower and often criminal classes of the great cities. Among eight hundred convicted French soldiers Lacassagne found 40 per cent tattooed. In the British army till 1879 the letters D. and B. C. for *Deserter* and *Bad Character* were tattooed with needles and Indian ink; and tattooing has often been used to identify criminals and slaves.

❧ **WAKE** (A.S. *wacan,* to "wake" or "watch"), a term now restricted to the Irish custom of an all-night "waking" or watching round a corpse before burial, but anciently used in the wider sense of a vigil kept as an annual church celebration in commemoration of the completion or dedication of the parish church. This strictly religious wake consisted in an all-night service of prayer and meditation in the church. These services, popularly known as "wakes," were officially termed *Vigiliae* by the church, and appear to have existed from the earliest days of Anglo-Saxon Christianity. Tents and booths were set up in the churchyard before the dawn which heralded in a day devoted to feasting, dancing and sports, each parish keeping the morrow of its vigil as a holiday. Wakes soon degenerated into fairs; people from neighbouring parishes journeyed over to join the merry-making, and as early as Edgar's reign (958–975) the revelry and drunkenness had become a scandal. The *vigiliae* usually fell on Sundays or saints' days, those being the days oftenest chosen for church dedications, and thus the abuse was the more scandalous. In 1445 Henry VI. attempted to suppress markets and fairs on Sundays and holy days. In 1536 an Act of Convocation ordered that the yearly "wake" should be held in every parish on the same day, viz. the first Sunday in October, but this regulation was disregarded. Wakes are specially mentioned in the *Book of Sports* of James I. and Charles I. among the feasts which should be observed.

Side by side with these church wakes there existed from the earliest times the custom of "waking" a corpse. The custom, as far as England was concerned, seems to have been older than Christianity, and to have been at first essentially Celtic. Doubtless it had a superstitious origin, the fear of evil spirits hurting or even removing the body, aided perhaps by the practical desire to keep away rats and other vermin. The Anglo-Saxons called the custom lich-wake or like-wake (A.S. *lic*, a corpse). With the introduction of Christianity the offering of prayer was added to the mere vigil, which until then had been characterized by formal mourning chants and recitals of the life story of the dead. As a rule the corpse, with a plate of salt on its breast, was placed under the table, on which was liquor for the watchers. These private wakes soon tended to become drinking orgies, and during the reign of Edward III. the provincial synod held in London proclaimed by its 10th canon the object of wakes to be the offering of prayer for the dead, and ordered that in future none but near relatives and friends of the deceased should attend. The penalty for disobedience was excommunication. With the Reformation and the consequent disuse of prayers for the dead the custom of "waking" in England became obsolete and died out. Many countries and peoples have been found to have a custom equivalent to "waking," which, however, must be distinguished from the funeral feasts pure and simple.

WINDOW TAX, a tax first levied in England in the year 1697 for the purpose of defraying the expenses and making up the deficiency arising from clipped and defaced coin in the recoinage of silver during the reign of William III. It was an assessed tax on the rental value of the house, levied according to the number of windows and openings on houses having more than six windows and worth more than £5 per annum. Owing to the method of assessment the tax fell with peculiar hardship on the middle classes, and to this day traces of the endeavours to lighten its burden may be seen in numerous bricked-up windows.

The revenue derived from the tax in the first year of its levy amounted to £1,200,000. The tax was increased no fewer than six times between 1747 and 1808, but was reduced in 1823. There was a strong agitation in favour of the abolition of the tax during the winter of 1850–1851, and it was accordingly repealed on the 24th of July 1851, and a tax on inhabited houses substituted. The tax contributed £1,856,000 to the imperial revenue the year before its repeal. There were in England in that year about 6000 houses having fifty windows and upwards; about 275,000 having ten windows and upwards, and about 725,000 having seven windows or less.

In France there is still a tax on doors and windows, and this forms an appreciable amount of the revenue.

THINGS OF THIS WORLD

The eleventh was nothing if not a collective stickler for significant and intriguing detail, and its many attractions owe much to the innumerable minutiae that editor Hugh Chisholm was willing to take an interest in and commission appropriately descriptive articles about. Nowhere is this more evident than in the sprightly details of life as lived that appear in our final collation, which has as its common theme "hearth and home." The attraction of such modest pieces often lies in their extreme precision and eloquence of language as the historical depth of the object is explored. This is certainly the case with "Bed," "Box," "Pillow," "Toast," "Laundry," and the complete history of the reception of tea in England. And it is good to note that, even in 1910–1911, in the article entitled "Cookery," the anonymous contributor feels constrained to admit that ". . . French cooking is admittedly the ideal of the culinary art, [and] directly we leave behind the plain roast and boiled."

BACKSCRATCHER, a long slender rod of wood, whalebone, tortoiseshell, horn or cane, with a carved human hand, usually of ivory, mounted at the extremity. Its name suggests the primary use of the implement, but little is known of its history, and it was unquestionably also employed as a kind of rake to keep in order the huge "heads" of powdered hair worn by ladies, during a considerable portion of the 18th and the early part of the 19th centuries. The backscratcher varies in length from 12 to 20 in., and the more elaborate examples, which were occasionally hung from the waist, are silver-mounted, and in rare instances the ivory fingers bear carved rings. The hand is sometimes outstretched, and sometimes the fingers are flexed; the modelling is frequently good, the fingers delicately formed and the nails well defined. As a rule the rod is finished off with a knob. The hand was now and again replaced by a rake or a bird's claw. The hand was indifferently dexter or sinister, but the Chinese variety usually bears a right hand. Like most of the obsolete appliances of daily life, the backscratcher, or scratch-back, as it is sometimes called, has become scarce, and it is one of the innumerable objects which attract the attention of the modern collector.

BED (a common Teutonic word, cf. German *Bett*, probably connected with the Indo-European root *bhodh*, seen in the Lat. *fodere*, to dig; so "a dug-out place" for safe resting, or in the same sense as a garden "bed"), a general term for a resting or sleeping

place for men and animals, and in particular for the article of household furniture for that object, and so used by analogy in other senses,
involving a supporting surface or layer. The accompaniments of a
domestic bed (bedding, coverlets, &c.) have naturally varied considerably in different times, and its form and decoration and social
associations have considerable historical interest. The Egyptians had
high bedsteads which were ascended by steps, with bolsters or pillows,
and curtains to hang round. Often there was a head-rest as well,
semi-cylindrical and made of stone, wood or metal. Assyrians, Medes
and Persians had beds of a similar kind, and frequently decorated
their furniture with inlays or *appliqués* of metal, mother-of-pearl and
ivory. The oldest account of a bedstead is probably that of Ulysses
which Homer describes him as making in his own house, but he also
mentioned the inlaying of the woodwork of beds with gold, silver
and ivory. The Greek bed had a wooden frame, with a board at the
head and bands of hide laced across, upon which skins were placed.
At a later period the bedstead was often veneered with expensive
woods; sometimes it was of solid ivory veneered with tortoise-shell
and with silver feet; often it was of bronze. The pillows and coverings
also became more costly and beautiful; the most celebrated places
for their manufacture were Miletus, Corinth and Carthage. Folding
beds, too, appear in the vase paintings. The Roman mattresses were
stuffed with reeds, hay, wool or feathers; the last was used towards
the end of the Republic, when custom demanded luxury. Small cushions were placed at the head and sometimes at the back. The bedsteads were high and could only be ascended by the help of steps.
They were often arranged for two persons, and had a board or railing
at the back as well as the raised portion at the head. The counterpanes
were sometimes very costly, generally purple embroidered with figures in gold; and rich hangings fell to the ground masking the front.
The bedsteads themselves were often of bronze inlaid with silver, and
Elagabalus, like some modern Indian princes, had one of solid silver.
In the walls of some of the houses at Pompeii bed niches are found
which were probably closed by curtains or sliding partitions. The
marriage bed, *lectus genialis,* was much decorated, and was placed in
the atrium opposite the door. A low pallet-bed used for sick persons
was known as *scimpodium.* Other forms of couch were called *lectus,*
but were not beds in the modern sense of the word except the *lectus
funebris,* on which the body of a dead person lay in state for seven
days, clad in a toga and rich garments, and surrounded by flowers
and foliage. This bed rested on ivory legs, over which purple blankets
embroidered with gold were spread, and was placed in the atrium

with the foot to the door and with a pan of incense by its side. The ancient Germans lay on the floor on beds of leaves covered with skins, or in a kind of shallow chest filled with leaves and moss. In the early middle ages they laid carpets on the floor or on a bench against the wall, placed upon them mattresses stuffed with feathers, wool or hair, and used skins as a covering. They appear to have generally lain naked in bed, wrapping themselves in the large linen sheets which were stretched over the cushions. In the 13th century luxury increased, and bedsteads were made of wood much decorated with inlaid, carved and painted ornament. They also used folding beds, which served as couches by day and had cushions covered with silk laid upon leather. At night a linen sheet was spread and pillows placed, while silk-covered skins served as coverlets. Curtains were hung from the ceiling or from an iron arm projecting from the wall. The Carolingian MSS. show metal bedsteads much higher at the head than at the feet, and this shape continued in use till the 13th century in France, many cushions being added to raise the body to a sloping position. In the 12th-century MSS. the bedsteads appear much richer, with inlays, carving and painting, and with embroidered coverlets and mattresses in harmony. Curtains were hung above the bed, and a small hanging lamp is often shone. In the 14th century the wood-work became of less importance, being generally entirely covered by hangings of rich materials. Silk, velvet and even cloth of gold were much used. Inventories from the beginning of the 14th century give details of these hangings lined with fur and richly embroidered. Then it was that the tester bed made its first appearance, the tester being slung from the ceiling or fastened to the walls, a form which developed later into a room within a room, shut in by double curtains, sometimes even so as to exclude all draughts. The space between bed and wall was called the *ruelle*, and very intimate friends were received there. In the 15th century beds became very large, reaching to 7 or 8 ft. by 6 or 7 ft. Viollet-le-Duc says that the mattresses were filled with pea-shucks or straw—neither wool nor horsehair is mentioned—but feathers also were used. At this time great personages were in the habit of carrying most of their property about with them, including beds and bed-hangings, and for this reason the bedsteads were for the most part mere frameworks to be covered up; but about the beginning of the 16th century bedsteads were made lighter and more decorative, since the lords remained in the same place for longer periods. In the museum at Nancy is a fine bedstead of this period which belonged to Antoine de Lorraine. It has a carved head and foot as well as the uprights which support the tester. Another is in the Musée Cluny ascribed to Pierre de Gondi, very architectural in design, with a bracketed cornice, and turned and carved posts; at the head figures of warriors watch the sleeper. Louis XIV. had an enormous number of sumptuous beds, as many as 413 being described in the inventories of his palaces. Some of them had embroideries enriched with pearls, and figures on a silver or golden ground. The carving was the work of Proux or Caffieri, and the gilding by La Baronnière. The great bed at Versailles had crimson velvet curtains on which "The Triumph of Venus" was embroidered. So much gold was used that the velvet scarcely showed. Under the influence of Madame de Maintenon "The Sacrifice of Abraham," which is now on the tester, replaced "The Triumph of Venus." In the 17th century, which has been called "the century of magnificent beds," the style *à la duchesse,* with tester and curtains only at the head, replaced the more enclosed beds in France; though they lasted much longer in England. In the 18th century feather pillows were first used as coverings in Germany, which in the fashions of the bed and the curious etiquette connected with the bedchamber followed France for the most part. The beds were *à la duchesse,* but in France itself there was great variety both of name and shape—the *lit à alcove, lit d'ange,* which had no columns, but a suspended tester with curtains drawn back, *lit à l'Anglaise,* which looked like a high sofa by day, *lit en baldaquin,* with the tester fixed against the wall, *lit à couronne* with a tester shaped like a crown, a style which appeared under Louis XVI., and was fashionable under the Restoration and Louis Philippe, and *lit à l'impériale,* which had a curved tester, are a few of their varieties. The *lit en baldaquin* of Napoleon I. is still at Fontainebleau, and the Garde Meuble contains several richly carved beds of a more modern date. The custom of the "bed of justice" upon which the king of France reclined when he was present in parliament, the princes being seated, the great officials standing, and the lesser officials kneeling, was held to denote the royal power even more than the throne. Louis XI. is credited with its first use and the custom lasted till the end of the monarchy. From the habit of using this bed to hear petitions, &c., came the usage of the *grand lit,* which was provided wherever the king stayed, called also *lit de parement* or *lit de parade,* rather later. Upon this bed the dead king lay in state. The beds of the king and queen were saluted by the courtiers as if they were altars, and none approached them even when there was no railing to prevent it. These railings were apparently placed for other than ceremonial reasons originally, and in the accounts of several castles in the 15th century mention is made of a railing to keep dogs from the bed. In the *chambre de parade,* where the ceremonial bed was placed, certain persons, such as ambassadors or great lords, whom it was desired to honour, were received in a more intimate fashion than the crowd of courtiers. The *petit lever* was held in the bedroom itself, the *grand lever* in the *chambre de parade.* At Versailles women received their friends in their beds, both before and after childbirth, during periods of mourning, and even directly after marriage—in fact in any circumstances, which were thought deserving of congratulation or condolence. During the 17th century this curious custom became general, perhaps to avoid the tiresome details of etiquette. Portable beds were used in high society in France till the end of the *ancien régime.* The earliest of which mention has been found belonged to Charles the Bold (see *Memoirs* of Philippe de Comines). They had curtains over a light framework, and were in their way as fine as the stationary beds. Iron beds appear in the 18th century; the advertisements recommend them as free from the insects which sometimes infested wooden bedsteads, but one is mentioned in the inventory of the furniture of the castle of Nerac in 1569, "un lit de fer et de cuivre, avec quatre petites colonnes de laiton, ensemble quatre satyres de laiton, quatre petits vases de laiton pour mettre sur les colonnes; dedans le dit lit il y a la figure d'Olopherne ensemble de Judith, qui sont d'albâtre." In Scotland, Brittany and Holland the closed bed with sliding or folding shutters has persisted till our own day, and in England—where beds were commonly quite simple in form—the four-poster, with tester and curtains all round, was the usual citizen's bed till the middle of the 19th century. Many fine examples exist of 17th-century carved oak bedsteads, some of which have found their way into museums. The later forms, in which mahogany was usually the wood employed, are much less architectural in design. Some exceedingly elegant mahogany bedsteads were designed by Chippendale, Hepplewhite and Sheraton, and there are signs that English taste is returning to the wooden bedstead in a lighter and less monumental form. (J.P.B.)

BOX, the most varied of all receptacles. A box may be square, oblong, round or oval, or of an even less normal shape; it usually opens by raising, sliding or removing the lid, which may be fastened by a catch, hasp or lock. Whatever its shape or purpose or the material of which it is fashioned, it is the direct descendant of the chest, one of the most ancient articles of domestic furniture. Its uses are infinite, and the name, preceded by a qualifying adjective, has been given to many objects of artistic or antiquarian interest.

Box 295

Of the boxes which possess some attraction beyond their immediate purpose the feminine work-box is the commonest. It is usually fitted with a tray divided into many small compartments, for needles, reels of silk and cotton and other necessaries of stitchery. The date of its introduction is in considerable doubt, but 17th-century examples have come down to us, with covers of silk, stitched with beads and adorned with embroidery. In the 18th century no lady was without her work-box, and, especially in the second half of that period, much taste and elaborate pains were expended upon the case, which was often exceedingly dainty and elegant. These boxes are ordinarily portable, but sometimes form the top of a table.

But it is as a receptacle for snuff that the box has taken its most distinguished and artistic form. The snuff-box, which is now little more than a charming relic of a disagreeable practice, was throughout the larger part of the 18th century the indispensable companion of every man of birth and breeding. It long survived his sword, and was in frequent use until nearly the middle of the 19th century. The jeweller, the enameller and the artist bestowed infinite pains upon what was quite as often a delicate bijou as a piece of utility; fops and great personages possessed numbers of snuff-boxes, rich and more ordinary, their selection being regulated by their dress and by the relative splendour of the occasion. From the cheapest wood that was suitable—at one time potato-pulp was extensively used—to a frame of gold encased with diamonds, a great variety of materials was employed. Tortoise-shell was a favourite, and owing to its limpid lustre it was exceedingly effective. Mother-of-pearl was also used, together with silver, in its natural state or gilded. Costly gold boxes were often enriched with enamels or set with diamonds or other precious stones, and sometimes the lid was adorned with a portrait, a classical vignette, or a tiny miniature, often some choice work by an old master. After snuff-taking had ceased to be general it lingered for some time among diplomatists, either because—as Talleyrand explained—they found a ceremonious pinch to be a useful aid to reflection in a business interview, or because monarchs retained the habit of bestowing snuff-boxes upon ambassadors and other intermediaries, who could not well be honoured in any other way. It is, indeed, to the cessation of the habit of snuff-taking that we may trace much of modern lavishness in the distribution of decorations. To be invited to take a pinch from a monarch's snuff-box was a distinction almost equivalent to having one's ear pulled by Napoleon. At the coronation of George IV. of England, Messrs Rundell & Bridge, the court jewellers, were paid £8205 for snuff-boxes for foreign ministers. Now that the snuff-box is no longer used it is collected by wealthy amateurs or deposited in museums, and especially artistic examples command large sums. George, duke of Cambridge (1819–1904), possessed an important collection; a Louis XV. gold box was sold by auction after his death for £2000.

A jewel-box is a receptacle for trinkets. It may take a very modest form, covered in leather and lined with satin, or it may reach the monumental proportions of the jewel cabinets which were made for Marie Antoinette, one of which is at Windsor, and another at Versailles, the work of Schwerdfeger as cabinet-maker, Degault as miniature-painter, and Thomire as chaser.

A strong-box is a receptacle for money, deeds and securities. Its place has been taken in modern life by the safe. Some of those which have survived, such as that of Sir Thomas Bodley in the Bodleian library, possess locks with an extremely elaborate mechanism contrived in the under-side of the lid.

The knife-box is one of the most charming of the minor pieces of furniture which we owe to the artistic taste and mechanical ingenuity of the English cabinet-makers of the last quarter of the 18th century. Some of the most elegant were the work of Adam, Hepplewhite and Sheraton. Occasionally flat-topped boxes, they were most frequently either vase-shaped, or tall and narrow with a sloping lid necessitated by a series of raised stages for exhibiting the handles of knives and the bowls of spoons. Mahogany and satinwood were the woods most frequently employed, and they were occasionally inlaid with marqueterie or edged with boxwood. These graceful receptacles still exist in large numbers; they are often converted into stationery cabinets.

The Bible-box, usually of the 17th century, but now and again more ancient, probably obtained its name from the fact that it was of a size to hold a large Bible. It often has a carved or incised lid.

The powder-box and the patch-box were respectively receptacles for the powder and the patches of the 18th century; the former was the direct ancestor of the puff-box of the modern dressing-table.

The *étui* is a cylindrical box or case of very various materials, often of pleasing shape or adornment, for holding sewing materials or small articles of feminine use.

COOKERY (Lat. *coquus*, a cook), the art of preparing and dressing food of all sorts for human consumption, of converting the raw materials, by the application of heat or otherwise, into a digestible and pleasing condition, and generally ministering to the satisfaction of the appetite and the delight of the palate. We may take it that some form of cookery has existed from the earliest times, and its progress has been from the simple to the elaborate, dominated partly by the foods accessible to man, partly by the stage of civilization he has attained, and partly by the appliances at his command for the purpose either of treating the food, or of consuming it when served.

The developed art of cookery is necessarily a late addition—if it may be considered to be included at all—to the list of "fine arts." Originally it is a purely industrial and useful art. Man, says a French writer, was born a roaster, and *"pour être cuisinier, il a besoin de le devenir."* The ancients were great eaters, but strangers to the subtler refinements of the palate. The gods were supposed to love the smell of fried meat, while their nectar and ambrosia represented an ideal, which, though preserved as a phrase, would hardly satisfy a modern epicure. The ancients were poorly provided with pots and pans, except of a simple order, or with the appurtenances of a kitchen, and they were sadly to seek in the requisites of a modern table. So long as men ate with their hands no dainty confection was suitable; the viands were set forth in a straightforward style fit for their requirements. "Plain cooking," which, after all, can never become obsolete, was the only sort. Oddities, no doubt, were the luxuries; and we can see to-day in the ethnological accounts of contemporary savages and backward civilizations, a fair representation of the cookeries of the ancients. The luxuries of the Chinese are, in their way, a survival of long ages of a cookery which to western civilization is grotesque. Even if it is an historic impertinence, it is impossible for the countries of western civilization to regard the fine flower of their own evolution as other than the highest pitch of progress. *Autres temps, autres mœurs.* To the Chinaman French cooking may possibly be as grotesque as to an Englishman the Chinaman's hundred-year-old buried egg, black and tasteless. The history of comparative cookery is bound up with the physical possibilities of each country and its products; and if we attempt to mark out stages in the evolution of cookery as a fine art, it is necessarily as understood by the so-called civilized peoples of the West in their culmination at the present day.

It is obvious that opportunity has dominated its history, for the art of cookery is to some extent the product of an increased refinement of taste, consequent on culture and increase of wealth. To this extent it is a decadent art, ministering to the luxury of man, and to his progressive inclination to be pampered and have his appetite tickled. It is thus only remotely connected with the mere necessities of nutrition, or the science of dietetics. Mere hunger, though the best sauce, will not produce cookery, which is the art of sauces.

COSTUME, dress or clothing, especially the distinctive clothing worn at different periods by different peoples or different classes of people. The word appears in English in the 18th century, and was first applied to the correct representation, in literature and art, of the manners, dress, furniture and general surroundings of the scene represented. By the early part of the 19th century it became restricted to the fashion or style of personal apparel, including the headdresses, jewelry and the like.

The subject of clothing is far wider than appears at first sight. To the average man there is a distinction between clothing and ornament, the first being regarded as that covering which satisfies the claims of modesty, the second as those appendages which satisfy the aesthetic sense. This distinction, however, does not exist for science, and indeed the first definition involves a fallacy of which it will be as well to dispose forthwith.

Modesty is not innate in man, and its conventional nature is easily seen from a consideration of the different ideas held by different races on this subject. With Mahommedan peoples it is sufficient for a woman to cover her face; the Chinese women would think it extremely indecent to show their artificially compressed feet, and it is even improper to mention them to a woman; in Sumatra and Celebes the wild tribes consider the exposure of the knee immodest; in central Asia the finger-tips, and in Samoa the navel are similarly regarded. In Tahiti and Tonga clothing might be discarded without offence, provided the individual were tattooed; and among the Caribs a woman might leave the hut without her girdle but not unpainted. Similarly, in Alaska, women felt great shame when seen without the plugs they carried in their lips. Europeans are considered indelicate in many ways by other races, and a remark of Peschel is to the point: "Were a pious Mussulman of Ferghana to be present at our balls and see the bare shoulders of our wives and daughters, and the semi-embraces of our round dances, he would silently wonder at the long-suffering of Allah who had not long ago poured fire and brimstone on this sinful and shameless generation." Another point of interest lies in the difference of outlook with which nudity is regarded by the English and Japanese. Among the latter it has been common for the sexes to take baths together without clothing, while in England mixed bathing, even in full costume, is even now by no means universal. Yet

in England the representation of the nude in art meets with no re-
proach, though considered improper by the Japanese. Even more
striking is the fact that in civilized countries what is permitted at
certain times is forbidden at others; a woman will expose far more
of her person at night, in the ballroom or theatre, than would be
considered seemly by day in the street; and a bathing costume which
would be thought modest on the beach would meet with reprobation
in a town.

Modesty therefore is highly conventional, and to discover its origin
the most primitive tribes must be observed. Among these, in Africa,
South America, Australia and so forth, where clothing is at a minimum, the men are always more elaborately ornamented than the
women. At the same time it is noticeable that no cases of spinsterhood
are found; celibacy, rare as it is, is confined to the male sex. It is
reasonable, therefore, to conclude that ornament is a stimulus to
sexual selection, and this conclusion is enforced by the fact that
among many comparatively nude peoples clothing is assumed at certain dances which have as their confessed object the excitation of the
passions of the opposite sex. Many forms of clothing, moreover, seem
to call attention to those parts of the body of which, under the conditions of Western civilization at the present day, it aims at the concealment; certain articles of dress worn by the New Hebrideans, the
Zulu-Xosa tribes, certain tribes of Brazil and others, are cases in point.
Clothing, moreover—and this is true also of the present day—almost
always tends to accentuate rather than to conceal the difference between the sexes. Looking at the question then from the point of view
of sexual selection it would seem that a stage in the progress of human
society is marked by the discovery that concealment affords a greater
stimulus than revelation; that the fact is true is obvious—even to
modern eyes a figure partially clad appears far more indecent than
a nude. That the stimulus is real is seen in the fact that among nude
races flagrant immorality is far less common than among the more
clothed; the contrast between the Polynesians and Melanesians, living
as neighbours under similar conditions, is striking evidence on this
point. Later, when the novelty of clothing has spent its force, the
stimulus is supplied by nudity complete or partial. (T.A.J.)

HEARTH (a word which appears in various
forms in several Teutonic languages, cf. Dutch *haard*, German *Herd*,
in the sense of "floor"), the part of a room where a fire is made,
usually constructed of stone, bricks, tiles or earth, beaten hard and

having a chimney above; the fire being lighted either on the hearth itself, or in a receptacle placed there for the purpose. Like the Latin *focus*, especially in the phrase for "hearth and home" answering to *pro aris et focis*, the word is used as equivalent to the home or household. The word is also applied to the fire and cooking apparatus on board ship; the floor of a smith's forge; the floor of a reverberatory furnace on which the ore is exposed to the flame; the lower part of a blast furnace through which the metal goes down into the crucible; in soldering, a portable brazier or chafing dish, and an iron box sunk in the middle of a flat iron plate or table. An "open-hearth furnace" is a regenerative furnace of the reverberatory type used in making steel, hence "open-hearth steel."

Hearth-money, hearth tax or chimney-money, was a tax imposed in England on all houses except cottages at a rate of two shillings for every hearth. It was first levied in 1662, but owing to its unpopularity, chiefly caused by the domiciliary visits of the collectors, it was repealed in 1689, although it was producing £170,000 a year. The principle of the tax was not new in the history of taxation, for in Anglo-Saxon times the king derived a part of his revenue from a *fumage* or tax of smoke farthings levied on all hearths except those of the poor. It appears also in the hearth-penny or tax of a penny on every hearth, which as early as the 10th century was paid annually to the pope.

LAUNDRY, a place or establishment where soiled linen, &c., is washed. The word is a contraction of an earlier form *lavendry*, from Lat. *lavanda*, things to be washed, *lavare*, to wash. "Launder," a similar contraction of *lavender*, was one (of either sex) who washes linen; from its use as a verb came the form "launderer," employed as both masculine and feminine in America, and the feminine form "laundress," which is also applied to a female caretaker of chambers in the Inns of Court, London.

Laundry-work has become an important industry, organized on a scale which requires elaborate mechanical plant very different from the simple appliances that once sufficed for domestic needs. For the actual cleansing of the articles, instead of being rubbed by the hand or trodden by the foot of the washer-woman, or stirred and beaten with a "dolly" in the wash-tub, they are very commonly treated in rotary washing machines driven by power. These machines consist of an outer casing containing an inner horizontal cylindrical cage, in which the clothes are placed. By the rotation of this cage, which is reversed by automatic gearing every few turns, they are rubbed and tumbled on each other in the soap and water which is contained in the outer casing and enters the inner cylinder through perforations. The outer casing is provided with inlet valves for hot and cold water, and with discharge valves; and often also arrangements are made for the admission of steam under pressure, so that the contents can be boiled. Thus the operations of washing, boiling, rinsing and blueing (this last being the addition of a blue colouring matter to mask the yellow tint and thus give the linen the appearance of whiteness) can be performed without removing the articles from the machine. For drying, the old methods of wringing by hand, or by machines in which the clothes were squeezed between rollers of wood or india-rubber, have been largely superseded by "hydro-extractors" or "centrifugals." In these the wet garments are placed in a perforated cage or basket, supported on vertical bearings, which is rotated at a high speed (1000 to 1500 times a minute) and in a short time as much as 85% of the moisture may thus be removed. The drying is often completed in an apartment through which dry air is forced by fans. In the process of finishing linen the old-fashioned laundress made use of the mangle, about the only piece of mechanism at her disposal. In the box-mangle the articles were pressed on a flat surface by rollers which were weighted with a box full of stones, moved to and fro by a rack and pinion. In a later and less cumbrous form of the machine they were passed between wooden rollers or "bowls" held close together by weighted levers. An important advance was marked by the introduction of machines which not only smooth and press the linen like the mangle, but also give it the glazed finish obtained by hot ironing. Machines of this kind are essentially the same as the calenders used in paper and textile manufacture. They are made in a great variety of forms, to enable them to deal with articles of different shapes, but they may be described generally as consisting either of a polished metal roller, heated by steam or gas, which works against a blanketted or felted surface in the form of another roller or a flat table, or, as in the Decoudun type, of a felted metal roller rotating against a heated concave bed of polished metal. In cases where hand-ironing is resorted to, time is economized by the employment of irons which are continuously heated by gas or electricity.

PILLOW (O. Eng. *pylu;* Lat. *pulvinus,* a cushion), a support for the head during sleep or rest. The pillow of Western nations is a cushion of linen or other material, stuffed with feathers, down, hair or wool. In the East it is a framework made of bamboo or rattan with a depression in the top to receive the neck; similarly blocks of wood with a concave-shaped top are used by the natives of other countries. The word is found in various technical uses for a block or support, as for a brass bearing for the journal of a shaft, and the like. In architecture the term "pillowed," or "pulvinated," is given to the frieze of an order which bulges out in the centre and is convex in section. It is found in friezes of some of the later works of the Roman school and is common in Italian practice.

TEA (Chinese *cha*, Amoy dialect *té*), the name given to the leaves of the tea bush (see below) prepared by decoction as a beverage. The term is by analogy also used for an infusion or decoction of other leaves, *e.g.* camomile tea; and similarly for the afternoon meal at which tea is served.

The early history of tea as a beverage is mainly traditional. The lack of accurate knowledge regarding the past of the Chinese Empire may possibly some day be supplied, as European scholars become more able to explore the unstudied stores in the great Chinese libraries, or as Chinese students ransack the records of their country for the facts of earlier periods. It may then be learnt who made the first cup of tea, who planted the earliest bushes, and how the primitive methods of manufacture were evolved. In the meantime knowledge on the subject is mingled with much that is obviously mythical and with gleanings from the casual references of travellers and authors.

According to Chinese legend, the virtues of tea were discovered by the Emperor Chinnung, 2737 B.C., to whom all agricultural and medicinal knowledge is traced. It is doubtfully referred to in the book of ancient poems edited by Confucius, all of which are previous in date to 550 B.C. A tradition exists in China that a knowledge of tea travelled eastward to and in China, having been introduced 543 A.D. by Bodhidharma, an ascetic who came from India on a missionary expedition, but that legend is also mixed with supernatural details. But it is quite certain, from the historical narrative of Lo Yu, who lived in the Tang dynasty (618–906 A.D.), that tea was already used as a beverage in the 6th century, and that during the 8th century its use had become so common that a tax was levied on its consumption in the 14th year of Tih Tsung (793). The use of tea in China in the middle of the 9th century is known from Arab sources (Reinaud, *Relation des Voyages*, 1845, p. 40). From China a knowledge of tea was carried into Japan, and there the cultivation was established during the 9th century. Seed was brought from China by the priest Miyoye, and planted first in the south island, Kiushiu, whence the cultivation spread northwards till it reached the high limit of 39° N.

It is somewhat curious that although many of the products of China were known and used in Europe at much earlier times, no reference to tea has yet been traced in European literature prior to 1588. No mention of it is made by Marco Polo, and no knowledge of the substance appears to have reached Europe till after the establishment of intercourse between Portugal and China in 1517. The Portuguese, however, did little towards the introduction of it into Europe, and it was not till the Dutch established themselves at Bantam early in the 17th century that these adventurers learned from the Chinese the habit of tea drinking and brought it into Europe.

The earliest mention of tea by an Englishman is probably that contained in a letter from Mr Wickham, an agent of the East India Company, written from Firando in Japan, on the 27th June 1615, to Mr Eaton, another officer of the company, resident at Macao, and asking for "a pot of the best sort of *chaw.*" How the commission was executed does not appear, but in Mr Eaton's subsequent accounts of expenditure occurs this item—"three silver porringers to drink chaw in."

It was not till the middle of the century that the English began to use tea, and they also received their supplies from Java till in 1686 they were driven out of the island by the Dutch. At first the price of tea in England ranged from £6 to £10 per lb. In the *Mercurius Politicus,* No. 435, of September 1658, the following advertisement occurs:— "That excellent and by all Physitians approved China Drink called by the Chineans *Tcha,* by other nations *Tay, alias Tee,* is sold at the Sultaness Head, a cophee-house in Sweetings Rents, by the Royal Exchange, London." Thomas Garway, the first English tea dealer, and founder of the well-known coffee-house, "Garraway's," in a curious broadsheet, *An Exact Description of the Growth, Quality and Virtues of the Leaf Tea,* issued in 1659 or 1660, writes, "in respect of its scarceness and dearness, it hath been only used as a regalia in high treatments and entertainments, and presents made thereof to princes and grandees." In that year he purchased a quantity of the rare and muchprized commodity, and offered it to the public, in the leaf, at fixed prices varying from 15s to 50s. the lb, according to quality, and also in the infusion, "made according to the directions of the most knowing merchants and travellers into those eastern countries." In 1660 an Act of the first parliament of the Restoration imposed a tax on "every gallon of chocolate, sherbet and tea, made and sold, to be paid by the maker thereof, eightpence" (12 Car. II. c. 23).

Pepys's often-quoted mention of the fact that on the 25th September 1660, "I did send for a cup of tee, a China drink of which I never had drunk before," proves the novelty of tea in England at that date. In 1664 we find that the East India Company presented the king with 2 lb and 2 oz. of "thea," which costs 40s. per lb, and two years afterwards with another parcel containing 22¾ lb, for which the directors paid 50s. per lb. Both parcels appear to have been purchased on the Continent. Not until 1677 is the Company recorded to have taken any steps for the importation of tea. The order then given to their agents was for "teas of the best kind to the amount of 100 dollars." But their instructions were considerably exceeded, for the quantity imported in 1678 was 4713 lb, a quantity which seems to have glutted the market for several years. The annals of the Company record that, in February 1684, the directors wrote thus to Madras:— "In regard thea is grown to be a commodity here, and we have occasion to make presents therein to our great friends at court, we would have you to send us yearly five or six canisters of the very best and freshest thea." Until the Revolution no duty was laid on tea other than that levied on the infusion as sold in the coffee-houses. By I William and Mary, c. 6, a duty of 5s. per lb and 5 per cent. on the value was imposed. For several years the quantities imported were very small, and consisted exclusively of the finer sorts. The first direct purchase in China was made at Amoy, the teas previously obtained by the Company's factors having been purchased in Madras and Surat, whither it was brought by Chinese junks after the expulsion of the British from Java. During the closing years of the century the amount brought over seems to have been, on the average, about 20,000 lb a year. The instructions of 1700 directed the supercargoes to send home 300 tubs of the finer green teas and 80 tubs of bohea. In 1703 orders were given for "75,000 lb Singlo (green), 10,000 lb imperial, and 20,000 lb bohea." The average price of tea at this period was 16s. per lb.

As the 18th century progressed the use of tea in England rapidly increased, and by the close of the century the rate of consumption exceeded an average of 2 lb per person except those of Mongol and Anglo-Saxon origin. The business being a monopoly of the East India Company, and a very profitable one, the company at an early stage of its development endeavoured to ascertain whether tea could not be grown within its own dominions. Difficulties with China doubtless showed the advisability of having an independent source of supply. In 1788 Sir Joseph Banks, at the request of the directors, drew up a memoir on the cultivation of economic plants in Bengal, in which he gave special prominence to tea, pointing out the regions most favourable for its cultivation. About the year 1820 Mr David Scott, the first commissioner of Assam, sent to Calcutta from Kuch Behar and Rangpur—the very districts indicated by Sir Joseph Banks as favourable for tea-growing—certain leaves, with a statement that they were said to belong to the wild tea-plant. The leaves were submitted to Dr Wallich, government botanist at Calcutta, who pronounced them to belong to a species of *Camellia,* and no result followed on Mr Scott's communication. These very leaves ultimately came into the herbarium of the Linnean Society of London, and have authoritatively been pronounced to belong to the indigenous Assam tea-plant. Dr Wallich's attribution of this and other specimens subsequently sent in to the genus *Camellia,* although scientifically defensible, unfortunately diverted attention from the significance of the discovery. It was not till 1834 that, overcome by the insistence of Captain Francis Jenkins, who maintained and proved that, called by the name *Camellia* or not, the leaves belonged to a tea-plant, Dr Wallich admitted "the fact of the genuine tea-plant being a native of our territories in Upper Assam as incontrovertibly proved." In the meantime a committee had been formed by Lord William Bentinck, the governor-general, for the introduction of tea culture into India, and an official had already been sent to the tea districts of China to procure seed and skilled Chinese workmen to conduct operations in the Himalayan regions. The discovery and reports of Captain Jenkins led to the investigation of the capacities of Assam as a tea-growing country by Lord William Bentinck's committee. Evidence of the abundant existence of the indigenous tea-tree was obtained; and the directors of the East India Company resolved to institute an experimental establishment in Assam for cultivating and manufacturing tea, leaving the industry to be developed by private enterprise should its practicability be demonstrated.

In 1834 the monopoly of the East India Company was abolished and an era of rapid progress in the new industry began. In 1836 there was sent to London 1 lb of tea made from indigenous leaves; in 1837 5 lb of Assam tea were sent; in 1838 the quantity sent was 12 small boxes, and 95 boxes reached London in 1839. In 1840 there were grown, and offered at public auction in Calcutta early the following year, 35 packages, chiefly green teas, stated to have been manufactured by a chief of the Singpho tribe aided by the government establishment. In the same auction catalogue were included 95 packages, "the produce of the Government Tea Plantation in Assam," many of which bore the Chubwa mark, one well known to this day.

This auction is most interesting as being the first of British-grown tea, and it included about 6000 lb. It is of interest also for the reference to the Singpho tribe, who are even now in small numbers in the same district, where they still produce in a primitive manner tea plucked from the indigenous trees growing in their jungles.

In January 1840 the Assam Company was formed to take over the early tea garden of the East India Company, and this, the premier company, is still in existence, having produced up to 1907 no less than 117,000,000 lb of tea and paid in dividends £1,360,000 or 730 per cent. on capital. It is no longer the first company in extent of yield, as the Consolidated Tea and Lands Company produced in 1907 about 15,000,000 lb of tea, besides other products. The introduction of Chinese seed and Chinese methods was a mistake, and there seems little reason to doubt that, in clearing jungle for tea planting, fine indigenous tea was frequently destroyed unwittingly in order to plant the inferior China variety. The period of unlearning the Chinese methods, and replacing the Chinese plants, had to be lived through. Vicissitudes of over-production and inflation came to interfere with an even course of success, but the industry developed and has increased enormously. From its point of origin in Assam, it has gradually spread to other districts with varying commercial success. The aggregate total of capital of the tea-producing companies in India and Ceylon now amounts to about £25,000,000.

The Dutch were rather earlier than the English in attempting to establish tea-growing in their eastern possessions. A beginning was made in Java in 1826, but probably because of the even more marked influence of Chinese methods and Chinese plant, the progress was slow and the results indifferent. Of late years, however, by the introduction of fine Assam seed and the adoption of methods similar to those in use in India, a marked improvement has taken place, and there seems little reason to doubt that, with the very rich soil and abundant cheap labour that the island of Java possesses, the relative progress there may be greater in future than in any other producing land.

Somewhere about 1860 the practical commercial growing of tea was introduced into the island of Formosa. The methods of cultivation and manufacture followed there differ in many ways from those of the other large producing countries, but the industry has been fairly successful throughout its history.

Attempts were repeatedly made to introduce tea culture in Ceylon, under both Dutch and British authority. No permanent success was attained till about 1876, when the disastrous effects of the coffee-leaf disease forced planters to give serious attention to tea. Since that period the tea industry has developed with marvellous rapidity, and now takes first rank in the commerce of the island.

TOAST, a slice of bread scorched brown on the two surfaces by the heat of a fire. The word was borrowed from the O. Fr. *toste,* Lat. *torrere, tostum,* to scorch, burn. It was formerly the custom to have pieces of toast floating in many kinds of liquor, especially when drunk hot. It is said to be from this custom that the word is used of the calling upon a company to drink the health of some person, institution or cause.

UMBRELLA, a portable folding protector from rain (Fr. *parapluie*), the name parasol being given to the smaller and more fanciful article carried by ladies as a sunshade, and the *en-tout-cas* being available for both purposes. Primarily the umbrella (*ombrella,* Ital. dim. from Lat. *umbra,* shade) was a sunshade alone—its original home having been in hot, brilliant climates. In Eastern countries from the earliest times the umbrella was one of the insignia of royalty and power. On the sculptured remains of ancient Nineveh and Egypt there are representations of kings and sometimes of lesser potentates going in procession with an umbrella carried over their heads; and throughout Asia the umbrella had, and still has, something of the same significance. The Mahratta princes of India had among their titles "lord of the umbrella." In 1855 the king of Burma in addressing the governor-general of India termed himself "the monarch who reigns over the great umbrella-wearing chiefs of the Eastern countries." The baldachins erected over ecclesiastical chairs, altars and portals, and the canopies of thrones and pulpits, &c., are in their origin closely related to umbrellas, and have the same symbolic significance. In each of the basilican churches of Rome there still hangs a large umbrella.

Among the Greeks and Romans the umbrella (σκιάζ, σκιάδειον, *umbraculum, umbella*) was used by ladies, while the carrying of it by men was regarded as a sign of effeminacy. Probably in these southern climes it never went out of use, and allusions by Montaigne show that in his day its employment as a sunshade was quite common in Italy. The umbrella was not unknown in England in the 17th century, and was already used as a rain protector. Michael Drayton, writing about the beginning of the 17th century, says, speaking of doves:—

> And, like umbrellas, with their feathers
> Shield you in all sorts of weathers.

Although it was the practice to keep an umbrella in the coffee-houses early in the 18th century, its use cannot have been very familiar, for in 1752 Colonel Wolfe, writing from Paris, mentions the carrying of them there as a defence against both rain and sun, and wonders that they are not introduced into England. The traveller Jonas Hanway, who died in 1786, is credited with having been the first Englishman who habitually carried an umbrella.

WIG (short for "periwig," an alternative form of "peruke," conjecturally derived from Lat. *pilus*), an artificial head of hair, worn as a personal adornment, disguise or symbol of office. The custom of wearing wigs is of great antiquity. If, as seems probable, the curious head-covering of a prehistoric ivory carving of a female head found by M. Piette in the cave of Brassempouy in the Landes represents a wig, the fashion is certainly some 100,000 years old. In historic times, wigs were worn among the Egyptians as a royal and official head-dress, and specimens of these have been recovered from mummies. In Greece they were used by both men and women. A reference in Xenophon (*Cyr.* i. 3. 2) to the false hair worn by Cyrus's grandfather "as is customary among the Medes," and also a story in Aristotle (*Oecon.* 4. 14), would suggest that wigs were introduced from Persia, and were in use in Asia Minor. Lucian, in the 2nd century, mentions wigs of both men and women as a matter of course. The theatrical wig was also in use in Greece, the various comic and tragic masks having hair suited to the character represented. A. E. Haigh (*Attic Theatre*, pp. 221, 239) refers to the black hair and beard of the tyrant, the fair curls of the youthful hero, and the red hair characteristic of the dishonest slave of comedy. These conventions appear to have been handed on to the Roman theatre.

At Rome wigs came into use certainly in the early days of the empire. They were also known to the Carthaginians; Polybius says that Hannibal used wigs as a means of disguise. The fashionable ladies of Rome were much addicted to false hair, and we learn from Ovid and Martial that the golden hair imported from Germany was most favoured. Juvenal shows us Messalina assuming a yellow wig for her visits to places of ill-fame, and the scholiast on the passage says that the yellow wig was characteristic of courtesans.

The first men's wigs would have been tight fur caps simulating hair, which would naturally suggest wigs of false hair. Otho wore a wig (Suetonius, *Otho* § 12), which could not be distinguished from real hair, while Nero wore a wig as a disguise, and Heliogabalus also wore one at times. Women continued to have wigs of different colours as part of their ordinary wardrobe, and Faustina, wife of Marcus Aurelius, is said to have had several hundred. An amusing development of this is occasionally found in portrait busts, *e.g.* that of Plautilla in the Louvre, in which the hair is made movable, so that by changing the wig of the statue from time to time it should never be out of fashion.

The Fathers of the Church violently attacked the custom of wearing wigs, Tertullian being particularly eloquent against them, but that they did not succeed in stamping out the custom was proved by the finding of an auburn wig in the grave of a Christian woman in the cemetery of St Cyriacus. In 672 a synod of Constantinople forbade the wearing of artificial hair.

Artificial hair has presumably always been worn by women when the fashion required abundant locks. Thus, with the development of elaborate coiffures in the 16th century, the wearing of false hair became prevalent among ladies in Europe; Queen Elizabeth had eighty attires of false hair, and Mary queen of Scots was also in the habit of varying the attires of hair she wore. The periwig in the 16th century, however, merely simulated real hair, either as an adornment or to supply the defects of nature. It was not till the 17th century that the peruke was worn as a distinctive feature of costume. The fashion started in France. In 1602 the abbé La Rivière appeared at the court of Louis XIII. in a periwig made to simulate long fair hair, and four years later the king himself, prematurely bald, also adopted one and thus set the fashion. Louis XIV., who was proud of his abundant hair, did not wear a wig till after 1670. Meanwhile, his courtiers had continued to wear wigs in imitation of the royal hair, and from Versailles the fashion spread through Europe. In England it came in with the Restoration; for though the prince of Wales (Charles I.), while in Paris on his way to Spain, had "shadowed himself the most he could under a burly perruque, which none in former days but bald-headed people used," he had dropped the fashion on returning to England, and he and his Cavaliers were distinguished from the "Roundheads" only by wearing their own flowing locks. Under Charles II. the wearing of the peruke became general. Pepys records that he parted with his own hair and "paid £3 for a periwigg"; and on going to church in one he says "it did not prove so strange as I was afraid it would." It was under Queen Anne, however, that the wig attained its maximum development, covering the back and shoulders and floating down over the chest. So far, indeed, whatever the exaggeration of its proportions, the wig had been a "counterfeit hair" intended to produce the illusion of abundant natural locks. But, to quote the inimitable author of *Plocacosmos,* "as the perukes became more common, their shape and forms altered. Hence we hear of the clerical, the physical, and the huge tie peruke for the man of law, the brigadier or major for the army and navy; as also the tremendous fox ear, or cluster of temple curls, with a pig-tail behind. The merchant, the man of business and of letters, were distinguished by the grave full bottom, or more moderate tie, neatly curled; the tradesman by the long bob, or natty scratch; the country gentleman by the natural fly and hunting peruke. All conditions of men were distinguished by the cut of the wig, and none more so than the coachman, who wore his, as there does some to this day, in imitation of the curled hair of a water-dog."

This differentiation of wigs according to class and profession explains why, when early in the reign of George III. the general fashion of wearing wigs began to wane and die out, the practice held its own among professional men. It was by slow degrees that doctors, soldiers and clergymen gave up the custom. In the Church it survived longest among the bishops, the wig ultimately becoming a sort of ensign of the episcopal dignity. Wigs were first discarded by the bishops, by permission of the king, at the coronation banquet of William IV., the weather being hot; and Greville comments on the odd appearance of the prelates with their cropped polls. At the coronation of Queen Victoria the archbishop of Canterbury, alone of the prelates, still wore a wig. Wigs are now worn as part of official costume only in the United Kingdom and its dependencies, their use being confined, except in the case of the speaker of the house of commons, and the clerks of parliament, to the lord chancellor, the judges and members of the bar. Wigs of course continue to be worn by many to make up for natural deficiencies; and on the stage the wig is, as in all times, an indispensable adjunct. Many of the modern stage wigs are made of jute, a fibre which lends itself to marvellously perfect imitations of human hair.

WINE-TABLE, a late 18th-century device for facilitating after-dinner drinking—the cabinetmakers called it a "Gentleman's Social Table." It was always narrow and of semicircular or horseshoe form, and the guests sat round the outer circumference.

In the earlier and simpler shapes metal wells for bottles and ice were sunk in the surface of the table; they were fitted with brass lids. In later and more elaborate examples the tables were fitted with a revolving wine-carriage, bottle-holder or tray working upon a balanced arm which enabled the bottles to be passed to any guest without shaking. The side opposite the guests was often fitted with a network bag. It has been conjectured that this bag was intended to hold biscuits, but it is much more likely that its function was to prevent glasses and bottles which might be upset from falling to the floor. That the wine-table might be drawn up to the fire in cold weather without inconvenience from the heat it was fitted with curtains hung upon a brass frame and running upon rings. Sometimes the table was accompanied by a circular bottle-stand supported on a tripod into which the bottles were deeply sunk to preserve them from the heat of the fire. Yet another form was circular with a socket in the centre for the bottle. Wine-tables followed the fashion of other tables and were often inlaid with wood or brass. They are now exceedingly scarce.

STYLE

BY EDMUND GOSSE

*A*though *no single figure dominated the English literary scene just before World War I in the same way that T. S. Eliot, Ezra Pound, and the Bloomsbury group held sway in the subsequent years, Ed-*

mund Gosse was one of the pivotal figures of the period. There are many reasons for his preeminence during the years of the making of the eleventh, the first decade of the twentieth century. He was not a new contributor to this edition—he had already done distinguished work for both the ninth and the tenth editions of the Britannica *before Chisholm's invitation to participate in the eleventh. Gosse was a cosmopolitan and continental figure within the often provincial and confined circles of the fin-de-siècle English literary world. He translated Ibsen's* Hedda Gabler *and later* The Master Builder, *carried on a long friendship and correspondence with André Gide, and wrote various full-length studies that later led to a reevaluation of metaphysical poetry and seventeenth-century writing in general, then long out of favor. His* Life and Letters of John Donne *dates from 1899, again, well outside of the reigning literary fashions, and this was followed by equally impressive studies dedicated to Jeremy Taylor and Sir Thomas Browne. These works of Edmund Gosse are often taken to be a major critical element in the reaction against romantic expression, which came into full flower with T. S. Eliot's early critical essays, later collected in* The Sacred Wood. *But Gosse was not just a critic; he is the author of one of the most discerning studies of a conflictive relationship within a family—*Father and Son: A Study of Two Temperaments, *first published anonymously in 1907. It is the book he is still remembered by.*

As an example of Gosse's wide readings and keen discrimination, we include his essay on "Style," where, among other points made, he happily reconsiders in a favorable light the delights of baroque expression, that of "vivid imagery and . . . graceful illumination." This reconsideration will form a part of the formalist campaign against nineteenth-century tastes in favor of the modernism that later triumphed in the twenties, both in England and in the United States.

STYLE, in literature a term which may be defined as language regarded from the point of view of the characteristics which it reveals; similarly, by analogy, in other arts, a mode or method of working characterized by distinctive features. The word (which is different from that used in architecture) is derived from the instrument *stilus* (wrongly spelled *stylus*), of metal, wood or ivory, by means of which, in classic times, letters and words were imprinted upon waxen tablets. By the transition of thought known as metonymy the word has been transferred from the object which makes the impression to the sentences which are impressed by it, and a mechanical observation has become an intellectual conception. To "turn the stylus" was to correct what had been written by the sharp end of the tool, by a judicious application of the blunt end, and this responds to that discipline and self-criticism upon which literary excellence depends. The energy of a deliberate writer would make a firm and full impression when he wielded the stylus. A scribe of rapid and fugitive habit would press more irregularly and produce a less consistent text. The varieties of writing induced by these differences of temperament would reveal the nature of the writer, yet they would be attributed, and with justice, to the implement which immediately produced them. Thus it would be natural for any one who examined several tablets of wax to say, "The writers of these inscriptions are revealed by their stylus"; in other words, the style or impression of the implement is the medium by which the temperament is transferred to the written speech.

If we follow this analogy, the famous phrase of Buffon becomes at once not merely intelligible but luminous—"le style est l'homme même." This axiom is constantly misquoted ("le style c'est l'homme"), and not infrequently miscomprehended. It is usual to interpret it as meaning that the style of a writer is that writer's self, that it reveals the essence of his individuality. That is true, and the statement of it is useful. But it is probably not the meaning, or at least not the original meaning, that Buffon had in mind. It should be recollected that Buffon was a zoologist, and that the phrase occurs in the course of his great *Natural History.* He was considering man in the abstract, and differentiating him from other genera of the animal kingdom. Hence, no doubt, he remarked that "style was man himself," not as every reviewer repeats the sentence to-day, "the man." He meant that style, in the variety and elaboration of it, distinguished the language of man *(Homo sapiens)* from the monotonous roar of the lion or the limited gamut of the bird. Buffon was engaged with biological, not with aesthetic ideas.

Nevertheless, the usual interpretation given to the phrase "le style est l'homme même" may be accepted as true and valuable. According to an Arab legend King Solomon inquired of a djinn, "What is language?" and received the answer, "a wind that passes." "But how," continued the wisest of men, "can it be held?" "By one art only," replied the djinn, "by the art of writing." It may be well to follow a little closely the processes of this art of writing. A human being in the artless condition, in whom, that is to say, the conception of personal expression has not been formed, uses written language to state primitive and general matters of fact. He writes, "The sea is rough to-day; the wind is cold." In these statements there is some observation, but as yet no personal note. We read them without being able to form the very smallest conjecture as to the character or condition of the writer. From these bald and plain words we may rise in degree until we reach Victor Hugo's celebrated parallel of the ocean with the genius of Shakespeare, where every phrase is singular and elaborate, and every element of expression redolent of Victor Hugo, but of no other person who ever lived. Another example, in its own way still more striking, is found in comparison of the famous paragraph which occurs in the *Cyrus-Garden* (1658) of Sir Thomas Browne. A primitive person would say, "But it is time to go to bed"; this statement is drawn out by Browne into the wonderful page beginning, "But the quincunx of Heaven runs low," and collects around it as it proceeds on its voluptuous course the five ports of knowledge, cables of cobwebs, the bed of Cleopatra, the ghost of a rose, the huntsmen of Persia, and a dozen other examples of prolific and ornamented style. In its final form it is so fully characteristic of its author that it may be justly said that the passage *is* Browne himself.

It follows from what has just been said that style appeals exclusively to those who read with attention and for the pleasure of reading. It is not even perceived by those who read primarily for information, and these form the great majority of readers. Even these have a glimmering impression that we must not live by bread alone; that the human heart, with its imagination, its curiosity and sensitiveness, cannot be satisfied by bald statements of fact delivered on the printed page as messages are shouted along the telephone. This instinct it is which renders the untaught liable to fall into those errors of false style to which we shall presently call attention. In the untrained there yet exists a craving for beauty, and the misfortune is that this craving is too easily met by gaudy rhetoric and vain repetitions. The effect on the nature of a human being which is produced by reading or listening to a book, or a passage from a book, which that being greatly admires, is often so violent as to resemble a physical shock to the nerves. It causes a spasm of emotion, which is betrayed by tears or laughter or a heightened pulse. This effect could not be produced by a statement of the fact conveyed in language, but is the result of the manner in which that fact is presented. In other words, it is the style which appeals so vividly to the physical and moral system of the reader—not the fact, but the ornament of the fact. That this emotion may be, and often is, caused by bad style, by the mere tinsel of rhetoric and jangle of alliteration, is not to the point. The important matter is that it is caused by style, whether good or bad. Those juvenile ardours and audacities of expression which so often amuse the wise man and exasperate the pedant are but the effects of style acting on a fervid and unripe imagination. The deep delight with which a grown man of experience reads Milton or Dante is but the same phenomenon produced in different conditions.

It is, however, desirable at the outset of an inquiry into the elements of style to insist on the dangers of a heresy which found audacious expression towards the close of the 19th century, namely, that style is superior to thought and independent of it. Against this may be set at once another of the splendid apothegms of Buffon, "Les idées seules forment le fond du style." Before there can be style, therefore, there must be thought, clearness of knowledge, precise experience, sanity of reasoning power. It is difficult to allow that there can be style where there is no thought, the beauty even of some poems, the sequence of words in which is intentionally devoid of meaning, being preserved by the characteristics of the metre, the rhymes, the asso-nances, all which are, in their degree, intellectual in character. A confusion between form and matter has often confused this branch of our theme. Even Flaubert, than whom no man ever gave closer attention to the question of style, seems to dislocate them. For him the *form* was the work itself: "As in living creatures, the blood, nour-ishing the body, determines its very contour and external aspect, just so, to his mind, the *matter,* the basis, is a work of art, imposed, nec-essarily, the unique, the just expression, the measure, the rhythm, the *form* in all its characteristics." This ingenious definition seems to strain language beyond its natural limits. If the adventures of an ordinary young man in Paris be the *matter* of *L'Éducation sentimentale* it is not easy to admit that they "imposed, necessarily," such a "unique" treatment of them as Flaubert so superlatively gave. They might have been recounted with feebler rhythm by an inferior novelist, with bad rhythm by a bad novelist and with no rhythm at all by a police-news reporter. What makes that book a masterpiece is not the basis of adventure, but the superstructure of expression. The expression, however, could not have been built up on no basis at all, and would have fallen short of Flaubert's aim if it had risen on an inadequate basis. The perfect union is that between adequate matter and an adequate form. We will borrow from the history of English literature an example which may serve to illuminate this point. Locke has no appreciable style; he has only thoughts. Berkeley has thoughts which are as valuable as those of Locke, and he has an exquisite style as well. From the artist's point of view, therefore, we are justified in giving the higher place to Berkeley, but in doing this we must not deny the importance of Locke. If we compare him with some pseudo-philosopher, whose style is highly ornamental but whose thoughts are valueless, we see that Locke greatly prevails. Yet we need not pretend that he rises to an equal height with Berkeley, in whom the basis is no less solid, and where the superstructure of style adds an emotional and aesthetic importance to which Locke's plain speech is a stranger. At the same time, an abstract style, such as that of Pascal, may often give extreme pleasure, in spite of its absence of ornament, by its precise and pure definition of ideas and by the just mental impression it supplies of its writer's distinguished vivacity of mind. The abstract or concrete style, moreover, what Rossetti called "fundamental brain-work," must always have a leading place.

When full justice has been done to the necessity of thought as the basis of style, it remains true that what is visible, so to speak, to the naked eye, what can be analysed and described, is an artistic arrangement of words. Language is so used as to awaken impressions of touch, taste, odour and hearing, and these are roused in a way peculiar to the genius of the individual who brings them forth. The personal aspect of style is therefore indispensable, and is not to be ignored even by those who are most rigid in their objection to mere ornament. Ornament in itself is no more style than facts, as such, constitute thought. In an excellent style there is an effect upon our senses of the mental force of the man who employs it. We discover himself in what he writes, as it was excellently said of Châteaubriand that it was into his phrases that he put his heart; again, D'Alembert said of Fontenelle that he had the style of his thought, like all good authors. In the words of Schopenhauer, style is the physiognomy of the soul. All these attempts at epigrammatic definition tend to show the sense that language ought to be, and even unconsciously is, the mental picture of the man who writes.

To attain this, however, the writer must be sincere, original and highly trained. He must be highly trained, because, without the exercise of clearness of knowledge, precise experience and the habit of expression, he will not be able to produce his soul in language. It will, at best, be perceived as through a glass, darkly. Nor can anyone who desires to write consistently and well, afford to neglect the laborious discipline which excellence entails. He must not be satisfied with his first sprightly periods; he must polish them, and then polish them again. He must never rest until he has attained a consummate adaptation of his language to his subject, of his words to his emotion. This is the most difficult aim which the writer can put before him, and it is a light that flits ever onward as he approaches. Perfection is impossible, and yet he must never desist from pursuing perfection. In this connexion the famous tirade of Tamburlaine in Marlowe's tragedy cannot be meditated upon too carefully, for it contains the finest definition which has been given in any language of style as the unapproachable fen-fire of the mind:—

> If all the pens that poets ever held
> Had fed the feeling of their master's thoughts,
> And every sweetness then inspired their hearts,
> Their minds, and muses, on admirèd themes—
> If all the heavenly quintessence they 'still
> From their immortal flowers of poesy,
> Wherein, as in a mirror, we perceive
> The highest reaches of a human wit—
> If those had made one poem's period,
> And all combined in beauty's worthiness,
> Yet should there hover in our restless heads
> One thought, one grace, one wonder, at the least.
> Which into words no virtue can digest.

Flaubert believed that every thought or grace or wonder had one word or phrase exactly adapted to express it, and could be "digested" by no other without loss of clearness and beauty. It was the passion of his life, and the despair of it, to search for this unique phrase in each individual case. Perhaps in this research after style he went too far, losing something of that simplicity and inevitability which is the charm of natural writing. It is boasted by the admirers of Flaubert that his style is an enamel, and those who say this perhaps forget that the beauty of an enamel resides wholly in its surface and not at all in the substance below it. This is the danger which lies in wait for those who consider too exquisitely the value and arrangement of their words. Their style becomes too glossy, too highly varnished, and attracts too much attention to itself. The greatest writing is that which in its magnificent spontaneity carries the reader with it in its flight; that which detains him to admire itself can never rise above the second place. Forgetfulness of self, absence of conceit and affectation, simplicity in the sense not of thinness or poorness but of genuineness—these are elements essential to the cultivation of a noble style. Here again, thought must be the basis, not vanity or the desire to astonish. We do not escape by our ingenuities from the firm principle of Horace, "scribendi *recti sapere* est et principium et fons."

In speaking of originality in style it must not be forgotten that memory exercises a strong and often an insidious effect upon writing. That which has been greatly admired will have a tendency to impregnate the mind, and its echo, or, what is worse, its cadence, will be unconsciously repeated. The *cliché* is the greatest danger which lies in wait for the vapid modern author, who is tempted to adopt, instead of the one fresh form which suits his special thought, a word or even a chain of words, which conventionally represents it. Thus "the devouring element" was once a striking variant for the short word "fire," and a dangerous hidden place was once well described as "a veritable death-trap," but these have long been *clichés* which can only be used by writers who are insincere or languid. Worse than these are continuous phrases, and even sentences, such as are met with in the leaders of daily newspapers, which might be lifted bodily from their places and inserted elsewhere, so completely have they lost all vitality and reality.

With regard to the training which those who wish to write well should resign themselves to undergo, there is some difference of opinion, based upon difference of temperament. There are those who believe that the gift of style is inborn, and will reveal itself at the moment of mental maturity without any external help. There are others who hold that no amount of labour is excessive, if it be directed to a study and an emulation of what are called "the best models." No doubt these theories are both admissible. If a man is not born to write well, no toil in the imitation of Addison or Ruskin will make his style a brilliant one; and a born writer will express himself with exactitude and fire even though he be but an idle student of the classics. Yet, on the other hand, the very large number of persons who have a certain aptitude for writing, yet no strong native gift, will undoubtedly cure themselves of faults and achieve skill and smoothness by the study of those writers who have most kinship with themselves. To be of any service, however, it seems that those writers must have used the same language as their pupils. Of the imitation of the ancients much has been written, even to the extent of the publication of manuals. But what is that imitation of the verse of Homer which leads to-day to Chapman and to-morrow to Pope? What the effect of the study of the prose of Theophrastus which results in the prose of Addison? The good poet or prose-man, however closely he studies an admirable foreign model, is really anxious to say something which has never before been said in his own language. The stimulus which he receives from any foreign predecessor must be in the direction of analogous or parallel effort, not in that of imitation.

The importance of words, indeed, is exemplified, if we regard it closely, in this very question, so constantly mooted, of the imitation of the ancients, by the loss of beauty fatally felt in a bad translation. The vocabulary of a great writer has been, as Pater says, "winnowed"; it is impossible to think of Sophocles or of Horace as using a word which is not the best possible for introduction at that particular point. But the translator has to interpret the ideas of these ancient writers into a vocabulary which is entirely different from theirs, and unless he has a genius of almost equal impeccability he will undo the winnowing work. He will scatter chaff and refuse over the pure grain which the classic poet's genius had so completely fanned and freed. The employment of vague and loose terms where the original author has been eclectic, and of a flood of verbiage where he has been frugal, destroys all semblance of style, although the meaning may be correctly preserved.

The errors principally to be avoided in the cultivation of a pure style are confusion, obscurity, incorrectness and affectation. To take the earliest of these first, no fault is so likely to be made by an impetuous beginner as a mingling together of ideas, images, propositions which are not on the same plane or have no proper relation. This is that mass of "stunning sounds and voices all confused" which Milton deprecates. One of the first lessons to be learned in the art of good writing is to avoid perplexity and fatigue in the mind of the reader by retaining clearness and order in all the segments of a paragraph, as well as propriety of grammar and metaphor in every phrase. Those who have overcome this initial difficulty, and have learned to avoid a jumble of misrelated thoughts and sentences, may nevertheless sin by falling into obscurity, which, indeed, is sometimes a wilful error and arises from a desire to cover poverty of thought by a semblance of profundity. The meaning of "obscurity" is, of course, in the first instance "darkness," but in speaking of literature it is used of a darkness which arises from unintelligibility, not from depth of expression, but from cloudiness and fogginess of idea.

Of the errors of style which are the consequences of bad taste, it is difficult to speak except in an entirely empirical spirit, because of the absence of any absolute standard of beauty by which artistic products can be judged. That kind of writing which in its own age is extravagantly cultivated and admired may, in the next age, be as violently repudiated; this does not preclude the possibility of its recovering critical if not popular favour. Perhaps the most remarkable instance of this is the revolution made against the cold and stately Ciceronian prose of the middle of the 16th century by the so-called Euphuists. This occurred almost simultaneously in several nations, but has been traced to its sources in the Spanish of Guevara and in his English imitators, North and Pettie, whom Lyly in his turn followed with his celebrated *Euphues*. Along with these may not unfairly be mentioned Montaigne in France and Castiglione in Italy, for, although these men were not proficients in Guevara's artificial manner, his *estilo alto,* still, by their easiness and brightness, their use of vivid imagery and their graceful illumination, they marked the universal revulsion against the Ciceronian stiffness. Each of these new manners of writing fell almost immediately into desuetude, and the precise and classic mode of writing in another form came into vogue (Addison, Bossuet, Vico, Johnson). But what was best in the ornamental writers of the 16th century is now once more fully appreciated, if not indeed admired to excess. A facility in bringing up before the memory incessant analogous metaphors is the property, not merely of certain men, but of certain ages; it flourished in the age of Marino and is welcomed again in that of Meredith. A vivid, concrete style, full of colour and images, is not to be condemned because it is not an abstract style, scholastic and systematic. It is to be judged on its own merits and by its own laws. It may be good or bad; it is not bad merely because it is metaphorical and ornate. The amazing errors which lie strewn along the shore of criticism bear evidence to the lack of sympathy which has not perceived this axiom and has wrecked the credit of dogmatists. To De Quincey, a convinced Ciceronian, the style of Keats "belonged essentially to the vilest collections of wax-work filagree or gilt gingerbread"; but to read such a judgment is to encourage a question whether all discussion of style is not futile. Yet that particular species of affectation which encourages untruth, affectation, parade for the mere purpose of producing an effect, must be wrong, even though Cicero be guilty of it.

The use of the word "style," in the sense of the present remarks, is not entirely modern. For example, the early English critic Puttenham says that "style is a constant and continual phrase or tenour of speaking and writing" (1589). But it was in France and in the great age of Louis XIV. that the art of writing began to be carefully studied and ingeniously described. Mme de Sévigné, herself mistress of a manner exquisitely disposed to reflect her vivacious, tender and eloquent character, is particularly fond of using the word "style" in its modern sense, as the expression of a complete and rich personality. She says, in a phrase which might stand alone as a text on the subject,

"Ne quittez jamais le naturel, votre tour s'y est formé, et cela compose un style parfait." Her contemporary, Boileau, contributed much to the study, and spoke with just pride of "mon style, ami de la lumière." The expression to form one's style, *à se faire un style,* appears, perhaps for the first time, in the works of the abbé d'Olivet (1682–1768), who was addicted to rhetorical speculation. Two great supporters of the pure art of writing, Swift and Voltaire, contributed much to the study of style in the 18th century. The former declared that "proper words in proper places make the true definition of a style"; the latter, more particularly, that "le style rend singulières les choses les plus communs, fortifie les plus faibles, donne de la grandeur aux plus simples." Voltaire speaks of "le mélange des styles" as a great fault of the age in which he lived; it has come to be looked upon as a principal merit of that in which we live.

The problem of how to obtain a style has frequently been treated in works of more or less ephemeral character. In France the treatises of M. Albalat have received a certain amount of official recognition, and may be mentioned here as containing a good deal of sound advice mixed with much that is jejune and pedagogic. If M. Albalat distributes a poison, the antidote is supplied by the wit of M. Remy de Gourmont; the one should not be imbibed without the other.

SAMUEL JOHNSON
BY LORD MACAULAY

*T*he inclusion of Lord Macaulay's rich evocation of the life and works of Samuel Johnson was never even a matter of debate among the editors; among such a plethora of literary appreciations in *the eleventh, this outstanding example of romantic critical appreciation stands alone. But there is some explaining to do as to the choice, since the eleventh was published in 1910 and early 1911, while Macaulay, a renowned and hallowed name in the essay and historiography of English romanticism, had died in 1859. Here we have one of the select examples where editor Hugh Chisholm decided to reprint, with only minor modifications executed by his collaborator Thomas Seccombe, a major entry from an earlier edition. Macaulay's "Samuel Johnson" comes down to us not from an immediately preceding edition of the Britannica such as the ninth, but from the seventh edition, composed of twenty-one volumes published between the years 1830 and 1842. Though it was not at all a habit of Chisholm's to carry over major treatments from earlier editions, the Macaulay contributions (on John Bunyan, Oliver Goldsmith, William Pitt, and of course Samuel Johnson) were deemed by successive editors and Chisholm to be irreplaceable, and they continued on being included up to and including the eleventh. It is nonetheless possible, as editor Seccombe pointedly reminds us, that "Macaulay exaggerated persistently the poverty of Johnson's pedigree, the squalor of his early married life, the grotesqueness of his entourage in Fleet Street, the decline and fall from complete virtue of Mrs. Thrale, the novelty and success of the Dictionary, the complete failure of the ("Prefaces to) Shakespeare and political tracts." Seccombe clearly quibbles too much; his objections come from a more limpid and less rotund kind of literary criticism. The Macaulay piece is unique. The splendid style and the overarching design of Macaulay's exercise in insight bring us to a refreshed appreciation of the power of romantic rhetoric, in the best sense of the much maligned noun "rhetoric"—the art of persuading the reader first, then to go back again to the major works of Johnson, to plunge again into that magnificence.*

⤜⤛ JOHNSON, SAMUEL (1709–1784), English

writer and lexicographer, was the son of Michael Johnson (1656–1731), bookseller and magistrate of Lichfield, who married in 1706 Sarah Ford (1669–1759). Michael's abilities and attainments seem to have been considerable. He was so well acquainted with the contents of the volumes which he exposed for sale that the country rectors of Staffordshire and Worcestershire thought him an oracle on points of learning. Between him and the clergy, indeed, there was a strong religious and political sympathy. He was a zealous churchman, and, though he had qualified himself for municipal office by taking the oaths to the sovereigns in possession, was to the last a Jacobite in heart. The social position of Samuel's paternal grandfather, William Johnson, remains obscure; his mother was the daughter of Cornelius Ford, "a little Warwickshire Gent."

At a house (now the Johnson Museum) in the Market Square, Lichfield, Samuel Johnson was born on the 18th of September 1709 and baptized on the same day at St Mary's, Lichfield. In the child the physical, intellectual and moral peculiarities which afterwards distinguished the man were plainly discernible: great muscular strength accompanied by much awkwardness and many infirmities; great quickness of parts, with a morbid propensity to sloth and pro-crastination; a kind and generous heart, with a gloomy and irritable temper. He had inherited from his ancestors a scrofulous taint, and his parents were weak enough to believe that the royal touch would cure him. In his third year he was taken up to London, inspected by the court surgeon, prayed over by the court chaplains and stroked and presented with a piece of gold by Queen Anne. Her hand was applied in vain. The boy's features, which were originally noble and not irregular, were distorted by his malady. His cheeks were deeply scarred. He lost for a time the sight of one eye; and he saw but very imperfectly with the other. But the force of his mind overcame every impediment. Indolent as he was, he acquired knowledge with such ease and rapidity that at every school (such as those at Lichfield and Stourbridge) to which he was sent he was soon the best scholar. From sixteen to eighteen he resided at home, and was left to his own devices. He learned much at this time, though his studies were without guid-ance and without plan. He ransacked his father's shelves, dipped into a multitude of books, read what was interesting, and passed over what was dull. An ordinary lad would have acquired litttle or no useful knowledge in such a way; but much that was dull to ordinary lads was interesting to Samuel. He read little Greek; for his proficiency in that language was not such that he could take much pleasure in the masters of Attic poetry and eloquence. But he had left school a good Latinist, and he soon acquired an extensive knowledge of Latin literature. He was peculiarly attracted by the works of the great res-torers of learning. Once, while searching for some apples, he found a huge folio volume of Petrarch's works. The name excited his curiosity, and he eagerly devoured hundreds of pages. Indeed, the diction and versification of his own Latin compositions show that he had paid at least as much attention to modern copies from the antique as to the original models.

While he was thus irregularly educating himself, his family was sinking into hopeless poverty. Old Michael Johnson was much better qualified to pore over books, and to talk about them, than to trade in them. His business declined; his debts increased; it was with difficulty that the daily expenses of his household were defrayed. It was out of his power to support his son at either university; but a wealthy neighbour offered assistance; and, in reliance on promises which proved to be of very little value, Samuel was entered at Pembroke College, Oxford. When the young scholar presented himself to the rulers of that society, they were amazed not more by his ungainly figure and eccentric manners than by the quantity of extensive and curious information which he had picked up during many months of desultory but not unprofitable study. On the first day of his residence he surprised his teachers by quoting Macrobius; and one of the most learned among them declared that he had never known a freshman of equal attainments.

At Oxford Johnson resided barely over two years, possibly less. He was poor, even to raggedness; and his appearance excited a mirth and a pity which were equally intolerable to his haughty spirit. He was driven from the quadrangle of Christ Church by the sneering looks which the members of that aristocratical society cast at the holes in his shoes. Some charitable person placed a new pair at his door; but he spurned them away in a fury. Distress made him, not servile, but reckless and ungovernable. No opulent gentleman commoner, panting for one-and-twenty, could have treated the academical authorities with more gross disrespect. The needy scholar was generally to be seen under the gate of Pembroke, a gate now adorned with his effigy, haranguing a circle of lads, over whom in spite of his tattered gown and dirty linen, his wit and audacity gave him an undisputed ascendancy. In every mutiny against the discipline of the college he was the ringleader. Much was pardoned, however, to a youth so highly distinguished by abilities and acquirements. He had early made himself known by turning Pope's "Messiah" into Latin verse. The style and rhythm, indeed, were not exactly Virgilian; but the translation found many admirers, and was read with pleasure by Pope himself.

The time drew near at which Johnson would, in the ordinary course of things, have become a Bachelor of Arts; but he was at the end of his resources. Those promises of support on which he had relied had not been kept. His family could do nothing for him. His debts to Oxford tradesmen were small indeed, yet larger than he could pay. In the autumn of 1731 he was under the necessity of quitting the university without a degree. In the following winter his father died. The old man left but a pittance; and of that pittance almost the whole was appropriated to the support of his widow. The property to which Samuel succeeded amounted to no more than twenty pounds.

His life, during the thirty years which followed, was one hard struggle with poverty. The misery of that struggle needed no aggravation, but was aggravated by the sufferings of an unsound body and an unsound mind. Before the young man left the university, his hereditary malady had broken forth in a singularly cruel form. He had become an incurable hypochondriac. He said long after that he had been mad all his life, or at least not perfectly sane; and, in truth, eccentricities less strange than his have often been thought ground sufficient for absolving felons and for setting aside wills. His grimaces, his gestures, his mutterings, sometimes diverted and sometimes terrified people who did not know him. At a dinner table he would, in a fit of absence, stoop down and twitch off a lady's shoe. He would amaze a drawing-room by suddenly ejaculating a clause of the Lord's Prayer. He would conceive an unintelligible aversion to a particular alley, and perform a great circuit rather than see the hateful place. He would set his heart on touching every post in the streets through which he walked. If by any chance he missed a post, he would go back a hundred yards and repair the omission. Under the influence of his disease, his senses became morbidly torpid, and his imagination morbidly active. At one time he would stand poring on the town clock without being able to tell the hour. At another he would distinctly hear his mother, who was many miles off, calling him by his name. But this was not the worst. A deep melancholy took possession of him, and gave a dark tinge to all his views of human nature and of human destiny. Such wretchedness as he endured has driven many men to shoot themselves or drown themselves. But he was under no temptation to commit suicide. He was sick of life; but he was afraid of death; and he shuddered at every sight or sound which reminded him of the inevitable hour. In religion he found but little comfort during his long and frequent fits of dejection; for his religion partook of his own character. The light from heaven shone on him indeed, but not in a direct line, or with its own pure splendour. The rays had to struggle through a disturbing medium; they reached him re-

fracted, dulled and discoloured by the thick gloom which had settled
on his soul, and, though they might be sufficiently clear to guide
him, were too dim to cheer him.

With such infirmities of body and of mind, he was left, at two-and-
twenty, to fight his way through the world. He remained during about
five years in the midland counties. At Lichfield, his birthplace and
his early home, he had inherited some friends and acquired others.
He was kindly noticed by Henry Hervey, a gay officer of noble family,
who happened to be quartered there. Gilbert Walmesley, registrar of
the ecclesiastical court of the diocese, a man of distinguished parts,
learning and knowledge of the world, did himself honor by patron-
izing the young adventurer, whose repulsive person, unpolished manners and squalid garb moved many of the petty aristocracy of the
neighbourhood to laughter or disgust. At Lichfield, however, Johnson
could find no way of earning a livelihood. He became usher of a
grammar school in Leicestershire; he resided as a humble companion
in the house of a country gentleman; but a life of dependence was
insupportable to his haughty spirit. He repaired to Birmingham, and
there earned a few guineas by literary drudgery. In that town he
printed a translation, little noticed at the time, and long forgotten,
of a Latin book about Abyssinia. He then put forth proposals for
publishing by subscription the poems of Politian, with notes containing a history of modern Latin verse; but subscriptions did not come
in, and the volume never appeared.

While leading this vagrant and miserable life, Johnson fell in love.
The object of his passion was Mrs Elizabeth Porter (1688–1752),
widow of Harry Porter (d. 1734), whose daughter Lucy was born
only six years after Johnson himself. To ordinary spectators the lady
appeared to be a short, fat, coarse woman, painted half an inch thick,
dressed in gaudy colours, and fond of exhibiting provincial airs and
graces which were not exactly those of the Queensberrys and Lepels.
To Johnson, however, whose passions were strong, whose eyesight was
too weak to distinguish rouge from natural bloom, and who had
seldom or never been in the same room with a woman of real fashion,
his Tetty, as he called her, was the most beautiful, graceful and accomplished of her sex. That his admiration was unfeigned cannot be
doubted; she had, however, a jointure of £600 and perhaps a little
more; she came of a good family, and her son Jervis (d. 1763) commanded H.M.S. "Hercules." The marriage, in spite of occasional
wranglings, proved happier than might have been expected. The
lover continued to be under the illusions of the wedding-day (July
9, 1735) till the lady died in her sixty-fourth year. On her monument

at Bromley he placed an inscription extolling the charms of her person and of her manners; and when, long after her decease, he had occasion to mention her, he exclaimed with a tenderness half ludicrous, half pathetic, "Pretty creature!"

His marriage made it necessary for him to exert himself more strenuously than he had hitherto done. He took a house at Edial near Lichfield and advertised for pupils. But eighteen months passed away, and only three pupils came to his academy. The "faces" that Johnson habitually made (probably nervous contortions due to his disorder) may well have alarmed parents. Good scholar though he was, these twitchings had lost him usherships in 1735 and 1736. David Garrick, who was one of the pupils, used, many years later, to throw the best company of London into convulsions of laughter by mimicking the master and his lady.

At length Johnson, in the twenty-eighth year of his age, determined to seek his fortune in London as a literary adventurer. He set out with a few guineas, three acts of his tragedy of *Irene* in manuscript, and two or three letters of introduction from his friend Walmesley. Never since literature became a calling in England had it been a less gainful calling than at the time when Johnson took up his residence in London. In the preceding generation a writer of eminent merit was sure to be munificently rewarded by the Government. The least that he could expect was a pension or a sinecure place; and, if he showed any aptitude for politics, he might hope to be a member of parliament, a lord of the treasury, an ambassador, a secretary of state. But literature had ceased to flourish under the patronage of the great, and had not yet begun to flourish under the patronage of the public. One man of letters, indeed, Pope, had acquired by his pen what was then considered as a handsome fortune, and lived on a footing of equality with nobles and ministers of state. But this was a solitary exception. Even an author whose reputation was established, and whose works were popular—such an author as Thomson, whose *Seasons* was in every library, such an author as Fielding, whose *Pasquin* had had a greater run than any drama since *The Beggar's Opera*—was sometimes glad to obtain, by pawning his best coat, the means of dining on tripe at a cookshop underground, where he could wipe his hands, after his greasy meal, on the back of a Newfoundland dog. It is easy, therefore, to imagine what humiliations and privations must have awaited the novice who had still to earn a name. One of the publishers to whom Johnson applied for employment measured with a scornful eye that athletic though uncouth frame, and exclaimed, "You had better get a porter's knot and carry trunks." Nor was the advice bad, for a porter was likely to be as plentifully fed, and as comfortably lodged, as a poet.

Some time appears to have elapsed before Johnson was able to form any literary connexion from which he could expect more than bread for the day which was passing over him. He never forgot the generosity with which Hervey, who was now residing in London, relieved his wants during this time of trial. "Harry Hervey," said Johnson many years later, "was a vicious man but he was very kind to me. If you call a dog Hervey, I shall love him." At Hervey's table Johnson sometimes enjoyed feasts which were made more agreeable by contrast. But in general he dined, and thought that he dined well, on sixpennyworth of meat and a pennyworth of bread at an alehouse near Drury Lane.

The effect of the privations and sufferings which he endured at this time was discernible to the last in his temper and his deportment. His manners had never been courtly. They now became almost savage. Being frequently under the necessity of wearing shabby coats and dirty shirts, he became a confirmed sloven. Being often very hungry when he sat down to his meals, he contracted a habit of eating with ravenous greediness. Even to the end of his life, and even at the tables of the great, the sight of food affected him as it affects wild beasts and birds of prey. His taste in cookery, formed in subterranean ordinaries and *à la mode* beef shops, was far from delicate. Whenever he was so fortunate as to have near him a hare that had been kept too long, or a meat pie made with rancid butter, he gorged himself with such violence that his veins swelled and the moisture broke out on his forehead. The affronts which his poverty emboldened stupid and low-minded men to offer to him would have broken a mean spirit into sycophancy, but made him rude even to ferocity. Unhappily the insolence which, while it was defensive, was pardonable, and in some sense respectable, accompanied him into societies where he was treated with courtesy and kindness. He was repeatedly provoked into striking those who had taken liberties with him. All the sufferers, however, were wise enough to abstain from talking about their beatings, except Osborne, the most rapacious and brutal of booksellers, who proclaimed everywhere that he had been knocked down by the huge fellow whom he had hired to puff the Harleian Library.

About a year after Johnson had begun to reside in London he was fortunate enough to obtain regular employment from Edward Cave on the *Gentleman's Magazine.* That periodical, just entering on the ninth year of its long existence, was the only one in the kingdom which then had what would now be called a large circulation. Johnson was engaged to write the speeches in the "Reports of the Debates of the Senate of Lilliput," under which thin disguise the proceedings of parliament were published. He was generally furnished with notes, meagre indeed and inaccurate, of what had been said; but sometimes he had to find arguments and eloquence both for the ministry and for the opposition. He was himself a Tory, not from rational conviction—for his serious opinion was that one form of government was just as good or as bad as another—but from mere passion, such as inflamed the Capulets against the Montagues, or the Blues of the Roman circus against the Greens. In his infancy he had heard so much talk about the villainies of the Whigs, and the dangers of the Church, that he had become a furious partisan when he could scarcely speak. Before he was three he had insisted on being taken to hear Sacheverel preach at Lichfield Cathedral, and had listened to the sermon with as much respect and probably with as much intelligence, as any Staffordshire squire in the congregation. The work which had been begun in the nursery had been completed by the university. Oxford, when Johnson resided there, was the most Jacobitical place in England; and Pembroke was one of the most Jacobitical colleges in Oxford. The prejudices which he brought up to London were scarcely less absurd than those of his own Tom Tempest. Charles II. and James II. were two of the best kings that ever reigned. Laud was a prodigy of parts and learning over whose tomb Art and Genius still continued to weep. Hampden deserved no more honourable name than that of the "zealot of rebellion." Even the ship-money Johnson would not pronounce to have been an unconstitutional impost. Under a government which allowed to the people an unprecedented liberty of speech and action, he fancied that he was a slave. He hated Dissenters and stock-jobbers, the excise and the army, septennial parliaments, and Continental connexions. He long had an aversion to the Scots, an aversion of which he could not remember the commencement, but which, he owned, had probably originated in his abhorrence of the conduct of the nation during the Great Rebellion. It is easy to guess in what manner debates on great party questions were likely to be reported by a man whose judgment was so much disordered by party spirit. A show of fairness was indeed necessary to the prosperity of the *Magazine*. But Johnson long afterwards owned that, though he had saved appearances, he had taken care that the Whig dogs should not have the best of it; and, in fact, every passage which has lived, every passage which bears the marks of his higher faculties, is put into the mouth of some member of the opposition.

A few weeks after Johnson had entered on these obscure labours, he published a work which at once placed him high among the writers of his age. It is probable that what he had suffered during his first year in London had often reminded him of some parts of the satire in which Juvenal had described the misery and degradation of a needy man of letters, lodged among the pigeons' nests in the tottering garrets which overhung the streets of Rome. Pope's admirable imitations of Horace's *Satires* and *Epistles* had recently appeared, were in every hand, and were by many readers thought superior to the originals. What Pope had done for Horace, Johnson aspired to do for Juvenal.

Johnson's *London* appeared without his name in May 1738. He received only ten guineas for his stately and vigorous poem; but the sale was rapid and the success complete. A second edition was required within a week. Those small critics who are always desirous to lower established reputations ran about proclaiming that the anonymous satirist was superior to Pope in Pope's own peculiar department of literature. It ought to be remembered, to the honour of Pope, that he joined heartily in the applause with which the appearance of a rival genius was welcomed. He made inquiries about the author of *London.* Such a man, he said, could not long be concealed. The name was soon discovered; and Pope, with great kindness, exerted himself to obtain an academical degree and the mastership of a grammar school for the poor young poet. The attempt failed, and Johnson remained a bookseller's hack.

It does not appear that these two men, the most eminent writer of the generation which was going out, and the most eminent writer of the generation which was coming in, ever saw each other. They lived in very different circles, one surrounded by dukes and earls, the other by starving pamphleteers and index-makers. Among Johnson's associates at this time may be mentioned Boyse, who, when his shirts were pledged, scrawled Latin verses sitting up in bed with his arms through two holes in his blanket, who composed very respectable sacred poetry when he was sober, and who was at last run over by a hackney coach when he was drunk; Hoole, surnamed the metaphysical tailor, who, instead of attending to his measures, used to trace geometrical diagrams on the board where he sat cross-legged; and the penitent impostor, George Psalmanazar, who, after poring all day, in a humble lodging, on the folios of Jewish rabbis and Christian fathers, indulged himself at night with literary and theological conversation at an alehouse in the City. But the most remarkable of the persons with whom at this time Johnson consorted was Richard Savage, an earl's son, a shoemaker's apprentice, who had seen life in all its forms, who had feasted among blue ribands in St James's Square, and had lain with fifty pounds weight of irons on his legs in the condemned ward of Newgate. This man had, after many vicissitudes of fortune, sunk at last into abject and hopeless poverty. His pen had failed him. His patrons had been taken away by death, or estranged by the riotous profusion with which he squandered their bounty, and the ungrateful insolence with which he rejected their advice. He now lived by begging. He dined on venison and champagne whenever he had been so fortunate as to borrow a guinea. If his questing had been unsuccessful, he appeased the rage of hunger with some scraps of broken meat, and lay down to rest under the piazza of Covent Garden in warm weather, and, in cold weather, as near as he could get to the furnace of a glass house. Yet in his misery he was still an agreeable companion. He had an inexhaustible store of anecdotes about that gay and brilliant world from which he was now an outcast. He had observed the great men of both parties in hours of careless relaxation, had seen the leaders of opposition without the mask of patriotism, and had heard the prime minister roar with laughter and tell stories not over-decent. During some months Savage lived in the closest familiarity with Johnson; and then the friends parted, not without tears. Johnson remained in London to drudge for Cave. Savage went to the west of England, lived there as he had lived everywhere, and in 1743 died, penniless and heartbroken, in Bristol Gaol.

Soon after his death, while the public curiosity was strongly excited about his extraordinary character and his not less extraordinary adventures, a life of him appeared widely different from the catchpenny lives of eminent men which were then a staple article of manufacture in Grub Street. The style was indeed deficient in ease and variety; and the writer was evidently too partial to the Latin element of our language. But the little work, with all its faults, was a masterpiece. No finer specimen of literary biography existed in any language, living or dead; and a discerning critic might have confidently predicted that the author was destined to be the founder of a new school of English eloquence.

The *Life of Savage* was anonymous; but it was well known in literary circles that Johnson was the writer. During the three years which followed, he produced no important work; but he was not, and indeed could not be, idle. The fame of his abilities and learning continued to grow. Warburton pronounced him a man of parts and genius; and the praise of Warburton was then no light thing. Such was Johnson's reputation that, in 1747, several eminent booksellers combined to employ him in the arduous work of preparing a *Dictionary of the English Language,* in two folio volumes. The sum which they agreed to pay him was only fifteen hundred guineas; and out of this sum he had to pay several poor men of letters who assisted him in the humbler parts of his task.

The prospectus of the *Dictionary* he addressed to the earl of Chesterfield. Chesterfield had long been celebrated for the politeness of his manners, the brilliance of his wit, and the delicacy of his taste. He was acknowledged to be the finest speaker in the House of Lords. He had recently governed Ireland, at a momentous conjuncture, with eminent firmness, wisdom and humanity; and he had since become secretary of state. He received Johnson's homage with the most winning affability, and requited it with a few guineas, bestowed doubtless in a very graceful manner, but was by no means desirous to see all his carpets blackened with the London mud, and his soups and wines thrown to right and left over the gowns of fine ladies and the waistcoats of fine gentlemen, by an absent, awkward scholar, who gave strange starts and uttered strange growls, who dressed like a scarecrow and ate like a cormorant. During some time Johnson continued to call on his patron, but, after being repeatedly told by the porter that his lordship was not at home, took the hint, and ceased to present himself at the inhospitable door.

Johnson had flattered himself that he should have completed his *Dictionary* by the end of 1750; but it was not till 1755 that he at length gave his huge volumes to the world. During the seven years which he passed in the drudgery of penning definitions and marking quotations for transcription, he sought for relaxation in literary labour of a more agreeable kind. In January 1749 he published *The Vanity of Human Wishes,* an excellent imitation of the tenth satire of Juvenal, for which he received fifteen guineas.

A few days after the publication of this poem, his tragedy of *Irene,* begun many years before, was brought on the stage by his old pupil, David Garrick, now manager of Drury Lane Theatre. The relation between him and his old preceptor was of a very singular kind. They repelled each other strongly, and yet attracted each other strongly. Nature had made them of very different clay; and circumstances had fully brought out the natural peculiarities of both. Sudden prosperity had turned Garrick's head. Continued adversity had soured Johnson's temper. Johnson saw with more envy than became so great a man the villa, the plate, the china, the Brussels carpet, which the little mimic had got by repeating, with grimaces and gesticulations, what wiser men had written; and the exquisitely sensitive vanity of Garrick was galled by the thought that, while all the rest of the world was applauding him, he could obtain from one morose cynic, whose opinion it was impossible to despise, scarcely any compliment not acidulated with scorn. Yet the two Lichfield men had so many early recollections in common, and sympathized with each other on so many points on which they sympathized with nobody else in the vast population of the capital, that, though the master was often provoked by the monkey-like impertinence of the pupil, and the pupil by the bearish rudeness of the master, they remained friends till they were parted by death. Garrick now brought *Irene* out, with alterations sufficient to displease the author, yet not sufficient to make the piece pleasing to the audience. After nine representations the play was withdrawn. The poet however cleared by his benefit nights, and by the sale of the copyright of his tragedy, about three hundred pounds, then a great sum in his estimation.

About a year after the representation of *Irene,* he began to publish a series of short essays on morals, manners and literature. This species of composition had been brought into fashion by the success of the *Tatler,* and by the still more brilliant success of the *Spectator.* A crowd of small writers had vainly attempted to rival Addison. The *Lay Monastery,* the *Censor,* the *Freethinker,* the *Plain Dealer,* the *Champion,* and other works of the same kind had had their short day. At length Johnson undertook the adventure in which so many aspirants had failed. In the thirty-sixth year after the appearance of the last number of the *Spectator* appeared the first number of the *Rambler.* From March 1750 to March 1752 this paper continued to come out every Tuesday and Saturday.

From the first the *Rambler* was enthusiastically admired by a few eminent men. Richardson, when only five numbers had appeared, pronounced it equal if not superior to the *Spectator.* Young and Hartley expressed their approbation not less warmly. In consequence probably of the good offices of Bubb Dodington, who was then the confidential adviser of Prince Frederick, two of his royal highness's gentlemen carried a gracious message to the printing office, and ordered seven copies for Leicester House. But Johnson had had enough of the patronage of the great to last him all his life, and was not disposed to haunt any other door as he had haunted the door of Chesterfield.

By the public the *Rambler* was at first very coldly received. Though the price of a number was only twopence, the sale did not amount to five hundred. The profits were therefore very small. But as soon as the flying leaves were collected and reprinted they became popular.

The author lived to see thirteen thousand copies spread over England alone. Separate editions were published for the Scotch and Irish markets. A large party pronounced the style perfect, so absolutely perfect that in some essays it would be impossible for the writer himself to alter a single word for the better. Another party, not less numerous, vehemently accused him of having corrupted the purity of the English tongue. The best critics admitted that his diction was too monotonous, too obviously artificial, and now and then turgid even to absurdity. But they did justice to the acuteness of his observations on morals and manners, to the constant precision and frequent brilliancy of his language, to the weighty and magnificent eloquence of many serious passages, and to the solemn yet pleasing humour of some of the lighter papers.

The last *Rambler* was written in a sad and gloomy hour. Mrs Johnson had been given over by the physicians. Three days later she died. She left her husband almost broken-hearted. Many people had been surprised to see a man of his genius and learning stooping to every drudgery, and denying himself almost every comfort, for the purpose of supplying a silly, affected old woman with superfluities, which she accepted with but little gratitude. But all his affection had been concentrated on her. He had neither brother nor sister, neither son nor daughter. Her opinion of his writings was more important to him than the voice of the pit of Drury Lane Theatre, or the judgment of the *Monthly Review*. The chief support which had sustained him through the most arduous labour of his life was the hope that she would enjoy the fame and the profit which he anticipated from his *Dictionary*. She was gone; and in that vast labyrinth of streets, peopled by eight hundred thousand human beings, he was alone. Yet it was necessary for him to set himself, as he expressed it, doggedly to work. After three more laborious years, the *Dictionary* was at length complete.

It had been generally supposed that this great work would be dedicated to the eloquent and accomplished nobleman to whom the prospectus had been addressed. Lord Chesterfield well knew the value of such a compliment; and therefore, when the day of publication drew near, he exerted himself to soothe, by a show of zealous and at the same time of delicate and judicious kindness, the pride which he had so cruelly wounded. Since the *Rambler* had ceased to appear, the town had been entertained by a journal called the *World*, to which many men of high rank and fashion contributed. In two successive numbers of the *World*, the *Dictionary* was, to use the modern phrase, puffed with wonderful skill. The writings of Johnson were warmly praised. It was proposed that he should be invested with the authority of a dictator, nay, of a pope, over our language, and that his decisions about the meaning and the spelling of words should be received as final. His two folios, it was said, would of course be bought by everybody who could afford to buy them. It was soon known that these papers were written by Chesterfield. But the just resentment of Johnson was not to be so appeased. In a letter written with singular energy and dignity of thought and language, he repelled the tardy advances of his patron. The *Dictionary* came forth without a dedication. In the Preface the author truly declared that he owed nothing to the great, and described the difficulties with which he had been left to struggle so forcibly and pathetically that the ablest and most malevolent of all the enemies of his fame, Horne Tooke, never could read that passage without tears.

Johnson's *Dictionary* was hailed with an enthusiasm such as no similar work has ever excited. It was indeed the first dictionary which could be read with pleasure. The defintions show so much acuteness of thought and command of language, and the passages quoted from poets, divines and philosophers are so skilfully selected, that a leisure hour may always be very agreeably spent in turning over the pages. The faults of the book resolve themselves, for the most part, into one great fault. Johnson was a wretched etymologist. He knew little or nothing of any Teutonic language except English, which indeed, as he wrote it, was scarcely a Teutonic language; and thus he was absolutely at the mercy of Junius and Skinner.

The *Dictionary*, though it raised Johnson's fame, added nothing to his pecuniary means. The fifteen hundred guineas which the booksellers had agreed to pay him had been advanced and spent before the last sheets issued from the press. It is painful to relate that twice in the course of the year which followed the publication of this great work he was arrested and carried to sponging-houses, and that he was twice indebted for his liberty to his excellent friend Richardson. It was still necessary for the man who had been formerly saluted by the highest authority as dictator of the English language to supply his wants by constant toil. He abridged his *Dictionary*. He proposed to bring out an edition of Shakespeare by subscription, and many subscribers sent in their names and laid down their money; but he soon found the task so little to his taste that he turned to more attractive employments. He contributed many papers to a new monthly journal, which was called the *Literary Magazine*. Few of these papers have much interest; but among them was one of the best things that he ever wrote, a masterpiece both of reasoning and of satirical pleasantry, the review of Jenyns' *Inquiry into the Nature and Origin of Evil.*

In the spring of 1758 Johnson put forth the first of a series of essays, entitled the *Idler.* During two years these essays continued to appear weekly. They were eagerly read, widely circulated, and indeed impudently pirated, while they were still in the original form, and had a large sale when collected into volumes. The *Idler* may be described as a second part of the *Rambler,* somewhat livelier and somewhat weaker than the first part.

While Johnson was busied with his *Idlers,* his mother, who had accomplished her ninetieth year, died at Lichfield. It was long since he had seen her, but he had not failed to contribute largely out of his small means to her comfort. In order to defray the charges of her funeral, and to pay some debts which she had left, he wrote a little book in a single week, and sent off the sheets to the press without reading them over. A hundred pounds were paid him for the copyright, and the purchasers had great cause to be pleased with their bargain, for the book was *Rasselas,* and it had a great success.

The plan of *Rasselas* might, however, have seemed to invite severe criticism. Johnson has frequently blamed Shakespeare for neglecting the proprieties of time and place, and for ascribing to one age or nation the manners and opinions of another. Yet Shakespeare has not sinned in this way more grievously than Johnson. Rasselas and Imlac, Nekayah and Pekuah, are evidently meant to be Abyssinians of the 18th century; for the Europe which Imlac describes is the Europe of the 18th century, and the inmates of the Happy Valley talk familiarly of that law of gravitation which Newton discovered and which was not fully received even at Cambridge till the 18th century. Johnson, not content with turning filthy savages, ignorant of their letters, and gorged with raw steaks cut from living cows, into philosophers as eloquent and enlightened as himself or his friend Burke, and into ladies as highly accomplished as Mrs Lennox or Mrs Sheridan, transferred the whole domestic system of England to Egypt. Into a land of harems, a land of polygamy, a land where women are married without ever being seen, he introduced the flirtations and jealousies of our ball-rooms. In a land where there is boundless liberty of divorce, wedlock is described as the indissoluble compact. "A youth and maiden meeting by chance, or brought together by artifice, exchange glances, reciprocate civilities, go home, and dream of each other. Such," says Rasselas, "is the common process of marriage." A writer who was guilty of such improprieties had little right to blame the poet who made Hector quote Aristotle, and represented Julio Romano as flourishing in the days of the Oracle of Delphi.

By such exertions as have been described Johnson supported himself till the year 1762. In that year a great change in his circumstancs took place. He had from a child been an enemy of the reigning dynasty. His Jacobite prejudices had been exhibited with little disguise both in his works and in his conversation. Even in his massy and elaborate *Dictionary* he had, with a strange want of taste and judgment, inserted bitter and contumelious reflexions on the Whig party. The excise, which was a favourite resource of Whig fanciers, he had designated as a hateful tax. He had railed against the commissioners of excise in language so coarse that they had seriously thought of prosecuting him. He had with difficulty been prevented from holding up the lord privy seal by name as an example of the meaning of the word "renegade." A pension he had defined as pay given to a state hireling to betray his country; a pensioner as a slave of state hired by a stipend to obey a master. It seemed unlikely that the author of these definitions would himself be pensioned. But that was a time of wonders. George III. had ascended the throne, and had, in the course of a few months, disgusted many of the old friends, and conciliated many of the old enemies of his house. The city was becoming mutinous; Oxford was becoming loyal. Cavendishes and Bentincks were murmuring; Somersets and Wyndhams were hastening to kiss hands. The head of the treasury was now Lord Bute, who was a Tory, and could have no objection to Johnson's Toryism. Bute wished to be thought a patron of men of letters; and Johnson was one of the most eminent and one of the most needy men of letters in Europe. A pension of three hundred a year was graciously offered, and with very little hesitation accepted.

This event produced a change in Johnson's whole way of life. For the first time since his boyhood he no longer felt the daily goad urging him to the daily toil. He was at liberty, after thirty years of anxiety and drudgery, to indulge his constitutional indolence, to lie in bed till two in the afternoon, and to sit up talking till four in the morning, without fearing either the printer's devil or the sheriff's officer.

One laborious task indeed he had bound himself to perform. He had received large subscriptions for his promised edition of Shakespeare; he had lived on those subscriptions during some years; and he could not without disgrace omit to perform his part of the contract. His friends repeatedly exhorted him to make an effort, and he repeatedly resolved to do so. But, notwitstanding their exhortations and his resolutions, month followed month, year followed year, and nothing was done. He prayed fervently against his idleness; he determined, as often as he received the sacrament, that he would no longer doze away and trifle away his time; but the spell under which he lay resisted prayer and sacrament. Happily for his honour, the charm which held him captive was at length broken by no gentle or friendly hand. He had been weak enough to pay serious attention to a story about a ghost which haunted a house in Cock Lane, and had actually gone himself, with some of his friends, at one in the morning, to St John's Church, Clerkenwell, in the hope of receiving a communication from the perturbed spirit. But the spirit, though adjured with all solemnity, remained obstinately silent; and it soon appeared that a naughty girl of eleven had been amusing herself by making fools of so many philosophers. Churchill, who, confident in his powers, drunk with popularity, and burning with party spirit, was looking for some man of established fame and Tory politics to insult, celebrated the Cock Lane ghost in three cantos, nicknamed Johnson Pomposo, asked where the book was which had been so long promised and so liberally paid for, and directly accused the great moralist of cheating. This terrible word proved effectual, and in October 1765 appeared, after a delay of nine years, the new edition of Shakespeare.

This publication saved Johnson's character for honesty, but added nothing to the fame of his abilities and learning. The Preface, though it contains some good passages, is not in his best manner. The most valuable notes are those in which he had an opportunity of showing how attentively he had during many years observed human life and human nature. The best specimen is the note on the character of Polonius. Nothing so good is to be found even in Wilhelm Meister's admirable examination of *Hamlet*. But here praise must end. It would be difficult to name a more slovenly, a more worthless edition of any great classic.[1] Johnson had, in his prospectus, told the world that he was peculiarly fitted for the task which he had undertaken, because he had, as a lexicographer, been under the necessity of taking a wider view of the English language than any of his predecessors. But, unfortunately, he had altogether neglected that very part of our literature with which it is especially desirable that an editor of Shakespeare should be conversant. In the two folio volumes of the *English Dictionary*

---

[1]This famous dictum of Macaulay, though endorsed by Lord Rosebery, has been energetically rebutted by Professor W. Raleigh and others, who recognize both sagacity and scholarship in Johnson's Preface and Notes. Johnson's wide grasp of the discourse and knowledge of human nature enable him in a hundred entangled passages to go straight to the dramatist's meaning.—(T. Se.)

there is not a single passage quoted from any dramatist of the Elizabethan age except Shakespeare and Ben Jonson. Even from Ben the quotations are few. Johnson might easily in a few months have made himself well acquainted with every old play that was extant. But it never seems to have occurred to him that this was a necessary preparation for the work he had undertaken. He would doubtless have admitted that it would be the height of absurdity in a man who was not familiar with the works of Aeschylus and Euripides to publish an edition of Sophocles. Yet he ventured to publish an edition of Shakespeare, without having ever in his life, as far as can be discovered, read a single scene of Massinger, Ford, Dekker, Webster, Marlowe, Beaumont or Fletcher. His detractors were noisy and scurrilous. He had, however, acquitted himself of a debt which had long lain heavy on his conscience and he sank back into the repose from which the sting of satire had roused him. He long continued to live upon the fame which he had already won. He was honoured by the university of Oxford with a doctor's degree, by the Royal Academy with a professorship, and by the king with an interview, in which his majesty most graciously expressed a hope that so excellent a writer would not cease to write. In the interval between 1765 and 1775 Johnson published only two or three political tracts.

But, though his pen was now idle, his tongue was active. The influence exercised by his conversation, directly upon those with whom he lived, and indirectly on the whole literary world, was altogether without a parallel. His colloquial talents were indeed of the highest order. He had strong sense, quick discernment, wit, humour, immense knowledge of literature and of life, and an infinite store of curious anecdotes. As respected style, he spoke far better than he wrote. Every sentence which dropped from his lips was as correct in structure as the most nicely balanced period of the *Rambler*. But in his talk there were no pompous triads, and little more than a fair proportion of words in *-osity* and *-ation*. All was simplicity, ease and vigour. He uttered his short, weighty, and pointed sentences with a power of voice, and a justness and energy of emphasis, of which the effect was rather increased than diminished by the rollings of his huge form, and by the asthmatic gaspings and puffings in which the peals of his eloquence generally ended. Nor did the laziness which made him unwilling to sit down to his desk prevent him from giving instruction or entertainment orally. To discuss questions of taste, of learning, of casuistry, in language so exact and so forcible that it might have been printed without the alteration of a word, was to him no exertion, but a pleasure. He loved, as he said, to fold his legs and have his talk out. He was ready to bestow the overflowings of his full mind on anybody who would start a subject: on a fellow-passenger in a stage coach, or on the person who sat at the same table with him in an eating-house. But his conversation was nowhere so brilliant and striking as when he was surrounded by a few friends, whose abilities and knowledge enabled them, as he once expressed it, to send him back every ball that he threw. Some of these, in 1764, formed them-selves into a club, which gradually became a formidable power in the commonwealth of letters. The verdicts pronounced by this conclave on new books were speedily known over all London, and were suf-ficient to sell off a whole edition in a day, or to condemn the sheets to the service of the trunkmaker and the pastrycook. Goldsmith was the representative of poetry and light literature, Reynolds of the arts, Burke of political eloquence and political philosophy. There, too, were Gibbon the greatest historian and Sir William Jones the greatest linguist of the age. Garrick brought to the meetings his inexhaustible pleasantry, his incomparable mimicry, and his consummate knowl-edge of stage effect. Among the most constant attendants were two high-born and high-bred gentlemen, closely bound together by friendship, but of widely different characters and habits—Bennet Langton, distinguished by his skill in Greek literature, by the ortho-doxy of his opinions, and by the sanctity of his life, and Topham Beauclerk, renowned for his amours, his knowledge of the gay world, his fastidious taste and his sarcastic wit.

Among the members of this celebrated body was one to whom it has owed the greater part of its celebrity, yet who was regarded with little respect by his brethren, and had not without difficulty obtained a seat among them. This was James Boswell, a young Scots lawyer, heir to an honourable name and a fair estate. That he was a coxcomb and a bore, weak, vain, pushing, curious, garrulous, was obvious to all who were acquainted with him.

To the man of Johnson's strong understanding and irritable tem-per, the silly egotism and adulation of Boswell must have been as teasing as the constant buzz of a fly. Johnson hated to be questioned; and Boswell was eternally catechizing him on all kinds of subjects, and sometimes propounded such questions as, "What would you do, sir, if you were locked up in a tower with a baby?" Johnson was a water-drinker and Boswell was a wine-bibber, and indeed little better than an habitual sot. It was impossible that there should be perfect harmony between two such companions. Indeed, the great man was sometimes provoked into fits of passion, in which he said things which the small man, during a few hours, seriously resented. Every quarrel, however, was soon made up. During twenty years the disciple continued to worship the master; the master continued to scold the disciple, to sneer at him, and to love him. The two friends ordinarily resided at a great distance from each other. Boswell practised in the Parliament House of Edinburgh, and could pay only occasional visits to London. During those visits his chief business was to watch Johnson, to discover all Johnson's habits, to turn the conversation to subjects about which Johnson was likely to say something remarkable, and to fill quarto notebooks with minutes of what Johnson had said. In this way were gathered the materials out of which was afterwards constructed the most interesting biographical work in the world.

Soon after the club began to exist, Johnson formed a connexion less important indeed to his fame, but much more important to his happiness, than his connexion with Boswell. Henry Thrale, one of the most opulent brewers in the kingdom, a man of sound and cultivated understanding, rigid principles, and liberal spirit, was married to one of those clever, kind-hearted, engaging, vain, pert young women who are perpetually doing or saying what is not exactly right, but who, do or say what they may, are always agreeable. In 1765 the Thrales became acquainted with Johnson, and the acquaintance ripened fast into friendship. They were astonished and delighted by the brilliancy of his conversation. They were flattered by finding that a man so widely celebrated preferred their house to any other in London. Johnson soon had an apartment in the brewery of Southwark, and a still more pleasant apartment at the villa of his friends on Streatham Common. A large part of every year he passed in those abodes, which must have seemed magnificent and luxurious indeed, when compared with the dens in which he had generally been lodged. But his chief pleasures were derived from what the astronomer of his Abyssinian tale called "the endearing elegance of female friendship." Mrs Thrale rallied him, soothed him, coaxed him, and if she sometimes provoked him by her flippancy, made ample amends by listening to his reproofs with angelic sweetness of temper. When he was diseased in body and in mind, she was the most tender of nurses. No comfort that wealth could purchase, no contrivance that womanly ingenuity, set to work by womanly compassion, could devise, was wanting to his sick room. It would seem that a full half of Johnson's life during about sixteen years was passed under the roof of the Thrales. He accompanied the family sometimes to Bath, and sometimes to Brighton, once to Wales and once to Paris. But he had at the same time a house in one of the narrow and gloomy courts on the north of Fleet Street. In the garrets was his library, a large and

miscellaneous collection of books, falling into pieces and begrimed
with dust. On a lower floor he sometimes, but very rarely, regaled a
friend with a plain dinner—a veal pie, or a leg of lamb and spinach,
and a rice pudding. Nor was the dwelling uninhabited during his
long absences. It was the home of the most extraordinary assemblage
of inmates that ever was brought together. At the head of the establishment Johnson had placed an old lady named Williams, whose
chief recommendations were her blindness and her poverty. But, in
spite of her murmurs and reproaches, he gave an asylum to another
lady who was as poor as herself, Mrs Desmoulins, whose family he
had known many years before in Staffordshire. Room was found for
the daughter of Mrs Desmoulins, and for another destitute damsel,
who was generally addressed as Miss Carmichael, but whom her generous host called Polly. An old quack doctor named Levett, who had
a wide practice, but among the very poorest class, poured out Johnson's tea in the morning and completed this strange menagerie. All
these poor creatures were at constant war with each other, and with
Johnson's negro servant Frank. Sometimes, indeed, they transferred
their hostilities from the servant to the master, complained that a
better table was not kept for them, and railed or maundered till their
benefactor was glad to make his escape to Streatham or to the Mitre
Tavern. And yet he, who was generally the haughtiest and most irritable of mankind, who was but too prompt to resent anything which
looked like a slight on the part of a purse-proud bookseller, or of a
noble and powerful patron, bore patiently from mendicants, who,
but for his bounty, must have gone to the workhouse, insults more
provoking than those for which he had knocked down Osborne and
bidden defiance to Chesterfield. Year after year Mrs Williams and
Mrs Desmoulins, Polly and Levett, continued to torment him and to
live upon him.

The course of life which has been described was interrupted in
Johnson's sixty-fourth year by an important event. He had early read
an account of the Hebrides, and had been much interested by learning that there was so near him a land peopled by a race which was
still as rude and simple as in the Middle Ages. A wish to become
intimately acquainted with a state of society so utterly unlike all that
he had ever seen frequently crossed his mind. But it is not probably
that his curiosity would have overcome his habitual sluggishness, and
his love of the smoke, the mud, and the cries of London, had not
Boswell importuned him to attempt the adventure, and offered to
be his squire. At length, in August 1773, Johnson crossed the Highland line, and plunged courageously into what was then considered,

by most Englishmen, as a dreary and perilous wilderness. After wandering about two months through the Celtic region, sometimes in rude boats which did not protect him from the rain, and sometimes on small shaggy ponies which could hardly bear his weight, he returned to his old haunts with a mind full of new images and new theories. During the following year he employed himself in recording his adventures. About the beginning of 1775 his *Journey to the Hebrides* was published, and was, during some weeks, the chief subject of conversation in all circles in which any attention was paid to literature. His prejudice against the Scots had at length become little more than matter of jest; and whatever remained of the old feeling had been effectually removed by the kind and respectful hospitality with which he had been received in every part of Scotland. It was, of course, not to be expected that an Oxonian Tory should praise the Presbyterian polity and ritual, or that an eye accustomed to the hedgerows and parks of England should not be struck by the bareness of Berwickshire and East Lothian. But even in censure Johnson's tone is not unfriendly. The most enlightened Scotsmen, with Lord Mansfield at their head, were well pleased. But some foolish and ignorant Scotsmen were moved to anger by a little unpalatable truth which was mingled with much eulogy, and assailed him whom they chose to consider as the enemy of their country with libels much more dishonourable to their country than anything that he had ever said or written. They published paragraphs in the newspapers, articles in the magazines, sixpenny pamphlets, five-shilling books. One scribbler abused Johnson for being blear-eyed, another for being a pensioner; a third informed the world that one of the doctor's uncles had been convicted of felony in Scotland, and had found that there was in that country one tree capable of supporting the weight of an Englishman. Macpherson, whose *Fingal* had been treated in the *Journey* as an impudent forgery, threatened to take vengeance with a cane. The only effect of this threat was that Johnson reiterated the charge of forgery in the most contemptuous terms, and walked about, during some time, with a cudgel.

Of other assailants Johnson took no notice whatever. He had early resolved never to be drawn into controversy; and he adhered to his resolution with a steadfastness which is the more extraordinary because he was, both intellectually and morally, of the stuff of which controversialists are made. In conversation he was a singularly eager, acute and pertinacious disputant. When at a loss for good reasons, he had recourse to sophistry; and when heated by altercation he made unsparing use of sarcasm and invective. But when he took his pen in his hand, his whole character seemed to be changed. A hundred bad writers misrepresented him and reviled him; but not one of the hundred could boast of having been thought by him worthy of a refutation, or even of a retort. One Scotsman, bent on vindicating the fame of Scots learning, defied him to the combat in a destestable Latin hexameter:—

Maxime, si tu vis, cupio contendere tecum.

But Johnson took no notice of the challenge. He always maintained that fame was a shuttlecock which could be kept up only by being beaten back as well as beaten forward, and which would soon fall if there were only one battledore. No saying was oftener in his mouth than that fine apophthegm of Bentley, that no man was ever written down but by himself.

Unhappily, a few months after the appearance of the *Journey to the Hebrides,* Johnson did what none of his envious assailants could have done, and to a certain extent succeeded in writing himself down. The disputes between England and her American colonies had reached a point at which no amicable adjustment was possible. War was evidently impending; and the ministers seem to have thought that the eloquence of Johnson might with advantage be employed to inflame the nation against the opposition at home, and against the rebels beyond the Atlantic. He had already written two or three tracts in defence of the foreign and domestic policy of the government; and those tracts, though hardly worthy of him, were much superior to the crowd of pamphlets which lay on the counters of Almon and Stockdale. But his *Taxation no Tyranny* was a pitiable failure. Even Boswell was forced to own that in this unfortunate piece he could detect no trace of his master's powers. The general opinion was that the strong faculties which had produced the *Dictionary* and the *Rambler* were beginning to feel the effect of time and of disease, and that the old man would best consult his credit by writing no more. But this was a great mistake. Johnson had failed, not because his mind was less vigorous than when he wrote *Rasselas* in the evenings of a week, but because he had foolishly chosen, or suffered others to choose for him, a subject such as he would at no time have been competent to treat. He was in no sense a statesman. He never willingly read or thought or talked about affairs of state. He loved biography, literary history, the history of manners; but political history was positively distasteful to him. The question at issue between the colonies and the mother country was a question about which he had really nothing to say. Happily, Johnson soon had an opportunity of proving most signally that his failure was not to be ascribed to intellectual decay.

On Easter Eve 1777 some persons, deputed by a meeting which consisted of forty of the first booksellers in London, called upon him. Though he had some scruples about doing business at that season, he received his visitors with much civility. They came to inform him that a new edition of the English poets, from Cowley downwards, was in contemplation, and to ask him to furnish short biographical prefaces. He readily undertook the task for which he was pre-eminently qualified. His knowledge of the literary history of England since the Restoration was unrivalled. That knowledge he had derived partly from books, and partly from sources which had long been closed: from old Grub Street traditions; from the talk of forgotten poetasters and pamphleteers, who had long been lying in parish vaults; from the recollections of such men as Gilbert Walmesley, who had conversed with the wits of Button, Cibber, who had mutilated the plays of two generations of dramatists, Orrery, who had been admitted to the society of Swift and Savage, who had rendered services of no very honourable kind to Pope. The biographer therefore sat down to his task with a mind full of matter. He had at first intended to give only a paragraph to every minor poet, and only four or five pages to the greatest name. But the flood of anecdote and criticism overflowed the narrow channel. The work, which was originally meant to consist only of a few sheets, swelled into ten volumes—small volumes, it is true, and not closely printed. The first four appeared in 1779, the remaining six in 1781.

The *Lives of the Poets* are, on the whole, the best of Johnson's works. The narratives are as entertaining as any novel. The remarks on life and on human nature are eminently shrewd and profound. The criticisms are often excellent, and, even when grossly and provokingly unjust, well deserve to be studied. *Savage's Life* Johnson reprinted nearly as it had appeared in 1744. Whoever, after reading that life, will turn to the other lives will be struck by the difference of style. Since Johnson had been at ease in his circumstances he had written little and had talked much. When therefore he, after the lapse of years, resumed his pen, the mannerism which he had contracted while he was in the constant habit of elaborate composition was less perceptible than formerly, and his diction frequently had a colloquial ease which it had formerly wanted. The improvement may be discerned by a skilful critic in the *Journey to the Hebrides,* and in the *Lives of the Poets* is so obvious that it cannot escape the notice of the most careless reader. Among the *Lives* the best are perhaps those of Cowley,

years, came close, the dark cloud passed away from Johnson's mind. Windham's servant, who sat up with him during his last night, declared that "no man could appear more collected, more devout or less terrified at the thoughts of the approaching minute." At hour intervals, often of much pain, he was moved in bed and addressed himself vehemently to prayer. In the morning he was still able to give his blessing, but in the afternoon he became drowsy, and at a quarter past seven in the evening on the 13th of December 1784, in his seventy-sixth year, he passed away. He was laid, a week later, in Westminister Abbey, among the eminent men of whom he had been the historian—Cowley and Denham, Dryden and Congreve, Gay, Prior and Addison.

ANTI-SEMITISM

BY LUCIEN WOLF

*F*ew Jewish intellectuals in the
London of his time were more fully cognizant of the history
of European Jewry and their perilous situation on the continent than Lucien Wolf, and few thus better prepared to

write the exhaustive and historically significant analysis of
the phenomenon of anti-Semitism especially for the eleventh edition of the Britannica. At the height of his fame,
at the time of the publication of the eleventh, Wolf was known
in both journalistic and governmental circles as "British
Jewry's secretary for foreign affairs," and it was no exaggeration, since he was both a practicing journalist and a
functioning, effective diplomatic presence and conscience
at the Versailles Peace Conference of 1919.

Born in London in 1857 of a family recently exiled from
Bohemia, Wolf was fluent in French and German and at
the early age of seventeen began one aspect of his life—as
observer of contemporary European politics, with a special
interest in the fate of the Jewish people in Russia and in
Rumania. Over the years he contributed to such journals
and newspapers as The Jewish World, The Daily Graphic,
The Fortnightly Review, and of course The Times, but that
was only one side of him—he was a scholar and a cultural
organizer, too.

This man of many parts was an expert on the history of
the Jews in England; while in his mid-twenties he had
written the centennial life of Sir Moses Haim Montefiore
(1784–1885), the banker-philanthropist; in 1887 he organized the Anglo-Jewish Historical Exhibition, and in
1893 founded the Anglo-Jewish Historical Society. In 1905
he edited and published the jubilee edition of the novels
of Benjamin Disraeli; he also had a passionate interest in
making scholarly contributions to the history of the Mar-
ranos in Spain and Portugal. Wolf also edited a valuable
documentary bulletin called Darkest Russia between 1912
and 1914, and in 1917 became the secretary of the Joint
Foreign Committee of the Anglo-Jewish Association. In
that capacity he forcefully intervened at the Versailles Peace
Conference with his paper "Notes on the Diplomatic History of the Jewish Question," and his skills brought about
the approval by the Allies of the "Minorities Treaties," intended to safeguard the civil and religious rights of Central
and East European Jews. Wolf also played a significant role
in the definitive debunking of the fraudulent anti-Semitic
tract called "Protocols of the Elders of Zion" in his 1921
essay "The Myth of the Jewish Menace in World Affairs."

Wolf was a good friend of Hugh Chisholm, since for

many years he had contributed to the old Saint James's Gazette, *and when the time came for the commissioning of articles for eleventh, Wolf was clearly Chisholm's man for the job. But the topic itself was not exactly a commonplace in most contemporary encyclopedias, and credit must be given to the editor for not only the choice of author, but the ample space given to develop the subject according to Wolf's needs and wishes. Wolf was not a liberal in every respect. Although he was on close personal terms with Theodor Herzl, Wolf opposed Zionism and Jewish nationalism in general, as one of his other contributions to the eleventh, "Zionism," makes abundantly clear.*

As for the retrospective drama of our reading in the 1990s a prescient document written in the first decade of this century, one can only take note of the implications, dire enough, of the last paragraph of Wolf's long essay:

> *Though Anti-Semitism has been unmasked and discredited, it is to be feared that its history is not yet at an end. While there remain in Russia and Rumania over six millions of Jews who are being systematically degraded, and who periodically overflow the western frontier, there must continue to be a Jewish question in Europe; and while there are weak governments, and ignorant and superstitious elements in the enfranchised classes of the countries affected, that question will seek to play a part in politics.*

Though hampered by blindness in the last thirty years of his life, Wolf was active until his death in 1930.

ANTI-SEMITISM.

In the political struggles of the concluding quarter of the 19th century an important part was played by a religious, political and social agitation against the Jews, known as "Anti-Semitism." The origins of this remarkable movement already threaten to become obscured by legend. The Jews contend that anti-Semitism is a mere atavistic revival of the Jew-hatred of the middle ages. The extreme section of the anti-Semites, who have given the movement its quasi-scientific name, declare that it is a racial struggle—an incident of the eternal conflict between Europe and Asia—and that the anti-Semites are engaged in an effort to prevent what is called the Aryan race from being subjugated by a Semitic immigration, and to save Aryan ideals from being modified by an alien and demoralizing oriental *Anschauung*. There is no essential foundation for either of these contentions. Religious prejudices reaching back to the dawn of history have been reawakened by the anti-Semitic agitation, but they did not originate it, and they have not entirely controlled it. The alleged racial divergence is, too, only a linguistic hypothesis on the physical evidence of which anthropologists are not agreed (Topinard, *Anthropologie*, p. 444; Taylor, *Origins of Aryans*, cap. i.), and, even if it were proved, it has existed in Europe for so many centuries, and so many ethnic modifications have occurred on both sides, that it cannot be accepted as a practical issue. It is true that the ethnographical histories of the Jews and the nations of Europe have proceeded on widely diverging lines, but these lines have more than once crossed each other and become interlaced. Thus Aryan elements are at the beginning of both; European morals have been ineradicably semitized by Christianity, and the Jews have been Europeans for over a thousand years, during which their character has been modified and in some respects transformed by the ecclesiastical and civil polities of the nations among whom they have made their permanent home. Anti-Semitism is then exclusively a question of European politics, and its origin is to be found, not in the long struggle between Europe and Asia, or between the Church and the Synagogue, which filled so much of ancient and medieval history, but in the social conditions resulting from the emancipation of the Jews in the middle of the 19th century.

If the emancipated Jews were Europeans in virtue of the antiquity of their western settlements, and of the character impressed upon them by the circumstances of their European history, they none the less presented the appearance of a strange people to their Gentile fellow-countrymen. They had been secluded in their ghettos for centuries, and had consequently acquired a physical and moral physiognomy differentiating them in a measure from their former oppressors. This peculiar physiognomy was, on its moral side, not essentially Jewish or even Semitic. It was an advanced development of the main attributes of civilized life, to which Christendom in its transition from feudalism had as yet only imperfectly adapted itself. The ghetto, which had been designed as a sort of quarantine to safeguard Christendom against the Jewish heresy, had in fact proved a storage chamber for a portion of the political and social forces which were destined to sweep away the last traces of feudalism from central Europe. In the ghetto, the pastoral Semite, who had been made a wanderer by the destruction of his nationality, was steadily trained, through centuries, to become an urban European, with all the parasitic activities of urban economics, and all the democratic tendencies of occidental industrialism. Excluded from the army, the land, the trade corporations and the artisan gilds, this quondam oriental peasant was gradually transformed into a commercial middleman and a practised dealer in money. Oppressed by the Church, and persecuted by the State, his theocratic and monarchical traditions lost their hold on his daily life, and he became saturated with a passionate devotion to the ideals of democratic politics. Finally, this former bucolic victim of Phoenician exploitation had his wits preternaturally sharpened, partly by the stress of his struggle for life, and partly by his being compelled in his urban seclusion to seek for recreation in literary exercises, chiefly the subtle dialectics of the Talmudists (Loeb, *Juif de l'histoire;* Jellinek, *Der Jüdische Stamm*). Thus, the Jew who emerged from the ghetto was no longer a Palestinian Semite, but an essentially modern European, who differed from his Christian fellow-countrymen only in the circumstances that his religion was of the older Semitic form, and that his physical type had become sharply defined through a slightly more rigid exclusiveness in the matter of marriages than that practised by Protestants and Roman Catholics (Andree, *Volkskunde der Juden,* p. 58).

Unfortunately, these distinctive elements, though not very serious in themselves, became strongly accentuated by concentration. Had it been possible to distribute the emancipated Jews uniformly throughout Christian society, as was the case with other emancipated religious denominations, there would have been no revival of the Jewish question. The Jews, however, through no fault of their own, belonged to only one class in European society—the industrial *bourgeoisie.* Into that class all their strength was thrown, and owing to their ghetto preparation, they rapidly took a leading place in it, politically and socially. When the mid-century revolutions made the *bourgeoisie* the ruling power in Europe, the semblance of a Hebrew domination presented itself. It was the exaggeration of this apparent domination, not by the *bourgeoisie* itself, but by its enemies among the vanquished reactionaries on the one hand, and by the extreme Radicals on the other, which created modern anti-Semitism as a political force.

The movement took its rise in Germany and Austria. Here the concentration of the Jews in one class of the population was aggravated by their excessive numbers. While in France the proportion to the total population was, in the early 'seventies, 0.14%, and in Italy, 0.12%, it was 1.22% in Germany, and 3.85% in Austria-Hungary; Berlin had 4.36% of Jews, and Vienna 6.62% (Andree, *Volkskunde,*

pp. 287, 291, 294, 295). The activity of the Jews consequently manifested itself in a far more intense form in these countries than elsewhere. This was apparent even before the emancipations of 1848.
Germany.—Towards the middle of the 18th century, a limited number
of wealthy Jews had been tolerated as *Schutz-Juden* outside the ghettos,
and their sons, educated as Germans under the influence of Moses
Mendelssohn and his school, supplied a majority of the leading spirits
of the revolutionary agitation. To this period belong the formidable
names of Ludwig Börne (1786–1837), Heinrich Heine (1799–1854),
Edward Ganz (1798–1839), Gabriel Riesser (1806–1863), Ferdinand
Lassalle (1825–1864), Karl Marx (1818–1883), Moses Hess (1812–
1875), Ignatz Kuranda (1811–1884), and Johann Jacobi (1805–
1877). When the revolution was completed, and the Jews entered in
a body the national life of Germany and Austria, they sustained this
high average in all the intellectual branches of middle-class activity.
Here again, owing to the accidents of their history, a further concentration became apparent. Their activity was almost exclusively
intellectual. The bulk of them flocked to the financial and the dis-
tributive (as distinct from the productive) fields of industry to which
they had been confined in the ghettos. The sharpened faculties of
the younger generation at the same time carried everything before
them in the schools, with the result that they soon crowded the professions, especially medicine, law and journalism (Nossig, *Statistik des
Jüd. Stammes*, pp. 33–37; Jacobs, *Jew. Statistics*, pp. 41–69). Thus the
"Semitic domination," as it was afterwards called, became every day
more strongly accentuated. If it was a long time in exciting resentment
and jealousy, the reason was that it was in no sense alien to the new
conditions of the national life. The competition was a fair one. The
Jews might be more successful than their Christian fellow-citizens,
but it was in virtue of qualities which complied with the national
standards of conduct. They were as law-abiding and patriotic as they
were intelligent. Crime among them was far below the average
(Nossig, p. 31). Their complete assimilation of the national spirit
was brilliantly illustrated by the achievements in German literature,
art and science of such men as Heinrich Heine and Berthold Auer-
bach (1812–1882), Felix Mendelssohn (-Bartholdy) (1809–1847), and
Jacob Meyerbeer (1794–1864), Karl Gustav Jacobi the mathematician
(1804–1851), Gabriel Gustav Valentin the physiologist (1810–1883),
and Moritz Lazarus (1824–1903) and Heymann Steinthal (1823–
1899) the national psychologists. In politics, too, Edward Lasker
(1829–1884) and Ludwig Bamberger (1823–1899) had shown how
Jews could put their country before party, when, at the turning-point

of German imperial history in 1866, they led the secession from the *Fortschritts-Partei* and founded the National Liberal party, which enabled Prince Bismarck to accomplish German unity. Even their financiers were not behind their Christian fellow-citizens in patriotism. Prince Bismarck himself confessed that the money for carrying on the 1866 campaign was obtained from the Jewish banker Bleichroeder, in face of the refusal of the money-market to support the war. Hence the voice of the old Jew-hatred—for in a weak way it was still occasionally heard in obscurantist corners—was shamed into silence, and it was only in the European twilight—in Russia and Rumania—and in lands where medievalism still lingered, such as northern Africa and Persia, that oppression and persecution continued to dog the steps of the Jews.

The signal for the change came in 1873, and was given unconsciously by one of the most distinguished Jews of his time, Edward Lasker, the gifted lieutenant of Bennigsen in the leadership of the National Liberal party. The unification of Germany in 1870, and the rapid payment of the enormous French war indemnity, had given an unprecedented impulse to industrial and financial activity throughout the empire. Money became cheap and speculation universal. A company mania set in which was favoured by the government, who granted railway and other concessions with a prodigal hand. The inevitable result of this state of things was first indicated by Jewish politicians and economists. On the 14th of January 1873, Edward Lasker called the attention of the Prussian diet to the dangers of the situation, while his colleague, Ludwig Bamberger, in an able article in the *Preussischen Jahrbücher,* condemned the policy which had permitted the milliards to glut the country instead of being paid on a plan which would have facilitated their gradual digestion by the economic machinery of the nation. Deeply impressed by the gravity of the impending crisis, Lasker instituted a searching inquiry, with the result that he discovered a series of grave company scandals in which financial promoters and aristocratic directors were chiefly involved. Undeterred by the fact that the leading spirit in these abuses, Bethel Henry Strousberg (1823–1884), was a Jew, Lasker presented the results of his inquiry to the diet on the 7th of February 1873, in a speech of great power and full of sensational disclosures. The dramatic results of this speech need not be dwelt upon here (for details see Blum, *Das deutsche Reich zur Zeit Bismarcks,* pp. 153–181). It must suffice to say that in the following May the great Vienna "Krach" occurred, and the colossal bubble of speculation burst, bringing with it all the ruin foretold by Lasker and Bamberger. From the position occupied by the Jews in the commercial class, and especially in the financial section of that class, it was inevitable that a considerable number of them should figure in the scandals which followed. At this moment an obscure Hamburg journalist, Wilhelm Marr, who as far back as 1862 had printed a still-born tract against the Jews (*Judenspiegel*), published a sensational pamphlet entitled *Der Sieg des Judenthums über das Germanthum* ("The Victory of Judaism over Germanism"). The book fell upon fruitful soil. It applied to the nascent controversy a theory of nationality which, under the great sponsorship of Hegel, had seized on the minds of the German youth, and to which the stirring events of 1870 had already given a deep practical significance. The state, according to the Hegelians, should be rational, and the nation should be a unit comprising individuals speaking the same language and of the same racial origin. Heterogeneous elements might be absorbed, but if they could not be reduced to the national type they should be eliminated. This was the pseudo-scientific note of the new anti-Semitism, the theory which differentiated it from the old religious Jew-hatred and sought to give it a rational place in modern thought. Marr's pamphlet, which reviewed the facts of the Jewish social concentration without noticing their essentially transitional character, proved the pioneer of this teaching. It was, however, in the passions of party politics that the new crusade found its chief sources of vitality. The enemies of the *bourgeoisie* at once saw that the movement was calculated to discredit and weaken the school of Manchester Liberalism, then in the ascendant. Agrarian capitalism, which had been dethroned by industrial capitalism in 1848, and had burnt its fingers in 1873, seized the opportunity of paying off old scores. The clericals, smarting under the *Kulturkampf*, which was supported by the whole body of Jewish liberalism, joined eagerly in the new cry. In 1876 another sensational pamphlet was published, Otto Glogau's *Die Börsen und Grundergeschwindel in Berlin* ("The Bourses and the Company Swindles in Berlin"), dealing in detail with the Jewish participation in the scandals first revealed by Lasker. The agitation gradually swelled, its growth being helped by the sensitiveness and *cacoëthes scribendi* of the Jews themselves, who contributed two pamphlets and a much larger proportion of newspaper articles for every one supplied by their opponents (Jacobs, *Bibliog. Jew. Question,* p. xi.). Up to 1879, however, it was more of a literary than a political agitation, and was generally regarded only as an ephemeral craze or a passing spasm of popular passion.

Toward the end of 1879 it spread with sudden fury over the whole of Germany. This outburst, at a moment when no new financial scandals or other illustrations of Semitic demoralization and domination were before the public, has never been fully explained. It is impossible to doubt, however, that the secret springs of the new agitation were more or less directly supplied by Prince Bismarck himself. Since 1877 the relations between the chancellor and the National Liberals had gradually become strained. The deficit in the budget had compelled the government to think of new taxes, and in order to carry them through the Reichstag the support of the National Liberals had been solicited. Until then the National Liberals had faithfully supported the chancellor in nursing the consolidation of the new empire, but the great dream of its leaders, especially of Lasker and Bamberger, who had learnt their politics in England, was to obtain a constitutional and economic *régime* similar to that of the British Isles. The organization of German unity was now completed, and they regarded the new overtures of Prince Bismarck as an opportunity for pressing their constitutional demands. These were refused, the Reichstag was dissolved and Prince Bismarck boldly came forward with a new fiscal policy, a combination of protection and state socialism. Lasker and Bamberger thereupon led a powerful secession of National Liberals into opposition, and the chancellor was compelled to seek a new majority among the ultra-Conservatives and the Roman Catholic Centre. This was the beginning of the famous "journey to Canossa." Bismarck did not hide his mortification. He began to recognize in anti-Semitism a means of "dishing" the Judaized liberals, and to his creatures who assisted him in his press campaigns he dropped significant hints in this sense (Busch, *Bismarck,* ii. 453–454, iii. 16). He even spoke of a new *Kulturkampf* against the Jews (*ibid.* ii. p. 484). How these hints were acted upon has not been revealed, but it is sufficiently instructive to notice that the final breach with the National Liberals took place in July 1879, and that it was immediately followed by a violent revival of the anti-Semitic agitation. Marr's pamphlet was reprinted, and within a few months ran through nine further editions. The historian Treitschke gave the sanction of his great name to the movement. The Conservative and Ultramontane press rang with the sins of the Jews. In October an anti-Semitic league was founded in Berlin and Dresden (for statutes of the league see *Nineteenth Century,* February 1881, p. 344).

The leadership of the agitation was now definitely assumed by a man who combined with social influence, oratorical power and inexhaustible energy, a definite scheme of social regeneration and an organization for carrying it out. This man was Adolf Stöcker (b. 1835), one of the court preachers. He had embraced the doctrines of Christian socialism which the Roman Catholics, under the guidance of Archbishop Ketteler, had adopted from the teachings of the Jew Lassalle (Nitti, *Catholic Socialism,* pp. 94–96, 122, 127), and he had formed a society called "The Christian Social Working-man's Union." He was also a conspicuous member of the Prussian diet, where he sat and voted with the Conservatives. He found himself in strong sympathy with Prince Bismarck's new economic policy, which, although also of Lassallian origin (Kohut, *Ferdinand Lassalle,* pp. 144 et seq.), was claimed by its author as being essentially Christian (Busch, P. 483). Under his auspices the years 1880–1881 became a period of bitter and scandalous conflict with the Jews. The Conservatives supported him, partly to satisfy their old grudges against the Liberal *bourgeoisie* and partly because Christian Socialism, with its anti-Semitic appeal to ignorant prejudice, was likely to weaken the hold of the Social Democrats on the lower classes. The Lutheran clergy followed suit, in order to prevent the Roman Catholics from obtaining a monopoly of Christian Socialism, while the Ultramontanes readily adopted anti-Semitism, partly to maintain their monopoly, and partly to avenge themselves on the Jewish and Liberal supporters of the *Kulturkampf.* In this way a formidable body of public opinion was recruited for the anti-Semites. Violent debates took place in the Prussian diet. A petition to exclude the Jews from the national schools and universities and to disable them from holding public appointments was presented to Prince Bismarck. Jews were boycotted and insulted. Duels between Jews and anti-Semites, many of them fatal, became of daily occurrence. Even unruly demonstrations and street riots were reported. Pamphlets attacking every phase and aspect of Jewish life streamed by the hundred from the printing-press. On their side the Jews did not want for friends, and it was owing to the strong attitude adopted by the Liberals that the agitation failed to secure legislative fruition. The crown prince (afterward Emperor Frederick) and crown princess boldly set themselves at the head of the party of protest. The crown prince publicly declared that the agitation was "a shame and a disgrace to Germany." A manifesto denouncing the movement as a blot on German culture, a danger to German unity and a flagrant injustice to the Jews themselves, was signed by a long list of illustrious men, including Herr von Forcken-beck, Professors Mommsen, Gneist, Droysen, Virchow, and Dr Werner Siemens (*Times,* November 18, 1880). During the Reichstag elections of 1881 the agitation played an active part, but without much effect, although Stöcker was elected. This was due to the fact that the great Conservative parties, so far as their political organizations were concerned, still remained chary of publicly identifying themselves with a movement which, in its essence, was of socialistic tendency. Hence the electoral returns of that year supplied no sure guide to the strength of anti-Semitic opinion among the German people.

The first severe blow suffered by the German anti-Semites was in 1881, when, to the indignation of the whole civilized world, the barbarous riots against the Jews in Russia and the revival of the medieval Blood Accusation in Hungary illustrated the liability of unreasoning mobs to carry into violent practice the incendiary doctrines of the new Jew-haters. From this blow anti-Semitism might have recovered had it not been for the divisions and scandals in its own ranks, and the artificial forms it subsequently assumed through factitious alliances with political parties bent less on persecuting the Jews than on profiting by the anti-Jewish agitation. The divisions showed themselves at the first attempt to form a political party on an anti-Semitic basis. Imperceptibly the agitators had grouped themselves into two classes, economic and ethnological anti-Semites. The impracticable racial views of Marr and Treitschke had not found favour with Stöcker and the Christian Socialists. They were disposed to leave the Jews in peace so long as they behaved themselves properly, and although they carried on their agitation against Jewish malpractices in a comprehensive form which seemed superficially to identify them with the root-and-branch anti-Semites, they were in reality not inclined to accept the racial theory with its scheme of revived Jewish disabilities (Huret, *La Question Sociale*—interview with Stöcker). This feeling was strengthened by a tendency on the part of an extreme wing of the racial anti-Semites to extend their campaign against Judaism to its offspring, Christianity. In 1879 Professor Sepp, arguing that Jesus was of no human race, had proposed that Christianity should reject the Hebrew Scriptures and seek a fresh historical basis in the cuneiform inscriptions. Later Dr Eugen Dühring, in several brochures, notably *Die Judenfrage als Frage des Rassencharakters* (1881, 5th ed. Berlin, 1901), had attacked Christianity as a manifestation of the Semitic spirit which was not compatible with the theological and ethical conceptions of the Scandinavian peoples. The philosopher Friedrich Nietzsche had also adopted the same view, without noticing that it was a *reductio ad absurdum* of the whole agitation, in his *Menschliches, Allzumenschliches* (1878), *Jenseits von Gut und Böse* (1886), *Genealogie der Moral* (1887). With these tendencies the Christian Socialists could have no sympathy, and the consequence was that when in March 1881 a political organization of anti-Semitism was attempted, two rival bodies were created, the "Deutsche Volksverein," under the Conservative auspices of Herr Liebermann von Sonnenberg (b. 1848) and Herr Förster, and the "Sociale Reichsverein," led by the racial and Radical anti-Semites, Ernst Henrici (b. 1854) and Otto Böckel (b. 1859). In 1886, at an anti-Semitic congress held at Cassel a reunion was effected under the name of the "Deutsche antisemitische Verein," but this only lasted three years. In June 1889 the anti-Semitic Christian Socialists under Stöcker again seceded.

Meanwhile racial anti-Semitism with its wholesale radical proposals had been making considerable progress among the ignorant lower classes. It adapted itself better to popular passions and inherited prejudice than the more academic conceptions of the Christian Socialists. The latter, too, were largely Conservatives, and their points of contact with the proletariat were at best artificial. Among the Hessian peasantry the inflammatory appeals of Böckel secured many adherents. This paved the way for a new anti-Semitic leader, Herrmann Ahlwardt (b. 1846), who, towards the end of the 'eighties, eclipsed all the other anti-Semites by the sensationalism and violence with which he prosecuted the campaign. Ahlwardt was a person of evil notoriety. He was loaded with debt. In the Manché decoration scandals it was proved that he had acted first as a corrupt intermediary and afterwards as the betrayer of his confederates. His anti-Semitism was adopted originally as a means of *chantage*, and it was only when it failed to yield profit in this form that he came out boldly as an agitator. The wildness, unscrupulousness, and full-bloodedness of his propaganda enchanted the mob, and he bid fair to become a powerful democratic leader. His pamphlets, full of scandalous revelations of alleged malpractices of eminent Jews, were read with avidity. No fewer than ten of them were written and published during 1892. Over and over again he was prosecuted for libel and convicted, but this seemed only to strengthen his influence with his followers. The Roman Catholic clergy and newspapers helped to inflame the popular passions. The result was that anti-Jewish riots broke out. At Neustettin the Jewish synagogue was burnt, and at Xanten the Blood Accusation was revived, and a Jewish butcher was tried on the ancient charge of murdering a Christian child for ritual purposes. The man was, of course, acquitted, but the symptoms it revealed of reviving medievalism strongly stirred the liberal and cultured mind of Germany. All protest, however, seemed powerless, and the barbarian movement appeared destined to carry everything before it.

German politics at this moment were in a very intricate state. Prince Bismarck had retired, and Count Caprivi, with a programme of general conciliation based on Liberal principles, was in power. Alarmed by the non-renewal of the anti-Socialist law, and by the conclusion of commercial treaties which made great concessions to German industry, the landed gentry and the Conservative party became alienated from the new chancellor. In January 1892 the split was completed by the withdrawal by the government of the Primary Education bill, which had been designed to place primary instruction on a religious basis. The Conservatives saw their opportunity of posing as the party of Christianity against the Liberals and Socialists, who had wrecked the bill, and they began to look towards Ahlwardt as a possible ally. He had the advantages over Stöcker that he was not a Socialist, and that he was prepared to lead his apparently large following to assist the agrarian movement and weaken the Social Democrats. The intrigue gradually came to light. Towards the end of the year Herr Liebknecht, the Social Democratic leader, denounced the Conservatives to the Reichstag as being concerned "in using the anti-Semitic movement as a bastard edition of Socialism for the use of stupid people." (1st December). Two days later the charge was confirmed. At a meeting of the party held on the 3rd of December the following plank was added to the Conservative programme: "We combat the oppressive and disintegrating Jewish influence on our national life; we demand for our Christian people a Christian magistracy and Christian teachers for Christian pupils; we repudiate the excesses of anti-Semitism." In pursuance of the resolution Ahlwardt was returned to the Reichstag at a by-election by the Conservative district of Arnswalde-Friedeberg. The coalition was, however, not yet completed. The intransigeant Conservatives, led by Baron von Hammerstein, the editor of the *Kreuz-Zeitung,* justly felt that the concluding sentence of the resolution of the 3rd of December repudiating "the excesses of anti-Semitism" was calculated to hinder a full and loyal co-operation between the two parties. Accordingly on the 9th of December another meeting of the party was summoned. Twelve hundred members met at the Tivoli Hall in Berlin, and with only seven dissentients solemnly expunged the offending sentence from the resolution. The history of political parties may be searched in vain for a parallel to this discreditable transaction.

The capture of the Conservative party proved the high-water mark of German anti-Semitism. From that moment the tide began to recede. All that was best in German national life was scandalized by the cynical tactics of the Conservatives. The emperor, strong Christian though he was, was shocked at the idea of serving Christianity by a compact with unscrupulous demagogues and ignorant fanatics. Prince Bismarck growled out a stinging sarcasm from his retreat at

Friedrichsruh. Even Stöcker raised his voice in protest against the "Ahlwardtismus" and "Böckelianismus," and called upon his Conservative colleagues to distinguish between "respectable and disreputable anti-Semitism." As for the Liberals and Socialists, they filled the air with bitter laughter, and declared from the housetops that the stupid party had at last been overwhelmed by its own stupidity. The Conservatives began to suspect that they had made a false step, and they were confirmed in this belief by the conduct of their new ally in the Reichstag. His début in parliament was the signal for a succession of disgraceful scenes. His whole campaign of calumny was transferred to the floor of the house, and for some weeks the Reichstag discussed little else than his so-called revelations. The Conservatives listened to his wild charges in uncomfortable silence, and refused to support him. Stöcker opposed him in a violent speech. The Radicals and Socialists, taking an accurate measure of the shallow vanity of the man, adopted the policy of giving him "enough rope." Shortly after his election he was condemned to five months' imprisonment for libel, and he would have been arrested but for the interposition of the Socialist party, including five Jews, who claimed for him the immunities of a member of parliament. When he moved for a commission to inquire into his revelations, it was again the Socialist party which supported him, with the result that all his charges, without exception, were found to be absolutely baseless. Ahlwardt was covered with ridicule, and when in May the Reichstag was dissolved, he was marched off to prison to undergo the sentence for libel from which his parliamentary privilege had up to that moment protected him.

His hold on the anti-Semitic populace was, however, not diminished. On the contrary, the action of the Conservatives at the Tivoli congress could not be at once eradicated from the minds of the Conservative voters, and when the electoral campaign began it was found impossible to explain to them that the party leaders had changed their minds. The result was that Ahlwardt, although in prison, was elected by two constituencies. At Arnswalde-Friedeberg he was returned in the teeth of the opposition of the official Conservatives, and at Neustettin he defeated no less a person than his anti-Semitic opponent Stöcker. Fifteen other anti-Semites, all of the Ahlwardtian school, were elected. This, however, represented little in the way of political influence; for henceforth, the party had to stand alone as one of the many minor factions in the Reichstag, avoided by all the great parties, and too weak to exercise any influence on the main course of affairs.

During the subsequent seven years it became more and more discredited. The financial scandals connected with Förster's attempt to found a Christian Socialist colony in Paraguay, the conviction of Baron von Hammerstein, the anti-Semitic Conservative leader, for forgery and swindling (1895–1896), and several minor scandals of the same unsavoury character, covered the party with the very obloquy which it had attempted to attach to the Jews. At the same time the Christian Socialists who had remained with the Conservative party also suffered. After the elections of 1893, Stöker was dismissed from his post of court preacher, and publicly reprimanded for speaking familiarly of the empress. Two years later the Christian Socialist, Pastor Neumann, observing the tendency of the Conservatives to coalesce with the moderate Liberals in antagonism to Social Democracy, declared against the Conservative party. The following year the emperor publicly condemned Christian Socialism and the "political pastors," and Stöcker was expelled from the Conservative party for refusing to modify the socialistic propaganda of his organ, *Das Volk*. His fall was completed by a quarrel with the Evangelical Social Union. He left the Union and appealed to the Lutheran clergy to found a new church social organization, but met with no response. Another blow to anti-Semitism came from the Roman Catholics. They had become alarmed by the unbridled violence of the Ahlwardtians, and when in 1894 Förster declared in an address to the German anti-Semitic Union that anarchical outrages like the murder of President Carnot were as much due to the "Anarchismus von oben" as the "Anarchismus von unten," the Ultramontane *Germania* publicly washed its hands of the Jew-baiters (1st of July 1894). Thus gradually German anti-Semitism became stripped of every adventitious alliance; and at the general election of 1898 it only managed to return twelve members to the Reichstag, and in 1903 its party strength fell to nine. A remarkable revival in its fortunes, however, took place between 1905 and 1907. Identifying itself with the extreme Chauvinists and Anglophobes it profited by the anti-national errors of the Clericals and Socialists, and won no fewer than twelve by-elections. At the general election of 1907 its jingoism and aggressive Protestantism were rewarded with twenty-five seats. It is clear, however, from the figures of the second ballots that these successes owed far more to the tendencies of the party in the field of general politics than to its anti-Semitism. Indeed the specifically anti-Semitic movement has shown little activity since 1893.

The causes of the decline of German anti-Semitism are not difficult to determine. While it remained a theory of nationality and a fad of the metaphysicians, it made considerable noise in the world, but without exercising much practical influence. When it attempted to play an active part in politics it became submerged by the ignorant and superstitious voters, who could not understand its scientific justification, but who were quite ready to declaim and riot against the Jew bogey. It thus became a sort of Jacquerie which, being exploited by unscrupulous demagogues, soon alienated all its respectable elements. Its moments of real importance have been due not to inherent strength but to the uses made of it by other political parties for their own purposes. These coalitions are no longer of perilous significance so far as the Jews are concerned, chiefly because, in face of the menace of democratic socialism and its unholy alliance with the Roman Catholic Centrum, all supporters of the present organization of society have found it necessary to sink their differences. The new social struggle has eclipsed the racial theory of nationality. The Social Democrat became the enemy, and the new reaction counted on the support of the rich Jews and the strongly individualist Jewish middle class to assist it in preserving the existing social structure. Hence in Prince Bülow's "Bloc" (1908) anti-Semites figured side by side with Judeophil Radicals.

More serious have been the effects of German anti-Semitic teachings on the political and social life of the countries adjacent to the empire—Russia, Austria and France.

Russia.—In Russia these effects were first seriously felt owing to the fury of autocratic reaction to which the tragic death of the tsar Alexander II. gave rise. This, however, like the Strousberg *Krach* in Germany, was only the proximate cause of the outbreak. There were other elements which had created a *milieu* peculiarly favourable to the transplantation of the German craze. In the first place the medieval anti-Semitism was still an integral part of the polity of the empire. The Jews were cooped up in one huge ghetto in the western provinces, "marked out to all their fellow-countrymen as aliens, and a pariah caste set apart for special and degrading treatment" (*Persecution of the Jews in Russia*, 1891, p. 5). In the next place, owing to the emancipation of the serfs which had half ruined the landowners, while creating a free but moneyless peasantry, the Jews, who could be neither nobles nor peasants, had found a vocation as moneylenders and as middlemen between the grain producers, and the grain consumers and exporters. There is no evidence that this function was performed, as a rule, in an exorbitant or oppressive way. On the contrary, the fall in the value of cereals on all the provincial markets, after the riots of 1881, shows that the Jewish competition had previously assured full prices to the farmers (Schwabacher, *Denk-schrift*, 1882, p. 27). Nevertheless, the Jewish activity or "exploitation," as it was called, was resented, and the ill-feeling it caused among landowners and farmers was shared by non-Jewish middlemen and merchants who had thereby been compelled to be satisfied with small profits. Still there was but little thought of seeking a remedy in an organized anti-Jewish movement. On the contrary, the abnormal situation aggravated by the disappointments and depression caused by the Turkish war, had stimulated a widespread demand for constitutional changes which would enable the people to adopt a state-machinery more exactly suited to their needs. Among the peasantry this demand was promoted and fomented by the Nihilists, and among the landowners it was largely adopted as a means of checking what threatened to become a new Jacquerie (Walcker, *Gegenwärtige Lage Russlands*, 1873; *Innere Krisis Russlands*, 1876). The tsar, Alexander II., strongly sympathized with this movement, and on the advice of Count Loris-Melikov and the council of ministers a rudimentary scheme of parliamentary government had been drafted and actually signed when the emperor was assassinated. Meanwhile a nationalist and reactionary agitation, originating like its German analogue in the Hegelianism of a section of the lettered public, had manifested itself in Moscow. After some early vicissitudes, it had been organized, under the auspices of Alexis Kireiev, Chomyakov, Aksakov and Ko-chelev, into the Slavophil party, with a Romanticist programme of reforms based on the old traditions of the pre-Petrine epoch. This party gave a great impetus to Slav nationalism. Its final possibilities were sanguinarily illustrated by Muraviev's campaign in Poland in 1863, and in the war against Turkey in 1877, which was exclusively its handiwork (Statement by General Kireiev: Schütz, *Das heutige Russ-land*, p. 104). After the assassination of Alexander II. the Slavophil teaching, as expounded by Ignatiev and Pobêdonostsev, became paramount in the government, and the new tsar was persuaded to cancel the constitutional project of his father. The more liberal views of a section of the Slavophils under Aksakov, who had been in favour of representative institutions on traditional lines, were displaced by the reactionary system of Pobêdonostsev, who took his stand on absolutism, orthodoxy and the racial unity of the Russian people. This was the situation on the eve of Easter 1881. The hardening nationalism above, the increasing discontent below, the economic activity of the Hebrew heretics and aliens, and the echoes of anti-Semitism from over the western border were combining for an explosion.

A scuffle in a tavern at Elisabethgrad in Kherson sufficed to ignite this combustible material. The scuffle grew into a riot, the tavern was sacked, and the drunken mob, hounded on by agitators who declared that the Jews were using Christian blood for the manufacture of their Easter bread, attacked and looted the Jewish quarter. The outbreak spread rapidly. On the 7th of May there was a similar riot at Smiela, near Cherkasy, and the following day there was a violent outbreak at Kiev, which left 2000 Jews homeless. Within a few weeks the whole of western Russia, from the Black Sea to the Baltic, was smoking with the ruins of Jewish homes. Scores of Jewish women were dishonoured, hundreds of men, women and children were slaughtered, and tens of thousands were reduced to beggary and left without a shelter. Murderous riots or incendiary outrages took place in no fewer than 167 towns and villages, including Warsaw, Odessa and Kiev. Europe had witnessed no such scenes of mob savagery since the Black Death massacres in the 14th century. As the facts gradually filtered through to the western capitals they caused a thrill of horror everywhere. An indignation meeting held at the Mansion House in London, under the presidency of the lord mayor, was the signal for a long series of popular demonstrations condemning the persecutions, held in most of the chief cities of England and the continent.

Except as stimulated by the Judeophobe revival in Germany the Russian outbreak in its earlier forms does not belong specifically to modern anti-Semitism. It was essentially a medieval uprising animated by the religious fanaticism, gross superstition and predatory instincts of a people still in the medieval stage of their development. This is proved by the fact that, although the Russian peasant was supposed to be a victim of unbearable Jewish "exploitation," he was not moved to riot until he had been brutalized by drink and excited by the old fable of the Blood Accusation. The modern anti-Semitic element came from above and followed closely on the heels of the riots. It has been freely charged against the Russian government that it promoted the riots in 1881 in order to distract popular attention from the Nihilist propaganda and from the political disappointments involved in the cancellation of the previous tsar's constitutional project (Lazare, *L'Antisémitisme,* p. 211). This seems to be true of General Ignatiev, then minister of the interior, and the secret police (Séménoff, *The Russian Government and the Massacres,* pp. 17, 32, 241). It is certain that the local authorities, both civil and military, favoured the outbreak, and took no steps to suppress it, and that the feudal bureaucracy who had just escaped a great danger were not sorry to see the discontented populace venting their passions on the Jews. In the higher circles of the government, however, other views prevailed. The tsar himself was at first persuaded that the riots were the work of Nihilists, and he publicly promised his protection to the Jews. On the other hand, his ministers, ardent Slavophils, thought they recognized in the outbreak an endorsement of the nationalist teaching of which they were the apostles, and, while reprobating the acts of violence, came to the conclusion that the most reasonable solution was to aggravate the legal disabilities of the persecuted aliens and heretics. To this view the tsar was won over, partly by the clamorous indignation of western Europe, which had wounded his national *amour propre* to the quick, and partly by the strongly partisan report of a commission appointed to inquire, not into the administrative complaisance which had allowed riot to run loose over the western and southern provinces, but into the "exploitation" alleged against the Jews, the reasons why "the former laws limiting the rights of the Jews" had been mitigated, and how these laws could be altered so as "to stop the pernicious conduct of the Jews" (Rescript of the 3rd of September 1881). The result of this report was the drafting of a "Temporary Order concerning the Jews" by the minister of the interior, which received the assent of the tsar on the 3rd of May 1882. This order, which was so little temporary that it has not yet been repealed, had the effect of creating a number of fresh ghettos within the pale of Jewish settlement. The Jews were cooped up within the towns, and their rural interests were arbitrarily confiscated. The doubtful incidence of the order gave rise to a number of judgments of the senate, by which all its persecuting possibilities were brought out, with the result that the activities of the Jews were completely paralysed, and they became a prey to unparalleled cruelty. As the gruesome effect of this legislation became known, a fresh outburst of horror and indignation swelled up from western Europe. It proved powerless. Count Ignatiev was dismissed owing to the protests of high-placed Russians, who were disgusted by the new *Kulturkampf*, but his work remained, and, under the influence of Pobêdonostsev, the procurator of the Holy Synod, the policy of the "May Laws," as they were significantly called, was applied to every aspect of Jewish life with pitiless rigour. The temper of the tsar may be judged by the fact that when an appeal for mercy from an illustrious personage in England was conveyed to him at Fredensborg through the gracious medium of the tsaritsa, he angrily exclaimed within the hearing of an Englishman in the ante-room who was the bearer of the message, "Never let me hear you mention the name of that people again!"

The Russian May Laws are the most conspicuous legislative monument achieved by modern anti-Semitism. It is true that they re-

enacted regulations which resemble the oppressive statutes introduced into Poland through the influence of the Jesuits in the 16th
century (Sternberg, *Gesch. d. Juden in Polen,* pp. 141 et seq.), but their
Orthodox authors were as little conscious of this irony of history as
they were of the Teutonic origins of the whole Slavophil movement.
These laws are an experimental application of the political principles
extracted by Marr and his German disciples from the metaphysics of
Hegel, and as such they afford a valuable means of testing the practical operation of modern anti-Semitism. Their result was a widespread commercial depression which was felt all over the empire.
Even before the May Laws were definitely promulgated the passport
registers showed that the anti-Semitic movement had driven 67,900
Jews across the frontier, and it was estimated that they had taken with
them 13,000,000 roubles, representing a minimum loss of 60,000,000
roubles to the annual turnover of the country's trade. Towards the
end of 1882 it was calculated that the agitation had cost Russia as
much as the whole Turkish war of 1877. Trade was everywhere paralysed. The enormous increase of bankruptcies, the transfer of in-
vestments to foreign funds, the consequent fall in the value of the
rouble and the prices of Russian stocks, the suspension of farming
operations owing to advances on growing crops being no longer available, the rise in the prices of the necessities of life, and lastly, the
appearance of famine, filled half the empire with gloom. Banks closed
their doors, and the great provincial fairs proved failures. When it
was proposed to expel the Jews from Moscow there was a loud outcry
all over the sacred city, and even the Orthodox merchants, realizing
that the measure would ruin their flourishing trade with the south
and west, petitioned against it. The Moscow Exhibition proved a
failure. Nevertheless the government persisted with its harsh policy,
and Jewish refugees streamed by tens of thousands across the western
frontier to seek an asylum in other lands. In 1891 the alarm caused
by this emigration led to further protests from abroad. The citizens
of London again assembled at Guildhall, and addressed a petition to
the tsar on behalf of his Hebrew subjects. It was handed back to the
lord mayor by the Russian ambassador, with a curt intimation that
the emperor declined to receive it. At the same time orders were
defiantly given that the May Laws should be strictly enforced. Meanwhile the Russian minister of finance was at his wits' ends for money.
Negotiations for a large loan had been entered upon with the house
of Rothschild, and a preliminary contract had been signed, when, at
the instance of the London firm, M. Wyshnigradski, the finance minister, was informed that unless the persecutions of the Jews were

stopped the great banking-house would be compelled to withdraw from the operation. Deeply mortified by this attempt to deal with him *de puissance à puissance*, the tsar peremptorily broke off the negotiations, and ordered that overtures should be made to a non-Jewish French syndicate. In this way anti-Semitism, which had already so profoundly influenced the domestic politics of Europe, set its mark on the international relations of the powers, for it was the urgent need of the Russian treasury quite as much as the termination of Prince Bismarck's secret treaty of mutual neutrality which brought about the Franco-Russian alliance (Daudet, *Hist. Dipl. de l' Alliance Franco-Russe*, pp. 259 et. seq.).

For nearly three years more the persecutions continued. Elated by the success of his crusade against the Jews, Pobêdonostsev extended his persecuting policy to other non-Orthodox denominations. The legislation against the Protestant Stundists became almost as unbearable as that imposed on the Jews. In the report of the Holy Synod, presented to the tsar towards the end of 1893, the procurator called for repressive measures against Roman Catholics, Moslems and Buddhists, and denounced the rationalist tendency of the whole system of secular education in the empire (*Neue Freie Presse*, 31st January 1894). A year later, however, the tsar died, and his successor, without repealing any of the persecuting laws, let it gradually be understood that their rigorous application might be mitigated. The country was tired and exhausted by the persecution, and the tolerant hints which came from high quarters were acted upon with significant alacrity.

A new era of conflict dawned with the great constitutional struggle towards the end of the century. The conditions, however, were very different from those which prevailed in the 'eighties. The May Laws had avenged themselves with singular fitness. By confining the Jews to the towns at the very moment that Count Witte's policy of protection was creating an enormous industrial proletariat they placed at the disposal of the disaffected masses an ally powerful in numbers and intelligence, and especially in its bitter sense of wrong, its reckless despair and its cosmopolitan outlook and connexions. As early as 1885 the Jewish workmen assisted by Jewish university students led the way in the formation of trades unions. They also became the *colporteurs* of western European socialism, and they played an important part in the organization of the Russian Social Democratic Federation which their "Arbeiter Bund" joined in 1898 with no fewer than 30,000 members. The Jewish element in the new democratic movement excited the resentment of the government, and under the minister of the interior, M. Sipiaguine, the persecuting laws were

once more rigorously enforced. The "Bund" replied in 1901 by proclaiming itself frankly political and revolutionary, and at once took
a leading place in the revolutionary movement. The reactionaries
were not slow to profit by this circumstance. With the support of M.
Plehve, the new minister of the interior, and the whole of the bu-
reaucratic class they denounced the revolution as a Jewish conspiracy,
engineered for exclusively Jewish purposes and designed to establish
a Jewish domination over the Russian people. The government and
even the intimates of the tsar became persuaded that only by the
terrorization of the Jews could the revolutionary movement be effectually dealt with. For this purpose a so-called League of True
Russians was formed. Under high patronage, and with the assistance
of the secret police and a large number of the local authorities, it set
itself to stir up the populace, chiefly the fanatics and the hooligans,
against the Jews. Incendiary proclamations were prepared and
printed in the ministry of the interior itself, and were circulated by
the provincial governors and the police (Prince Urussov's speech in
the Duma, June 8 (21), 1906). The result was another series of massacres which began at Kishinev in 1903 and culminated in wholesale
butchery at Odessa and Bielostok in October 1905. An attempt was
made to picture and excuse these outbreaks as a national upheaval
against the Jew-made revolution but it failed. They only embittered
the revolutionists and "intellectuals" throughout the country, and won
for them a great deal of outspoken sympathy abroad. The artificiality
of the anti-Jewish outbreak was illustrated by the first Duma elections.
Thirteen Jews were elected and every constituency which had been
the scene of a *pogrom* returned a liberal member. Unfortunately the
Jews benefited little by the new parliamentary constitution. The privileges of voting for members of the Duma and of sitting in the new
assembly were granted them, but all their civil and religious disabilities were maintained. Both the first and the second Duma proposed
to emancipate them, but they were dissolved before any action could
be taken. By the modification of the electoral law under which the
third Duma was elected the voting power of the Jews was diminished
and further restrictions were imposed upon them through official
intimidation during the elections. The result was that only two Jews
were elected, while the reactionary tendency of the new electorate
virtually removed the question of their emancipation from the field
of practical politics.

Rumania.—The only other country in Europe in which a legalized
anti-Semitism exists is Rumania. The conditions are very similar to
those which obtain in Russia, with the important difference that Ru-

mania is a constitutional country, and that the Jewish persecutions are the work of the elected deputies of the nation. Like the *Bourgeois Gentilhomme* who wrote prose all his life without knowing it, the Rumanians practised the nationalist doctrines of the Hegelian anti-Semites unconsciously long before they were formulated in Germany. In the old days of Turkish domination the lot of the Rumanian Jews was not conspicuously unhappy. It was only when the nation began to be emancipated, and the struggle in the East assumed the form of a crusade against Islam that the Jews were persecuted. Rumanian politicians preached a nationalism limited exclusively to indigenous Christians, and they were strongly supported by all who felt the commercial competition of the Jews. Thus, although the Jews had been settled in the land for many centuries, they were by law declared aliens. This was done in defiance of the treaty of Paris of 1856 and the convention of 1858 which declared all Rumans to be equal before the law. Under the influence of this distinction the Jews became persecuted, and sanguinary riots were of frequent occurrence. The realization of a Jewish question led to legislation imposing disabilities on the Jews. In 1878 the congress of Berlin agreed to recognize the independence of Rumania on condition that all religious disabilities were removed. Rumania agreed to this condition, but ultimately persuaded the powers to allow her to carry out the emancipation of the Jews gradually. Persecutions, however, continued, and in 1902 they led to a great exodus of Jews. The United States addressed a strong remonstrance to the Rumanian government, but the condition of the Jews was in no way improved. Their emancipation was in 1908 as far off as ever, and their disabilities heavier than those of their brethren in Russia. For this state of things the example of the anti-Semites in Germany, Russia, Austria and France was largely to blame, since it had justified the intolerance of the Rumans. Owing, also, to the fact that of late years Rumania had become a sort of *annexe* of the Triple Alliance, it was found impossible to induce the signatories of the treaty of Berlin to take action to compel the state to fulfil its obligations under that treaty.

Austria-Hungary.—In Austria-Hungary the anti-Semitic impulses came almost simultaneously from the North and East. Already in the 'seventies the doctrinaire anti-Semitism of Berlin had found an echo in Budapest. Two members of the diet, Victor Istoczy and Geza Onody, together with a publicist named Georg Marczianyi, busied themselves in making known the doctrine of Marr in Hungary. Marczianyi, who translated the German Judeophobe pamphlets into Magyar, and the Magyar works of Onody into German, was the chief medium between the northern and southern schools. In 1880 Istoczy tried to establish a "Nichtjuden Bund" in Hungary, with statutes literally translated from those of the German anti-Semitic league. The movement, however, made no progress, owing to the stalwart Liberalism of the predominant political parties, and of the national principles inherited from the revolution of 1848. The large part played by the Jews in that struggle, and the fruitful patriotism with which they had worked for the political and economic progress of the country, had created, too, a strong claim on the gratitude of the best elements in the nation. Nevertheless, among the ultramontane clergy, the higher aristocracy, the ill-paid minor officials, and the ignorant peasantry, the seeds of a tacit anti-Semitism were latent. It was probably the aversion of the nobility from anything in the nature of a demogogic agitation which for a time prevented these seeds from germinating. The news of the uprising in Russia and the appearance of Jewish refugees on the frontier, had the effect of giving a certain prominence to the agitation of Istoczy and Onody and of exciting the rural communities, but it did not succeed in impressing the public with the pseudo-scientific doctrines of the new anti-Semitism. It was not until the agitators resorted to the Blood Accusation—that never-failing decoy of obscurantism and superstition—that Hungary took a definite place in the anti-Semitic movement. The outbreak was short and fortunately bloodless, but while it lasted its scandals shocked the whole of Europe.

Dr August Rohling, professor of Hebrew at the university of Prague, a Roman Catholic theologian of high position but dubious learning, had for some years assisted the Hungarian anti-Semites with *réchauffés* of Eisenmenger's *Entdecktes Judenthum* (Frankfurt a/M. 1700). In 1881 he made a solemn deposition before the Supreme Court accusing the Jews of being bound by their law to work the moral and physical ruin of non-Jews. He followed this up with an offer to depose on oath that the murder of Christians for ritual purposes was a doctrine secretly taught among Jews. Professor Delitzsch and other eminent Hebraists, both Christian and Jewish, exposed and denounced the ignorance and malevolence of Rohling, but were unable to stem the mischief he was causing. In April 1882 a Christian girl named Esther Sobymossi was missed from the Hungarian village of Tisza Eszlar, where a small community of Jews were settled. The rumor got abroad that she had been kidnapped and murdered by the Jews, but it remained the burden of idle gossip, and gave rise to neither judicial complaint nor public disorders. At this moment the question of the Bosnian Pacification credits was before the diet. The unpopularity of the task assumed by Austria-Hungary, under the treaty of Berlin, which was calculated to strengthen the disaffected Croat element in the empire, had reduced the government majority to very small proportions, and all the reactionary factions in the country were accordingly in arms. The government was violently and unscrupulously attacked on all sides. On the 23rd of May there was a debate in the diet when M. Onody, in an incendiary harangue, told the story of the missing girl at Tisza Eszlar, and accused ministers of criminal indulgence to races alien to the national spirit. In the then excited state of the public mind on the Croat question, the manoeuvre was adroitly conceived. The government fell into the trap, and treated the story with lofty disdain. Thereupon the anti-Semites set to work on the case, and M. Joseph Bary, the magistrate at Nyiregyhaza, and a noted anti-Semite, was induced to go to Tisza Eszlar and institute an inquiry. All the anti-liberal elements in the country now became banded together in this effort to discredit the liberal government, and for the first time the Hungarian anti-Semites found themselves at the head of a powerful party. Fifteen Jews were arrested and thrown into prison. No pains were spared in preparing the case for trial. Perjury and even forgery were freely resorted to. The son of one of the accused, a boy of fourteen, was taken into custody by the police, and by threats and cajoleries prevailed upon to give evidence for the prosecution. He was elaborately coached for the terrible *rôle* he was to play. The trial opened at Nyiregyhaza on the 19th of June, and lasted till the 3rd of August. It was one of the most dramatic *causes célèbres* of the century. Under the brilliant cross-examination of the advocates for the defence the whole of the shocking conspiracy was gradually exposed. The public prosecutor thereupon withdrew from the case, and the four judges—the chief of whom held strong anti-Semitic opinions—unanimously acquitted all the prisoners. The case proved the death-blow of Hungarian anti-Semitism. Although another phase of the Jewish question, which will be referred to presently, had still to occupy the public mind, the shame brought on the nation by the Tisza Eszlar conspiracy effectually prevented the anti-Semites from raising their voices with any effect again.

Meanwhile a more formidable and complicated outburst was preparing in Austria itself. Here the lines of the German agitation were closely followed, but with far more dramatic results. It was exclusively political—that is to say, it appealed to anti-Jewish prejudices for party purposes while it sought to rehabilitate them on a pseudo-scientific basis, racial and economic. At first it was confined to sporadic pamphleteers. By their side there gradually grew up a school of Christian Socialists, recruited from the ultra-Clericals, for the study and application of the doctrines preached at Mainz by Archbishop Ketteler. This constituted a complete Austrian analogue to the Evangelical-Socialist movement started in Germany by Herr Stöcker. For some years the two movements remained distinct, but signs of approximation were early visible. Thus one of the first complaints of the anti-Semites was that the Jews were becoming masters of the soil. This found an echo in the agrarian principles of the Christian Socialists, as expounded by Rudolph Meyer, in which individualism in landed property was admitted on the condition that the landowners were "the families of the nation" and not "cosmopolitan financiers." A further indication of anti-Semitism is found in a speech delivered in 1878 by Prince Alois von Liechtenstein (b. 1846), the most prominent disciple of Rudolph Meyer, who denounced the national debt as a tribute paid by the state to cosmopolitan *rentiers* (Nitti, *Catholic Socialism*, pp. 200, 201, 211, 216). The growing disorder in parliament, due to the bitter struggle between the German and Czech parties, served to bring anti-Semitism into the field of practical politics. Since 1867 the German Liberals had been in power. They had made enemies of the Clericals by tampering with the concordat, and they had split up their own party by the federalist policy adopted by Count Taaffe. The Radical secessionists in their turn found it difficult to agree, and an ultra-national German wing formed itself into a separate party under the leadership of Ritter von Schönerer (b. 1842), a Radical nationalist of the most violent type. In 1882 two anti-Semitic leagues had been founded in Vienna, and to these the Radical nationalists now appealed for support. The growing importance of the party led the premier, Count Taaffe, to angle for the support of the Clericals by accepting a portion of the Christian Socialist programme. The hostility this excited in the liberal press, largely written by Jews, served to bring the feudal Christian Socialists and Radical anti-Semites together. In 1891 these strangely assorted factions became consolidated, and during the elections of that year Prince Liechtenstein came forward as an anti-Semitic candidate and the acknowledged leader of the party. The elections resulted in the return of fifteen anti-Semites to the Reichsrath, chiefly from Vienna.

Although Prince Liechtenstein and the bulk of the Christian Socialists had joined the anti-Semites with the support of the Clerical organ, the *Vaterland*, the Clerical party as a whole still held aloof from the Jew-baiters. The events of 1892–1895 put an end to their hesitation. The Hungarian government, in compliance with long-standing pledges to the liberal party, introduced into the diet a series of ecclesiastical reform bills providing for civil marriage, freedom of worship, and the legal recognition of Judaism on an equality with other denominations. These proposals, which synchronized with Ahlwardt's turbulent agitation in Germany, gave a great impulse to anti-Semitism and served to drive into its ranks a large number of Clericals. The agitation was taken in hand by the Roman Catholic clergy, and the pulpits resounded with denunciations of the Jews. One clergyman, Father Deckert, was prosecuted for preaching the Blood Accusation and convicted (1894). Cardinal Schlauch, bishop of Grosswardein, declared in the Hungarian House of Magnates that the Liberals were in league with "cosmopolitans" for the ruin of the country. In October 1894 the magnates adopted two of the ecclesiastical bills with amendments, but threw out the Jewish bill by a majority of six. The crown sided with the magnates, and the ministry resigned, although it had a majority in the Lower House. An effort was made to form a Clerical cabinet, but it failed. Baron Banffy was then entrusted with the construction of a fresh Liberal ministry. The announcement that he would persist with the ecclesiastical bills lashed the Clericals and anti-Semites into a fury, and the agitation broke out afresh. The pope addressed a letter to Count Zichy encouraging the magnates to resist, and once more two of the bills were amended, and the third rejected. The papal nuncio, Mgr. Agliardi, now thought proper to pay a visit to Budapest, where he allowed himself to be interviewed on the crisis. This interference in the domestic concerns of Hungary was deeply resented by the Liberals, and Baron Banffy requested Count Kalnoky, the imperial minister of foreign affairs, to protest against it at the Vatican. Count Kalnoky refused and tendered his resignation to the emperor. Clerical sympathies were predominant in Vienna, and the emperor was induced for a moment to decline the count's resignation. It soon became clear, however, that the Hungarians were resolved to see the crisis out, and that in the end Vienna would be compelled to give way. The emperor accordingly retraced his steps, Count Kalnoky's resignation was accepted, the papal nuncio was recalled, a batch of new magnates were created, and the Hungarian ecclesiastical bills passed.

Simultaneously with the crisis another startling phase of the anti-Semitic drama was being enacted in Vienna itself. Encouraged by the support of the Clericals the anti-Semites resolved to make an effort to carry the Vienna municipal elections. So far the alliance of the Clericals with the anti-Semites had been unofficial, but on the eve of the elections (January 1895) the pope, influenced partly by the Hungarian crisis and partly by an idea of Cardinal Rampolla that the best antidote to democratic socialism would be a clerically controlled fusion of the Christian Socialists and anti-Semites, sent his blessing to Prince Liechtenstein and his followers. This action alarmed the government and a considerable body of the higher episcopate, who felt assured that any permanent encouragement given to the anti-Semites would in the end strengthen the parties of sedition and disorder. Cardinal Schönborn was despatched in haste to Rome to expostulate with the pontiff, and his representations were strongly supported by the French and Belgian bishops. The mischief was however, done, and although the pope sent a verbal message to Prince Liechtenstein excluding the anti-Semites from his blessing, the elections resulted in a great triumph for the Jew-haters. The municipal council was immediately dissolved by the government, and new elections were ordered, but these only strengthened the position of the anti-Semites, who carried 92 seats out of a total of 138. A cabinet crisis followed, and the premiership was entrusted to the Statthalter of Galicia, Count Badeni, who assumed office with a pledge of war to the knife against anti-Semitism. In October the new municipal council elected as burgomaster of Vienna Dr Karl Lueger (b. 1844), a vehement anti-Semite, who had displaced Prince Liechtenstein as leader of the party. The emperor declined to sanction the election, but the council repeated it in face of the imperial displeasure. Once more a dissolution was ordered, and for three months the city was governed by administrative commissioners. In February 1896 elections were again held, and the anti-Semites were returned with an increased majority. The emperor then capitulated, and after a temporary arrangement, by which for one year Dr Lueger acted as vice-burgomaster and handed over the burgomastership to an inoffensive nominee, permitted the municipal council to have its way. The growing anarchy in parliament at this moment served still further to strengthen the anti-Semites, and their conquest of Vienna was speedily followed by a not less striking conquest of the Landtag of Lower Austria (November 1896).

Since then a reaction of sanity has slowly but surely asserted itself. In 1908 the anti-Semites had governed Vienna twelve years, and, although they had accomplished much mischief, the millennium of which they were supposed to be the heralds had not dawned. On the contrary, the commercial interests of the city had suffered and the rates had been enormously increased (*Neue Freie Presse*, 29th March 1901), while the predatory hopes which secured them office had only been realized on a small and select scale. The spectacle of a Clerico-anti-Semitic tammany in Vienna had strengthened the resistance of the better elements in the country. Time had also shown that Christian Socialism is only a disguise for high Toryism, and that the German Radicals who were originally induced to join the anti-Semites had been victimized by the Clericals. The fruits of this disillusion began to show themselves in the general elections of 1900–1901, when the anti-Semites lost six seats in the Reichsrath. The elections were followed (26th January 1901) by a papal encyclical on Christian democracy, in which Christian Socialism was declared to be a term unacceptable to the Church, and the faithful were adjured to abstain from agitation of a demagogic and revolutionary character, and "to respect the rights of others." Nevertheless, in 1907 the Christian Socialists trebled their representation in the Reichsrath. This, however, was due more to their alliance with the German national parties than to any large increase of anti-Semitism in the electorate.

France.—The last country in Europe to make use of the teachings of German anti-Semitism in its party politics was France. The fact that the movement should have struck root in a republican country, where the ideals of democratic freedom have been so passionately cultivated, has been regarded as one of the paradoxes of our latterday history. As a matter of fact, it is more surprising that it was not adopted earlier. All the social and political conditions which produced anti-Semitism in Germany were present in France, but in an aggravated form due primarily to the very republican *régime* which at first sight seemed to be a guarantee against it. In the monarchical states the dominance of the *bourgeoisie* was tempered in a measure by the power of the crown and the political activity of the aristocracy, which carried with them a very real restraining influence in the matter of political honour and morality. In France these restraining influences were driven out of public life by the republic. The nobility both of the *ancien régime* and the empire stood aloof, and politics were abandoned for the most part to professional adventurers, while the *bourgeoisie* assumed the form of an omnipotent plutocracy. This naturally attracted to France all the financial adventurers in Europe, and in the train of the immigration came not a few German Jews, alienated from their own country by the agitation of Marr and Stöcker. Thus the *bourgeoisie* was not only more powerful in France than in other countries, but the obnoxiousness of its Jewish element was accentuated by a tinge of the national enemy. The anti-clericalism of the *bouregois* republic and its unexampled series of financial scandals, culminating in the Panama "Krach," thus sufficed to give anti-Semitism a strong hold on the public mind.

Nevertheless, it was not until 1882 that the anti-Jewish movement was seriously heard of in France. Paul Bontoux (b. 1820), who had formerly been in the employ of the Rothschilds, but had been obliged to leave the firm in consequence of his disastrous speculations, had joined the Legitimist party, and had started the Union Générale with funds obtained from his new allies. Bontoux promised to break up the alleged financial monopoly of the Jews and Protestants and to found a new plutocracy in its stead, which should be mainly Roman Catholic and aristocratic. The bait was eagerly swallowed. For five years the Union Générale, with the blessing of the pope, pursued an apparently prosperous career. Immense schemes were undertaken, and the 125-fr. shares rose gradually to 3200 francs. The whole structure, however, rested on a basis of audacious speculation, and in January 1882 the Union Générale failed, with liabilities amounting to 212,000,000 francs. The cry was at once raised that the collapse was due to the manoeuvres of the Jews, and a strong anti-Semitic feeling manifested itself in clerical and aristocratic circles. In 1886 violent expression was given to this feeling in a book since become famous, *La France juive*, by Edouard Drumont (b. 1844). The author illustrated the theories of German anti-Semitism with a *chronique scandaleuse* full of piquant personalities, in which the corruption of French national life under Jewish influences was painted in alarming colours. The book was read with avidity by the public, who welcomed its explanations of the obviously growing debauchery. The Wilson scandals and the suspension of the Panama Company in the following year, while not bearing out Drumont's anti-Semitism, fully justified his view of the prevailing corruption. Out of this condition of things rose the Boulangist movement, which rallied all the disaffected elements in the country, including Drumont's following of anti-Semites. It was not, however, until the flight of General Boulanger and the ruin of his party that anti-Semitism came forward as a political movement.

The chief author of the rout of Boulangism was a Jewish politician and journalist, Joseph Reinach (b. 1856), formerly private secretary to Gambetta, and one of the ablest men in France. He was a Frenchman by birth and education, but his father and uncles were Germans, who had founded an important banking establishment in Paris. Hence he was held to personify the alien Jewish domination in France, and the ex-Boulangists turned against him and his co-religionists with fury. The Boulangist agitation had for a second time involved the Legitimists in heavy pecuniary losses, and under the leadership of the marquis de Morès they now threw all their influence on the side of Drumont. An anti-Semitic league was established, and with Royalist assistance branches were organized all over the country. The Franco-Russian alliance in 1891, when the persecutions of the Jews by Po-bêdonostsev were attracting the attention of Europe, served to invest Drumont's agitation with a fashionable and patriotic character. It was a sign of the spiritual approximation of the two peoples. In 1892 Drumont founded a daily anti-Semitic newspaper, *La Libre Parole*. With the organization of this journal a regular campaign for the discovery of scandals was instituted. At the same time a body of aristocratic swashbucklers, with the marquis de Morès and the comte de Lamase at their head, set themselves to terrorize the Jews and provoke them to duels. At a meeting held at Neuilly in 1891, Jules Guérin, one of the marquis de Morès's lieutenants, had demanded rhetorically *un cadavre de Juif*. He had not long to wait. Anti-Semitism was most powerful in the army, which was the only branch of the public service in which the reactionary classes were fully represented. The republican law compelling the seminarists to serve their term in the army had strengthened its Clerical and Royalist elements, and the result was a movement against the Jewish officers, of whom 500 held commissions. A series of articles in the *Libre Parole* attacking these officers led to a number of ferocious duels, and these culmi-nated in 1892 in the death of an amiable and popular Jewish officer, Captain Armand Mayer, of the Engineers, who fell, pierced through the lungs by the marquis de Morès. This tragedy, rendered all the more painful by the discovery that Captain Mayer had chivalrously fought to shield a friend, aroused a great deal of popular indignation against the anti-Semites, and for a moment it was believed that the agitation had been killed with its victim.

Towards the end of 1892, the discovery of the widespread cor-ruption practised by the Panama Company gave a fresh impulse to anti-Semitism. The revelations were in a large measure due to the industry of the *Libre Parole;* and they were all the more welcome to the readers of that journal since it was discovered that three Jews were implicated in the scandals, one of whom, baron de Reinach, was uncle and father-in-law to the hated destroyer of Boulangism. The escape of the other two, Dr Cornelius Herz and M. Arton, and the difficulties experienced in obtaining their extradition, deepened the popular conviction that the authorities were implicated in the scan-dals, and kept the public eye for a long time absorbed by the otherwise restricted Jewish aspects of the scandals. In 1894 the military side of the agitation was revived by the arrest of a prominent Jewish staff officer, Captain Alfred Dreyfus, on a charge of treason. From the beginning the hand of the anti-Semite was flagrant in the new sensation. The first hint of the arrest appeared in the *Libre Parole;* and before the facts had been officially communicated to the public that journal was busy with a campaign against the war minister, based on the apprehension that, in conspiracy with the *Juiverie* and his republican colleagues, he might exert himself to shield the traitor. Anti-Semitic feeling was now thoroughly aroused. Panama had prepared the people to believe anything; and when it was announced that a court-martial, sitting in secret, had convicted Dreyfus, there was a howl of execration against the Jews from one end of the country to the other, although the alleged crime of the convict and the evidence by which it was supported were quite unknown. Dreyfus was degraded and transported for life amid unparalleled scenes of public excitement.

The Dreyfus Case registers the climax not only of French, but of European anti-Semitism. It was the most ambitious and most unscrupulous attempt yet made to prove the nationalist hypothesis of the anti-Semites, and in its failure it afforded the most striking illustration of the dangers of the whole movement by bringing France to the verge of revolution. For a few months after the Dreyfus court-martial there was a comparative lull; but the highly strung condition of popular passion was illustrated by a violent debate on "The Jewish Peril" in the Chamber of Deputies (25th April 1895), and by two outrages with explosives at the Rothschild bank in Paris. Meanwhile the family of Dreyfus, absolutely convinced of his innocence, were casting about for the means of clearing his character and securing his liberation. They were wealthy, and their activity unsettled the public mind and aroused the apprehensions of the conspirators. Had the latter known how to preserve silence, the mystery would perhaps have been yet unsolved; but in their anxiety to allay all suspicions they made one false step, which proved the beginning of their ruin. Through their friends in the press they secured the publication of a facsimile of a document known as the *Bordereau*—a list of documents supposed to be in Dreyfus's handwriting and addressed apparently to the military attaché of a foreign power, which was alleged to constitute the chief evidence against the convict. It was hoped by this publication to put an end to the doubts of the so-called Dreyfusards. The result, however, was only to give them a clue on which they worked with remarkable ingenuity. To prove that the *Bordereau* was not in Dreyfus's handwriting was not difficult. Indeed, its authorship was recognized almost on the day of publication; but the Dreyfusards held their hands in order to make assurance doubly sure by further evidence. Meanwhile one of the officers of the general staff, Colonel

Picquart, had convinced himself by an examination of the *dossier* of the trial that a gross miscarriage of justice had taken place. On mentioning his doubts to his superiors, who were animated partly by anti-Semitic feeling and partly by reluctance to confess to a mistake, he was ordered to the Tunisian hinterland on a dangerous expedition. Before leaving Paris, however, he took the precaution to confide his discovery to his legal adviser. Harassed by their anxieties, the conspirators made further communications to the newspapers; and the government, questioned and badgered in parliament, added to the revelations. The new disclosures, so far from stopping the Dreyfusards, proved to them, among other things, that the conviction had been partially based on documents which had not been communicated to the counsel for the defence, and hence that the judges had been tampered with by the ministry of war behind the prisoner's back. So far, too, as these documents related to correspondence with foreign military attachés, it was soon ascertained that they were forgeries. In this way a terrible indictment was gradually drawn up against the ministry of war. The first step was taken towards the end of 1897 by a brother of Captain Dreyfus, who, in a letter to the minister of war, denounced Major Esterhazy as a real author of the *Bordereau*. The authorities, supported by parliament, declined to reopen the Dreyfus Case, but they ordered a court-martial on Esterhazy, which was held with closed doors and resulted in his acquittal. It now became clear that nothing short of an appeal to public opinion and a full exposure of all the iniquities that had been perpetrated would secure justice at the hands of the military chiefs. On behalf of Dreyfus, Emile Zola, the eminent novelist, formulated the case against the general staff of the army in an open letter to the president of the republic, which by its dramatic accusations startled the whole world. The letter was denounced as wild and fantastic even by those who were in favour of revision. Zola was prosecuted for libel and convicted, and had to fly the country; but the agitation he had started was taken in hand by others, notably M. Clemenceau, M. Reinach and M. Yves Guyot. In August 1898 their efforts found their first reward. A reexamination of the documents in the case by M. Cavaignac, then minister of war, showed that one was undoubtedly forged. Colonel Henry, of the intelligence department of the war office, then confessed that he had fabricated the document, and, on being sent to Mont Valérien under arrest, cut his throat.

In spite of this damaging discovery the war office still persisted in believing Dreyfus guilty, and opposed a fresh inquiry. It was supported by three successive ministers of war, and apparently an overwhelming body of public opinion. By this time the question of the guilt or innocence of Dreyfus had become an altogether subsidiary issue. As in Germany and Austria, the anti-Semitic crusade had passed into the hands of the political parties. On the one hand the Radicals and Socialists, recognizing the anti-republican aims of the agitators and alarmed by the clerical predominance in the army, had thrown in their lot with the Dreyfusards; on the other the reactionaries, anxious to secure the support of the army, took the opposite view, denounced their opponents as *sans patrie,* and declared that they were conspiring to weaken and degrade the army in the face of the national enemy. The controversy was, consequently, no longer for or against Dreyfus, but for or against the army, and behind it was a life-or-death struggle between the republic and its enemies. The situation became alarming. Rumours of military plots filled the air. Powerful leagues for working up public feeling were formed and organized; attempts to discredit the republic and intimidate the government were made. The president was insulted; there were tumults in the streets, and an attempt was made by M. Déroulède to induce the military to march on the Elysée and upset the republic. In this critical situation France, to her eternal honour, found men with sufficient courage to do the right. The Socialists, by rallying to the Radicals against the reactionaries, secured a majority for the defence of the republic in parliament. Brisson's cabinet transmitted to the court of cassation an application for the revision of the case against Dreyfus; and that tribunal, after an elaborate inquiry, which fully justified Zola's famous letter, quashed and annulled the proceedings of the court-martial, and remitted the accused to another court-martial, to be held at Rennes. Throughout these proceedings the military party fought tooth and nail to impede the course of justice; and although the innocence of Dreyfus had been completely established, it concentrated all its efforts to secure a fresh condemnation of the prisoner at Rennes. Popular passion was at fever heat, and it manifested itself in an attack on M. Labori, one of the counsel for the defence, who was shot and wounded on the eve of his cross-examination of the witnesses for the prosecution. To the amazement and indignation of the whole world outside France, the Rennes court-martial again found the prisoner guilty; but all reliance on the conscientiousness of the verdict was removed by a rider, which found "extenuating circumstances," and by a reduction of the punishment to ten years' imprisonment, to which was added a recommendation to mercy. The verdict was evidently an attempt at a compromise, and the government resolved to advise the president of the republic to pardon Dreyfus.

This lame conclusion did not satisfy the accused; but his innocence had been so clearly proved, and on political grounds there were such urgent reasons for desiring a termination of the affair, that it was accepted without protest by the majority of moderate men.

The rehabilitation of Dreyfus, however, did not pass without another effort on the part of the reactionaries to turn the popular passions excited by the case to their own advantage. After the failure of Déroulède's attempt to overturn the republic, the various Royalist and Boulangist leagues, with the assistance of the anti-Semites, organized another plot. This was discovered by the government, and the leaders were arrested. Jules Guérin, secretary of the anti-Semitic league, shut himself up in the league offices in the rue Chabrol, Paris, which had been fortified and garrisoned by a number of his friends, armed with rifles. For more than a month these anti-Semites held the authorities at bay, and some 5000 troops were employed in the siege. The conspirators were all tried by the senate, sitting as a high court, and Guérin was sentenced to ten years' imprisonment. The evidence showed that the anti-Semitic organization had taken an active part in the anti-republican plot (see the report of the Commission d'Instruction in the *Petit Temps,* 1st November 1899).

The government now resolved to strike at the root of the mischief by limiting the power of the religious orders, and with this view a drastic Association bill was introduced into the chambers. This anti-clerical move provoked the wildest passions of the reactionaries, but it found an overwhelming support in the elections of 1902 and the bill became law. The war thus definitely reopened soon led to a revival of the Dreyfus controversy. The nationalists flooded the country with incendiary defamations of "the government of national treason," and Dreyfus on his part loudly demanded a fresh trial. It was clear that conciliation and compromise were useless. Early in 1905 M. Jaurès urged upon the chamber that the demand of the Jewish officer should be granted if only to tranquillize the country. The necessary *faits nouveaux* were speedily found by the minister of war, General André, and having been examined by a special commission of revision were ordered to be transmitted to the court of cassation for final adjudication. On the 12th of July 1906, the court, all chambers united, gave its judgment. After a lengthy review of the case it declared unanimously that the whole accusation against Dreyfus had been disproved, and it quashed the judgment of the Rennes court-martial *sans renvoi.* The explanation of the whole case is that Esterhazy and Henry were the real culprits; that they had made a trade of supplying the German government with military documents; and that once the *Bordereau* was discovered they availed themselves of the anti-Jewish agitation to throw suspicion on Dreyfus.

Thus ended this famous case, to the relief of the whole country and with the approval of the great majority of French citizens. Except a knot of anti-Semitic monomaniacs all parties bowed loyally to the judgment of the court of cassation. The government gave the fullest effect to the judgment. Dreyfus and Picquart were restored to the active list of the army with the ranks respectively of major and general of brigade. Dreyfus was also created a knight of the Legion of Honour, and received the decoration in public in the artillery pavilion of the military school. Zola, to whose efforts the triumph of truth was chiefly due, had not been spared to witness the final scene, but the chambers decided to give his remains a last resting-place in the Pantheon. When three months later M. Clémenceau formed his first cabinet he appointed General Picquart minister of war. Nothing indeed was left undone to repair the terrible series of wrongs which had grown out of the Dreyfus case. Nevertheless its destructive work could not be wholly healed. For over ten years it had been a nightmare to France, and it now modified the whole course of French history. In the ruin of the French Church, which owed its disestablishment very largely to the Dreyfus conspiracy, may be read the most eloquent warning against the demoralizing madness of anti-Semitism.

In sympathy with the agitation in France there has been a similar movement in Algeria, where the European population have long resented the admission of the native Jews to the rights of French citizenship. The agitation has been marked by much violence, and most of the anti-Semitic deputies in the French parliament, including M. Drumont, have found constituencies in Algeria. As the local anti-Semites are largely Spaniards and Levantine riff-raff, the agitation has not the peculiar nationalist bias which characterizes continental anti-Semitism. Before the energy of the authorities it has lately shown signs of subsiding.

Great Britain, & c.—While the main activity of anti-Semitism has manifested itself in Germany, Russia, Rumania, Austria-Hungary and France, its vibratory influences have been felt in other countries when conditions favourable to its extension have presented themselves. In England more than one attempt to acclimatize the doctrines of Marr and Treitschke has been made. The circumstance that at the time of the rise of German anti-Semitism a premier of Hebrew race, Lord Beaconsfield, was in power first suggested the Jewish bogey to English political extremists. The Eastern crisis of 1876–1878, which was regarded by the Liberal party as primarily a struggle between Christianity, as represented by Russia, and a degrading Semitism, as represented by Turkey, accentuated the anti-Jewish feeling, owing to the anti-Russian attitude adopted by the government. Violent expression to the ancient prejudices against the Jews was given by Sir J. G. Tollemache Sinclair (*A Defence of Russia*, 1877). Mr. T. P. O'Connor, in a life of Lord Beaconsfield (1878), pictured him as the instrument of the Jewish people, "moulding the whole policy of Christendom to Jewish aims." Professor Goldwin Smith, in several articles in the *Nineteenth Century* (1878, 1881 and 1882), sought to synthetize the growing anti-Jewish feeling by adopting the nationalist theories of the German anti-Semites. This movement did not fail to find an equivocal response in the speeches of some of the leading Liberal statesmen; but on the country generally it produced no effect. It was revived when the persecutions in Russia threatened England with a great influx of Polish Jews, whose mode of life was calculated to lower the standard of living in the industries in which they were employed, and it has left its trace in the anti-alien legislation of 1905. In 1883 Stöcker visited London, but received a very unflattering reception. Abortive attempts to acclimatize anti-Semitism have also been made in Switzerland, Belgium, Greece and the United States.

Anti-Semitism made a great deal of history during the thirty years up to 1908, but has left no permanent mark of a constructive kind on the social and political evolution of Europe. It is the fruit of a great ethnographic and political error, and it has spent itself in political intrigues of transparent dishonesty. Its racial doctrine is at best a crude hypothesis: its nationalist theory has only served to throw into striking relief the essentially economic bases of modern society, while its political activity has revealed the vulgarity and ignorance which constitute its main sources of strength. So far from injuring the Jews, it has really given Jewish racial separatism a new lease of life. Its extravagant accusations, as in the Tisza Eszlar and Dreyfus cases, have resulted in the vindication of the Jewish character. Its agitation generally, coinciding with the revival of interest in Jewish history, has helped to transfer Jewish solidarity from a religious to a racial basis. The bond of a common race, vitalized by a new pride in Hebrew history and spurred on to resistance by the insults of the anti-Semites, has given a new spirit and a new source of strength to Judaism at a moment when the approximation of ethical systems and the revolt against dogma were sapping its essentially religious foundations. In the whole history of Judaism, perhaps, there have been no more numerous or remarkable instances of reversions to the faith than in the period in question. The reply of the Jews to anti-Semitism

has taken two interesting practical forms. In the first place there is
the so-called Zionist movement, which is a kind of Jewish nationalism
and is vitiated by the same errors that distinguish its anti-Semitic
analogue. In the second place, there is a movement represented by
the Maccabaeans' Society in London, which seeks to unite the Jewish
people in an effort to raise the Jewish character and to promote a
higher consciousness of the dignity of the race. It lays no stress on
orthodoxy, but welcomes all who strive to render Jewish conduct an
adequate reply to the theories of the anti-Semites. Both these movements are elements of fresh vitality to Judaism, and they are probably
destined to produce important fruit in future years. A splendid spirit
of generosity has also been displayed by the Jewish community in
assisting and relieving the victims of the Jew-haters. Besides countless
funds raised by public subscription, Baron de Hirsch founded a colossal scheme for transplanting persecuted Jews to new countries
under new conditions of life, and endowed it with no less a sum than
£9,000,000.

Though anti-Semitism has been unmasked and discredited, it is
to be feared that its history is not yet at an end. While there remain
in Russia and Rumania over six millions of Jews who are being systematically degraded, and who periodically overflow the western frontier, there must continue to be a Jewish question in Europe; and while
there are weak governments, and ignorant and superstitious elements
in the enfranchized classes of the countries affected, that question
will seek to play a part in politics.

CHARLES DICKENS

BY THOMAS SECCOMBE

*T*homas Seccombe was a little-
noticed master whose contributions to the Dictionary of
National Biography *and the eleventh were always duly*

praised for their terseness, wit, and critical insight, but who somehow has today been entirely forgotten.

Born in 1866, Seccombe was educated at Oxford, where he graduated with honors, having submitted a paper on "Political Satire in England in the Eighteenth Century." He was soon employed by Sir Sidney Lee, who in 1891 had succeeded Sir Leslie Stephen as editor of the Dictionary of National Biography. *He remained with that project all through the decade, contributing some seven hundred biographies to the first series of the DNB, which ended with the death of Queen Victoria and the extensive note by Lee himself on the life of the queen. Seccombe also contributed to the second series, but after the turn of the century he concentrated on critical appreciations of his own or in collaboration. He was hardly a stuffy lexicographer or inflated literary critic—early on, in 1894, he had edited the* Lives of Twelve Bad Men, *a collection of necromancers, witchfinders, unjust judges, poisoners, libertines, and highwaymen, which he dedicated to "Barry Lyndon, Esquire." Although he did not write any of the twelve pieces, he had brought together "original studies of eminent scoundrels by various hands," and that was more than enough for him. In 1909 he published a major study,* The Age of Johnson 1748–1798, *in 1910 an anthology of prose and verse,* In Praise of Oxford, *and throughout his life enjoyed editing texts of a rollicking and humorous nature—those of Baron Munchausen, Smollett's* Travels Through France and Italy. *For the eleventh, he contributed some sixteen profiles of individual authors, and we have already included the incomparable "Tichborne Claimant." It is clear from his work for the* Dictionary of National Biography *and the eleventh that he felt most at home in the eighteenth century, a leaning that may account for his adverse but well-argued treatment of the work of Charles Dickens. At heart, Seccombe loved the briskness and lack of pomp in the best of the eighteenth century; and two sentences from his article on Sir Leslie Stephen for the eleventh may well be applied to Seccombe himself. "For blowing the froth off the flagon of extravagant or inflated eulogy he certainly met no equal in his generation. Voluminous as his work is, it is never dull."*

Seccombe spent his life in the lower echelons of British

academe—posts at East London College, the Royal Military College at Sandhurst, occasional lecturer at Oxford. In 1921 he accepted a chair of English letters at Kingston, Ontario, but soon fell ill, returning to England where he died in 1923.

‿❦‿ DICKENS, CHARLES JOHN HUFFAM

(1812–1870), English novelist, was born on the 7th of February 1812 at a house in the Mile End Terrace, Commercial Road, Landport (Portsea)—a house which was opened as a Dickens Museum on 22nd July 1904. His father John Dickens (d. 1851), a clerk in the navy-pay office on a salary of £80 a year, and stationed for the time being at Portsmouth, had married in 1809 Elizabeth, daughter of Thomas Barrow, and she bore him a family of eight children, Charles being the second. In the winter of 1814 the family moved from Portsea in the snow, as he remembered, to London, and lodged for a time near the Middlesex hospital. The country of the novelist's childhood, however, was the kingdom of Kent, where the family was established in proximity to the dockyard at Chatham from 1816 to 1821. He looked upon himself in later years as a man of Kent, and his capital abode as that in Ordnance Terrace, or 18 St Mary's Place, Chatham, amid surroundings classified in Mr Pickwick's notes as "appearing" to be soldiers, sailors, Jews, chalk, shrimps, officers and dockyard men. He fell into a family the general tendency of which was to go down in the world, during one of its easier periods (John Dickens was now fifth clerk on £250 a year), and he always regarded himself as belonging by right to a comfortable, genteel, lower middle-class stratum of society. His mother taught him to read; to his father he appeared very early in the light of a young prodigy, and by him Charles was made to sit on a tall chair and warble popular ballads, or even to tell stories and anecdotes for the benefit of fellow-clerks in the office. John Dickens, however, had a small collection of books which were kept in a little room upstairs that led out of Charles's own, and in this attic the boy found his true literary instructors in *Roderick Random, Peregrine Pickle, Humphry Clinker, Tom Jones, The Vicar of Wakefield, Don Quixote, Gil Blas* and *Robinson Crusoe.* The story of how he played at the characters in these books and sustained his idea of Roderick Random for a month at a stretch is picturesquely told in *David Copperfield.* Here as well as in his first and last books and in what many regard as his best, *Great Expectations,* Dickens returns with unabated fondness and mastery to the surroundings of his childhood. From seven to nine years he was at a school kept in Clover Lane, Chatham, by a Baptist minister named William Giles, who gave him Goldsmith's *Bee* as a keepsake when the call to Somerset House necessitated the removal of the family from Rochester to a shabby house in Bayham Street, Camden Town. At the very moment when a consciousness of capacity was beginning to plump his youthful ambitions, the whole flattering dream vanished and left not a rack behind. Happiness and Chatham had been left behind together, and Charles was about to enter a school far sterner and also far more instructive than that in Clover Lane. The family income had been first decreased and then mortgaged; the creditors of the "prodigal father" would not give him time; John Dickens was consigned to the Marshalsea; Mrs Dickens started an "Educational Establishment" as a forlorn hope in Upper Gower Street; and Charles, who had helped his mother with the children, blacked the boots, carried things to the pawnshop and done other menial work, was now sent out to earn his own living as a young hand in a blacking warehouse, at Old Hungerford Stairs, on a salary of six shillings a week. He tied, trimmed and labelled blacking pots for over a year, dining off a saveloy and a slice of pudding, consorting with two very rough boys, Bob Fagin and Pol Green, and sleeping in an attic in Little College Street, Camden Town, in the house of Mrs Roylance (Pipchin), while on Sunday he spent the day with his parents in their comfortable prison, where they had the services of a "marchioness" imported from the Chatham workhouse.

Already consumed by ambition, proud, sensitive and on his dignity to an extent not uncommon among boys of talent, he felt his position keenly, and in later years worked himself up into a passion of self-pity in connexion with the "degradation" and "humiliation" of this episode. The two years of childish hardship which ate like iron into his soul were obviously of supreme importance in the growth of the novelist. Recollections of the streets and the prison and its purlieus supplied him with a store of literary material upon which he drew through all the years of his best activity. And the bitterness of such an experience was not prolonged sufficiently to become sour. From 1824 to 1826, having been rescued by a family quarrel and by a windfall in the shape of a legacy to his father, from the warehouse, he spent two years at an academy known as Wellington House, at the corner of Granby Street and the Hampstead Road (the lighter traits of which are reproduced in Salem House), and was there known as a merry and rather mischievous boy. Fortunately he learned nothing there to compromise the results of previous instruction. His father had now emerged from the Marshalsea and was seeking employment as a parliamentary reporter. A Gray's Inn solicitor with whom he had had dealings was attracted by the bright, clever look of Charles, and took him into his office as a boy at a salary of thirteen and sixpence (rising to fifteen shillings) a week. He remained in Mr Blackmore's office from May 1827 to November 1828, but he had lost none of his eager thirst for distinction, and spent all his spare time mastering Gurney's shorthand and reading early and late at the British Museum. A more industrious apprentice in the lower grades of the literary profession has never been known, and the consciousness of opportunities used to the most splendid advantage can hardly have been absent from the man who was shortly to take his place at the head of it as if to the manner born. Lowten and Guppy, and Swiveller had been observed from this office lad's stool; he was now greatly to widen his area of study as a reporter in Doctors' Commons and various police courts, including Bow Street, working all day at law and much of the night at shorthand. Some one asked John Dickens, during the first eager period of curiosity as to the man behind "Pickwick," where his son Charles was educated. "Well really," said the prodigal father, "he may be said—haw—haw—to have educated himself." He was one of the most rapid and accurate reporters in London when, at nineteen years of age, in 1831, he realized his immediate ambition and "entered the gallery" as parliamentary reporter to the *True Sun*. Later he was reporter to the *Mirror of Parliament* and then to the *Morning Chronicle*. Several of his earliest letters are concerned with his exploits as a reporter, and allude to the experiences he had, travelling fifteen miles an hour and being upset in almost every description of known vehicle in various parts of Britain between 1831 and 1836. The family was now living in Bentwick Street, Manchester Square, but John Dickens was still no infrequent inmate of the sponging-houses. With all the accessories of these places of entertainment his son had grown to be excessively familiar. Writing about 1832 to his school friend Tom Mitton, Dickens tells him that his father has been arrested at the suit of a wine firm, and begs him go over to Cursitor Street and see what can be done. On another occasion of a paternal disappearance he observes: "I own that his absence does not give me any great uneasiness, knowing how apt he is to get out of the way when anything goes wrong." In yet another letter he asks for a loan of four shillings.

In the meanwhile, however, he had commenced author in a more creative sense by penning some sketches of contemporary London life, such as he had attempted in his school days in imitation of the sketches published in the *London* and other magazines of that day. The first of these appeared in the December number of the *Old*

Monthly Magazine for 1833. By the following August, when the signature "Boz" was first given, five of these sketches had appeared. By the end of 1834 we find him settled in rooms in Furnival's Inn, and a little later his salary on the *Morning Chronicle* was raised, owing to the intervention of one of its chiefs, George Hogarth, the father of (in addition to six sons) eight charming daughters, to one of whom, Catherine, Charles was engaged to be married before the year was out. Clearly as his career now seemed designated, he was at this time or a little before it coquetting very seriously with the stage: but circumstances were rapidly to determine another stage in his career. A year before Queen Victoria's accession appeared in two volumes *Sketches by Boz, Illustrative of Everyday Life and Everyday People.* The book came from a prentice hand, but like the little tract on the Puritan abuse of the Sabbath entitled, "Sunday under three Heads" which appeared a few months later, it contains in germ all, or almost all, the future Dickens. Glance at the headings of the pages. Here we have the Beadle and all connected with him, London streets, theatres, shows, the pawnshop, Doctors' Commons, Christmas, Newgate, coaching, the river. Here comes a satirical picture of parliament, fun made of cheap snobbery, a rap on the knuckles of sectarianism. And what could be more prophetic than the title of the opening chapter— Our Parish? With the Parish—a large one indeed—Dickens to the end concerned himself; he began with a rapid survey of his whole field, hinting at all he might accomplish, indicating the limits he was not to pass. This year was to be still more momentous to Dickens, for, on the 2nd of April 1836, he was married to George Hogarth's eldest daughter Catherine. He seems to have fallen in love with the daughters collectively, and, judging by subsequent events, it has been suggested that perhaps he married the wrong one. His wife's sister Mary was the romance of his early married life, and another sister, Georgina, was the dearest friend of his last ten years.

A few days before the marriage, just two months after the appearance of the *Sketches*, the first part of *The Posthumous Papers of the Pickwick Club* was announced. One of the chief vogues of the day was the issue of humorous, sporting or anecdotal novels in parts, with plates, and some of the best talent of the day, represented by Ainsworth, Bulwer, Marryat, Maxwell, Egan, Hook and Surtees, had been pressed into this kind of enterprise. The publishers of the day had not been slow to perceive Dickens's aptitude for this species of "letterpress." A member of the firm of Chapman & Hall called upon him at Furnival's Inn in December 1835 with a proposal that he should write about a Nimrod Club of amateur sportsmen, foredoomed to perpetual ignominies, while the comic illustrations were to be etched by Seymour, a well-known rival of Cruikshank (the illustrator of *Boz*). The offer was too tempting for Dickens to refuse, but he changed the idea from a club of Cockney sportsmen to that of a club of eccentric peripatetics, on the sensible grounds, first that sporting sketches were stale, and, secondly, that he knew nothing worth speaking of about sport. The first seven pictures appeared with the signature of Seymour and the letterpress of Dickens. Before the eighth picture appeared Seymour had blown his brains out. After a brief interval of Buss, Dickens obtained the services of Hablot K. Browne, known to all as "Phiz." Author and illustrator were as well suited to one another and to the common creation of a unique thing as Gilbert and Sullivan. Having early got rid of the sporting element, Dickens found himself at once. The subject exactly suited his knowledge, his skill in arranging incidents—nay, his very limitations too. No modern book is so incalculable. We commence laughing heartily at Pickwick and his troupe. The laugh becomes kindlier. We are led on through a tangle of adventure, never dreaming what is before us. The landscape changes: Pickwick becomes the symbol of kind-heartedness, simplicity and innocent levity. Suddenly in the Fleet Prison a deeper note is struck. The medley of human relationships, the loneliness, the mystery and sadness of human destinies are fathomed. The tragedy of human life is revealed to us amid its most farcical elements. The droll and laughable figure of the hero is transfigured by the kindliness of human sympathy into a beneficent and bespectacled angel in shorts and gaiters. By defying accepted rules, Dickens had transcended the limited sphere hitherto allotted to his art: he had produced a book to be enshrined henceforth in the inmost hearts of all sorts and conditions of his countrymen, and had definitely enlarged the boundaries of English humour and English fiction. As for Mr Pickwick, he is a fairy like Puck or Santa Claus, while his creator is "the last of the mythologists and perhaps the greatest."

When *The Pickwick Papers* appeared in book form at the close of 1837 Dickens's popular reputation was made. From the appearance of Sam Weller in part v. the universal hunger for the monthly parts had risen to a furore. The book was promptly translated into French and German. The author had received little assistance from press or critics, he had no influential connexions, his class of subjects was such as to "expose him at the outset to the fatal objections of vulgarity," yet in less than six months from the appearance of the first number, as the *Quarterly Review* almost ruefully admits, the whole reading world was talking about the Pickwickians. The names of Winkle,

Wardle, Weller, Jingle, Snodgrass, Dodson & Fogg, were as familiar as household words. Pickwick chintzes figured in the linendrapers' windows, and Pickwick cigars in every tobacconist's; Weller corduroys became the stock-in-trade of every breeches-maker; Boz cabs might be seen rattling through the streets, and the portrait of the author of *Pelham* and *Crichton* was scraped down to make way for that of the new popular favourite on the omnibuses. A new and original genius had suddenly sprung up, there was no denying it, even though, as the *Quarterly* concluded, "it required no gift of prophecy to foretell his fate—he has risen like a rocket and he will come down like the stick." It would have needed a very emphatic gift of prophecy indeed to foretell that Dickens's reputation would have gone on rising until at the present day (after one sharp fall, which reached an extreme about 1887) it stands higher than it has ever stood before.

Dickens's assumption of the literary purple was as amazing as anything else about him. Accepting the homage of the luminaries of the literary, artistic and polite worlds as if it had been his natural due, he arranges for the settlement of his family, decrees, like another Edmund Kean, that his son is to go to Eton, carries on the most complicated negotiations with his publishers and editors, presides and orates with incomparable force at innumerable banquets, public and private, arranges elaborate villegiatures in the country, at the seaside, in France or in Italy, arbitrates in public on every topic, political, ethical, artistic, social or literary, entertains and legislates for an increasingly large domestic circle, both juvenile and adult, rules himself and his time-table with a rod of iron. In his letter-writing alone, Dickens did a life's literary work. Nowadays no one thinks of writing such letters; that is to say, letters of such length and detail, for the quality is Dickens's own. He evidently enjoyed this use of the pen. Page after page of Forster's *Life* (750 pages in the *Letters* edited by his daughter and sister-in-law) is occupied with transcription from private correspondence, and never a line of this but is thoroughly worthy of print and preservation. If he makes a tour in any part of the British Isles, he writes a full description of all he sees, of everything that happens, and writes it with such gusto, such mirth, such strokes of fine picturing, as appear in no other private letters ever given to the public. Naturally buoyant in all circumstances, a holiday gave him the exhilaration of a schoolboy. See how he writes from Cornwall, when on a trip with two or three friends, in 1843. "Heavens! if you could have seen the necks of bottles, distracting in their immense variety of shape, peering out of the carriage pockets! If you could have witnessed the deep devotion of the post-boys, the maniac glee of the waiters! If you could have followed us into the earthy old churches we visited, and into the strange caverns on the gloomy seashore, and down into the depths of mines, and up to the tops of giddy heights, where the unspeakably green water was roaring, I don't know how many hundred feet below. . . . I never laughed in my life as I did on this journey. It would have done you good to hear me. I was choking and gasping and bursting the buckles off the back of my stock, all the way. And Stanfield"—the painter—"got into such apoplectic entanglements that we were obliged to beat him on the back with portmanteaus before we could recover him."

The animation of Dickens's look would attract the attention of any one, anywhere. His figure was not that of an Adonis, but his brightness made him the centre and pivot of every society he was in. The keenness and vivacity of his eye combined with his inordinate appetite for life to give the unique quality to all that he wrote. His instrument is that of the direct, sinewy English of Smollett, combined with much of the humorous grace of Goldsmith (his two favourite authors), but modernized to a certain extent under the influence of Washington Irving, Sydney Smith, Jeffrey, Lamb, and other writers of the *London Magazine*. He taught himself to speak French and Italian, but he could have read little in any language. His ideas were those of the inchoate and insular liberalism of the 'thirties. His unique force in literature he was to owe to no supreme artistic or intellectual quality, but almost entirely to his inordinate gift of observation, his sympathy with the humble, his power over the emotions and his incomparable endowment of unalloyed human fun. To contemporaries he was not so much a man as an institution, at the very mention of whose name faces were puckered with grins or wreathed in smiles. To many his work was a revelation, the revelation of a new world and one far better than their own. And his influence went further than this in the direction of revolution or revival. It gave what were then universally referred to as "the lower orders" a new sense of self-respect, a new feeling of citizenship. Like the defiance of another Luther, or the Declaration of a new Independence, it emitted a fresh ray of hope across the firmament. He did for the whole English-speaking race what Burns had done for Scotland—he gave it a new conceit of itself. He knew what a people wanted and he told what he knew. He could do this better than anybody else because his mind was theirs. He shared many of their "great useless virtues," among which generosity ranks before justice, and sympathy before truth, even though, true to his middle-class vein, he exalts piety, chastity and honesty in a manner somewhat alien to the mind of the low-bred man. This is what makes Dickens such a demigod and his public success such a marvel, and this also is why any exclusively literary criticism of his work is bound to be so inadequate. It should also help us to make the necessary allowances for the man. Dickens, even the Dickens of legend that we know, is far from perfect. The Dickens of reality to which Time may furnish a nearer approximation is far less perfect. But when we consider the corroding influence of adulation, and the intoxication of unbridled success, we cannot but wonder at the rel-atively high level of moderation and self-control that Dickens almost invariably observed. Mr G. K. Chesterton remarks suggestively that Dickens had all his life the faults of the little boy who is kept up too late at night. He is overwrought by happiness to the verge of exas-peration, and yet as a matter of fact he does keep on the right side of the breaking point. The specific and curative in his case was the work in which he took such anxious pride, and such unmitigated delight. He revelled in punctual and regular work; at his desk he was often in the highest spirits. Behold how he pictured himself, one day at Broadstairs, where he was writing *Chuzzlewit*. "In a bay-window in a one-pair sits, from nine o'clock to one, a gentleman with rather long hair and no neckcloth, who writes and grins, as if he thought he was very funny indeed. At one he disappears, presently emerges from a bathing-machine, and may be seen, a kind of salmon-colour porpoise, splashing about in the ocean. After that, he may be viewed in another bay-window on the ground-floor eating a strong lunch; and after that, walking a dozen miles or so, or lying on his back on the sand reading a book. Nobody bothers him, unless they know he is disposed to be talked to, and I am told he is very comfortable indeed. He's as brown as a berry, and they do say he is as good as a small fortune to the innkeeper, who sells beer and cold punch." Here is the secret of such work as that of Dickens; it is done with delight—done (in a sense) easily, done with the mechanism of mind and body in splendid order. Even so did Scott write; though more rapidly and with less conscious care: his chapter finished before the world had got up to breakfast. Later, Dickens produced novels less excellent with much more of mental strain. The effects of age could not have shown themselves so soon, but for the unfortunate loss of energy involved in his non-literary labours.

While the public were still rejoicing in the first sprightly runnings of the "new humour," the humorist set to work desperately on the grim scenes of *Oliver Twist*, the story of a parish orphan, the nucleus of which had already seen the light in his *Sketches*. The early scenes are of a harrowing reality, despite the germ of forced pathos which the observant reader may detect in the pitiful parting between Oliver and little Dick; but what will strike every reader at once in this book is the directness and power of the English style, so nervous and unadorned: from its unmistakable clearness and vigour Dickens was to travel far as time went on. But the full effect of the old simplicity is felt in such masterpieces of description as the drive of Oliver and Sikes to Chertsey, the condemned-cell ecstasy of Fagin, or the unforgettable first encounter between Oliver and the Artful Dodger. Before November 1837 had ended, Charles Dickens entered on an engagement to write a successor to *Pickwick* on similar lines of publication. *Oliver Twist* was then in mid-career; a *Life of Grimaldi* and *Barnaby Rudge* were already convenanted for. Dickens forged ahead with the new tale of *Nicholas Nickleby* and was justified by the results, for its sale far surpassed even that of *Pickwick*. As a conception it is one of his weakest. An unmistakably 18th-century character pervades it. Some of the vignettes are among the most piquant and besetting ever written. Large parts of it are totally unobserved conventional melodrama; but the Portsmouth Theatre and Dotheboys Hall and Mrs Nickleby (based to some extent, it is thought, upon Miss Bates in *Emma*, but also upon the author's Mamma) live for ever as Dickens conceived them in the pages of *Nicholas Nickleby*.

Having got rid of *Nicholas Nickleby* and resigned his editorship of *Bentley's Miscellany*, in which *Oliver Twist* originally appeared, Dickens conceived the idea of a weekly periodical to be issued as *Master Humphrey's Clock*, to comprise short stories, essays and miscellaneous papers, after the model of Addison's *Spectator*. To make the weekly numbers "go," he introduced Mr Pickwick, Sam Weller and his father in friendly intercourse. But the public requisitioned "a story," and in No. 4 he had to brace himself up to give them one. Thus was commenced *The Old Curiosity Shop,* which was continued with slight interruptions, and followed by *Barnaby Rudge*. For the first time we find Dickens obsessed by a highly complicated plot. The tonality achieved in *The Old Curiosity Shop* surpassed anything he had attempted in this difficult vein, while the rich humour of Dick Swiveller and the Marchioness, and the vivid portraiture of the wandering Bohemians, attain the very highest level of Dickensian drollery; but in the lamentable tale of Little Nell (though Landor and Jeffrey thought the character-drawing of this infant comparable with that of Cordelia), it is generally admitted that he committed an indecent assault upon the emotions by exhibiting a veritable monster of piety and long-suffering in a child of tender years. In *Barnaby Rudge* he was manifestly affected by the influence of Scott, whose achievements he always regarded with a touching veneration. The plot, again, is of the utmost complexity, and Edgar Allen Poe (who predicted the conclusion) must be one of the few persons who ever really mastered it. But few of Dickens's books are written in a more admirable style.

Master Humphrey's Clock concluded, Dickens started in 1842 on his first visit to America—an episode hitherto without parallel in English literary history, for he was received everywhere with popular acclamation as the representative of a grand triumph of the English language and imagination, without regard to distinctions of nationality. He offended the American public grievously by a few words of frank description and a few quotations of the advertisement columns of American papers illustrating the essential barbarity of the old slave system (*American Notes*). Dickens was soon pining for home—no English writer is more essentially and insularly English in inspiration and aspiration than he is. He still brooded over the perverseness of America on the copyright question, and in his next book he took the opportunity of uttering a few of his impressions about the objectionable sides of American democracy, the result being that "all Yankee-doodle-dom blazed up like one universal soda bottle," as Carlyle said. *Martin Chuzzlewit* (1843–1844) is important as closing his great character period. His *sève originale,* as the French would say, was by this time to a considerable extent exhausted, and he had to depend more upon artistic elaboration, upon satires, upon *tours de force* of description, upon romantic and ingenious contrivances. But all these resources combined proved unequal to his powers as an original observer of popular types, until he reinforced himself by autobiographic reminiscence, as in *David Copperfield* and *Great Expectations,* the two great books remaining to his later career.

After these two masterpieces and the three wonderful books with which he made his début, we are inclined to rank *Chuzzlewit.* Nothing in Dickens is more admirably seen and presented than Todgers's, a bit of London particular cut out with a knife. Mr Pecksniff and Mrs Gamp, Betsy Prig and "Mrs Harris" have passed into the national language and life. The coach journey, the windy autumn night, the stealthy trail of Jonas, the undertone of tragedy in the Charity and Mercy and Chuffey episodes suggest a blending of imaginative vision and physical penetration hardly seen elsewhere. Two things are specially notable about this novel—the exceptional care taken over it (as shown by the interlineations in the MS.) and the caprice or nonchalance of the purchasing public, its sales being far lower than those of any of its monthly predecessors.

At the close of 1843, to pay outstanding debts of his now lavish housekeeping, he wrote that pioneer of Christmas numbers, that national benefit as Thackeray called it, *A Christmas Carol*. It failed to realize his pecuniary anticipations, and Dickens resolved upon a drastic policy of retrenchment and reform. He would save expense by living abroad and would punish his publishers by withdrawing his custom from them, at least for a time. Like everything else upon which he ever determined, this resolution was carried out with the greatest possible precision and despatch. In June 1844 he set out for Marseilles with his now rapidly increasing family (the journey cost him £200). In a villa on the outskirts of Genoa he wrote *The Chimes*, which, during a brief excursion to London before Christmas, he read to a select circle of friends (the germ of his subsequent lecture-audiences), including Forster, Carlyle, Stanfield, Dyce, Maclise and Jerrold. He was again in London in 1845, enjoying his favourite diversion of private theatricals; and in January 1846 he experimented briefly as the editor of a London morning paper—the *Daily News*. By early spring he was back at Lausanne, writing his customary vivid letters to his friends, craving as usual for London streets, commencing *Dombey and Son*, and walking his fourteen miles daily. The success of *Dombey and Son* completely rehabilitated the master's finances, enabled him to return to England, send his son to Eton and to begin to save money. Artistically it is less satisfactory; it contains some of Dickens's prime curios, such as Cuttle, Bunsby, Toots, Blimber, Pipchin, Mrs MacStinger and young Biler; it contains also that masterpiece of sentimentality which trembles upon the borderland of the sublime and the ridiculous, the death of Paul Dombey ("that sweet Paul," as Jeffrey, the "critic laureate," called him), and some grievous and unquestionable blemishes. As a narrative, moreover, it tails off into a highly complicated and exacting plot. It was followed by a long rest at Broadstairs before Dickens returned to the native home of his genius, and early in 1849 "began to prepare for *David Copperfield*."

"Of all my books," Dickens wrote, "I like this the best; like many fond parents I have my favourite child, and his name is David Copperfield." In some respects it stands to Dickens in something of the same relation in which the contemporary *Pendennis* stands to Thackeray. As in that book, too, the earlier portions are the best. They gained in intensity by the autobiographical form into which they are thrown; as Thackeray observed, there was no writing against such power. The tragedy of Emily and the character of Rosa Dartle are stagey and unreal; Uriah Heep is bad art; Agnes, again, is far less convincing as a consolation than Dickens would have us believe; but these are more than compensated by the wonderful realization of early boyhood in the book, by the picture of Mr Creakle's school, the Peggottys, the inimitable Mr Micawber, Betsy Trotwood and that monument of selfish misery, Mrs Gummidge.

At the end of March 1850 commenced the new twopenny weekly called *Household Words,* which Dickens planned to form a direct means of communication between himself and his readers, and as a means of collecting around him and encouraging the talents of the younger generation. No one was better qualified than he for this work, whether we consider his complete freedom from literary jealousy or his magical gift of inspiring young authors. Following the somewhat dreary and incoherent *Bleak House* of 1852, *Hard Times* (1854)—an anti-Manchester School tract, which Ruskin regarded as Dickens's best work—was the first long story written for *Household Words.* About this time Dickens made his final home at Gad's Hill, near Rochester, and put the finishing touch to another long novel published upon the old plan, *Little Dorrit* (1855–1857). In spite of the exquisite comedy of the master of the Marshalsea and the final tragedy of the central figure, *Little Dorrit* is sadly deficient in the old vitality, the humour is often a mock reality, and the repetition of comic catchwords and overstrung similes and metaphors is such as to affect the reader with nervous irritation. The plot and characters ruin each other in this amorphous production. The *Tale of Two Cities,* commenced in *All the Year Round* (the successor of *Household Words*) in 1859, is much better: the main characters are powerful, the story genuinely tragic, and the atmosphere lurid; but enormous labour was everywhere expended upon the construction of stylistic ornament.

The *Tale of Two Cities* was followed by two finer efforts at atmospheric delineation, the best things he ever did of this kind: *Great Expectations* (1861), over which there broods the mournful impression of the foggy marshes of the Lower Thames; and *Our Mutual Friend* (1864–1865), in which the ooze and mud and slime of Rotherhithe, its boatmen and loafers, are made to pervade the whole book with cumulative effect. The general effect produced by the stories is, however, very different. In the first case, the foreground was supplied by autobiographical material of the most vivid interest, and the lucidity of the creative impulse impelled him to write upon this occasion with the old simplicity, though with an added power. Nothing therefore, in the whole range of Dickens surpassed the early chapters of *Great Expectations* in perfection of technique or in mastery of all the resources of the novelist's art. To have created Abel Magwitch alone is to be a god indeed, says Mr Swinburne, among the creators of deathless men. Pumblechook is actually better and droller and truer to imaginative life than Pecksniff; Joe Gargery is worthy to have been praised and loved at once by Fielding and by Sterne: Mr Jaggers and his clients, Mr Wemmick and his parent and his bride, are such figures as Shakespeare, when dropping out of poetry, might have created, if his lot had been cast in a later century. "Can as much be said," Mr Swinburne boldly asks, "for the creatures of any other man or god?"

In November 1867 Dickens made a second expedition to America, leaving all the writing that he was ever to complete behind him. He was to make a round sum of money, enough to free him from all embarrassments, by a long series of exhausting readings, commencing at the Tremont Temple, Boston, on the 2nd of December. The strain of Dickens's ordinary life was so tense and so continuous that it is, perhaps, rash to assume that he broke down eventually under this particular stress; for other reasons, however, his persistence in these readings, subsequent to his return, was strongly deprecated by his literary friends, led by the arbitrary and relentless Forster. It is a long testimony to Dickens's self-restraint, even in his most capricious and despotic moments, that he never broke the cord of obligation which bound him to his literary mentor, though sparring matches between them were latterly of frequent occurrence. His farewell reading was given on the 15th of March 1870, at St James's Hall. He then vanished from "those garish lights," as he called them, "for evermore." Of the three brief months that remained to him, his last book, *The Mystery of Edwin Drood*, was the chief occupation. It hardly promised to become a masterpiece (Longfellow's opinion) as did Thackeray's *Denis Duval*, but contained much fine descriptive technique, grouped round a scene of which Dickens had an unrivalled sympathetic knowledge.

In March and April 1870 Dickens, as was his wont, was mixing in the best society; he dined with the prince at Lord Houghton's and was twice at court, once at a long deferred private interview with the queen, who had given him a presentation copy of her *Leaves from a Journal of our Life in the Highlands* with the inscription "From one of the humblest of authors to one of the greatest"; and who now begged him on his persistent refusal of any other title to accept the nominal distinction of a privy councillor. He took for four months the Milner Gibsons' house at 5 Hyde Park Place, opposite the Marble Arch, where he gave a brilliant reception on the 7th of April. His last public appearance was made at the Royal Academy banquet early in May. He returned to his regular methodical routine of work at Gad's Hill on the 30th of May, and one of the last instalments he wrote of *Edwin Drood* contained an ominous speculation as to the next two people to die at Cloisterham: "Curious to make a guess at the two, or say at one of the two." Two letters bearing the well-known superscription "Gad's Hill Place, Higham by Rochester, Kent" are dated the 8th of June, and, on the same Thursday, after a long spell of writing in the Châlet where he habitually wrote, he collapsed suddenly at dinner. Startled by the sudden change in the colour and expression of his face, his sister-in-law (Miss Hogarth) asked him if he was ill; he said "Yes, very ill," but added that he would finish dinner and go on afterwards to London. "Come and lie down," she entreated; "Yes, on the ground," he said, very distinctly; these were the last words he spoke, and he slid from her arms and fell upon the floor. He died at 6-10 P.M. on Friday, the 9th of June, and was buried privately in Poets' Corner, Westminster Abbey, in the early morning of the 14th of June. One of the most appealing memorials was the drawing by his "new illustrator" Luke Fildes in the *Graphic* of "The Empty Chair; Gad's Hill: ninth of June, 1870." "Statesmen, men of science, philanthropists, the acknowledged benefactors of their race, might pass away, and yet not leave the void which will be caused by the death of Charles Dickens" (*The Times*). In his will he enjoined his friends to erect no monument in his honour, and directed his name and dates only to be inscribed on his tomb, adding this proud provision, "I rest my claim to the remembrance of my country on my published works."

Dickens had no artistic ideals worth speaking about. The sympathy of his readers was the one thing he cared about and, like Cobbett, he went straight for it through the avenue of the emotions. In personality, intensity and range of creative genius he can hardly be said to have any modern rival. His creations live, move and have their being about us constantly, like those of Homer, Virgil, Chaucer, Rabelais, Cervantes, Shakespeare, Bunyan, Molière and Sir Walter Scott. As to the books themselves, the backgrounds on which these mighty figures are projected, they are manifestly too vast, too chaotic and too unequal ever to become classics. Like most of the novels constructed upon the unreformed model of Smollett and Fielding, those of Dickens are enormous stock-pots into which the author casts every kind of autobiographical experience, emotion, pleasantry, anecdote, adage or apophthegm. The fusion is necessarily very incomplete and the hotch-potch is bound to fall to pieces with time. Dickens's plots, it must be admitted, are strangely unintelligible, the repetitions and stylistic decorations of his work exceed all bounds, the form is unmanageable and insignificant. The diffuseness of the English novel, in short, and its extravagant didacticism cannot fail to be most prejudicial to its perpetuation. In these circumstances there is very little fiction that will stand concentration and condensation so well as that of Dickens.

For these reasons among others our interest in Dickens's novels as integers has diminished and is diminishing. But, on the other hand, our interest and pride in him as a man and as a representative author of his age and nation has been steadily augmented and is still mounting. Much of the old criticism of his work, that it was not up to a sufficiently high level of art, scholarship or gentility, that as an author he is given to caricature, redundancy and a shameless subservience to popular caprice, must now be discarded as irrelevant.

As regards formal excellence it is plain that Dickens labours under the double disadvantage of writing in the least disciplined of all literary genres in the most lawless literary milieu of the modern world, that of Victorian England. In spite of these defects, which are those of masters such as Rabelais, Hugo and Tolstoy, the work of Dickens is more and more instinctively felt to be true, original and ennobling. It is already beginning to undergo a process of automatic sifting, segregation and crystallization, at the conclusion of which it will probably occupy a larger segment in the literary consciousness of the English-spoken race than ever before.

INDEX OF ARTICLES

INDEX OF AUTHORS

Most of the articles are anonymous. Those ending with a combination of initials are identified alphabetically below, beginning with the first initial of the FIRST name of the contributor, as was the custom with all indices of authors in the eleventh.

A.N. Alfred Newton, professor of zoology and comparative anatomy, University of Cambridge; author of *Dictionary of Birds.* (Canary; Nidification; Song of Birds, The)

A.Sy. Arthur Symons, author of *Poems, The Symbolist Movement in Literature, Studies in Two Literatures, Studies in Prose and Verse,* and *A Study in Pathology.* (Mallarmé, Stéphane)

C.Ar. Channing Arnold, barrister-at-law, author of *The American Egypt.* (Australian, Aboriginal)

C.Pf. Christian Pfister, professor at the Sorbonne. (Fredegond)

C.W.W. Sir Charles William Wilson, major-general, Royal Engineers; British commissioner on the Servian (Serbian) Boundary Commission; author of *From Korti to Khartum* and *Life of Clive.* (Armenians)

D.H. David Hannay, formerly vice-consul at Barcelona, author of *Short History of the Royal Navy.* (Hamilton, Emma; Pepys, Samuel)

D.Mn. Rev. Dugald MacFadyen, minister of South Grove Congregational Church, Highgate; director of the London Missionary Society. (Cruden, Alexander)

E.B.   Edward Breck, former foreign correspondent for *The New York Herald* and *The New York Times;* author of *Wilderness Pets*. (Base-Ball)

E.B.P.   Edward Bagnall Poulton, Hope Professor of zoology at the University of Oxford, author of *Essays on Evolution* and *Darwin and the Original Species*. (Darwin, Charles)

E.Bra.   Edwin Bramwell, assistant physician, Royal Infirmary, Edinburgh. (Hysteria)

E.G.   Edmund Gosse, poet and critic, author of *Seventeenth-Century Studies, A History of Eighteenth-Century Literature, French Profiles*, and *Father and Son*. (Andersen, Hans Christian; Bouts-Rimés; Diary; Herrick, Robert; Stevenson, Robert Louis)

E.H.C.   Ernest Hartley Coleridge, editor of *Byron's Poems* and the *Letters of Samuel Taylor Coleridge*. (Lord Byron)

E.M.T.   Sir Edward Maunde Thompson, director and principal libarian, British Museum; author of *Handbook of Greek and Latin Paleography*. (Palimpsest)

E.Tn.   Rev. Ethelred Leonard Taunton, author of *The English Black Monks of St. Benedict* and *History of the Jesuits in England*. (Campion, Edmund)

E.V.L.   E. V. Lucas, author of *Life of Charles Lamb, Reading, Writing and Remembering*, and *Letters of Charles and Mary Lamb* (ed.). (Austen, Jane)

F.By.   Captain Frank Brinkley, correspondent of *The Times* in Japan, editor of the *Japan Mail*, formerly professor of mathematics at the Imperial Engineering College, Tokyo; author of *Japan*. (Japanese)

F.L.   Sir Franklin Lushington, formerly chief magistrate of London. (Lear, Edward)

F.P.   Frank Podmore, author of *Studies in Psychical Research* and *Modern Spiritualism.* (Automatic Writing; Premonition)

F.R.C.   Frank R. Cana, author of *South Africa from the Great Trek to the Union.* (Egyptians)

G.   Count Albert Edward Wilfred Gleichen, colonel, Grenadier Guards, mission to Abyssinia, 1897. (Abyssinians)

G.Sa.   George Saintsbury, author of *A Short History of French Literature, History of Criticism and Literary Taste in Europe from the Earliest Texts to the Present Day, Loci Critici,* etc. Chair of rhetoric and English literature, Edinburgh University. (Voltaire)

H.F.G.   Hans Friedrich Gadow, Strickland Curator and Lecturer on zoology, University of Cambridge; author of *Amphibia and Reptiles.* (Chameleon; Migration of Birds)

H.St.   Henry Stuart, author of *The Idea of a Free Church* and *Personal Idealism.* (Metempsychosis)

I.A.   Israel Abrahams, reader in Talmudic and rabbinic literature at the University of Cambridge, formerly president of the Jewish Historical Society of England, author of *A Short History of Jewish Literature* and *Jewish Life in the Middle Ages.* (Circumcision)

J.B.B.   John Bagnall Bury, Regius Professor of modern history, University of Cambridge; author of *History of Greece to the Death of Alexander the Great* and *History of the Roman Empire 27 B.C.–180 A.D.;* editor of Gibbon's *Decline and Fall of the Roman Empire.* (Gibbon, Edward)

J.B.T.   Sir John Batty Tuke, president of the Neurological Society of the United Kingdom. (Hysteria)

J.D.B. James David Bourchier, correspondent of *The Times* in southeastern Europe, commander of the Orders of Prince Danilo of Montenegro and of the Saviour of Greece, and officer of the Order of St. Alexander of Bulgaria. (Greeks; Montenegrins)

J.G.M. John Gray McKendrick, emeritus professor of physiology, University of Glasgow; author of *Life of Helmholtz*. (Sleep)

J.G.Sc. Sir James George Scott, superintendent and political officer, Southern Shan States; author of *Burma* and *The Upper Burma Gazetteer*. (Wa)

J.L.W. Jessie L. Weston, author of *Arthurian Romances Unrepresented in Malory* and *From Ritual to Romance*. (Merlin; Tristan)

J.M.M. John Malcolm Mitchell, sometime scholar of Queen's College, Oxford; joint editor of Grote's *History of Greece*. (Harem)

J.P.B. James George Joseph Penderel-Brodhurst, editor of the *Guardian* (London). (Bed; Pawnbroking)

J.P.E. Jean Paul Hippolyte Emmanuel Adhemar Esmein, professor of law at the University of Paris; author of *Cours élémentaire d'histoire de droit français*. (Lettres de cachet)

L.V. Luigi Villari, Italian Foreign Office. (Accoramboni, Vittoria; Cappello, Bianca)

M. Lord Thomas Babington Macaulay, author of *History of England from the Accession of James II*. (Goldsmith, Oliver)

N.W.T. Northcote Whitbridge Thomas, government anthropologist to southern Nigeria, author of *Thought Transference* and *Kinship and Marriage in Australia*. (Animal Worship; Lycanthropy; Medium)

P.C.Y. Philip Chesney York, Magdalen College, Oxford University. (Anne of Cleves; Boleyn, Anne)

R.R.   Reinhold Rose, secretary of the Royal Asiatic Society, librarian at the India Office, London, 1869–1893. (Thugs)

T.A.J.   Thomas Athol Joyce, assistant in the Department of Ethnography, British Museum. (Costume; Negro)

T.H.H.   Colonel Sir Thomas Hungerford Holdich, superintendent, frontier surveys, India, 1892–1898; author of *The Indian Borderland, India,* and *Tibet.* (Afghans)

T.Se.   Thomas Seccombe, lecturer, East London and Birkbeck Colleges; assistant editor, *Dictionary of National Biography,* 1891–1901. (Tichborne Claimant, The)

W.A.L.   William Alexander Lindsay, bencher of the Middle Temple, peerage counsel; author of *The Royal Household,* 1837–1897. (Precedence)

W.Hy.   William Henry, founder and chief secretary to the Royal Life Saving Society. (Swimming)

W.L.F.   Walter Lynwood Fleming, professor of history at Louisiana State University; author of *Documentary History of Reconstruction.* (Lynch Law; McGillivray, Alexander)

W.M.C.   Sir W. Martin Conway, Slade Professor of fine arts, University of Cambridge; author of *The Alps from End to End, The First Crossing of Spitsbergen,* and *The Bolivian Andes.* (Mountaineering)

INDEX